1989 Supplement

Cases and Text on PROPERTY

1989 Supplement

Casner and Leach
Cases and Text on PROPERTY

Third Edition

A. James Casner

Austin Wakeman Scott Professor of Law, Emeritus
Harvard University

Little, Brown and Company   *Boston   Toronto   London*

Library of Congress Catalog Card No. 83-82695

ISBN 0-316-13238-1

Fourth Printing

EB

Published simultaneously in Canada
by Little, Brown & Company (Canada) Limited

PRINTED IN THE UNITED STATES OF AMERICA

Contents

Table of Cases   *ix*

PART 1.   PROBLEMS IN POSSESSION   1

Chapter Two.   Acquiring Title to Wild Animals   2

    Dorman v. Satti   2
    Glave v. Michigan Terminix Company   2
    Varga v. Welsh   4

Chapter Three.   Types of Possession   5

    United States v. Stubbs   *8*

PART 2.   GIFTS OF PERSONAL PROPERTY   13

Chapter Seven.   Retention of Rights by the Donor   14

    Gruen v. Gruen   *14*
    Lyle v. Durham   21
    Wion v. Henderson   21

Chapter Eight.   Oral Trusts Compared   23

    Elyacher v. Gerel Corporation   *23*

PART 4.   ESTATES IN LAND   45

Chapter Twelve.   Historical Background of Real
           Property Law   46

Note   46

Chapter Thirteen.   The Types of Estates in Land   47

Uniform Marital Property Act   47
Hewitt v. Hewitt   *47*
Estate of Leo Black   *57*
Drapek v. Drapek   *66*
Stevens v. Stevens   72
Garner v. Gerrish   *72*

Chapter Fourteen.   Concurrent Ownership   77

Harms v. Sprague   77

**PART 5.   BEFORE AND AFTER THE STATUTE OF
USES**   79

**Chapter Fifteen.   Conveyancing and Future Interests
Before the Statute of Uses**   80

Harrison v. Marcus   *80*

PART 6.   LANDLORD AND TENANT   87

**Chapter Eighteen.   Means Available to Assure Lease
Performance**   88

Vinton v. Demetrion   88
Castenholz v. Caira   88

**Chapter Nineteen.   When Parties Are Excused From
Performance**   89

Hilder v. St. Peter   *89*
Note: Implied Warranty of Habitability — the Minority
   Viewpoint   98
Berman v. Jefferson   *100*
Becker v. IRM Corporation   *106*
Feld v. Merriam   *138*
Scofield v. Berman and Sons   144

Contents

Note 144
Halet v. Wend Inv. Co. 145

PART 7.   THE MODERN LAND TRANSACTION 153

Chapter Twenty-five.   The Contract for the Sale of Land (Herein the Law of Vendor and Purchaser) 154

Bennett v. McCabe 155
Note 155
Johnson v. United States 155
Layman v. Binns 158
Freyfogle, Real Estate Sales and the New Implied
    Warranty of Lawful Use 162
Note: Return Required in the Case of Real Estate
    Transactions 162

Chapter Twenty-seven.   The Deed 163

Bernard v. Nantucket Boys' Club, Inc. 163

Chapter Twenty-eight.   Recording (Herein Bona Fide Purchaser of Real Property) 169

In re Walker 169

PART 8.   LAND USE PLANNING AND DEVELOPMENT 177

Chapter Thirty-two.   Private Law Devices 178

Revenue Ruling 85-132 178
Manning v. New England Mutual Life Insurance Co. 180
Malley v. Hanna 185
Granite Properties Limited Partnership v. Manns 188

Chapter Thirty-three.   Public Law Devices 201

Note: Right-to-Farm Laws 201

Williamson County Regional Planning Commission v.
  Hamilton Bank   *201*
Pennell v. City of San Jose   *220*
First English Evangelical Lutheran Church of Glendale
  v. County of Los Angeles, California   235
Hawaii Housing Authority v. Midkiff   *235*

PART 9.   RIGHTS INCIDENT TO OWNERSHIP OF
LAND   247

Chapter Thirty-five.   Water Rights   248

Utah Division of State Lands v. United States   248
United States v. Louisiana   *248*
United States v. Louisiana   *264*
Philips Petroleum Company v. Mississippi   *268*
Von Henneberg v. Generazio   *285*

PART 10.   TAXATION   295

Chapter Thirty-seven.   A-B-C of Taxes for Property
Lawyers (as of January 1989)   296

Notes on Tax Material to Update through January,
  1989   296

Table of Cases

Italics indicate principal cases.

Becker v. IRM Corporation, 106
Bennett v. McCabe, 155
Berman v. Jefferson, 100
Bernard v. Nantucket Boys' Club, Inc., 163
Black, Estate of Leo, 57
Castenholz v. Caira, 88
Dorman v. Satti, 2
Drapek v. Drapek, 66
Elyacher v. Gerel Corp., 23
Feld v. Merriam, 138
First English Evangelical Lutheran Church of Glendale v.
   County of Los Angeles, California, 235
Garner v. Gerrish, 72
Glave v. Michigan Terminix Company, 2
Gruen v. Gruen, 14
Granite Properties Limited Partnership v. Manns, 188
Halet v. Wend Inv. Co., 145
Harms v. Sprague, 77
Harrison v. Marcus, 80
Hawaii Hous. Auth. v. Midkiff, 235
Hewitt v. Hewitt, 47
Hilder v. St. Peter, 89
Johnson v. United States, 155
Layman v. Binns, 158
Leo Black, Estate of, 57
Louisiana, United States v., (470 U.S. 93 (1985)) 248
Louisiana, United States v., (108 S. Ct. 901 (1988)) 264
Lyle v. Durham, 21
Malley v. Hanna, 185
Manning v. New England Mutual Life Insurance Co., 180
Miles v. Shauntee, 98

Pennell v. City of San Jose, 220
Philips Petroleum Company v. Mississippi, 268
Scofield v. Berman and Sons, 144
Stevens v. Stevens, 72
Stubbs, United States v., 8
Utah Division of State Lands v. United States
Varga v. Welsh, 4
Vinton v. Demetrion, 88
Von Henneberg v. Generazio, 285
Walker, In re, 169
Williamson County Regional Planning Commn. v. Hamilton Bank, 201
Wion v. Henderson, 21

Acknowledgments

We wish to thank the authors and copyright holders of the following works, who have permitted their inclusion in this book.

Derrynaflan Finders Awarded £50,000 And Costs, The Irish Times, December 17, 1987, p. 7, cols. 2-8.

Massachusetts Conveyancers Association, offer to Purchase Real Estate. Copyright © 1987.

1989 Supplement

Cases and Text on PROPERTY

Part 1
Problems in Possession

Chapter Two

Acquiring Title to Wild Animals

Insert the following material after the New York Times article on page 17.

See Dorman v. Satti, 678 F. Supp. 375 (D. Conn. 1988), which held that Connecticut's Hunter Harrassment Act was invalid as a violation of free speech.

Insert following material on page 28.

Case involving liability for spraying building to drive away pigeons, which then caused damage to neighborhoods to which pigeons retreated.

GLAVE v. MICHIGAN TERMINIX COMPANY

Michigan Court of Appeals, 1987
159 Mich. App. 537, 407 N.W.2d 36

WEAVER, Judge

Plaintiff Peggy Glave appeals as of right from the order of the Kalamazoo Circuit Court granting summary disposition pursuant to MCR 2.116(C)(8) in favor of all defendants. We affirm.

Plaintiff sought damages for a medical condition she developed subsequent to efforts by the City of Battle Creek, the Michigan Terminix Company, and the Michigan Terminix Pest Control Company, beginning in 1974, to spray certain city buildings so that the pigeons inhabiting them would depart. Plaintiff alleged that this spraying caused the pigeons to flock to her neighborhood and home, thereby directly and proximately causing her to contract histoplasmosis, a fungal infection.

Plaintiff's complaint alleged the intentional tort of nuisance. Plaintiff also alleged that defendants had negligently chased the birds into residential neighborhoods when they should have killed them, trapped them, or left them where they were and that defendants negligently failed to consider the health hazard to area residents, failed to prevent the pigeons from relocating in residential neighborhoods, and failed to remove the pigeons once they were there.

When defendants Michigan Terminix Company and Michigan Terminix Pest Control Company requested summary disposition for failure to state a claim upon which relief could be granted, MCR 2.116(C)(8), plaintiff failed to answer, nor did plaintiff answer when defendant City of Battle Creek filed a similar motion. The circuit court granted summary disposition in favor of all defendants, holding that, because pigeons are ferae naturae (wild things) and the defendants never had control of them, plaintiff had no cause of action. Plaintiff appeals as of right.

On appeal, plaintiff argues that the court erred (1) by determining the pigeons to be ferae naturae and (2) by adjudicating the facts when it granted summary disposition. As to plaintiff's first argument, there appear to be no Michigan cases dealing with the question of whether pigeons are ferae naturae. However, "wild game" belongs to the state and is subject to the state's power of regulation and control, an individual acquiring in such game only the qualified property interest which the state permits. Aikens v. Dep't of Conservation, 387 Mich. 495, 502, 198 N.W.2d 304 (1972). By asserting dominion over a wild animal and keeping it, an individual may be held liable for personal injuries caused by the animal's conduct. Marquet v. LaDuke, 96 Mich. 596, 599, 55 N.W. 1006 (1893).[1] This is in consonance with Koop v. United States, 296 F.2d 53 (CA8, 1961), which declined to concede any property interest in wild animals or birds until human control is exercised by taming or confinement. Even if assumed, control is lost upon relinquishment. Id., pp. 59-60.

Here, no one owned the pigeons, and defendants never tamed, confined or otherwise controlled the pigeons. On the contrary, rather than trying to tame or confine them, defendants encouraged their departure. Hence, even assuming that defendants once had control (which was not alleged), such control was lost when defendants sent the birds away. Therefore, the trial court did not err by determining as a matter of law that the pigeons were wild. See Seaboard Air Line R. Co. v. Richmond-Petersburg Turnpike Authority, 202 Va. 1029, 121 S.E.2d 499 (1961).

This case is unlike Andrews v. Andrews, 242 N.C. 382, 88 S.E.2d 88 (1955), upon which plaintiff relies. In Andrews, the defendant deliberately attracted large numbers of wild geese to a large artificial pond constructed within four hundred feet of plaintiffs' lands, and over a period of years the pond became a base for the ever-widening and in-

---

1. As for domestic animals, an owner or custodian possessing knowledge of their vicious propensities is liable for injuries caused by their escape. Papke v. Tribbey, 68 Mich. App. 130, 136, 242 N.W.2d 38 (1976); lv. den. 399 Mich. 834 (1977).

creasingly expensive predations of the geese on plaintiffs' crops. Here, defendants merely encouraged the departure of wild pigeons from city buildings. Defendants never asserted dominion over the birds or reduced them to possession; hence the birds remained free, and the defendants were not responsible for their migrations. Sickman v. United States, 184 F.2d 616, 618 (CA7, 1950). To hold otherwise would put the imagination to ludicrous shifts.

As for appellant's second argument, it is true that the trial court must limit its consideration of motions for summary disposition to the pleadings alone. Allinger v. Kell, 102 Mich. App. 798, 806-807, 302 N.W.2d 576 (1981), *modified on other grounds,* 411 Mich. 1053, 309 N.W.2d 547 (1981). Therefore, the trial court erred by improperly basing its decision, in part, on a determination that plaintiff never showed defendants to have control over the pigeons. However, because the court was correct in determining as a matter of law that pigeons are wild things, defendants could not be liable without exercising dominion, control or possession over the birds. Since plaintiff did not allege such dominion, control or possession, she failed to state a claim upon which relief could be granted, and the error was harmless. Gilbert v. Grand Trunk W.R. Co., 95 Mich. App. 308, 313, 290 N.W.2d 426 (1980), *lv. den. sub. nom.* Gilbert v. Criswell, 410 Mich. 854 (1980).

Affirmed.

Insert the following material on page 28 after Glave v. Michigan Terminix Company.

See Varga v. Welsh, 27 Ohio App. 3d 386, 501 N.E.2d 668 (1986), which involved a motorist who was injured in an automobile accident when she struck a duck, lost control of her car and struck a telephone pole. Ducks in that area used ponds on neighboring property. Motorist sued owner of property on which ponds were located. Should she recover?

Chapter Three

Types of Possession

Insert the following material on page 35 after Problem 3.4.

The Irish Times reported the following account of the discovery of the Derrynaflan hoard. Did the court decision reported in the news story expand the law of treasure trove?

DERRYNAFLAN FINDERS AWARDED £50,000 AND COSTS

The Irish Times, Dec. 17, 1987, 7, col. 2

The Supreme Court in Dublin held yesterday that the State owns the Derrynaflan hoard and that the finders, a father and son, are to get a reward of £25,000 each. The State was also ordered to pay all costs.

The five judges gave a unanimous decision in favour of the State which had appealed against a High Court decision that Mr. Michael T. S. Webb (50), a company director, and his son, Mr. Michael O'Connell Webb (23), of Croan House, Coleville Road, Clonmel, Co. Tipperary could either keep the treasure or take its value of £5.5 million.

The two men found the treasures on February 7th, 1980 using metal detectors near a national monument at Derrynaflan Island in Littleton bog, Co. Tipperary.

The find consists of a chalice, silver paten, silver and bronze paten stand, gilt bronze strainer and a bronze basin. It has been described as one of the most significant discoveries ever made of Christian art.

The Webbs sent the find to the National Museum on the day after the discovery. They refused a government offer of £10,000. The owners of the land, Mr. Denis O'Brien and Mr. John O'Leary, got £25,000 each and the Government bought the title to the chattels found on the land.

The treasures which required preservation work by the British Museum have been in the National Museum of Ireland since their discovery.

The Chief Justice, Mr. Justice Finlay giving a reserved judgment with which Mr. Justice Henchy and Mr. Justice Griffin agreed, said the Webbs did not seek permission from the owners of the land before entering them. The director of the National Museum, Dr. Breandan O. Riordain had said they would be treated honourably.

He said that on the facts of the case there could not be implied in the arrangements between the Webbs and the State surrounding the deposit of the hoard with the museum, any term establishing a title in the Webbs to the hoard.

Mr. Justice Finlay said in his opinion the owners of the lands, Mr. O'Brien and Mr. O'Leary had a right to possession of the find, superior to that of the Webbs, who were the finders, and that the agreements made by the State with the landowners meant that these rights had become vested in the State.

He said the general principle of public policy seemed clearly to be that the Webbs should not, because of their trespass on the lands, acquire any rights of ownership to the land or things found on it.

They had behaved extremely responsibly once they found the hoard, and their subsequent conduct was exemplary. But the fact that they were finders by an act of trespass would disentitle them to any objects found, certainly as between them and the owners of the land.

He was satisfied that Mr. O'Brien and Mr. O'Leary conveyed owner-ship of the chattels found on their lands to the State, and once that was done the State became entitled to possession of these objects subject to some person establishing title as "true owner."

"In other words," said the Chief Justice, "it would be necessary . . . for a person to assert and establish that he was validly the successor in title to the person who owned the objects and was entitled to possession of them at the time they were . . . concealed in the pit of the bank."

Dealing with the question of treasure trove, the Chief Justice said it would appear that at common law the payment of a reward to the finder was an act of grace and did not confer any right enforceable at law.

He said it would now be universally accepted, certainly by the people of Ireland, and by people of most modern states, that one of the most important national assets belonging to the people is their heritage and knowledge of its true origins and the buildings and objects which consti-tute keys to their ancient heritage.

"If this be so then it would appear to me to follow," said Mr. Justice Finlay, "that a necessary ingredient of sovereignty in a modern state and certainly in this State, having regard to the terms of the Constitution, with emphasis on its historical origins and a constant concern for the common good, is and should be an ownership by the State of objects which constitute antiquities of importance which are discovered and which have no known owner."

He concluded that there did exist in this State since the 1922 Constitution a right or prerogative of treasure trove, which had the characteristics of the right of trove at common law and included the practice of rewarding a diligent and honest finder.

He said he was satisfied that the unqualified assurance of the director of the National Museum to Mr. Webb that he would be honourably treated was an integral part of the transaction under which the hoard was deposited in the museum and accepted on behalf of the State, and that the State could not now go back on the assurance.

"It would be inequitable and unjust if the State were allowed to repudiate that assurance and give only a meagre and disproportionate award. For the State to avoid giving the Webbs a reasonable reward would not be to treat them honourably," said the judge.

Evidence of amount paid for previous finds did not assist the court. The only comparable find was the Ardagh Chalice and the evidence indicated that the amounts paid in respect of that find showed a total lack of absence of the relationship between the true market value and the amounts paid.

Mr. Justice Finlay said in the absence of legislation to cover what is a proper and reasonable reward, it would appear the relevant factors were the value and importance of the find; how they were found; and rewards given in other instances. Lastly, there was the attitude and conduct of the finders.

In the case of the Webbs he said £50,000 would be assessed as the reward and the amount be divided equally among them.

On the question of treasure trove he said the circumstances of this case might be thought to point to the necessity for legislation. The right as outlined by him in his judgment was an outmoded remnant of the medieval prerogatives which were vested at common law in the monarch.

It might be thought proper, for instance, to provide that all articles of archaeological, historical, antiquarian or cultural value or interest should, when apparently ownerless, be deemed to vest in the State. It would be desirable to have a system of reward and that could be counterbalanced by penalties for improper excavation.

Mr. Justice Walsh, in a judgment, said the people of Ireland had the right and duty to exercise dominion over all objects forming part of the national heritage, whether found or not, subject to the lawful title of a true owner.

On the question of reward, he said there was evidence that in other countries the more generous the reward the greater was the assurance of the continued availability or even survival of such objects.

While it was hoped the State in any legislation it introduced, would see matters the same way, that was a matter for the Oireachtas.

In the third judgment of the court, Mr. Justice McCarthy said that whatever criticism might be made of the plaintiffs in the use of metal detectors or for the fact that they dug below the surface in order to retrieve the Derrynaflan Hoard, their subsequent conduct and attitude had been entirely praiseworthy.

The Judge added: "I would wish that I could say the same of those responsible for assessing the offer of £10,000 made to the Webbs, when the owners of the land, ignorant of the existence of the treasure until found by the plaintiffs, and who had done nothing whatever save own the land, [were] each paid the sum of £25,000 from the same source."

Insert the following material on page 63 before the note on adverse possession of chattels.

Case concerned with acquisition of title by adverse possession by the United States (also effect of deed to estate of deceased person).

UNITED STATES v. STUBBS

United States Court of Appeals, Tenth Circuit, 1985
776 F.2d 1472

LOGAN, Circuit Judge.

This appeal arises out of a dispute over title to an eighty-acre tract of land in a national forest in Utah.[1] This is the second time the dispute has been before us. In Stubbs v. United States, 620 F.2d 775 (10th Cir. 1980), we denied relief to Lloyd R. Stubbs in his quiet title suit against the United States on the ground that it was barred by the twelve-year statute of limitations in 28 U.S.C. §2409a(f). Thereafter, Stubbs apparently persisted in asserting rights to the property, and now the United States has sued him seeking to quiet its title to the tract.

On stipulated facts, the district court entered judgment in favor of the United States. Stubbs appealed. We affirm.

The district court in the instant case rejected defendant Stubbs' contention that a 1926 deed by which the land's owner, John R. Stubbs, and his wife conveyed title "to The Estate of Jesse G. Stubbs, deceased, Grantee," was void. It then found that Clifford Stubbs, to whom the real estate was distributed pursuant to the final settlement order in the Jesse Stubbs

---

1. The tract is legally described as the East half of the Northeast quarter, of Section 18, in Township Six South Range Three East of the Salt Lake Base and Meridian, in Utah County, State of Utah.

probate proceeding, had good title, which he conveyed when he sold the land to the United States in 1937. The district court treated the other issues raised—whether the United States had acquired title by its own adverse possession, the adverse possession of its predecessor in title, or a combination of both—as moot.

Defendant Stubbs claims to hold his title through a quitclaim deed signed by the heirs of John R. Stubbs, which he recorded in 1960. Most of the relevant stipulated facts are detailed in our earlier opinion, see 620 F.2d at 777-79, and will be repeated here only as necessary to our decision.

I

Stubbs bases his argument that the deed to the deceased Jesse Stubbs estate was void principally on dictum in Nilson v. Hamilton, 53 Utah 594, 174 P. 624 (1918). In that case patentees who had acquired land under the homestead act conveyed their land in 1876 to "James L. Hamilton, or the estate of James L. Hamilton, deceased." Id. at 624 (quoting the court's description, and not the deed itself). Hamilton had died in 1875. The court found that Hamilton had occupied the land during the period in which the patentees were seeking to perfect their homestead titles and had arranged to have the patentees convey the land to him once they acquired their patents. See id. at 625. The court found the deeds to be invalid because the arrangement was against public policy:

> The title granted by the homestead act gives to the patentee both the legal and equitable estate, and any prior arrangement made by him with any one concerning the title of any such premises is against the public policy of the government, is illegal, and not enforceable. It is immaterial whether the patentees, the parties to such agreement, are willing and ready to carry into effect such contract or agreements. The fact remains that it gives to the other party no legal or equitable right recognized by the courts, or which could or would be enforced. Neither did it give to the contracting party any enforceable right which he could transmit, by assignment or succession, to any one. In other words, Hamilton in this case had absolutely no right which he could enforce, or which he could transfer, and therefore had no devisable interest, and any one attempting to claim or take from him by purchase or inheritance would stand in no better position or relation than he himself, and would therefore acquire no right which the courts would recognize or enforce. Id. at 625-26 (citation omitted).

Significant for our purposes here is what the court then said in dictum:

We need to stop to discuss or declare that the attempted conveyances of 1876 to James L. Hamilton, who was then deceased, or to the estate of James L. Hamilton, deceased, did not convey any title to any one. There was no person in existence in law, named in the deed, authorized to receive, or who had the legal capacity to receive the title to the premises. It must therefore be concluded that these attempted conveyances of the several patentees in 1876 were mere nullities. 13 Cyc. 527; Rixford v. Zeigler et al., 150 Cal. 535, 88 Pac. 1092, 119 Am. St. Rep. 229; McInerney v. Beck, 10 Wash. 515, 39 Pac. 130; 1 Devlin, Deeds (3d Ed.) §187. It necessarily follows, from the foregoing, that the deceased, James L. Hamilton, at the date of his death, had no devisable interest in the premises, and the appellants acquire no title or interest in the premises by reason of his will. Id. at 626.

Neither party has cited, and we have not been able to find, any other Utah case treating the validity of a deed to a deceased person or to a decedent's estate—although Utah State Bar Title Standard Rule 12 declares a deed to an estate of a deceased person a "nullity," citing the *Hamilton* dictum as its authority.

The ancient black letter law is that a deed to the estate of a deceased person is void for want of a grantee in being capable of taking the estate. See, e.g., Simmons v. Spratt, 1 So. 860, 862 (Fla. 1887); In re Reason's Estate, 276 Mich. 376, 267 N.W. 863, 865 (1936); Kenaston v. Lorig, 81 Minn. 454, 84 N.W. 323, 323-24 (1900); 3 American Law of Property §12.40, at 282 (Casner ed. 1952); 6 G. Thomspon, Commentaries on the Modern Law of Real Property §3005, at 340-343 (1962); 23 Am. Jur. 2d §29 (1983). Nevertheless, even the cases stating this rule often gave equitable rights to reformation. See Life Insurance Co. v. Page, 178 Miss. 287, 172 So. 873, 876 (1937) (implying court might uphold conveyance if the grantor's intended beneficiary had been sufficiently disclosed to constitute constructive notice of the deed's contents); 3 American Law of Property 282. And the trend in the more recent cases is to try to honor the intention of a grantor executing such a conveyance. See Holder v. Elmwood Corp., 231 Ala. 411, 165 So. 235, 236-37 (1936) (considering deed to person's estate to be color of title); Crouch v. Crouch, 241 Ark. 447, 408 S.W.2d 495, 497 (1966) (deed to person's estate valid under some circumstances); McCollum v. Loveless, 187 Ga. 262, 200 S.E.115, 117-18 (1939) (permitting reformation of deed to person's estate); Fisher v. Standard Investment Co., 145 Neb. 80, 15 N.W.2d 355, 358-59 (1944) (deed to estate of a deceased person reformed to show executor of the estate as grantee); Haile v. Holtzclaw, 414 S.W.2d 916, 927 (Tex. 1967) (deed to person's estate is valid); see also Matthews v. Greer, 260 S.W. 53, 54 (Mo. 1924) (deed to the heirs of a person is valid); Wilson v. Dearing, Inc., 415 S.W.2d 475, 477-78 (Tex. Civ. App. 1967) (deed to dead person construed in accord with grantor's intent); Fidelity Securities Co. v.

Martin, 117 Wash. 323, 201 P. 301, 304 (1921) (deed to dead person construed in accord with grantor's intent); City Bank v. Plank, 141 Wis. 653, 124 N.W. 1000, 1001-02 (1910) (adopting "more rational" modern view that deed to dead person should be construed to follow parties' intent); Black v. Beagle, 59 Wyo. 268, 139 P.2d 439, 444 (1943) (deed to dead person conveys equitable title to person's heirs).

These cases ignore, if necessary, the conceptual problem that confounded the medieval conveyancers, who required an identifiable existing person to receive seisin at the time a deed was exectuted and title passed. The apparent willingness in these cases to honor substance over form is consistent with the practical realities of modern law. Today, a probate estate is a legal entity. It files tax returns; it operates businesses; and, acting through its administrator or executor, it commonly both conveys and receives real and personal property during the period of administration. These more liberal cases comport with the legal trend that permits former nonentities such as partnerships to hold title to land in the partnership name. See Utah Code Ann. §48-1-5 (following general Uniform Partnership Act rule).

Recent Utah Supreme Court decisions endorse the principle that a court should construe an ambiguous deed in a way that gives effect to the parties' intentions. See Chournos v. D'Agnillo, 642 P.2d 710, 712 (Utah 1982); Russell v. Geyser-Marion Gold Mining Co., 18 Utah 2d 363, 423 P.2d 487, 490 (1967). In the instant case it is clear that the grantor knew of the death and intended the property to pass to the decedent's estate. The grantee was the "Estate of Jesse G. Stubbs, deceased"; Jessie G. Stubbs was the grantor's son who had died about six weeks before the execution of the deed. A probate proceeding in Jesse Stubbs' estate already had been opened, and an administrator had been appointed before the deed was executed. The deed was recorded at the request of the administrator and at the estate's expense. The purpose of the conveyance presumably was to cause the property to pass with the other assets of the son's estate in the same manner as if it had been owned by the son immediately before the son's death. The district court considered it significant in this regard that the son's beneficiaries "were clearly known and undisputed" at the time the grantor executed the deed.

Further, Nilson v. Hamilton, *supra,* the source of the dictum Stubbs relies on, is distinguishable. There the grantor conveyed to a named person *or* his estate, apparently not knowing whether that grantee was living or dead. We are not certain how Utah courts would or should rule if a deed were made to a decedent's estate under circumstances substantially different from those in the case at bar. But we agree with the district court that if the Utah Supreme Court was to rule on the case before us it probably would apply the more generous trend of other states and uphold the validity of the deed when surrounding circumstances indicate the grantor intended that result, as they do here.

II

The United States has suggested that we might certify this question to the Supreme Court of Utah for its definitive answer. We do not do so because we are satisfied that even if we have erroneously interpreted Utah law on this issue, the stipulated facts sufficiently establish that the United States had acquired good title by adverse possession by 1955. See Utah Code Ann. §78-12-7 (seven year adverse possession statute). Stubbs' claim therefore must fail regardless.

From at least 1937 until 1955 only the United States and the predecessor who conveyed to it acted as owners of this property. Because Utah cannot tax the United States, it is no infirmity that the government did not pay real estate taxes on the land after acquiring what it thought was good title. See Farrer v. Johnson, 2 Utah 2d 189, 271 P.2d 462, 466 (1954). No other person paid real estate taxes on the tract. That the United States believed it had good title does not prevent its possession from being adverse to the rest of the world. The limitations statute is one of repose, to "quiet" challenges to the land's occupant claiming of right. Further, once the United States' title did mature, Stubbs could not similarly acquire ownership right by adverse possession against the government. 28 U.S.C. §2409a(g).

Consequently we agree with the district court's determination that the United States holds valid title.

Affirmed.[2]

Add the following material at the end of page 64.

In regard to O'Keefe v. Snyder, see Franzese, "Georgia on My Mind"—Reflections on O'Keefe v. Snyder, 19 Seton Hall L. Rev. 1 (1989).

---

2. See State ex rel. A.A.A. Inv. v. City of Columbus, 17 Ohio St. 3d 151, 478 N.E.2d 773 (1985), which held that a municipal corporation could acquire title to private property by adverse possession and that the city's acquisition of property by adverse possession did not constitute a "taking" requiring compensation pursuant to the state constitution. — ED.

Part 2
Gifts of Personal Property

Chapter Seven

Retention of Rights by the Donor

Insert the following material on page 113 before the problems.

Case involving gift of painting with reservation of life interest in donor.

GRUEN v. GRUEN

Court of Appeals of New York, 1986
68 N.Y.2d 48, 496 N.E.2d 869

SIMONS, Judge.

Plaintiff commenced this action seeking a declaration that he is the rightful owner of a painting which he alleges his father, now deceased, gave to him. He concedes that he has never had possession of the painting but asserts that his father made a valid gift of the title in 1963 reserving a life estate for himself. His father retained possession of the painting until he died in 1980. Defendant, plaintiff's stepmother, has the painting now and has refused plaintiff's requests that she turn it over to him. She contends that the purported gift was testamentary in nature and invalid insofar as the formalities of a will were not met or, alternatively, that a donor may not make a valid inter vivos gift of a chattel and retain a life estate with a complete right of possession. Following a seven-day nonjury trial, Special Term found that plaintiff had failed to establish any of the elements of an inter vivos gift and that in any event an attempt by a donor to retain a present possessory life estate in a chattel invalidated a purported gift of it. The Appellate Division held that a valid gift may be made reserving a life estate and, finding the elements of a gift established in this case, it reversed and remitted the matter for a determination of value (104 A.D.2d 171, 488 N.Y.S.2d 401). That determination has now been made and defendant appeals directly to this court, pursuant to CPLR 5601(d), from the subsequent final judgment entered in Supreme Court awarding plaintiff $2,500,000 in damages representing the value of the painting, plus interest. We now affirm.

The subject of the dispute is a work entitled "Schloss Kammer am Attersee II" painted by a noted Austrian modernist, Gustav Klimt. It was purchased by plaintiff's father, Victor Gruen, in 1959 for $8,000. On April 1, 1963 the elder Gruen, a successful architect with offices and residences in both New York City and Los Angeles during most of the time involved in this action, wrote a letter to plaintiff, then an undergraduate student at Harvard, stating that he was giving him the Klimt painting for his birthday but that he wished to retain the possession of it for his lifetime. This letter is not in evidence, apparently because plaintiff destroyed it on instructions from his father. Two other letters were received, however, one dated May 22, 1963 and the other April 1, 1963. Both had been dictated by Victor Gruen, and sent together to plaintiff on or about May 22, 1963. The letter dated May 22, 1963 reads as follows:

Dear Michael:

I wrote to you at the time of your birthday about the gift of the painting by Klimt.

Now my lawyer tells me that because of the existing tax laws, it was wrong to mention in that letter that I want to use the painting as long as I live. Though I still want to use it, this should not appear in the letter. I am enclosing, therefore, a new letter, and I ask you to send the old one back to me so that it can be destroyed.

I know this is all very silly, but the lawyer and our accountant insist that they must have in their possession copies of a letter which will serve the purpose of making it possible for you, once I die, to get this picture without having to pay inheritance taxes on it.

Love,
s/Victor.

Enclosed with this letter was a substitute gift letter, dated April 1, 1963, which stated:

Dear Michael:

The 21st birthday, being an important event in life, should be celebrated accordingly. I therefore wish to give you as a present the oil painting by Gustav Klimt of Schloss Kammer which now hangs in the New York living room. You know that Lazette and I bought it some 5 or 6 years ago, and you always told us how much you liked it.

Happy birthday again.

Love,
s/Victor.

Plaintiff never took possession of the painting nor did he seek to do so. Except for a brief period between 1964 and 1965 when it was on loan to art exhibits and when restoration work was performed on it, the painting remained in his father's possession, moving with him from New York City to Beverly Hills and finally to Vienna, Austria, where Victor Gruen died on February 14, 1980. Following Victor's death plaintiff requested possession of the Klimt painting, and when defendant refused, he commenced this action.

The issues framed for appeal are whether a valid inter vivos gift of a chattel may be made where the donor has reserved a life estate in the chattel and the donee never has had physical possession of it before the donor's death and, if it may, which factual findings on the elements of a valid inter vivos gift more nearly comport with the weight of the evidence in this case, those of Special Term or those of the Appellate Division. The latter issue requires application of two general rules. First, to make a valid inter vivos gift there must exist the intent on the part of the donor to make a present transfer; delivery of the gift, either actual or constructive to the donee; and acceptance by the donee (Matter of Szabo, 10 N.Y.2d 94, 98, 217 N.Y.S.2d 593, 176 N.E.2d 395; Matter of Kelly, 285 N.Y. 139, 150, 33 N.E.2d 62 [dissenting in part opn]; Matter of Van Alstyne, 207 N.Y. 298, 306, 100 N.E. 802; Beaver v. Beaver, 117 N.Y. 421, 428, 22 N.E. 940). Second, the proponent of a gift has the burden of proving each of these elements by clear and convincing evidence (Matter of Kelly, *supra*, 285 N.Y. at p. 150, 33 N.E.2d 62; Matter of Abramowitz, 38 A.D.2d 387, 389-390, 329 N.Y.S.2d 932, *affd. on opn.* 32 N.Y.2d 654, 342 N.Y.S.2d 855, 295 N.E.2d 654).

Donative Intent

There is an important distinction between the intent with which an inter vivos gift is made and the intent to make a gift by will. An inter vivos gift requires that the donor intend to make an irrevocable present transfer of ownership; if the intention is to make a testamentary disposition effective only after death, the gift is invalid unless made by will (see McCarthy v. Pieret, 281 N.Y. 407, 409, 24 N.E.2d 102; Gannon v. McGuire, 160 N.Y. 476; 481, 55 N.E.7; Martin v. Funk, 75 N.Y. 134, 137-138).

Defendant contends that the trial court was correct in finding that Victor did not intend to transfer any present interest in the painting to plaintiff in 1963 but only expressed an intention that plaintiff was to get the painting upon his death. The evidence is all but conclusive, however, that Victor intended to transfer ownership of the painting to plaintiff in 1963 but to retain a life estate in it and that he did, therefore, effectively transfer a remainder interest in the painting to plaintiff at that time. Although the original letter was not in evidence, testimony of its contents was received along with the substitute gift letter and its covering letter dated May 22, 1963. The three letters should be considered together as a single instrument (see Matter of Brandreth, 169 N.Y. 437, 440, 62 N.E. 563) and when they are they unambiguously establish that Victor Gruen intended to make a present gift of title to the painting at that time. But there was other evidence for after 1963 Victor made several statements orally and in writing indicating that he had previously given plaintiff the painting and that plaintiff owned it. Victor Gruen retained possession of the property, insured it, allowed others to exhibit it and made necessary repairs to it but those acts are not inconsistent with his retention of a life estate. Furthermore, whatever probative value could be attached to his statement that he had bequeathed the painting to his heirs, made 16 years later when he prepared an export license application so that he could take the painting out of Austria, is negated by the overwhelming evidence that he had intended a present transfer of title in 1963. Victor's failure to file a gift tax return on the transaction was partially explained by allegedly erroneous legal advice he received, and while that omission sometimes may indicate that the donor had no intention of making a present gift, it does not necessarily do so and it is not dispositive in this case.

Defendant contends that even if a present gift was intended, Victor's reservation of a lifetime interest in the painting defeated it. She relies on a statement from Young v. Young, 80 N.Y. 422 that " '[a]ny gift of chattels which expressly reserves the use of the property to the donor for a certain period, or . . . as long as the donor shall live, is ineffectual' " (id., at p. 436, quoting 2 Schouler, Personal Property, at 118). The statement was dictum, however, and the holding of the court was limited to a determination that an attempted gift of bonds in which the donor reserved the interest for life failed because there had been no delivery of the gift, either actual or constructive (see, id., at p. 434; see also Speelman v. Pascal, 10 N.Y.2d 313, 319-320, 222 N.Y.S.2d 324, 178 N.E.2d 723). The court expressly left undecided the question "whether a remainder in a chattel may be created and given by a donor by carving out a life estate for himself and transfering the remainder" (Young v. Young, *supra*, at p.440). We answered part of that question in Matter of Brandreth, 169 N.Y. 437, 441-442, 62 N.E. 563, *supra*) when we held that "[in] this state a life estate and remainder can be created in a chattel or a fund the same as in real property." The case did not require us to decide whether there could be a valid gift of the remainder.

Defendant recognizes that a valid inter vivos gift of a remainder interest can be made not only of real property but also of such intangibles as stocks and bonds. Indeed, several of the cases she cites so hold. That being so, it is difficult to perceive any legal basis for the distinction she urges which would permit gifts of remainder in those properties but not of remainder interests in chattels such as the Klimt painting here. The only reason suggested is that the gift of a chattel must include a present right to possession. The application of *Brandreth* to permit a gift of the remainder in this case, however, is consistent with the distinction, well recognized in the law of gifts as well as in real property law, between ownership and possession or enjoyment (see Speelman v. Pascal, 10 N.Y.2d 313, 318, 222 N.Y.S.2d 324, 178 N.E.2d 723, *supra;* McCarthy v. Pieret, 281 N.Y. 407, 409-411, 24 N.E.2d 102, *supra;* Matter of Brandreth, 169 N.Y. 437, 442, 62 N.E. 563, *supra*). Insofar as some of our cases purport to require that the donor intend to transfer both title and possession immediately to have a valid inter vivos gift (see Gannon v. McGuire, 160 N.Y. 476, 481, 55 N.E. 7, *supra;* Young v. Young, 80 N.Y. 422, 430, *supra*), they state the rule too broadly and confuse the effectiveness of a gift with the transfer of the possession of the subject of that gift. The correct test is " 'whether the maker intended the [gift] to have *no effect* until after the maker's death, or whether he intended it to transfer *some present interest*' " (McCarthy v. Pieret, 281 N.Y. 407, 409, 24 N.E.2d 102, *supra* [emphasis added]; see also 25 N.Y. Jur., Gifts. §14, at 156-157). As long as the evidence establishes an intent to make a present and irrevocable transfer of title or the right of ownership, there is a present transfer of some interest and the gift is effective immediately (see Matter of Brady, 228 App. Div. 56, 60, 239 N.Y.S. 5, *aff'd no opn.* 254 N.Y. 590, 173 N.E. 879; In re Sussman's Estate, 125 N.Y.S.2d 584, 589-591, *affd. no opn.* 283 App. Div. 1051, 134 N.Y.S.2d 586, Matter of Valentine, 122 Misc. 486, 489, 204 N.Y.S. 284; Brown, Personal Property §48, at 133-136 [2d ed.]; 25 N.Y. Jur., Gifts, §30, at 173-174; see also Farmers' Loan & Trust Co. v. Winthrop, 238 N.Y. 477, 485-486, 144 N.E. 686). Thus, in Speelman v. Pascal, *supra,* we held valid a gift of a percentage of the future royalties to the play "My Fair Lady" before the play even existed. There, as in this case, the donee received title or the right of ownership to some property immediately upon the making of the gift but possession or enjoyment of the subject of the gift was postponed to some future time.

Defendant suggests that allowing a donor to make a present gift of a remainder with the reservation of a life estate will lead courts to effectuate otherwise invalid testamentary dispositions of property. The two have entirely different characteristics, however, which make them distinguishable. Once the gift is made it is irrevocable and the donor is limited to the rights of a life tenant, not an owner. Moreover, with the gift of a remainder title vests immediately in the donee and any possession is postponed until the donor's death whereas under a will neither title nor possession vests immediately. Finally, the postponement of enjoyment of the gift is produced by the express terms of the gift not by the nature of the instrument as it is with a will (see Robb v. Washington & Jefferson Coll., 185 N.Y. 485, 493, 78 N.E. 359).

Delivery

In order to have a valid inter vivos gift, there must be a delivery of the gift, either by a physical delivery of the subject of the gift or a constructive or symbolic delivery such as by an instrument of gift, sufficient to divest the donor of dominion and control over the property (see Matter of Szabo, 10 N.Y.2d 94, 98-99, 217 N.Y.S.2d 593, 176 N.E.2d 395, *supra;* Speelman v. Pascal, 10 N.Y.2d 313, 318-320, 222 N.Y.S.2d 324, *supra;* Beaver v. Beaver, 117 N.Y. 421, 428-429, 22 N.E. 940, *supra;* Matter of Cohn, 187 App. Div. 392, 395, 176 N.Y.S.2d 225). As the statement of the rule suggests, the requirement of delivery is not rigid or inflexible, but is to be applied in light of its purpose to avoid mistakes by donors and fraudulent claims by donees (see Matter of Van Alstyne, 207 N.Y. 298, 308, 100 N.E. 802, *supra;* Matter of Cohn, *supra,* 187 App. Div. at pp. 395-396, 176 N.Y.S.2d 255; Mechem, Requirement of Delivery in Gifts of Chattels and of Choses in Actions Evidenced by Commercial Instruments, 21 Ill. L. Rev. 341, 348-349). Accordingly, what is sufficient to constitute delivery "must be tailored to suit the circumstances of the case" (Matter of Szabo, *supra,* 10 N.Y.2d at p.98, 217 N.Y.S.2d 593, 176 N.E.2d 395). The rule requires that " '[t]he delivery necessary to consummate a gift must be as perfect as the nature of the property and the circumstances and surroundings of the parties will reasonably permit" (id.; Vincent v. Rix, 248 N.Y. 78, 83, 161 N.E. 425; Matter of Van Alstyne, *supra,* 207 N.Y. at p.309, 100 N.E. 802; see Beaver v. Beaver, *supra,* 117 N.Y. at p.428; 22 N.E. 940).

Defendant contends that when a tangible piece of personal property such as a painting is the subject of a gift, physical delivery of the painting itself is the best form of delivery and should be required. Here, of course, we have only delivery of Victor Gruen's letters which serve as instruments of gift. Defendant's statement of the rule as applied may be generally true, but it ignores the fact that what Victor Gruen gave plaintiff was not all rights to the Klimt painting, but only title to it with no right of possession until his death. Under these circumstances, it would be illogical for the law to require the donor to part with possession of the painting when that is exactly what he intends to retain.

Nor is there any reason to require a donor making a gift of a remainder interest in a chattel to physically deliver the chattel into the donee's hands only to have the donee redeliver it to the donor. As the facts of this case demonstrate, such a requirement could impose practical burdens on the parties to the gift while serving the delivery requirement poorly. Thus, in order to accomplish this type of delivery the parties would have been required to travel to New York for the symbolic transfer and redelivery of the Klimt painting which was hanging on the wall of Victor Gruen's Manhattan apartment. Defendant suggests that such a requirement would be stronger evidence of a completed gift, but in the absence of witnesses to the event or any written confirmation of the gift it would provide less protection against fraudulent claims than have the written instruments of gift delivered in this case.

Acceptance

Acceptance by the donee is essential to the validity of an inter vivos gift, but when a gift is of value to the donee, as it is here, the law will presume an acceptance on his part (Matter of Kelsey, 26 N.Y.2d 792, 309 N.Y.S.2d 219, 257 N.E.2d 663, *aff'g on opn.*, at 29 A.D.2d 450, 456, 289 N.Y.S.2d 314; Beaver v. Beaver, 117 N.Y. 421, 429, 22 N.E. 940, *supra*). Plaintiff did not rely on this presumption alone but also presented clear and convincing proof of his acceptance of a remainder interest in the Klimt painting by evidence that he had made several contemporaneous statements acknowledging the gift to his friends and associates, even showing some of them his father's gift letter, and that he had retained both letters for over 17 years to verify the gift after his father died. Defendant relied exclusively on affidavits filed by plaintiff in a matrimonial action with his former wife, in which plaintiff failed to list his interest in the painting as an asset. These affidavits were made over 10 years after acceptance was complete and they do not even approach the evidence in Matter of Kelly (285 N.Y.139, 148-149, 33 N.E.2d 62 [dissenting in part opn.], *supra*) where the donee, immediately upon delivery of a diamond ring, rejected it as "too flashy." We agree with the Appellate Division that interpretation of the affidavit was too speculative to support a finding of rejection and overcome the substantial showing of acceptance by plaintiff.

Accordingly, the judgment appealed from and the order of the Appellate Division brought up for review should be affirmed, with costs.

WACHTLER, C.J., and MEYER, KAYE, ALEXANDER, TITONE, and HANCOCK, JJ., concur.

Judgment appealed from and order of the Appellate Division brought up for review affirmed, with costs.

Insert the following material on page 113 at the end of the first paragraph of Problem 7.2.

Lyle v. Durham, 16 Ohio App. 3d 1, 473 N.E.2d 1216 (1984), held that in the absence of an agreement between the parties to the contrary, an engagement ring must be returned to the donor upon the termination of the engagement regardless of fault. This was recognized as a minority position. The court said:

> The engagement ring is a symbol of the coming marriage, given in contemplation of it. The ring is given as a unique type of conditional gift, and when the condition of marriage is not fulfilled, the ring (or its value) should be returned to the donor. It does not matter who broke the engagement or caused it to be broken; the important fact is that the ring was given in contemplation of a marriage that never came about.

Compare Wion v. Henderson, 24 Ohio App. 3d 207, 494 N.E.2d 133 (1985).

Chapter Eight

Oral Trusts Compared

Insert the following material at the end of page 135.

Case considering various aspects of gift of corporate stock, including finding that trust created by donor with retention by donor of certain controls.

ELYACHER v. GEREL CORPORATION

The United States District Court (S.D.N.Y. 1984)
583 F. Supp. 923

SOFAER, District Judge.

This is an action by two sons, Daniel and Ralph Elyachar, to compel their 85-year old father, Colonel Jehiel R. Elyachar, to deliver to them certain stock certificates. They claim their father long ago gave them the interests represented by the certificates, but now refuses physically to deliver the certificates because he wants to revoke the gifts he made. The father contends he never made the gifts claimed by his sons, and that his failure to deliver the certificates proves his intent. These differences resulted in an eight-day trial to ascertain the father's intentions from his statements and actions. The evidence establishes that Colonel Elyachar intended to create and created irrevocable, intervivos trusts (or remainder interests), whereby he implicitly declared himself trustee of the shares he gave to his children and grandchildren as beneficial owners, with full control over the interests to pass to them only upon the Colonel's death or resignation.

Jehiel Elyachar was born in Jerusalem in 1898. He left what was then Palestine around 1928 to come to this country. He became an engineer, and then a builder and owner of office and apartment buildings in Manhattan. He enlisted in the war against Hitler, joining General Patton's army in its march across Europe into the Nazi homeland, and helping to construct the bridges used by Patton's troops in their advance.

His service earned him promotion to the rank of full Colonel, as well as the Bronze Star from the United States Army and the Legion of Honor from the French Government. After the war, Colonel Elyachar returned to his real estate business in New York. Over the years he built and managed several valuable properties. He also built a family—twin sons, the plaintiffs in this case, and a daughter named Ruth, who has interests similar to those of her brothers, but who has refused to join a suit against her father.

I. Jurisdictional Defenses

Defendants contend that diversity of citizenship is absent here, because Daniel and Ralph are domiciliaries of New York, where their father also lives. The evidence establishes, however, that the sons are domiciled in Florida. Daniel has lived in Florida for over ten years, Ralph for over five. They run a real estate business there, as partners in two companies that operate only in Florida. Both have been registered to vote there for several years, and both hold Florida drivers' licenses. The fact that they rent and do not own their homes in Florida has little significance, in that many bona fide domiciliaries rent their homes. Ralph and Dan appear from the record to have economic constraints on their ability to buy homes at this time, given their other Florida land holdings. They left New York in part because their father cannot constructively work with them in running the family real estate. The Colonel himself recognized at trial that his sons "live in Florida." Tr. 867; see Tr. 831, 834.

Defendants argue that Ralph owns a Scarsdale home worth over $250,000, that he has spent substantial time there, see Tr. 585, 587-88, 592-93, that Ralph's wife has retained her New York citizenship, and that Ralph and his wife filed a verified complaint in a personal injury action in October 1981 in New York County Supreme Court reciting that they reside in the Scarsdale home. In fact, Ralph's wife Alice does regard herself as a New York resident, and while she lives with her husband in Florida she apparently does so with the hope that he will someday return to New York. Alice, however, and not Ralph, owns the Scarsdale home, see Tr. 584; and Alice filed the complaint alleging that she and her husband were residents of New York without consulting Ralph or obtaining his authorization for such a statement, see Tr. 589-90. Defendants also refer to statements that indicate that plaintiffs intend to return to New York, particularly if they succeed in this suit and assume control of significant properties. Defendants failed to prove, however, that plaintiffs have formed an intent to return to New York at any specific time. Plaintiffs have made a *bona fide* change in their domicile, and the fact that they might be inclined to return to New York under circumstances that may or may not ever come about does not nullify their present intent to live in Florida, which is potentially unlimited in time. See generally 1 Moore's Federal Practice ¶0.74[3-4] (2d ed. 1983).

The suggestion that plaintiffs are guilty of laches or should be estopped from bringing this suit is untenable. Plaintiffs have always understood that their father retained control of the business in which they argue he gave them ownership interests. They have also understood and agreed that they had no right to sell or pledge the stock, all in the Colonel's possession and control, in their names. Until recently, the Colonel gave no hint that he intended to revoke what his sons thought were gifts. In 1982, for example, when the Colonel stopped payment on dividend checks from Gerel Corporation his sons demanded the dividends as owners of "20 percent of the Gerel Corporation," and new checks were then issued at the Colonel's direction. See PX 74; see Tr. 458, PX 47. The Colonel has not been prejudiced by the alleged delay, moreover. He has voluntarily continued running the family businesses, and would have done so even if he had known all along that some of his companies were irrevocably owned by his children and grandchildren. The missing documents and faded memories encountered at the trial were partially if not exclusively the product of the Colonel's willful suppression of evidence. Had he produced the missing documents they would have established even more clearly that he intended to convey ownership interests to his children and grandchildren. In addition, he failed to call some available witnesses who have intimate knowledge of his intentions, and the evidence of record provides no reason to believe that the potential witnesses who have died would have supported the Colonel's position.

Defendants also argue that plaintiffs are barred by the applicable statute of limitations, having sought delivery of the certificates for over 10 years and having been denied delivery or use of the stock during that period. The earlier requests that the Colonel deliver the certificates were not demands, however, but only suggestions that he arrange his affairs to avoid estate tax problems. No demand for the certificates was made until the Colonel recently made clear that he wanted to deny his sons the interests he and the family had always treated as theirs. When that repudiation occurred, plaintiffs promptly made the formal demands that led to this litigation.

II. Relevant History and Findings

Plaintiffs claim that their father made them outright gifts of the stock certificates they now seek to have delivered. To establish their claim they must prove the requisites of a valid, intervivos gift of stock. In New York, these are an intention on the part of the donor to make a gift, delivery of the property, and acceptance by the donee. In re Estate of Szabo, 10 N.Y.2d 94, 98, 176 N.E.2d 395, 396, 217 N.Y.S.2d 593, 595 (1961); In re Van Alstyne, 207 N.Y. 298, 306, 100 N.E. 802, 804-05 (1913). Defendants assert that the Colonel never intended to make a present gift of the stock, that the stock has never been delivered to plaintiffs, and that plaintiffs have never accepted the certificates. Plaintiffs alternatively argue that their father made them gifts of ownership interests in the defendant corporations to the extent reflected by the certificates, retaining for himself the power to control the corporations during his lifetime. This claim was raised and advanced well before trial, and defendants have presented their evidence and argument against it. Plaintiffs' motion to deem the complaint amended to conform to the proof supporting this claim is therefore granted. See Fed. R. Civ.P. 15(b).

The Colonel decided early in his career to place each of the buildings he owned in a separate corporation. Huguel Corporation, for example, owns a building on East 56th Street; Timston Corporation owns a building at Second Avenue and 39th Street; Ruradan Corporation owns a building on East 48th Street; and Gerel Corporation owns a building on Madison Avenue. When Ruradan, Huguel, and Timston were formed, in about 1935, 1938, and 1945 respectively, Colonel Elyachar had not yet given his children ownership interests in those entities. In 1948, however, he arranged through his attorney and accountant to transfer all the stock of Ruradan (a name based on the names of Ruth, Ralph, and Dan) to the Drell Corporation, which at that time was owned by his three children. PX 58-61. Thereafter, on December 29, 1948, the original stock certificates issued for Ruradan were cancelled, and four new certificates were issued, reflecting 20 shares to J. R. Elyachar and 10 shares each to the three children. Each 10-share block was "in exchange for 10 shares of Drell Corporation." DX 1003, Certificate Nos. 4-7. The Colonel placed or arranged to have placed on each certificate the stock transfer tax stamps required under New York law for such transfers. See N.Y. Tax Law §270 (McKinney's 1966 & Supp. 1983). All three of the children's certificates were countersigned some time after June 1949 by the Colonel's daughter, Ruth Elyachar, who had by that time married Spencer Dvorkin. Tr. 373-74. Some time during the same year, Colonel Elyachar also told his sons Daniel and Ralph that he had given them stock in Ruradan, for which they thanked him. Tr. 426, 566. The Colonel did not give physical control of the certificates in Ruradan to his children, however; rather, he retained them, completely executed in the corporation's stock book, which he kept in a closet or desk at the office from which he managed his real estate business.

During 1950, Daniel and Ralph began working full time with their father in the family business. In February 1950, the Colonel issued 20 shares of stock in Gerel Corporation to himself, 40 shares to his daughter, and 20 shares to each son. DX 1001. In December 1952, the Colonel began to distribute the 10 shares of Huguel Corporation, initially issued to himself in 1938. Colonel Elyachar retained six Huguel shares, and certificates for one share each were issued to his three children and to his son-in-law, Spencer Dvorkin. DX 1002. In December 1953, the Colonel cancelled his six-share certificate in Huguel, issued himself one certificate for two shares, and issued certificates for one share each to the same four beneficiaries of his 1953 transfer. In December 1954, he cancelled his remaining two-share certificate and issued certificates for one share each to his daughter and son-in-law. Ruth Dvorkin countersigned five of the preceding certificates, which are still in the stock book, and probably signed the missing certificates as well. See Tr. 372-73. The Colonel's 10-share certificate in Timston, issued in 1945, was cancelled on October 4, 1955. He issued himself a certificate for five shares, and issued certificates for two shares each to his sons and one share to his daughter. Daniel countersigned the last three certificates. Tr. 427. Stock transfer tax stamps were attached to the stubs of all the certificates issued by all three corporations (Gerel, Huguel, and Timston), but the Colonel kept all the shares in his possession. The children knew of some or all the Colonel's actions transferring shares to them, and thanked him contemporaneously for what they believed were gifts. See Tr. 426 (Daniel); Tr. 566 (Ralph); Tr. 371-76 (Ruth).

Other transfers of stock in the corporations occurred in the 1950s. During 1955 two of the three Huguel shares in Spencer Dvorkin's name were transferred to two of Dvorkin's children, and on December 22, 1958, Dvorkin's third Huguel share was transferred to two other Dvorkin children. These transfers were accomplished unilaterally by the Colonel, who had not told Dvorkin that any shares were in his name. Dvorkin found out in the late 1970s that shares had been in his name, when he examined the books at the Colonel's request. At that time he made notations on the certificate stubs, at the Colonel's direction, to conform "the stubs to the certificates." Tr. 180. In 1958 the Colonel also transferred his five remaining shares in Timston to eight of his grandchildren. All the certificates issued in the 1950s contained stock transfer stamps.

In 1975 the Colonel began a series of annual transfers of his 20 remaining shares in Ruradan. During that year he announced to Spencer Dvorkin, who had been working in the Colonel's office since 1960, that "I'm giving five of my shares to Ralph, Dan, and my grandchildren." Tr. 60. He instructed Dvorkin to prepare the necessary papers, including new certificates reducing the Colonel's shares by five, and reflecting the

27

other transfers. Dvorkin filled in the shares and stubs in accord with the Colonel's instructions, and both the Colonel and Dvorkin signed the certificates, on each of which was affixed the necessary stock transfer tax stamps. Dvorkin also drafted a letter for the Colonel to the Colonel's accountant, dated December 9, 1975, which enclosed "a list of 20 people to each of whom I have given ¼ of a share of Ruradan Corporation stock as a gift . . . . Please figure out what the tax is and prepare the necessary papers for filing." PX 82. The accountant thereupon prepared and the Colonel signed and filed a federal gift tax return for the quarter ending December 1975, reflecting the one-quarter share gifts to 20 people, including Ralph and Dan, on which the Colonel paid a gift tax of $2,569. PX 14; see PX 83.

In 1976 and 1977 the Colonel again gave one-quarter share interests in Ruradan to 20 family members. On both occasions he asked Dvorkin to make all the necessary arrangements, signed all the necessary stock certificates, instructed his accountant to implement his "gifts," filed gift tax returns reflecting the transfers made, and paid the required tax. PX 84-88, 18. During 1977 and 1978 the IRS audited the 1975 and 1976 gift tax returns and assessed deficiencies. The deficiencies were based on a valuation of Ruradan, derived from data supplied by the Colonel and his accountant, all of which assumed that 50 shares were outstanding, and that each transfer of one-quarter share therefore represented 0.5% of the company's stock. In a letter responding to an IRS request that he provide a "list of all stockholders and their holdings," PX 19, the Colonel reported that, as of December 31, 1976, 50 shares were outstanding of which Ralph and Dan each owned 10. PX 21. The value of the shares was revised upward by agreement, and the Colonel paid gift tax deficiencies, based on the revised values of his gifts, of $2,071 for 1975 and $7,831.43 for 1976. See Tr. 682, 692-94, 699; PX 17-24, 85, 91, 106.

In 1978 the Colonel transferred four of his remaining Ruradan shares to 20 Elyachar family members, including Ralph and Dan. Dvorkin made the necessary arrangements, pursuant to the Colonel's instructions, and the Colonel announced to his accountant in a letter dated December 28, 1978:

> Today I have given one-fifth of a share of Ruradan Corporation to each of the following people . . . . Will you please prepare the necessary tax returns reflecting this gift. PX 26.

A gift tax return was duly prepared, and Colonel Elyachar signed and filed it. The return reflected gifts in exactly the proportion he had ordered, and called for payment of a tax of $1,079. PX 108, 109.

In 1978 the Colonel also began to have dividends issued by the corporate defendants. He had been made aware at about that time that if the corporations continued to retain all earnings they would be classified as personal holding companies. His accountants told him that the holding company classification, and consequential tax, could be avoided if the companies distributed certain amounts of earnings as dividends to shareholders. Tr. 741-43. Colonel Elyachar decided to have the dividends issued. He ordered Spencer Dvorkin to compile from the stock books the names of all shareholders and their holdings, and to draw up checks to them in proportion to their stock ownership. Tr. 82-83.

The first distribution was from Huguel. Ralph and Daniel received $2,195.40 each, 20% of the total amount paid out, precisely proportionate to their ownership in the company as reflected in the stock books in the Colonel's possession. This payment enabled Huguel to file a "Claim for Deficiency Dividends Deduction" to recover the tax which would have been lost but for the 1978 payment. Colonel Elyachar signed the return and listed his sons as each owning two of the 10 outstanding shares. A resolution attached to the form recited that Huguel had "authorize[d] payment of a dividend totalling $10,977 to the shareholders of Huguel Corporation pro-rata, payable immediately," and was signed by J. R. Elyachar, Ruth Dvorkin, and Spencer Dvorkin. PX 104.

In 1979, 1980, and 1981, dividend distributions were made to the plaintiffs and others by all four companies, and in 1982 by Gerel. Every distribution was exactly proportional to the percentage of the recipients' stock ownership as reflected in the stock books. Each company reported these dividend distributions in its federal income tax returns. E.g., PX 4-7, 38-39, 105, DX 1042-44. Each company's financial statements reflected these payments as dividends to stockholders. PX 63-64, 68-72. The payment checks frequently had "dividend" written on them. PX 2, 27, 32, 36. The companies also often filed forms or resolutions with the IRS reporting the dividend payments. PX 3, 28, 30, 33, 37; Tr. 87-88, 760-61. In 1979 the Timston tax return included forms for both Ralph and Daniel entitled "Consent of Shareholder to Include Specific Amount in Gross Income." PX 105. Ralph and Ruth reported these dividend payments as income in the year of their receipt; Daniel reported the dividends soon after he was informed in 1981 that the payments were in fact dividends. See PX 40, 54-56, 76-79, DX 1064, 1067-68; Tr. 379, 443-45. All the dividend checks were signed by Colonel Elyachar and were issued at his direction. Finally, when the Colonel stopped payment on the 1982 dividend checks from Gerel, Ralph and Daniel wrote to him as owners of "20 percent stock of the Gerel Corporation" demanding the dividends be reissued to them. PX 74. New dividend checks were issued and sent to plaintiffs by Colonel Elyachar after his sons' demand. Tr. 458.

Throughout the entire period during which these transfers occurred,

Colonel Elyachar retained the stock certificates and exercised exclusive control over the corporations involved. At various times the Colonel's sons and son-in-law worked with him, but always at his pleasure. The Colonel repeatedly ejected his sons from the office, often after having invited or even urged them to return. At times the Colonel has wanted his sons to take over control and invited them into the business with that purpose in mind. While he purportedly found them incompetent, the evidence also demonstrates that he would simply change his mind and realize that he wanted to remain in control. The buildings are his "children," and he seems to feel that if he quits working he will die. The Colonel also never permitted anyone to share his complete authority. He demanded and received from his children stock powers signed in blank, though no specific purpose for such powers was ever demonstrated. Finally, while his sons were well aware that certificates in the Colonel's possession described them as the owners of stock in the four corporations at issue, they agreed with the Colonel that they would never attempt to pledge or otherwise use these corporate interests without the Colonel's consent. Tr. 498.

The Colonel's first wife, Jean—the mother of his children—died in 1972, after which he married his second wife, Anna. The record also shows that in recent years the Colonel has become increasingly involved in charitable causes. He has established the Elyachar Welfare Fund, to which he has made and continues to make gifts, and he directs the distribution of the Fund's assets. The Colonel's sons appear less enthusiastic about giving away large portions of the family wealth, and seem resentful of their father's shift in interest from them to other causes. These factors, the Colonel's lack of faith in his sons' abilities, and the stress that sometimes accompanies father-son relationships all appear to have contributed to the Colonel's decision—gradually formed over the last few years—to cancel all the stock transfers he made to his children and grandchildren during the family's closer times. He testified that this decision does not necessarily mean he intends to leave nothing to his family, although he believes he has more than fulfilled his financial responsibilities to his children. Rather, he wants to replace what he now describes as the testamentary plan reflected in part by the stock transfers with an overall plan consistent with his present interests and desires.

The Colonel's determination to annul his prior acts emerged in several relatively recent events. First, he indicated the lengths to which he would go to cancel prior transfers in a heated dispute he had on February 26, 1981, with Spencer Dvorkin. After calling Dvorkin arrogant, insolent, and incompetent, he announced "[I will] go to the lawyers, go to jail if necessary, and spend $1 million to cancel everything [I have] ever done for [you and your] children." Tr. 116-17. The last dividend payment to Ralph and Dan from Gerel in early 1982 was also a major turning point. The sons for the first time squarely challenged the Colonel's authority, after he stopped payments on checks he had issued. He then sent replacement checks, but with obvious resentment. He wrote:

Dear Ralph and Dan:

I am enclosing a dividend check from Gerel for each of you.
The least you can do is send a receipt, *and* a thank you note, and also a check for the Elyachar Welfare Fund. This is very important to me. Ruth has sent her check.
I would like an answer by return mail. PX 47.

Dvorkin testified to the Colonel's penchant for secrecy. He often had Dvorkin, rather than the secretary, type confidential letters, and he even kept some information from his accountant. Dvorkin believed the Colonel engaged in this type of behavior because he wanted to be able to disavow everything. Tr. 337. In fact, when the Colonel made his decision to disavow all the transfers of stock in the defendant corporations, he did so with the purpose of destroying evidence that he thought might have limited the effectiveness of his decision. He placed "X" marks through some stock certificates he wished to cancel, and destroyed or hid others. He also appears to have thrown away letters and other documents that might have shown even more conclusively than has been demonstrated by the remaining records that the transfers were intended as gifts and were effectively delivered and accepted.

III. Nature of the Transfers

This case presents a conflict that is painful, but not uncommon. Courts have long had to deal with situations where a person indicates at one point in time that he or she intends a gift, but later disclaims having made it. A gift, like a sale, is a transfer of property. But gifts are transfers without consideration. When a gift is enforced, therefore, the donor suffers an outright forfeiture of property. Furthermore, gifts are usually claimed to have occurred by persons having a strong interest in the outcome, and often long after the donor has died. Courts discount the value of oral testimony about gifts by donors no longer present to dispute the claims. In fact, what an alleged donor might have said about a gift and what he or she might actually have intended can differ, since these matters often concern closely related individuals, who might have great difficulty in being forthright as to their intentions.

A. THE COLONEL'S INTENT

The Colonel correctly contends that, to establish a gift, plaintiffs must show that he intended to make a gift to them of a *present* interest in the companies, not a gift to take place in the future. He argues that the arrangements he made with respect to the certificates were part of a testamentary plan, to take effect upon his death in the event he had not in the meantime altered it. He claims the evidence establishes that he never intended to surrender control of the corporations to his sons, and therefore that no present interest was conveyed.

The principle espoused by the Colonel was clearly articulated in Young v. Young, 80 N.Y. 422, 430 (1880), where Judge Rapallo found that the donor had manifested his intention to give his sons ownership in certain stock, retaining for himself only a life interest. The donor's declarations, however, stated that the interest due was " '*owned and reserved*' by the donor for so long as he shall live, and that the bonds are not to belong 'wholly' or 'absolutely' to the donees till after his death." Id. 431-32 (emphasis in original). While the donor's stated desire to make a gift led the Court of Appeals to examine "the case with a strong disposition to effectuate that intention and sustain the gift, if possible," the donor could not effectively make a gift to take effect in the future without any written transfer of ownership delivered to the donee, or without unambiguously declaring a trust. Id. at 430, 435-438. Compare In re King, 230 A.D. 160, 244 N.S.S. 228 (3d Dept. 1930) (retention of income with unconditional delivery did not invalidate gift). Furthermore, the bonds at issue were retained by the donor, along with the coupons, and since the duration of his life was uncertain he might have collected the principal on some or all of the bonds before his death. "The reservation accompanying the gift would entitle the donor to possession of the fund." *Young,* 80 N.Y. at 434-35. A gift of the remainder interest in stock would not as likely be subject to complete depletion as the bonds in *Young.* See, e.g., In re Brandreth, 169 N.Y. 437, 62 N.E. 563 (1902).

The present case differs materially from *Young.* Documents and other objective evidence establish that the Colonel intended to give his children and grandchildren gifts of present interests in the corporate defendants. He referred to these transfers as "gifts" in letters, in tax filings, and in corporate reports. While Spencer Dvorkin and the Colonel's accountants were responsible for preparing some of these documents, the Colonel ordered them prepared in the form they took, read them, understood them, and signed them. Furthermore, the Colonel ordered careful and complete changes in the stock books of the companies to reflect the gifts announced to the world in writings. Pursuant to the Colonel's instructions, Dvorkin or some other members of Colonel Elyachar's family or staff recorded each and every transfer on the books by cancelling existing certificates and preparing new ones. Extra certificates were purchased when the Ruradan stock book ran out. All the certificates were duly stamped, and were signed by the Colonel and usually by another family member. The gifts were therefore not a secret to the Colonel's children, who have known since 1949 that gifts of stock were being made to them by their father. Finally, the Colonel ordered "dividends" paid to plaintiffs and other shareholders in the corporations when it became clear that further accumulation of income would result in taxes.

The Colonel contends that he never intended his gifts to be irrevocable. He claims he retained possession of the shares so that he unilaterally could change the plan of distribution they represented. He testified that the shares were made out prior to trips he took to Europe, and were a testamentary device in lieu of a will. He notes that at no time did he permit plaintiffs to exercise any of the normal incidents of ownership in the companies involved. He completely controlled the companies, and plaintiffs have always acquiesced in his control. He recognizes that he represented in sworn statements to the United States Government that his sons owned stock in the companies and that he had made "gifts" to them and others. And he acknowledges that the monies paid periodically to them were "dividends" paid by the companies directly as opposed to gifts of his own income from those companies. But he is willing to suffer the consequences of these misstatements, he states, rather than the unwarranted forfeiture of property he never intended to convey.

The Colonel did, however, intend to make present, irrevocable gifts to his sons. He transferred the shares at issue during a period when he was close to his sons, or had his sons working with him in the business. The transfers no doubt represented a plan for passing on his property, but they were not made in lieu of or because he lacked a will. The Colonel's keen practical sense, and his practice of seeking and accepting expert legal and accounting advice, make his claim not to have had a will unbelievable. He no doubt had prior wills, but kept them out of evidence. The Colonel's willingness to concede that he lied to our government is more probative of his present state of mind than his conduct or beliefs when the tax and other filings took place a few years ago. The Colonel's love for this country, the gratitude he feels toward it for his security and success, and the debt he knows his people owe the United States for the victory over fascism in which he played no small part, make untenable his present claim of having engaged in fraud with likely criminal consequences. See, e.g., 26 U.S.C. §7206(1); 18 U.S.C. §1001; Balter, Tax Fraud and Evasion, †11.03 (5th ed. 1983). He did not lie and would not have lied. Only the pain and anguish of the virtually total alienation from his children that this suit represents could have led him to suggest that he cheated the United States.

The Colonel's claim to have retained full control of the companies is significantly overstated. Over the years, he repeatedly sought the signatures of his children as shareholders on loan authorizations and other commercial documents. Nor is it accurate to state that he denied his children all the benefits and rights of ownership. They received their fair proportion of all dividends paid out by the companies. The Colonel saw fit to obtain his son's commitment not to pledge their stock interests, reflecting his realization that they might as beneficial owners possess that power, and as indicated above he reissued dividend checks from Gerel when his sons protested "as owners" his cancellation of earlier checks.

While the Colonel's memory was selective, and his testimony incredible as to his claim that he never intended to make irrevocable gifts, he was entirely convincing in claiming that he has never intended to surrender control of the companies during his lifetime. The Colonel is deeply attached to his work, and retained the certificates as well as operating control of the companies because he intended to keep running them until he either died or voluntarily relinquished their management. His children have always recognized this intent. They have never questioned their father's right to operate the companies, and still do not do so explicitly. Each time the Colonel threw them out of his office, they left. When he told them to sign corporate papers, they signed. When he told them not to pledge or otherwise rely upon their stock interests in the companies, they complied.

Under these circumstances, while the evidence overwhelmingly establishes intent to make present and irrevocable gifts, the gifts intended were of an ownership interest to the extent reflected in the shares transferred, but without control. The Colonel intended that, if he died, his children would assume complete control of the interests he had transferred. He also intended that they would acquire beneficial ownership immediately upon the transfer of shares, including the right to their fair proportion of dividends, and of capital in the event a corporate distribution or sale were made. But he never intended to convey a power to vote, pledge, or otherwise use the shares to interfere with his management of the companies. As one of Mr. Elyachar's accountants testified: "He really wanted to keep control. That was his overall [objective] during his life." Tr. 816. The Colonel's intention, therefore, was to convey present and complete beneficial ownership, but without control during his life. Whether the Colonel implemented this intention in a legally enforceable and irrevocable manner are issues dealt with below. But the law recognizes in principle that interests in property may be divided in the manner intended here, if the other requisites of a binding transfer are found to have occurred.

B. DELIVERY OF THE INTENDED INTERESTS

The law requires proof of the delivery of gifts to protect alleged donors and their estates from "ill-founded and fraudulent claims of gift, resting only on the assertion of oral words of gift, concerning which evidence may be doubtful or open to controversy." R. Brown, The Law of Personal Property §7.2, at 78 (3d ed. 1975). The requirement is a relatively objective test that protects against false claims of interest, and even against concessions or statements by alleged donors who decide not to implement the gifts they state they have made or will make. In re Van Alstyne, 207 N.Y. 298, 100 N.E. 802 (1913), for example, involved a husband who assured his wife that he would waive a debt that she owed him, but then failed to prepare the necessary papers or to deliver to her the notes and trust deeds that reflected the obligation. Uncontroverted proof of the husband's statements was held insufficient to establish a gift of the debt. The Court explained:

> Because many gifts are sought to be shown by oral evidence after the donor's death, it is necessary for the public good to require clear and satisfactory evidence of the fact to prevent fraud and perjury. There must be a delivery which results in a present change of dominion and ownership. Intention or mere words cannot supply the place of an actual surrender of control and authority over the thing intended to be given. 207 N.Y. at 308, 100 N.E. 802.

The most definitive evidence of delivery is a physical transfer of the gift to the donee. The *Van Alstyne* Court noted that "physical delivery of a note or other writing constituting a chose in action, with intent to vest in a donee a gift of the indebtedness represented thereby, is the most complete delivery that can be made, and consequently it is sufficient to establish the gift." Id. Physical delivery is not always required, however. "The delivery necessary to consummate a gift must be as perfect as the nature of the property and the circumstances and surroundings of the parties will reasonably permit." Id. at 309, 100 N.E. 802. The Court found in the facts of *Van Alstyne*

> no possible reason for a symbolical delivery. The testator had the immediate actual possession of the notes and trust deeds[;] . . . there could have been no reason why he should not have canceled the notes by some appropriate writing thereon or by actually delivering the notes and trust deeds into the physical possession and control of the respondent. Id at 309-10, 100 N.E. 802.

Where good reason exists for the physical retention by a donor of the subject matter of a gift, however, a good delivery can be shown by other circumstances. Thus, Chief Judge Desmond explained in distinguishing several earlier cases, including *Young:*

In each of those instances the attempted gifts failed because there had not been such a completed and irrevocable delivery of the subject matter of the gift as to put the gift beyond cancellation by the donor. In every such case the question must be as to whether there was a completed delivery of a kind appropriate to the subject property. Speelman v. Pascal, 10 N.Y.2d 313, 319, 178 N.E.2d 723, 725, 222 N.Y.S.2d 324, 328 (1961).

In *Speelman,* the delivery by Pascal to his secretary of a letter "giving" a percentage of his "share of profits" from the stage and film versions of "My Fair Lady" was found sufficient, even though at the time no arrangements had been made which gave tangible meaning to the interests granted. "In our present case there was nothing left for Pascal to do in order to make an irrevocable transfer to plaintiff of part of Pascal's right to receive royalties from the productions." 10 N.Y.2d at 320, 178 N.E.2d 723, 222 N.Y.S.2d 324.

Colonel Elyachar claims no adequate delivery occurred of the stock certificates, and therefore of the ownership interests at issue. The Colonel carefully retained control of the stock certificate books and he deliberately determined not to deliver physical possession of the certificates. Tr. 153-54, 461-63, 841-45, DX 1032, 1034-35, 1107. He rejected suggestions and requests that he deliver the certificates to his sons. He did so, moreover, because he intended thereby to continue to exercise without interference the power to manage the companies, which he believed he might lose by delivering the certificates. The record is also clear that he exercised virtually all the powers associated with the stock, and intended to continue to do so until he either stepped down voluntarily or died.

These circumstances establish that the Colonel failed to deliver *present* control of the interests represented by the certificates. They are consistent, however, with his intention to give his sons beneficial ownership interests in the corporations to the extent reflected by the certificates, but without control. Indeed, the Colonel delivered the interest he intended to convey — beneficial ownership — to the fullest extent practicable in light of his intention to retain management control.

The Court of Appeals has stressed that "[t]he delivery required must be such as to vest the donee with control and dominion over the property but this requirement must be tailored to suit the circumstances of the case." In re Estate of Szabo, 10 N.Y.2d 94, 98, 176 N.E.2d 395, 396, 217 N.Y.S.2d 593, 595 (1961). With respect to the "transfer of a part interest in stock certificates . . . , a symbolical delivery would be sufficient for it is the only kind of delivery that would be practicable under the circumstances where undoubtedly the donor would want to retain possession of the certificate." Id. The Court of Appeals in *Szabo,* however, made clear that even a "symbolical" delivery must proceed to a point of no return, and this point can only be reached when there is a transfer of record on the stock books of the company. Obviously the donor does not surrender dominion and control of a part interest until the transfer of record is made because up until that time he may change his mind and withdraw his directive to the transfer agent. Id.

Other decisions make clear that, while even the transfer of a corporate interest on the books is alone insufficient to establish delivery of ownership, a valid and irrevocable gift is found if the transfer is coupled with other acts representing tangible expressions implementing the donor's intent. See, e.g., Richardson v. Emmett, 61 A.D. 205, 70 N.Y.S. 546 (1st Dept. 1901), *rev'd on other grounds*, 170 N.Y. 412, 63 N.E. 440 (1902).

A particularly significant decision is In re Babcock's Estate, 85 Misc., 256, 147 N.Y.S. 168 (Sur. Ct. Lewis Co. 1914), *aff'd*, 169 A.D. 903, 153 N.Y.S. 1105 (3d Dept., *aff'd*, 216 N.Y. 717, 111 N.E. 1084 (1915), decided only two years after *Van Alstyne*. There, a father transferred stock on the books of a closely held corporation to his daughter, but put them in a safe in their home to which the daughter had no access. Thereafter the father, who controlled the corporation, caused dividends to be issued to the daughter in proportion to the shares transferred in her name. The New York courts found that, despite the donor's subsequent effort to deny having delivered the stock to his daughter, a valid and irrevocable gift had occurred. "Delivery may be actual, symbolical, or constructive, but must be such as to divest the donor of the possession, control and dominion over the thing given." 147 N.Y.S. at 171. Stock certificates are not themselves interests in property, but only evidence of such interests. Delivery of the property interests involved was established in *Babcock* by, among other things, the donor's deliberate transfer of those stock interests on the corporate books, issuance of certificates in her name, and the payment of dividends directly to her in proportion to the interests transferred. See id. at 175. The father's desire to continue to exercise management control made his retention of the physical certificates in his safe consistent with a transfer of beneficial ownership, and the steps he took to implement his intention proved delivery to the extent the circumstances required. See id. at 176.

In the present case the Colonel's conduct established far more than a symbolical or constructive delivery of the interests he intended to convey. When he decided to place various corporate interests in his children's names he carefully completed all the requisite formalities for stock transfers. He cancelled his own shares, filled in new certificates for himself and his children based on the number of shares transferred, purchased and affixed stock transfer tax stamps, and had the new certificates signed by the requisite corporate officers, in some instances his own children. He kept the certificates in his control, but made no secret of the fact that transfers had been made. When the stock transfers were substantial enough in value to require payment of a gift tax, the Colonel filed the required returns and paid the tax. Those filings required him to prepare lists of the stock ownership in the corporations at issue, which he physically gave to his accountants and thereafter used for the purposes of deciding the proportions in which dividends should be issued. The gift tax returns also required the Colonel to affirm on pain of civil and criminal sanctions that all the information submitted to the government was true and correct. When the companies' earnings made it financially responsible to issue dividends, the Colonel instructed that the "dividends" be paid to his sons and other donees directly, as the corporate "shareholders," in the exact proportion of their ownership, and the dividend payments were actually delivered to them.

The Colonel also treated his donees as the beneficial owners of the shares he transferred in other significant ways. He not only told his children he had given them shares, but declared this fact to his own accountants and lawyers. When the signatures of stockholders were required, the Colonel obtained signatures from his children, as in filing a "Consent of Shareholder to Include Specific Amount in Gross Income" and in complying with bank requests for stockholder consent signatures for loans. See PX 105, 110. These numerous accounts of delivery and acknowledgment and the Colonel's proven intent to make the gifts he declared and to which he swore establish an actual or "symbolical" delivery to the donees of beneficial ownership in the shares, including the right to receive any dividends or other payments made by the corporations to their owners.

In this evidentiary context, the Colonel's failure and refusal to deliver physical possession of the certificates reflects, not a retention of beneficial ownership or the power to revoke incomplete gifts, but his intention to manage and control the corporations until he dies or voluntarily surrenders control. He viewed possession of the stock as the physical manifestation of his determination that the donees should have no capacity to interfere with his management of the corporations. He so much as said this to his sons when he insisted they make no effort to pledge their interests in the corporations. He showed this was his purpose by repeatedly inviting his sons into the business in the unfulfilled hope that he would be able to surrender control, and always with the expectation that they would eventually take over. That Colonel Elyachar is the plaintiffs' father also lends support to the finding that he held the shares for his childrens' ultimate benefit, and because he wanted to remain in control. See In re Estate of Brady, 228 A.D. 56, 61, 239 N.Y.S. 5, 10 (3d Dept.), *aff'd*, 254 N.Y. 590, 173 N.E. 879 (1930) (natural for husband and father to hold stock he has given to wife and children; "reservation of the right to vote the stock [of closely-held corporation] for his children to avoid voting complications was not inconsistent with the absolute character of the gift"). Given the interests he wished to convey, and the powers he wanted to reserve, Colonel Elyachar's delivery could not have been more complete.

C.   ACCEPTANCE OF THE GIFTS

Defendants contend that Daniel and Ralph have failed to meet their burden of proving they accepted the gifts conferred by the Colonel. E.g., *Szabo,* 10 N.Y.2d at 98, 176 N.E.2d 395, 217 N.Y.S.2d 593; In re Harter's Estate, 24 A.D.2d 681, 682, 261 N.Y.S.2d 431, 432-33 (3d Dept. 1965). The Colonel's sons acted as shareholders only when asked to do so. They never attended meetings, and made no business decisions. Rather, they submitted to their father's orders and agenda, and even left their father's office when ordered out. Furthermore, they made no effort to pledge the shares, or even to claim ownership of them, prior to the events immediately before this lawsuit. See DX 1071-78. Daniel on one occasion in October 1971 wrote to his father, in an attempt to obtain delivery, that the certificates in three of the four corporations at issue were "in your name." DX 1011. On several occasions between 1976 and 1982 Ralph proposed changes in the operation of the business, each time assuring his father that his suggestions "would pertain only to the management and not to ownership" of the business. DX 1012, 1017, 1114, 1027, 1031. Finally, Daniel, Ralph, and Ruth each completed several stock powers in blank many years ago at their father's request. The Colonel testified that he obtained these powers because he feared his children might attempt to convert his testamentary plan into ownership claims and that his children knew that he wanted to be able to change any gift he had made them into gifts directly to their children. Tr. 861, 932.

Plaintiffs' lack of involvement in the corporate defendants' affairs establishes only their realization that their father had retained control. They were given, and accepted, beneficial ownership of the shares. When the Colonel told them he had given them shares, they thanked him. When he arranged to issue them dividends, they cashed the checks they received, and declared the sums on their tax returns. If the Colonel is to be believed, his sons' problem is their eagerness to receive his wealth, not their reticence. While they readily conceded control, they have at all appropriate occasions persisted in claiming ownership, as this suit reflects. Daniel's 1971 letter was, as he claimed, an unintended mischaracterization; he meant that his father controlled the corporations and insofar as the public was concerned they were in the Colonel's name. Ralph most certainly did not intend to suggest in his proposals between

1976 and 1982 that the Colonel owned the corporations; he was simply making it clear that ownership was a separate issue from the management issue, which was the subject of his proposals.

The stock power forms, signed in blank, provide no evidence of a failure to accept the gifts. To begin with, if the Colonel in fact asked his children to sign them so he could retransfer the shares, his actions indicate that he regarded the gifts he had made as complete and subject to cancellation only on consent of his children. Furthermore, even if the Colonel attempted thus to reserve the right to take back the shares, his children nevertheless accepted the gifts; his actions would only have made the gifts revocable. The evidence showed, in any event, that the children did not consent to the revocation of the gifts they had received. The Colonel's testimony was unconvincing insofar as he suggested that they so agreed. He was convincing in claiming that they had aquiesced in his transferring any of their stock to their respective children, and both Ruth and Ralph have agreed to such transfers in the past. Tr. 406; DX 1102. But none of his children agreed in signing the certificates to allow the Colonel to act as he chose with what all three have long regarded as their property.

A stock power signed in blank authorizes only what the signatory intended to permit, and must be shown to relate to specific stock to be effective. See, e.g., Larsen v. Long Island Natl. Bank, 38 Misc. 2d 877-78, 239 N.Y.S.2d 85 (Sup. Ct. Nassau Cy. 1963). The Colonel testified that he simply put the powers before his children and they signed, without any discussion or instruction. Tr. 931-32. This scenario, even if true, would at most authorize the Colonel to act only as a trustee in his children's interests. Finally, the Colonel failed to exercise whatever authority may have been conveyed by the powers. The powers remain unexercised, after a period of many years, and were not relied upon by the Colonel in his actual effort to cancel the gifts he made. Indeed, although he initially testified that he had not cancelled his gifts to his grandchildren, he later conceded that he had done so, even though they signed no stock powers authorizing him to take back or transfer their shares. Tr. 927-30.

D.   IMPLIED TRUST OR RETAINED LIFE INTEREST

The question remains whether Colonel Elyachar could effectively withhold delivery of the power to control the corporate interests reflected by the certificates. Two equally plausible bases exist for upholding this effort on his part. First, nothing in property law prevents an owner from separating beneficial ownership from control. A person can convey an ownership interest in personal property—in effect the remainder interest—along with the right to receive all income or profits, while at the same time retaining a life interest in its use or control. "Not only may the donor defer the enjoyment of the donee until the death of the donor, but he may also reserve to himself the use and enjoyment of the property during his life without affecting the present character of the gift to the donee of the future enjoyment or invalidating the donation." Brown, The Law of Personal Property §48, at 134 (2d ed. 1936); see, e.g., In re Estate of Valentine, 122 Misc. 486, 204 N.Y.S. 284 (Sur. Ct. N.Y. Cy. 1924) (donor effectively made gift of ownership of stock upon his death to his wife and daughters by delivering document proving absolute gift, despite reservation of control and income for donor's life); In re Estate of Hendricks, 163 A.D. 413, 148 N.Y.S. 511 (1st Dept. 1914), *aff'd*, 214 N.Y. 663, 108 N.E. 1095 (1915) (gift of beneficial ownership in stock upheld, though voting power and control reserved); In re Estate of Bullard, 76 A.D. 207, 78 N.Y.S. 491 (3rd Dept. 1902) (gift upheld where donor transferred stock certificates to his grandson, but retained control, dividends, and voting power and held office for long periods by virtue of stock control).

Dividing the incidents of property in the manner contemplated by Colonel Elyachar is uncommon with respect to some forms of property, but entirely familiar in connection with ownership interests in corporations. The separation of ownership and control in corporate affairs is the rule rather than the exception in our economy, and stock ownership is often unaccompanied by meaningful authority other than the right to a due proportion of such payments as the corporate directors choose to order. W. Cary & M. Eisenberg, Corporations 208-11 (5th ed. 1980). The analogy to this case is obviously imperfect, but it is advanced here only to show that the Colonel's plan sought an allocation of property interests that is far from unusual in our society. In light of the Colonel's lifetime involvement with his buildings, moreover, his plan to give away interests in them, while retaining control, is an allocation of ownership interests that advances reasonable economic expectations in a manner consistent with property law principles.

The Colonel's plan can also be upheld as an intervivos trust, in which he gave beneficial ownership of the shares to his children, while retaining physical possession of the certificates as trustee for his life or for such shorter period as he elected. A trust is "a fiduciary relationship in which one person holds a property interest, subject to an equitable obligation to keep or use that interest for the benefit of another." G. Bogert, The Law of Trusts & Trustees §1 (2d ed. 1965). Usually the settlor delivers the trust res to a trustee pursuant to a written document describing the transfer. But a trust may be established through an oral declaration or other conduct, even though the settlor does not use the words "trust" or "trustee."

Although a trust is created only if the settlor properly manifests an intention to create a trust, it is immaterial whether or not he knows that the relationship which he intends to create is called a trust, and whether or not he knows the precise characteristics of the relationship which is called a trust. In many cases the owner of property in disposing of it has no very clear idea of the precise nature of the disposition which he intends to make. 1 Scott on Trusts §23, at 191 (3d ed. 1967).

In New York a trust in personal property can be created or proved by parol, and no requirement exists that particular words be used. "The law will delineate a trust where, in view of sufficiently manifested purpose or intent, that is the appropriate instrumentality, even though its creator calls it something else, or doesn't call it anything." In re Will of Douglas, 195 Misc. 661, 665, 89 N.Y.S.2d 498, 503 (Sur. Ct. Broome Cy. 1949); see 61 N.Y. Jur. Trusts §57 (1968) ("the court will find that a trust is created where it appears that such was the intention of the parties, and where the nature of the transaction justifies or requires it"). To protect the alleged donor, however, New York law requires that his intent to create a trust must be established beyond any reasonable doubt. The words and acts relied upon must be unequivocal in nature and admit of no other interpretation than that the property was to be held in trust. There must be either an express declaration of trust or facts and circumstances which show that the putative settlor intended to create a trust relationship. In re Estate of Fontanella, 33 A.D.2d 29, 31, 304 N.Y.S.2d 829, 831 (3d Dept. 1969) (beyond reasonable doubt); Beaver v Beaver, 117 N.Y. 421, 428, 22 N.E. 940, 941 (1889).

In this case the Colonel's intention to create a trust is "implied from [his] acts or words . . . [and] arises as a necessary inference therefrom and is unequivocal." Wadd v. Hazelton, 137 N.Y. 215, 219, 33 N.E. 143, 144 (1893). His acts and words established his intention to give beneficial ownership, presently and absolutely, to those in whose names he issued certificates and to whom he paid dividends as shareholders. At the same time, his acts and words also established his intention to retain the power to control the corporations involved. These intended objectives strongly indicate a desire on his part to manage the property for the ultimate benefit of the beneficial owners. Furthermore, his conduct until his recent attempt to repudiate the gifts was entirely consistent with that of a trustee. He paid out all dividends to the beneficial owners, and when his sons protested his attempt to withhold a dividend, he acquiesced and paid the dividend declared. Some years before this litigation, Daniel instinctively described the nature of his interest in the corporation when he stated in a financial report that "[n]o New York Property has been included in this Statement, as it is involved with a large Family Trust, presently controlled by father, J. R. Elyachar." DX 1071; see Tr. 496.

The rule requiring proof beyond a reasonable doubt of an intention to create a trust has been satisfied here, if trusts may truly be implied from conduct without regard to form. To the extent any doubt exists, moreover, the rule must be applied with a view to its purpose rather than in a mechanical manner. That purpose is to avoid the instability to titles and the danger of perjury that would occur if courts could convert imperfect gifts into valid declarations of trust. See *Young*, 80 N.Y. at 437; see also Hamer v. Sidway, 124 N.Y. 538, 27 N.E. 256 (1891); Tsai v. Tsai, 39 A.D.2d 652, 331 N.Y.S.2d 691, 692 (1st Dept. 1972); *Fontanella*, 33 A.D. at 31, 304 N.Y.S.2d at 831. To apply the rule here, and thereby to invalidate the trust, would serve no such purpose. The gifts made by Colonel Elysachar were intended, delivered, and accepted so they have become present and irrevocable. A trust is implied in this case not to save a future or revocable gift but to give effect to the Colonel's equally clear intent to reserve to himself powers of management and control, powers that would be lost under these circumstances if no trust (or life interest) were implied. The dangers of fraud and perjury that exist when purported donees claim they were delivered property in trust are therefore not present in this case. While the situation is apparently one of first impression, it appears reasonable to assume that the courts of New York would more readily find a trust in order to effectuate a donor's intent to reserve a property interest than to render complete at a donee's behest an intended but undelivered gift.

IV. Conclusion

In light of the findings and conclusions recited above, Daniel and Ralph Elyachar are each hereby declared the beneficial owners of 20% of the outstanding shares of Gerel Corporation, 20% of the outstanding shares of Huguel Corporation, 20% of the outstanding shares of Timston Corporation, and 21.9% of the outstanding shares of Ruradan Corporation. Defendants are ordered to prepare the necessary documents and certificates properly to reflect plaintiffs' interests, which must be accomplished within thirty days of the entry of final judgment in this case, after all appeals are exhausted. Colonel Elyachar will continue to manage and control these corporations for his life, as fiduciary or trustee for the beneficial owners. The request that the certificates be surrendered to plaintiffs is therefore denied. The Court retains jurisdiction to enforce this judgment through appropriate proceedings and decrees.

So ordered.

Chapter Twelve

Historical Background of Real Property Law

Insert the following material on page 203 after the problem.

Note

For income tax purposes, the Maryland ground rent system operates as a mortgage. See John Howard Burbage, 82 T.C. 546 (1984).

Chapter Thirteen

The Types of Estates in Land

Add the following on page 241 at the end of the note on the Uniform Marital Property Act.

The Uniform Marital Property Act has been enacted in Wisconsin, effective January 1, 1986. In regard to this act, see Wellman, Third Party Interests Under the Uniform Marital Property Act, 21 Hous. L. Rev. 717 (1984).

Insert the following material at the end of page 242.

Case considering property rights where couple live together openly as husband and wife and have children but were never married.

HEWITT v. HEWITT

Supreme Court of Illinois, 1979
77 Ill. 2d 49, 394 N.E.2d 1204

UNDERWOOD, Justice:

The issue in this case is whether plaintiff Victoria Hewitt, whose complaint alleges she lived with defendant Robert Hewitt from 1960 to 1975 in an unmarried, family-like relationship to which three children have been born, may recover from him "an equal share of the profits and properties accumulated by the parties" during that period.

Plaintiff initially filed a complaint for divorce, but at a hearing on defendant's motion to dismiss, admitted that no marriage ceremony had taken place and that the parties had never obtained a marriage license. In dismissing that complaint the trial court found that neither a ceremonial nor a common law marriage existed; that since defendant admitted the paternity of the minor children, plaintiff need not bring a separate action under the Paternity Act (Ill. Rev. Stat. 1975, ch. 106¾, par. 51. et seq.) to have the question of child support determined; and directed plaintiff to make her complaint more definite as to the nature of the property of which she was seeking division.

Plaintiff thereafter filed an amended complaint alleging the following bases for her claim: (1) that because defendant promised he would "share his life, his future, his earnings and his property" with her and all of defendant's property resulted from the parties' joint endeavors, plaintiff is entitled in equity to a one-half share; (2) that the conduct of the parties evinced an implied contract entitling plaintiff to one-half the property accumulated during their "family relationship"; (3) that because defendant fraudulently assured plaintiff she was his wife in order to secure her services, although he knew they were not legally married, defendant's property should be impressed with a trust for plaintiff's benefit; (4) that because plaintiff has relied to her detriment on defendant's promises and devoted her entire life to him, defendant has been unjustly enriched.

The factual background alleged or testified to is that in June 1960, when she and defendant were students at Grinnell College in Iowa, plaintiff became pregnant; that defendant thereafter told her that they were husband and wife and would live as such, no formal ceremony being necessary, and that he would "share his life, his future, his earnings and his property" with her; that the parties immediately announced to their respective parents that they were married and thereafter held themselves out as husband and wife; that in reliance on defendant's promises she devoted her efforts to his professional education and his establishment in the practice of pedodontia, obtaining financial assistance from her parents for this purpose; that she assisted defendant in his career with her own special skills and although she was given payroll checks for these services she placed them in a common fund; that defendant, who was without funds at the time of the marriage, as a result of her efforts now earns over $80,000 a year and has accumulated large amounts of property, owned either jointly with her or separately; that she has given him every assistance a wife and mother could give, including social activities designed to enhance his social and professional reputation.

The amended complaint was also dismissed, the trial court finding that Illinois law and public policy require such claims to be based on a valid marriage. The appellate court reversed, stating that because the parties had outwardly lived a conventional married life, plaintiff's conduct had not "so affronted public policy that she should be denied any and all relief" (62 Ill. App. 3d 861, 869, 20 Ill. Dec. 476, 482, 380 N.E.2d 454, 460), and that plaintiff's complaint stated a cause of action on an express oral contract. We granted leave to appeal. Defendant apparently does not contest his obligation to support the children, and that question is not before us.

The appellate court, in reversing, gave considerable weight to the fact that the parties had held themselves out as husband and wife for over 15 years. The court noted that they lived "a most conventional, respectable and ordinary family life" (62 Ill. App. 3d 861, 863, 20 Ill. Dec. 476, 478, 380 N.E.2d 454, 457) that did not openly flout accepted standards, the "single flaw" being the lack of a valid marriage. Indeed the appellate court went so far as to say that the parties had "lived within the legitimate bounds of a marriage and family relationship of a most conventional sort" (62 Ill. App. 3d 861, 864, 20 Ill. Dec. 476, 479, 380 N.E.2d 454, 457), an assertion which that court cannot have intended to be taken literally. Nothing that the Illinois Marriage and Dissolution of Marriage Act (Ill. Rev. Stat. 1977, ch. 40, par. 101 et seq.) does not prohibit nonmarital cohabitation and that the Criminal Code of 1961 (Ill. Rev. Stat. 1977, ch. 38, par. 11-8(a)) makes fornication an offense only if the behavior is open and notorious, the appellate court concluded that plaintiff should not be denied relief on public policy grounds.

In finding that plaintiff's compliant stated a cause of action on an express oral contract, the appellate court adopted the reasoning of the California Supreme Court in the widely publicized case of Marvin v. Marvin (1976), 18 Cal. 3d 660, 134 Cal. Rptr. 815, 557 P.2d 106, quoting extensively therefrom. In *Marvin,* Michelle Triola and defendant Lee Marvin lived together for 7 years pursuant to an alleged oral agreement that while "the parties lived together they would combine their efforts and earnings and would share equally any and all property accumulated as a result of their efforts whether individual or combined." (18 Cal. 3d 660, 666, 134 Cal. Rptr. 815, 819, 557 P.2d 106, 110.) In her complaint she alleged that, in reliance on this agreement, she gave up her career as a singer to devote herself full time to defendant as "companion, home-maker, housekeeper and cook." (18 Cal. 3d 660, 666, 134 Cal. Rptr. 815, 819, 557 P.2d 106, 110.) In resolving her claim for one-half the property accumulated in defendant's name during that period the California court held that "The courts should enforce express contracts between nonmarital partners except to the extent that the contract is explicitly founded on the consideration of meretricious sexual services" and that

> In the absence of an express contract, the courts should inquire into the conduct of the parties to determine whether that conduct demonstrates an implied contract, agreement of partnership or joint venture, or some other tacit understanding between the parties. The courts may also employ the doctrine of quantum meruit, or equitable remedies such as constructive or resulting trusts, when warranted by the facts of the case. (18 Cal. 3d 660, 665, 134 Cal. Rptr. 815, 819, 557 P.2d 106, 110.)

The court reached its conclusions because:

In summary, we believe that the prevalence of nonmarital relationships in modern society and the social acceptance of them, marks this as a time when our courts should by no means apply the doctrine of the unlawfulness of the so-called meretricious relationship to the instant case. . . .

The mores of the society have indeed changed so radically in regard to cohabitation that we cannot impose a standard based on alleged moral considerations that have apparently been so widely abandoned by so many. (18 Cal. 3d 660, 683-84, 134 Cal. Rptr. 815, 831, 557 P.2d 106, 122.)

It is apparent that the *Marvin* court adopted a pure contract theory, under which, if the intent of the parties and the terms of their agreement are proved, the pseudo-conventional family relationship which impressed the appellate court here is irrelevant; recovery may be had unless the implicit sexual relationship is made the explicit consideration for the agreement. In contrast, the appellate court here, as we understand its opinion, would apply contract principles only in a setting where the relationship of the parties outwardly resembled that of a traditional family. It seems apparent that the plaintiff in *Marvin* would not have been entitled to recover in our appellate court because of the absence of that outwardly appearing conventional family relationship.

The issue of whether property rights accrue to unmarried cohabitants cannot, however, be regarded realistically as merely a problem in the law of express contracts. Plaintiff argues that because her action is founded on an express contract, her recovery would in no way imply that unmarried cohabitants acquire property rights merely by cohabitation and subsequent separation. However, the *Marvin* court expressly recognized and the appellate court here seems to agree that if common law principles of express contract govern express arrangements between unmarried cohabitants, common law principles of implied contract, equitable relief and constructive trust must govern the parties' relations in the absence of such an agreement. (18 Cal. 3d 660, 678, 134 Cal. Rptr. 815, 827, 557 P.2d 106, 118; 62 Ill. App. 3d 861, 867-68, 20 Ill. Dec. 476, 380 N.E.2d 454.) In all probability the latter case will be much the more common, since it is unlikely that most couples who live together will enter into express agreements regulating their property rights. (Bruch, Property Rights of De Facto Spouses, Including Thoughts on the Value of Homemakers' Services, 10 Fam. L. Q. 101, 102 (1976).) The increasing incidence of nonmarital cohabitation referred to in *Marvin* and the variety of legal remedies therein sanctioned seem certain to result in substantial amounts of litigation, in which, whatever the allegations regarding an oral contract, the proof will necessarily involve details of the parties' living arrangements.

Apart, however, from the appellate court's reliance upon *Marvin* to reach what appears to us to be a significantly different result, we believe there is a more fundamental problem. We are aware, of course, of the increasing judicial attention given the individual claims of unmarried cohabitants to jointly accumulated property, and the fact that the majority of courts considering the question have recognized an equitable or contractual basis for implementing the reasonable expectations of the parties unless sexual services were the explicit consideration. (See cases collected in Annot., 31 A.L.R.2d 1255 (1953) and A.L.R.2d Later Case Service supplementing vols. 25 to 31.) The issue of unmarried cohabitants' mutual property rights, however, as we earlier noted, cannot appropriately be characterized solely in terms of contract law, nor is it limited to considerations of equity or fairness as between the parties to such relationships. There are major public policy questions involved in determining whether, under what circumstances, and to what extent it is desirable to accord some type of legal status to claims arising from such relationships. Of substantially greater importance than the rights of the immediate parties is the impact of such recognition upon our society and the institution of marriage. Will the fact that legal rights closely resembling those arising from conventional marriages can be acquired by those who deliberately choose to enter into what have heretofore been commonly referred to as "illicit" or "meretricious" relationships encourage formation of such relationships and weaken marriage as the foundation of our family-based society? In the event of death shall the survivor have the status of a surviving spouse for purposes of inheritance, wrongful death actions, workmen's compensation, etc.? And still more importantly: what of the children born of such relationships? What are their support and inheritance rights and by what standards are custody questions resolved? What of the sociological and psychological effects upon them of that type of environment? Does not the recognition of legally enforceable property and custody rights emanating from nonmarital cohabitation in practical effect equate with the legalization of common law marriage—at least in the circumstances of this case? And, in summary, have the increasing numbers of unmarried cohabitants and changing mores of our society (Bruch, Property Rights of De Facto Spouses Including Thoughts on the Value of Homemakers' Services, 10 Fam. L.Q. 101, 102-03 (1976); Nielson, In re Cary: A Judicial Recognition of Illicit Cohabitation, 25 Hastings L.J. 1226 (1974)) reached the point at which the general welfare of the citizens of this State is best served by a return to something resembling the judicially created common law marriage our legislature outlawed in 1905?

Illinois' public policy regarding agreements such as the one alleged here was implemented long ago in Wallace v. Rappleye (1882), 103 Ill. 229, 249, where this court said: "An agreement in consideration of future illicit cohabitation between the plaintiffs is void." This is the traditional rule, in force until recent years in all jurisdictions. (See, e.g., Gauthier v. Laing (1950), 96 N.H. 80, 70 A.2d 207; Grant v. Butt (1941), 198 S.C. 298, 17 S.E.2d 689.) Section 589 of the Restatement of Contracts (1932) states, "A bargain in whole or in part for or in consideration of illicit sexual intercourse or of a promise thereof is illegal." See also 6A Corbin, Contracts sec. 1476 (1962), and cases cited therein.

It is true, of course, that cohabitation by the parties may not prevent them from forming valid contracts about independent matters, for which it is said the sexual relations do not form part of the consideration. (Restatement of Contracts secs. 589, 597 (1932); 6A Corbin, Contracts sec. 1476 (1962).) Those courts which allow recovery generally have relied on this principle to reduce the scope of the rule of illegality. Thus, California courts long prior to *Marvin* held that an express agreement to pool earnings is supported by independent consideration and is not invalidated by cohabitation of the parties, the agreements being regarded as simultaneous but separate. (See, e.g., Trutalli v. Meraviglia (1932), 215 Cal. 698, 12 P.2d 430; see also Annot., 31 A.L.R.2d 1255 (1953), and cases cited therein.) More recently, several courts have reasoned that the rendition of housekeeping and homemaking services such as plaintiff alleges here could be regarded as the consideration for a separate contract between the parties, severable from the illegal contract founded on sexual relations. (Kozlowski v. Kozlowski (1979), 80 N.J. 378, 403 A.2d 902; Marvin v. Marvin (1976), 18 Cal. 3d 660, 670 n.5, 134 Cal. Rptr. 815, 822 n.5, 557 P.2d 106, 113 n.5; Tyranski v. Piggins (1973), 44 Mich. App. 570, 205 N.W.2d 595, 597; contra, Rehak v. Mathis (1977), 239 Ga. 541 238 S.E.2d 81.) In Latham v. Latham (1976), 274 Or. 421, 547 P.2d 144, and Carlson v. Olson (Minn.1977), 256 N.W.2d 249, on allegations similar to those in this case, the Minnesota Supreme Court adopted *Marvin* and the Oregon court expressly held that agreements in consideration of cohabitation were not void, stating:

> We are not validating an agreement in which the only or primary consideration is sexual intercourse. The agreement here contemplated all the burdens and amenities of married life. 274 Or. 421, 427, 547 P.2d 144, 147.

The real thrust of plaintiff's argument here is that we should abandon the rule of illegality because of certain changes in societal norms and attitudes. It is urged that social mores have changed radically in recent years, rendering this principle of law archaic. It is said that because there are so many unmarried cohabitants today the courts must confer a legal status on such relationships. This, of course, is the rationale underlying some of the decisions and commentaries. (See, e.g., Marvin v. Marvin (1976), 18 Cal. 3d 660, 683, 134 Cal. Rptr. 815, 831, 557 P.2d 106, 122;

Beal v. Beal (1978), 282 Or. 115, 577 P.2d 507; Kay & Amyx, Marvin v. Marvin: Preserving the Options, 65 Cal. L. Rev. 937 (1977).) If this is to be the result, however, it would seem more candid to acknowledge the return of varying forms of common law marriage than to continue displaying the naivete we believe involved in the assertion that there are involved in these relationships contracts separate and independent from the sexual activity, and the assumption that those contracts would have been entered into or would continue without that activity.

Even if we were to assume some modification of the rule of illegality is appropriate, we return to the fundamental question earlier alluded to: If resolution of this issue rests ultimately on grounds of public policy, by what body should that policy be determined? *Marvin* viewing the issue as governed solely by contract law, found judicial policy-making appropriate. Its decision was facilitated by California precedent and that State's no-fault divorce law. In our view, however, the situation alleged here was not the kind of arm's length bargain envisioned by traditional contract principles, but an intimate arrangement of a fundamentally different kind. The issue, realistically, is whether it is appropriate for this court to grant a legal status to a private arrangement substituting for the institution of marriage sanctioned by the State. The question whether change is needed in the law governing the rights of parties in this delicate area of marriage-like relationships involves evaluations of sociological data and alternatives we believe best suited to the superior investigative and fact-finding facilities of the legislative branch in the exercise of its traditional authority to declare public policy in the domestic relations field. (Strukoff v. Strukoff (1979), 76 Ill. 2d 53, 27 Ill. Dec. 762, 389 N.E.2d 1170; Siegall v. Solomon (1960), 19 Ill. 2d 145, 166 N.E.2d 5.) That belief is reinforced by the fact that judicial recognition of mutual property rights between unmarried cohabitants would, in our opinion, clearly violate the policy of our recently enacted Illinois Marriage and Dissolution of Marriage Act. Although the Act does not specifically address the subject of nonmarital cohabitation, we think the legislative policy quite evident from the statutory scheme.

The Act provides:

> This Act shall be liberally construed and applied to promote its underlying purposes, which are to:
> (1) provide adequate procedures for the solemnization and registration of marriage;
> (2) strengthen and preserve the integrity of marriage and safeguard family relationships. (Ill. Rev. Stat. 1977, ch. 40, par. 102.)

We cannot confidently say that judicial recognition of property rights between unmarried cohabitants will not make that alternative to marriage more attractive by allowing the parties to engage in such relationships with greater security. As one commentator has noted, it may make this alternative especially attractive to persons who seek a property arrangement that the law does not permit to marital partners. (Comment, 90 Harv. L. Rev. 1708, 1713 (1977).) This court, for example, has held void agreements releasing husbands from their obligation to support their wives. (Vock. v. Vock (1937), 365 Ill. 432, 6 N.E.2d 843; VanKoten v. VanKoten (1926), 323 Ill. 323, 154 N.E. 146; see also Rhodes v. Rhodes (1967), 82 Ill. App. 2d 435, 225 N.E.2d 802; Restatement of Contracts sec. 587 (1932); Weitzman, Legal Regulation of Marriage: Tradition and Change, 62 Cal. L. Rev. 1169, 1259-63 (1974).) In thus potentially enhancing the attractiveness of a private arrangement over marriage, we believe that the appellate court decision in this case contravenes the Act's policy of strengthening and preserving the integrity of marriage.

The Act also provides: "Common law marriages contracted in this State after June 30, 1905 are invalid." (Ill. Rev. Stat. 1977, ch. 40, par. 214.) The doctrine of common law marriage was a judicially sanctioned alternative to formal marriage designed to apply to cases like the one before us. In Port v. Port (1873), 70 Ill. 484, this court reasoned that because the statute governing marriage did not "prohibit or declare void a marriage not solemnized in accordance with its provisions, a marriage without observing the statutory regulations, if made according to the common law, will still be a valid marriage." (70 Ill. 484, 486.) This court held that if the parties declared their present intent to take each other as husband and wife and thereafter did so a valid common law marriage existed. (Cartwright v. McGown (1887), 121 Ill. 388, 398, 12 N.E. 737.) Such marriages were legislatively abolished in 1905, presumably because of the problems earlier noted, and the above-quoted language expressly reaffirms that policy.

While the appellate court denied that its decision here served to rehabilitate the doctrine of common law marriage, we are not persuaded. Plaintiff's allegations disclose a relationship that clearly would have constituted a valid common law marriage in this State prior to 1905. The parties expressly manifested their present intent to be husband and wife; immediately thereafter they assumed the marital status; and for many years they consistently held themselves out to their relatives and the public at large as husband and wife. Revealingly, the appellate court relied on the fact that the parties were, to the public, husband and wife in determining that the parties living arrangement did not flout Illinois public policy. It is of course true, as plaintiff argues, that unlike a common law spouse she would not have full marital rights in that she could not, for example, claim her statutory one-third share of defendant's property on his death. The distinction appears unimpressive, however, if she can claim one-half of his property on a theory of express or implied contract.

Further, in enacting the Illinois Marriage and Dissolution of Marriage Act, our legislature considered and rejected the "no-fault" divorce concept that has been adopted in many other jurisdictions, including California. (See Uniform Marriage and Divorce Act secs. 302, 305.) Illinois appears to be one of three States retaining fault grounds for dissolution of marriage. (Ill. Rev. Stat. 1977, ch. 40, par. 401; Comment, Hewitt v. Hewitt, Contract Cohabitation and Equitable Expectations Relief for Meretricious Spouses, 12 J. Mar. J. Prac. & Proc. 435, 452-53 (1979).) Certainly a significantly stronger promarriage policy is manifest in that action, which appears to us to reaffirm the traditional doctrine that marriage is a civil contract between three parties — the husband, the wife and the State. (Johnson v. Johnson (1942), 381 Ill. 362, 45 N.E.2d 625; VanKoten v. VanKoten (1926), 323 Ill. 323, 154 N.E. 146.) The policy of the Act gives the State a strong continuing interest in the institution of marriage and prevents the marriage relationship from becoming in effect a private contract terminable at will. This seems to us another indication that public policy disfavors private contractual alternatives to marriage.

Lastly, in enacting the Illinois Marriage and Dissolution of Marriage Act, the legislature adopted for the first time the civil law concept of the putative spouse. The Act provides that an unmarried person may acquire the rights of a legal spouse only if he goes through a marriage ceremony and cohabits with another in the good-faith belief that he is validly married. When he learns that the marriage is not valid his status as a putative spouse terminates; common law marriages are expressly excluded. (Ill. Rev. Stat. 1977, ch. 40, par. 305.) The legislature thus extended legal recognition to a class of nonmarital relationships, but only to the extent of a party's good-faith belief in the existence of a valid marriage. Moreover, during the legislature's deliberations on the Act *Marvin* was decided and received wide publicity. (See Note, 12 J. Mar. J. Prac. & Proc. 435, 450 (1979).) These circumstances in our opinion constitute a recent and unmistakeable legislative judgment disfavoring the grant of mutual property rights to knowingly unmarried cohabitants. We have found no case in which recovery has been allowed in the face of a legislative declaration as recently and clearly enacted as ours. Even if we disagreed with the wisdom of that judgment, it is not for us to overturn or erode it. Davis v. Commonwealth Edison Co. (1975), 61 Ill. 2d 494, 496-97, 336 N.E.2d 881.

Actually, however, the legislature judgment is in accord with the history of common law marriage in this country. "Despite its judicial acceptance in many states, the doctrine of common-law marriage is generally frowned on in this country, even in some of the states that have accepted it." (52 Am. Jur. 2d 902 Marriage sec. 46 (1970).) Its origins, early history and problems are detailed in In re Estate of Soeder (1966), 7 Ohio App. 2d 271, 220 N.E.2d 547, where that court noted that some 30 States did not authorize common law marriage. Judicial criticism has been widespread even in States recognizing the relationship. (See, e.g., Baker v. Mitchell (1941), 143 Pa. Super. 50, 54, 17 A.2d 738, 741, "a fruitful source of perjury and fraud . . ."; Sorensen v. Sorensen (1904), 68 Neb. 500, 100 N.W. 930.) "It tends to weaken the public estimate of the sanctity of the marriage relation. It puts in doubt the certainty of the rights of inheritance. It opens the door to false pretenses of marriage and the imposition of estates on supposititious heirs." 7 Ohio App. 2d 271, 290, 220 N.E.2d 547, 561.

In our judgment the fault in the appellate court holding in this case is that its practical effect is the reinstatement of common law marriage, as we earlier indicated, for there is no doubt that the alleged facts would, if proved, establish such a marriage under our pre-1905 law. (Cartwright v. McGown (1887), 121 Ill. 388, 12 N.E. 737.) The concern of both the *Marvin* court and the appellate court on this score is manifest from the circumstance that both courts found it necessary to emphasize marital values ("the structure of society itself largely depends upon the institution of marriage" (Marvin v. Marvin (1976), 18 Cal. 3d 660, 684, 134 Cal. Rptr. 815, 831, 557 P.2d 106, 122) and to deny any intent to "derogate from" (18 Cal. 3d 660, 684, 134 Cal. Rptr. 815, 831, 557 P.2d 106, 122) or "denigrate" (Hewitt v. Hewitt (1978), 62 Ill. App. 3d 861, 868, 20 Ill. Dec. 476, 380 N.E.2d 454) that institution. Commentators have expressed greater concern: "[T]he effect of these cases is to reinstitute common-law marriage in California after it has been abolished by the legislature." (Clark, The New Marriage, Williamette L.J. 441, 449 (1976).) "[*Hewitt*] is, if not a direct resurrection of common-law marriage contract principles, at least a large step in that direction." Reiland, Hewitt v. Hewitt: Middle America, *Marvin* and Common-Law Marriage, 60 Chi. B. Rec. 84, 88-90 (1978).

We do not intend to suggest that plaintiff's claims are totally devoid of merit. Rather, we believe that our statement in Mogged v. Mogged (1973), 55 Ill. 2d 221, 225, 302 N.E.2d 293, 295, made in deciding whether to abolish a judicially created defense to divorce, is appropriate here:

> Whether or not the defense of recrimination should be abolished or modified in Illinois is a question involving complex public-policy considerations as to which compelling arguments may be made on both sides. For the reasons stated hereafter, we believe that these questions are appropriately within the province of the legislature, and that, if there is to be a change in the law of this State on this matter, it is for the legislature and not the courts to bring about that change."

We accordingly hold that the plaintiff's claims are unenforceable for the reason that they contravene the public policy, implicit in the statutory scheme of the Illinois Marriage and Dissolution of Marriage Act, disfavoring the grant of mutually enforceable property rights to knowingly unmarried cohabitants. The judgment of the appellate court is reversed and the judgment of the circuit court of Champaign County is affirmed.

Appellate court reversed; circuit court affirmed.

Case considering whether asserting Marvin-*type claim violated no-contest provision in decedent's will.*

ESTATE OF LEO BLACK

California Court of Appeals (Fifth District 1984)
160 Cal. App. 3d 584, 206 Cal. Rptr. 663

HANSON, Associate Justice.

In this probate proceeding, we hold that petitioner, a beneficiary under the will and alleged unmarried partner of decedent, may seek a determination of claimed property rights arising during the couple's lengthy relationship without forfeiting, by operation of the will's no-contest clause, the specific gift of their residence. We reach this conclusion based upon our independent interpretation of the language of the will in light of uncontradicted facts of the pleadings; the merits of petitioner's claims to a partnership interest in property in the estate are not before us.

Both sides appeal from an order of the probate court under Probate Code sections 588 and 1080[1] ruling upon the petition of Donna Graham "For Determination of Interest Under the Will and for Interpretation of the Will" of decedent Leo Black and the response of the coexecutors seeking instructions. Graham, a beneficiary and the alleged unmarried cohabitant of the deceased, sought a ruling that the filing of a proposed section 851.5 petition to determine an interest in property in the estate under theories of express or implied domestic partnership (Marvin v. Marvin (1976) 18 Cal. 3d 660, 134 Cal. Rptr. 815, 557 P.2d 106)[2] would not violate the in terrorem or no-contest clause of the will. A copy of the proposed pleading was attached to the section 1080 petition.

---

1. All statutory references are to the Probate Code unless otherwise indicated.

2. In the *Marvin* decision, the California Supreme Court held that a party to a nonmarital living arrangement may be entitled to enforce property rights based upon express or implied-in-fact agreement with the cohabitant, and that other equitable remedies may be available to protect the reasonable expectations of a nonmarital partner.

Donna F. Roberts and Thomas O. Gilbert, coexecutors of the estate, filed opposition contending the filing of the section 1080 petition itself triggered the in terrorem clause.

Following a hearing, the court ruled by minute order that "the filing of the instant petition did not violate the in terrorem clause in the will; however, the subsequent filing of the proposed petition or an independent action under a *Marvin* theory would do so." A formal order stating these rulings was entered.

Graham appealed from the portion of the court's order determining that the filing of the proposed petition or an independent action would violate the in terrorem clause.[3] The executors filed a "Notice of Cross-Appeal" attacking the portion of the order holding the filing of the section 1080 petition did not violate the no-contest clause.

Facts

The petition was tried upon the documents and arguments of counsel and presents issues of law arising from basically uncontested facts. No question concerning the merits of the *Marvin* claim was litigated.

Leo Black, a widower with five children, lived with Donna Graham, to whom he was not married, from 1965 until his death on May 19, 1983, or nearly 18 years. Also living in the household during this time was Graham's adopted daughter, born in 1960. The proposed petition under section 851.5 alleges Black agreed to

> support petitioner and her minor child and provide a home in which they all would reside, and . . . petitioner agreed to perform all the necessary functions of a typical housewife, including entertaining decedent's business acquaintances. . . .
>
> [Petitioner did in fact provide] a home and family for decedent until his death. . . .

Sixteen days before his death, Black executed a will which gave to Graham "if she shall survive me," a mobile home (according to the executors, the residence of Black and Graham), and placed $50,000 in trust to provide for expenses for the home during the life of Graham "[s]o long as [she] is . . . using said mobile home, or a replacement thereof, as her primary residence. . . ." The will further provided that the trust principal and income could be utilized, in the discretion of the trustees (executors Roberts and Gilbert), to provide for other needs of Graham "after

---

3. The court's order is appealable under section 1240, subdivisions (*l*) and (*o*). (See *Estate of Friedman* (1979) 100 Cal. App. 3d 810, 813-14, fn. 2, 161 Cal. Rptr. 311.)

taking into consideration any income or other means of health, education, support or maintenance available to her. . . ."[4]

The residue of the estate, which we are informed is valued at more than $900,000 including the remainder interest in the $50,000 trust, was left to Black's five children. Paragraph Seventh of the will provides as follows:

> If any beneficiary under this will in any manner, directly or indirectly, contests or attacks this will or any of its provisions, any share or interest in my estate given to that contesting beneficiary under this will is revoked and shall be disposed of in the same manner provided herein as if that contesting beneficiary had predeceased me.

Decedent's will was admitted to probate and letters testamentary issued on June 27, 1983. On August 15, 1983, Graham filed the instant petition under section 1080; attached as Exhibit "A" is a proposed pleading under section 851.5, claiming an undivided 50 percent interest in all the property held by Black at his death on the theory of a "*Marvin*-type domestic partnership implied in law. . . ."

Discussion

These appeals present two interrelated questions: (1) Did the filing of Graham's proposed section 1080 petition violate the no-contest clause of the will? (2) Would the filing of Graham's proposed section 851.5 petition claiming one-half the property possessed by decedent at his death on a theory of implied domestic partnership violate the no contest clause? We answer both questions in the negative, affirming in part and reversing in part the order of the probate court.[5]

The obvious purpose of no-contest ("in terrorem") clauses is to discourage will contests by imposing a penalty of forfeiture against beneficiaries who challenge the will. No-contest clauses are valid in California and have been said to be favored by the public policies of discouraging litigation and giving effect to the purposes expressed by the testator. (Estate of Hite (1909) 155 Cal. 436, 439-441, 101 P. 443.) However, "it is also the

---

4. The brief of the executors alleges Graham has a permanent disability in the nature of epilepsy and has no income except social security and welfare disability payments. Although these matters are not part of the record, counsel for Graham makes no objection and incorporates the additional facts into his reply argument.

5. As no issues of fact are involved, we independently determine the effect of the will's provisions in light of the uncontradicted allegations in the pleadings. (Estate of Dodge (1971) 6 Cal. 3d 311, 318, 98 Cal. Rptr. 801, 491 P.2d 385; Estate of Friedman, *supra*, 100 Cal. App. 3d at p. 815, fn. 4, 161 Cal. Rptr. 311.)

rule, and a salutory one, that such provision — being by way of forfeiture and condition subsequent — is to be strictly construed and not extended beyond what was plainly the testator's intent." (Estate of Bergland (1919) 180 Cal. 629, 633 182 P. 277.)

> The policy against forfeitures is so strong that our courts, following the universal rule in this country, insist upon a clear and unequivocal attack upon the will before invoking the penalty contained in the *in terrorem* clause; . . . (Estate of Miller (1963) 212 Cal. App. 2d. 284, 298, 27 Cal. Rptr. 909.)

California courts have accommodated these competing policies by determining on a case-by-case basis the crucial question of what constitutes a contest. (See Selvin, Comment: Terror in Probate (1964) 16 Stan. L. Rev. 355, 356-359, 362; Tucker, If a Will Is Contested . . . (1975) 50 State Bar J. 382, 407.)

> Whether there has been a contest within the meaning of the language used in a particular no-contest clause is determined according to the circumstances of the particular case. [Citations.] Thus, the answer cannot be sought in a vacuum, but must be gleaned from a consideration of the purpose that the testatrix sought to attain by the provisions of her will. (Estate of Kazian (1976) 59 Cal. App. 3d 797, 802, 130 Cal. Rptr. 908; Estate of Hite, *supra*, 155 Cal. 436, 441-444, 101 P. 443.)

In Estate of Hite, *supra*, 155 Cal. at pp. 438-439, 101 P. 443, the decedent had executed various codicils altering the amount of legacies given to various individuals in the original will. Etta Gross, one of the affected legatees, filed a "Contest of Codicil" opposing probate of the particular codicil reducing her inheritance on grounds of nonexecution, want of mental capacity and undue influence. The contest was settled prior to hearing but the Supreme Court found Gross had forfeited her rights under the will even though she abandoned the legal proceedings after the favorable settlement. The court explained:

> It does not follow herefrom that the mere filing of a paper contest, which has been abandoned without action and has not been employed to thwart the testator's expressed wishes, need be judicially declared a contest. But wherever an opponent uses the appropriate machinery of the law to the thwarting of the testator's expressed wishes, whether he succeed or fail, his action is a contest. (Id., at p. 444, 101 P. 443.)

The *type* of attack involved in *Hite* is clearly a "contest" within any provision forbidding "contests," because the grounds there alleged are expressly included among the grounds for opposing or revoking probate under the Probate Code chapter entitled "Contests of Wills" (§§370-385). (See Estate of Basore (1971) 19 Cal. App. 3d. 623, 630, 96 Cal. Rptr. 874.) In contrast, other types of claims and proceedings raising questions not "substantially affecting the validity of the will" (§371) have been held not to constitute contests under even very broad in terrorem clauses. (See Estate of Dow (1957) 149 Cal. App. 2d 47, 51, 53-57, 308 P.2d 475, and cases discussed therein; Estate of Schreck (1975) 47 Cal. App. 3d 693, 695, fn. 2., 697-698, 121 Cal. Rptr. 218; Estate of Basore, *supra,* 19 Cal. App. 3d 623, 629-631, 96 Cal. Rptr. 874.)

The executors contend, contrary to the determination of the trial court, that Graham's action of filing the section 1080 petition itself trigered the no-contest clause of the will and should result in forfeiture of the bequests to Graham. We disagree. Numerous cases hold that neither a petition under section 1080 to determine heirship nor a petition seeking construction or interpretation of a will is a "contest," although such proceedings might result in invalidation of certain of the will's provisions. (Estate of Basore, *supra,* 19 Cal. App. 3d at pp. 639-631, 96 Cal. Rptr. 874; Estate of Zappettini (1963) 223 Cal. App. 2d 424, 426-429, 35 Cal. Rptr. 844; Estate of Harrison (1937) 22 Cal. App. 2d 28, 32-33, 41, 70 P.2d 522; Estate of Kline (1934) 138 Cal. App. 514, 517, 521-523, 32 P.2d 677, and cases cited therein. Estate of Goyette (1968) 258 Cal. App. 2d 768, 66 Cal. Rptr. 103 and Estate of Harvey (1958) 164 Cal. App. 2d 330, 332, 330 P.2d 478, reach contrary results.)

In Estate of Kruse (1970) 7 Cal. App. 3d 471, 476, 86 Cal. Rptr. 491, this court quoted its earlier opinion in Estate of Miller (1964) 230 Cal. App. 2d 888, 903, 41 Cal. Rptr. 410, holding that instituting a proceeding for construction of the provisions of a will ordinarily does not violate a no-contest clause.

[S]eeking an interpretation of a will does not in and of itself constitute an attempt to thwart the will of the testator. In *Miller,* page 903 [41 Cal. Rptr. 410], we said, "Furthermore, it is the privilege and right of a party beneficiary to an estate at all times to seek a construction of the provisions of the will. An action brought to construe a will is not a contest within the meaning of the usual forfeiture clause, because it is obvious that the moving party does not by such means seek to set aside or annul the will, but rather to ascertain the true meaning of the testatrix and to enforce what she desired."

The executors argue that Graham's section 1080 petition should be held to violate the no-contest provision because it is in the nature of a declaratory relief action and has occasioned the expense and delay of a will contest.

Given [Graham's] appeal, what she is really seeking is a substantive decision on the merits of her proposed *Marvin* claim. She was plainly seeking more than a mere "interpretation of the will" by her Probate Code section 1080 petition, which might otherwise not constitute an attack on the will. The section 1080 petition was clearly designed to *result in* a much larger share of the estate going to the appellant than the decedent gave her by the unequivocal terms of his will.

We find the argument unconvincing. As previously stated, the merits of Graham's proposed *Marvin* claim are not at issue in this proceeding. Rather, Graham sought a ruling by the probate court whether, in light of the no-contest clause, the filing of such a claim would cause her to lose the mobile home which was given to her in the will. Such a determination requires interpretation of the will to ascertain the testator's intent and in no way frustrates the testamentary scheme. (See Estate of Vanderhurst (1915) 171 Cal. 553, 558-559, 154 P. 5.) That litigation of the section 1080 petition may entail substantial cost does not, without more, bring the proceeding within the scope of the forfeiture clause.[6]

Here, the wording of the in terrorem clause prohibits "contests or attacks" by a beneficiary upon the will "directly or indirectly. . . ." Both logic and the weight of authority hold that the bringing of a proceeding to determine the effect of such language should Graham file the proposed *Marvin* claim does not trigger a forfeiture. (Estate of Miller, *supra*, 230 Cal. App. 2d 888, 903, 41 Cal. Rptr. 410; see Estate of Basore, *supra*, 19 Cal. App. 3d 623, 630-631, 96 Cal. Rptr. 874.) In this case, as in Estate of Bullock (1968) 264 Cal. App. 2d 197, 202, 70 Cal. Rptr. 239, "a proper and straightforward question . . . should not be prevented nor should access to the probate court be impeded by any threat of reprisal."

It would be manifestly unjust, as well as going far beyond the plain import of the testator's language, to impose a forfeiture where a beneficiary is "simply asking the probate court to state or instruct whether a forfeiture of a valuable right will ensue" (Estate of Bullock, *supra*, 264 Cal. App. 2d 197, 202, 70 Cal. Rptr. 239) if she brings an action to establish an interest in property held by decedent which arose independently of the will. Accordingly, we uphold the trial court's ruling on this point.

Graham appeals from the portion of the trial court's order determining that the filing of Graham's proposed section 851.5 petition or a separate *Marvin*-type action would violate the no-contest clause. Graham contends an action to establish an implied domestic partnership under

---

6. Furthermore, in response to the petition, the executors not only requested the court to find that the filing of the proposed section 851.5 petition would constitute a violation of the in terrorem clause, but also sought a ruling that the filing of the section 1080 petition itself triggered the no-contest provision. The request for a determination of these matters was tantamount to a petition for instructions under section 588, and necessarily submitted to the court the question of the proper construction of the provisions of the will. Under the circumstances, the expense and delay attributable to litigation of this issue are not solely chargeable to Graham's action.

Marvin v. Marvin, *supra*, 18 Cal. 3d 660, 134 Cal. Rptr. 815, 557 P.2d 106 is not a "contest[ ] or attack[ ]" on decedent's will, because the claim is based upon an alleged source of right independent of the will, and the claim is brought in good faith upon probable cause. (See Estate of Dow, *supra*, 149 Cal. App. 2d 47, 53-57, 308 P.2d 475.) For the reasons explained below, we conclude that the proposed claim does not invoke a forfeiture under the terms of decedent's will.

Proceedings by beneficiaries to assert claims to property based on a source of right independent of the will have been held not to be "contests" under a variety of forfeiture clauses. (See, e.g., Estate of Schreck, *supra*, 47 Cal. App. 3d 693, 121 Cal. Rptr. 218, holding that a no-contest clause similar to one herein did not prevent a beneficiary who was the widow of the testator from claiming rights to joint tenancy property, which the testator had attempted to dispose of by will, or her statutory rights to a homestead; Estate of Dow, *supra*, 149 Cal. App. 2d 47, 308 P.2d 475, in which a widow's claim to establish that property otherwise disposed of by will was community property was held not to violate the in terrorem clause. Estate v. Miller, *supra*, 230 Cal. App. 2d 888, 41 Cal. Rptr. 410, holding that an action to establish a prior oral contract did not violate the no-contest clause; cf. Estate of Madansky (1938) 29 Cal. App. 2d 685, 85 P.2d 576; but see Estate of Kazian, *supra*, 59 Cal. App. 3d 797, 130 Cal. Rptr. 908 and Estate of Howard (1945) 68 Cal. App. 2d 9, 155 P.2d 841, reaching contrary results.) Graham's proposed claim is founded upon her economic contribution as a homemaker to the nonmarital partnership (Marvin v. Marvin, *supra*, 18 Cal. 3d at pp. 679-684, 134 Cal. Rptr. 815, 557 P.2d 106; Watkins v. Watkins (1983) 143 Cal. App. 3d 651, 653-654, 192 Cal. Rptr. 54) and is analogous to a surviving spouse's claim to community or joint tenancy property outside the will. However, even if Graham were a surviving spouse, her ability to assert a claim to property standing in the testator's name without invoking the in terrorem clause would depend upon the language of the will expressing the testator's intent.

In Estate of Kazian, *supra*, 59 Cal. App. 3d 797, 130 Cal. Rptr. 908, cited by both parties, the decedent's will gave a modest amount to her surviving husband and left the bulk of the substantial estate in trust to her three children from a former marriage and to her grandchildren. The will specifically declared:

> [A]ll property in which I have an interest or which now stands in my name, or my former name, . . . is my sole and separate property, having been owned by me prior to my marriage to Bill Kazian, or having been acquired subsequent to my marriage to him, but from the proceeds of property owned by me prior to said marriage. (Id., at p. 800, 130 Cal. Rptr. 908.)

The will further provided that any beneficiary would forfeit his interest if the will or any of its parts or provisions were contested. (Ibid.) The court held that the independent action filed by the husband to establish all of the property in the estate was community property "was a proceeding intended to thwart the decedent's wishes as expressed in her will to which the no-contest clause contained in that will properly applied." (Id., at p. 802, fn. omitted, 130 Cal. Rptr. 908.)

In reaching this result, the *Kazian* court relied upon the context of the particular no-contest clause and specifically the testatrix' unequivocal declaration that all property disposed was her separate property. (See also Estate of Howard, *supra,* 68 Cal. App. 2d 9, 10, fn. 1, 12, 155 P.2d 841, reaching the same result on similar facts, and a very comprehensive in terrorem provision.) The holdings in the *Howard* and *Kazian* cases were predicated upon the exact wording of the wills involved, and do not require a similar result here.

While the executors contend the proposed *Marvin* action is " 'designed to result in the thwarting of the testator's wishes' " (Estate of Howard, *supra,* 68 Cal. App. 2d at p. 11, 155 P.2d 841) and therefore the trial court properly held it would violate the no-contest clause, decedent Black's wishes, particularly his intention concerning the scope of the no-contest clause, are expressed very differently from those of the testator in the *Howard* case. Decedent's will includes this statement:

> It is my intention to dispose of all my property, both real and personal, which I have the right to dispose of by will, including any and all property as to which I may have a power of appointment by Will.

Graham contends that under the rationale of *Marvin,* the decedent did not have the right and did not intend to dispose by will of that property which represents her partnership interest based on the lengthy unmarried relationship, and which she was entitled to claim regardless of the will. We find this interpretation persuasive. The will does not declare an intention to distribute an estate totalling $900,000 in the manner described in the will; the expressed intent is to dispose of that property of the decedent which he had the *right* to dispose of by will. This frames a different situation from that found in Estate of Kazian, *supra,* 59 Cal. App. 3d at p. 800, 130 Cal. Rptr. 908 and Estate of Howard, *supra,* 68 Cal. App. 2d at p. 12, 155 P.2d 841, where the wills expressly referred to designated property as separate property.

In Estate of Schreck, *supra,* 47 Cal. App. 3d 693, 121 Cal. Rptr. 218, the court strictly construed, to avoid a forfeiture, a similar no-contest clause where the testator's widow claimed as surviving joint tenant the remaining one-half interest in their Cadillac and successfully petitioned the probate court to set apart a probate homestead. The clause in *Schreck* provided:

> If any person shall, in any manner whatsoever, directly or indirectly, attack, oppose or contest this will, or seek to invalidate it or any portion thereof, or seek to succeed to any part of my estate except through this will, then I give to each such person the sum of One Dollar ($1.00) only, in lieu of any, other, and all provisions made for such persons hereunder. . . . (Id., at p. 695, fn. 2, 121 Cal. Rptr. 218.)

Although the will directed that the testator's tangible property be sold and the proceeds placed in a testamentary trust, the court flatly stated:

> We think it clear that under . . . a strict construction the widow's challenged conduct does not come within the first clause of the provision at issue dealing with direct and indirect attacks upon the validity of the will or any part thereof. Moreover, her conduct did not come within the second clause . . . relating to succession to any part of the testator's estate except through his will. . . . Certainly the widow's establishing her ownership as surviving joint tenant of the remaining one-half interest in the Cadillac (once erroneously included within the reported estate of the testator) is not a succession to any part of the testator's estate. The widow merely claimed what was already her own. (Id., at p. 697, 121 Cal. Rptr. 218.)

Here, the decedent did not express a clear intent to forfeit the residuary legatees the limited provision made for his surviving partner of nearly 18 years by reason of her attempt to establish independently of the will an interest in property held by decedent at his death. Under the reasoning of *Schreck,* Graham should suffer no penalty for asserting a claim to property which, assuming she prevails in her *Marvin* action, already belongs to her. It is reasonable to conclude the decedent did not intend to preclude Graham, ill and without adequate funds, from receiving the use of the mobile home if she pursued her implied contract rights.

Finally, we note the decedent's will was drafted by an attorney several years after *Marvin* became the law of California. If the testator had wished to provide that a *Marvin* claim would trigger the provisions of the in terrorem clause, he could have done so.[7]

The portion of the court's order determining that the filing of Graham's section 1080 petition did not violate the no-contest clause of the

7. The executors contend for the first time on appeal that decedent intentionally adopted the provisions of the will because he was aware that (1) estate taxes and costs would reduce the amount of each child's share; and (2) Graham's right to receive social security and/or disability payments was subject to income limits. However, these "facts" are contained nowhere in the record and are not properly before us.

* Assigned by the Chairperson of the Judicial Council.

will is affirmed. The portion of the order challenged by Graham is reversed with directions to enter an order declaring that the filing of the proposed *Marvin* claim does not constitute a violation of the in terrorem clause.

FRANSON, Acting P.J., and ARDAIZ,* J., concur.

Insert the following material after the note on page 243.

Case that considers whether husband's estate on divorce includes his medical degree, which his wife helped him obtain.

DRAPEK v. DRAPEK

Supreme Judicial Court of Massachusetts, 1987
399 Mass. 240, 503 N.E.2d 946.

LYNCH, Justice:

Mark Joseph Drapek appeals from a judgment of divorce nisi granting Celia Mae Drapek a divorce and ordering Mark to pay Celia $42,024.50 in annual installments, and 9.35 percent of his gross earnings or $60,000 whichever is greater, for a period of sixty months. His wife also appeals. Judgment of divorce nisi was originally granted on April 11, 1984. On August 17, 1984, the judgment of April 11, 1984, was vacated and an amended judgment was entered clarifying that the husband's payment of 9.35 percent of his gross earnings was to be considered alimony terminating at death or remarriage of the wife, but changing the payment from 9.35 percent of gross earnings to 9.35 percent of gross earnings or $60,000, whichever is greater.

The Probate Court judge found the following facts: The parties were married for approximately eight years. At the time of the divorce Mark was twenty-eight years old, Celia was twenty-seven years old. During the marriage, the husband obtained his medical degree while the wife worked to support the household and also provided the bulk of the homemaking services. During the marriage the wife's financial contributions exceeded the husband's by $8,534. The joint funds of the marriage were used to pay the husband's tuition. The judge determined that one-half of the husband's tuition expense, plus the amount that the wife's financial contribution exceeded the husband's was the wife's excess financial contribution which he calculated to be $22,024.50. At the time of the divorce, the husband was employed as a senior resident in internal medicine at University Hospital in Boston; the wife was temporarily employed as a service representative with New England Telephone Company.

The husband primarily challenges the judges' finding that the "husband's estate consists of . . . A license to practice medicine through which I find he is capable of earning the median salary for physicians. . . ." The judge did not decide whether the degree was "property" but did characterize it as "part of [the husband's] estate and its future worth, while perhaps not presently determinable, is capable of being equitably assigned."

In order to enable the wife to rehabilitate her own skills and to compensate her for contributing to her husband's career, the judge decided that she is entitled to participate in her husband's increased earning capacity "at least until such time as she has been rehabilitated and self-sufficient." He therefore ordered the husband to pay the wife $42,024.50 ($22,024.50 excess financial contribution and $20,000 value of homemaking services), plus 9.35 percent of his gross earnings for five years.

Mark contends that the judge erred in finding that Mark's medical degree and resulting increased earning capacity were part of his estate subject to equitable assignment under G.L. c.208, §34.[1] He further contends that the judge erred in awarding Celia a lump sum for her excess financial contributions and homemaking services; that the factual findings regarding Celia's excess financial contributions and Mark's homemaking contributions were clearly erroneous; and that the amount of the alimony awarded was an abuse of discretion. Celia contends that the judge did not err except that he failed to include the totality of her financial contributions. She further contends that the judge abused his discretion in awarding too low an amount of alimony and in denying her request for an award of counsel fees.

---

1. General Laws, c.208, §34 (1984 ed.), provides:

Upon divorce or upon a complaint in an action brought at any time after a divorce, whether such a divorce has been adjudged in this commonwealth or another jurisdiction, the court of the commonwealth, provided there is personal jurisdiction over both parties, may make a judgment for either of the parties to pay alimony to the other. In addition to or in lieu of a judgment to pay alimony, the court may assign to either husband or wife all or any part of the estate of the other. In determining the amount of alimony, if any, to be paid, or in fixing the nature and value of the property, if any, to be so assigned, the court, after hearing the witnesses, if any, of each party, shall consider the length of the marriage, the conduct of the parties during the marriage, the age, health, station, occupation, amount and sources of income, vocational skills, employability, estate, liabilities and assets of each of the parties and the opportunity of each for future acquisition of capital assets and income. The court may also consider the contribution of each of the parties in the acquisition, preservation or appreciation in value of their respective estates and the contribution of each of the parties as a homemaker to the family unit. When the court makes an order for alimony on behalf of a spouse, and such spouse is not covered by a private group health insurance plan, said court shall determine whether the obligor under such order has health insurance on a group plan available to him through an employer or organization that may be extended to cover the spouse for whom support is ordered. When said court has determined that the obligor has such insurance, such court shall include in the support order a requirement that the obligor exercise the option of additional coverage in favor of such spouse.

General Laws c.208, §34, confers broad discretion on a judge in awarding alimony and making equitable property divisions. Loud v. Loud, 386 Mass. 473, 474, 436 N.E.2d 164 (1982). Rice v. Rice, 372 Mass. 398, 400-401, 361 N.E.2d 1305 (1977). Newman v. Newman, 11 Mass. App. Ct. 903, 414 N.E.2d 627 (1981). Under the statute, the trial judge *must* consider "the length of the marriage, the conduct of the parties during the marriage, the age, health, station, occupation, amount and sources of income, vocational skills, employability, estate, liabilities and needs of each of the parties and the opportunity of each for future acquisition of capital assets and income." G.L. c.208, §34.

In addition to the mandatory factors, the judge may, in his or her discretion, consider "the contribution of each of the parties in the acquisition, preservation or appreciation in value of their respective estates and the contribution of each of the parties as a homemaker to the family unit." Id. The judge's findings must indicate that he or she has weighed all the statutory factors. Loud v. Loud, *supra*. Bianco v. Bianco, 371 Mass. 420, 423, 358 N.E.2d 243 (1976).

1. Mark's medical degree as part of his estate under G.L. c. 208, §34.

General Laws, c. 208, §34, provides: "In addition to or in lieu of a judgment to pay alimony, the court may assign to either husband or wife all or any part of the estate of the other." Under Massachusetts law "[a] party's 'estate' by definition includes all property to which he holds title, however acquired. Therefore, this provision gives the trial judge discretion to assign to one spouse property of the other spouse whenever and however acquired." Rice v. Rice, *supra* 372 Mass. at 400, 361 N.E.2d 1305, citing Bianco v. Bianco, *supra* 371 Mass. at 422, 358 N.E.2d 243. Mark argues that because his professional degree is not an asset of the marriage subject to equitable assignment the lump sum award of $42,024.50 should be set aside.

The Appeals Court has held that a judge may decline to treat as a marital asset the present value of future earning potential. Cabot v. Cabot, 18 Mass. App. Ct. 903, 904, 462 N.E.2d 1128 (1984). That court reasoned that future earnings were too speculative and subject to variables the least of which being that they may never be achieved due to "death, illness, or simply market factors." Id. Earning capacity, however, could be considered in awarding alimony. Id.

We agree that the present value of future earned income is not subject to equitable assignment under G.L. c.208, §34. To adopt a rule that would subject such an item to distribution upon divorce would foreclose consideration of the effect of future events on the individual's earning capacity. Unlike alimony, a property settlement is not subject to modification. See G.L. c.208, §37;[2] Dumont v. Godbey, 382 Mass. 234, 238, 415 N.E.2d 188 (1981). See also Mahoney v. Mahoney, 91 N.J. 488, 498, 453 A.2d 527 (1982). The judge may, of course, consider the earning capacity of both parties in determining an award for alimony, or assignment of estate pursuant to G.L. c. 208, §34. See Schuler v. Schuler, 382 Mass. 366, 373-374, 416 N.E.2d 197 (1981); Rice v. Rice, *supra* 372 Mass. at 402, 361 N.E.2d 1305; Cabot v. Cabot, *supra* 18 Mass. App. Ct. at 904, 462 N.E.2d 1128. See also G.L. c.208, §34. Since assigning a present value to a professional degree would involve evaluating the earning potential created by that degree, we also decline to include the professional degree or license as a marital asset subject to division under G.L. c.208, §34.

This appears to be the prevailing view in other jurisdictions. Only one jurisdiction has held that a professional license is property subject to equitable distribution pursuant to the State's domestic relations laws. O'Brien v. O'Brien, 66 N.Y.2d 576, 498 N.Y.S.2d 743, 489 N.E.2d 712 (1985). That decision was based upon a statute in which the court found a clear mandate by the Legislature to include an interest in a profession or professional career as marital property. O'Brien v. O'Brien, *supra* at 585-586, 498 N.Y.S.2d 743, 489 N.E.2d 712.[3]

General Laws c.208, §34, does not contain such a mandate. It merely requires consideration of various factors including "amount and sources of income" and "the opportunity of each for future acquisition of capital assets and income" and allows consideration of "the contribution of each of the parties in the acquisition, preservation or appreciation in value of their respective estates and the contribution of each of the parties as a homemaker to the family unit." Id.

2. General Laws c.208, §37 (1984 ed.), provides in pertinent part: "After a judgment for alimony or an annual allowance for the spouse or children, the court may, from time to time, upon the action for modification of either party, revise and alter its judgment relative to the amount of such alimony or annual allowance and the payment thereof, and may make any judgment relative thereto which it might have made in the original action."

3. New York Domestic Relations Law §236(B) (McKinney's Supp.1986) allows for consideration of "any equitable claim to, interest in, or direct or indirect contribution made to the acquisition of such marital property by the party not having title, including joint efforts or expenditures and contributions and services as a spouse, parent, wage earner and homemaker, and to the career or career potential of the other party [and] . . . the impossibility or difficulty of evaluating any component asset or any interest in a business, corporation or *profession* . . ." Id. at §236(B)(5)(d)(6), [9] (emphasis added). It further provides that where the court "shall determine that an equitable distribution is appropriate but would be impractical or burdensome or where *the distribution of an interest in a business, corporation or profession* would be contrary to law, the court in lieu of such equitable distribution shall make a distributive award in order to achieve equity between the parties." Id. at §236[B][5][e] (emphasis added).

As noted above, the prevailing view is that a professional license or degree is not property subject to equitable distribution upon divorce or dissolution. See, e.g., Graham v. Graham, 194 Colo. 429, 574 P.2d 75 (1978); Hughes v. Hughes, 438 So. 2d 146, 150 (Fla. Dist. Ct. App.1983); Marriage of Jannsen, 348 N.W.2d 251, 253-254 (Iowa 1984); Inman v. Inman, 648 S.W.2d 847, 852 (Ky.1983); Olah v. Olah, 135 Mich. App. 404, 410, 354 N.W.2d 359 (1984); Grosskopf v. Grosskopf, 677 P.2d 814, 822 (Wyo. 1984). Many courts that have so held, however, have further held that the earning capacity of the degree holder and the contributions of the nondegree holder may be considered in awarding alimony and in dividing property. See, e.g., *Graham, supra,* 194 Colo. at 433, 574 P.2d 75; Lovett v. Lovett, 688 S.W.2d 329 (Ky. 1985), citing *Inman, supra; Olah, supra* 135 Mich. App. at 410, 354 N.W.2d 359; *Grosskopf, supra* at 823.

Some courts allow reimbursement of actual money contributed, regardless of the nondegree holder's entitlement to alimony. See DeLaRosa v. DeLaRosa, 309 N.W.2d 755, 758-759 (Minn. 1981); Mahoney v. Mahoney, 91 N.J. 488, 492-501, 453 A.2d 527 (1982); Hubbard v. Hubbard, 603 P.2d 747, 752 (Okla. 1979).

General Laws c.208, §34, is clearly broad enough to allow courts to consider the increased earning potential engendered by a professional degree in determining an award of alimony and assignment of the estates of the parties. Neither the degree or license, however, nor the increased earning capacity of the degree holder is an asset subject to assignment.

The Probate Court judge clarified that a portion of the judgment awarded to Celia was alimony. He did not so characterize the lump sum of $42,024.50, although such an award would have been warranted. Klar v. Klar, 322 Mass. 59, 60, 76 N.E.2d 5 (1947), citing Baird v. Baird, 311 Mass. 329, 333, 41 N.E.2d 5 (1942). See Surabian v. Surabian, 362 Mass. 342, 348, 285 N.E.2d 909 (1972). It appears that the award of $42,024.50 was in the nature of an assignment of the estate. Since we hold that Mark's medical degree and enhanced earning capacity are not part of his estate, any assignment of such degree or earning capacity must be set aside. Similarly, since we have no way of determining the effect of the error in calculating any alimony awarded, the award of alimony must also be set aside. The portion of the judgment granting the divorce is affirmed. The case is remanded for the judge to amend the award of alimony and assignment of assets consistent with this opinion.

We will address some of the remaining issues raised by the parties as they may arise on remand. General Laws c.208, §34, *requires* consideration of vocational skill, the conduct of the parties, employability, and the opportunity of each party for future acquisition of capital assets and income. The statute allows consideration of the contribution of the parties to the "acquisition, preservation or appreciation in value of their respective estates" and of "the contribution of each of the parties as a homemaker to the family unit." Thus, the trial judge was not in error in considering Celia's financial contributions to Mark's attainment of his medical degree, and her homemaking services. The judge could consider these factors, with relation to not only the assignment of the estates of the parties, but also the award of alimony. Similarly, there was no error in the judge's assigning a monetary value to Celia's homemaking services based on expert testimony. See Lombard, Family Law § 2056 (Supp. 1984). The only error in relation to these factors was that they were inextricably mixed with an assignment of Mark's medical degree and enhanced future earning capacity.

2. Factual findings.

A. CELIA'S EXCESS FINANCIAL CONTRIBUTIONS.

In determining Celia's financial contributions, there was no error in the judge's not including other items requested by Celia, i.e., lost income due to the move to Massachusetts, cost of the move and increased living expenses, one-half of the income Mark would have received if he had not attended medical school and her lost income due to the separation.

Mark claims error in the probate judge's calculation of his educational expenses. Because we hold that excess financial contributions are merely a factor to be considered in awarding alimony or assigning an estate, minor errors in the judge's calculations of the figures are insignificant. To the extent that any such errors exist in this case, the parties can call these errors to the attention of the judge on remand.

B. MARK'S HOMEMAKING SERVICES.

The judge was not clearly erroneous in characterizing Mark's homemaking services as "de minimis." The finding was based upon Celia's testimony, which the judge was entitled to credit.

3. Abuse of discretion.

As stated previously, the trial judge is given broad discretion under G.L. c.208, §34. The judgment dated April 11, 1984, although subsequently amended, clearly shows that the Probate Court judge weighed the statutory factors, as is required by this court. See Loud v. Loud, 386 Mass. 473, 474, 436 N.E.2d 164 (1982); Bianco v. Bianco, 371 Mass. 420, 423, 358 N.E.2d 243 (1976). The amounts awarded to the wife were not an abuse of discretion except to the extent that they were influenced by the erroneous conclusion that the medical degree was an asset subject to assignment. Mark was a physician employed as a senior resident at University Hospital in Boston. His income in the future will be significant. The judge found that Celia had postponed her educational and professional plans in order to put her husband through school. He further found that it was possible that in five years she might be able to rehabilitate her skills and that she was entitled to an award of alimony that would allow her to do so. There was no abuse of discretion in the award of 9.35 percent of gross income or at least $60,000. The award was time limited to five years, the amount of time determined to be necessary for Celia's rehabilitation. Further, Mark could, with approval of the court, defer one-half of any monthly payment for an additional five years.

4. Attorney's fees.

Celia claims that she should have been awarded attorney's fee. General Laws c.208, §38, allows the judge, in his discretion, to award counsel fees to either party in a divorce proceeding. See House v. House, 368 Mass. 120, 330 N.E.2d 152 (1975). The matter is within the discretion of the trial judge. Clifford v. Clifford, 354 Mass. 545, 548, 238 N.E.2d 522 (1968). In the present case the judge acted within his discretion in declining to award the wife attorney's fees.

The case is remanded to the Probate Court for further proceedings consistent with this opinion.

So ordered.

Note

See also, on the matter discussed in the Drapek case, Stevens v. Stevens, 23 Ohio St.2d 115, 492 N.E.2d 131 (1986).

Insert the following material on page 247 before the problems.

Case that considers whether tenancy terminable at the will of the tenant is also terminable at the will of the landlord.

GARNER v. GERRISH

Court of Appeals of New York, 1984
63 N.Y.2d 575, 473 N.E.2d 223

WACHTLER, Judge.

The question on this appeal is whether a lease which grants the tenant the right to terminate the agreement at a date of his choice creates a determinable life tenancy on behalf of the tenant or merely establishes a tenancy at will. The courts below held that the lease created a tenancy at will permitting the current landlord to evict the tenant. We granted the tenant's motion for leave to appeal and now reverse the order appealed from.

In 1977 Robert Donovan owned a house located in Potsdam, New York. On April 14 of that year he leased the premises to the tenant Lou Gerrish. The lease was executed on a printed form and it appears that neither side was represented by counsel. The blanks on the form were filled in by Donovan who provided the names of the parties, described the property and fixed the rent at $100 a month. With respect to the duration of the tenancy the lease provides it shall continue "for and during the term of *quiet enjoyment* from the *first* day of *May,* 1977 which term will end — *Lou Gerrish has the privilege of termination [sic] this agreement at a date of his own choice*" (emphasis added to indicate handwritten and typewritten additions to the printed form). The lease also contains a standard reference to the landlord's right to reentry if the rent is not timely paid, which is qualified by the handwritten statement: "Lou has thirty days grace for payment."

Gerrish moved into the house and continued to reside there, apparently without incident, until Donovan died in November of 1981. At that point David Garner, executor of Donovan's estate, served Gerrish with a notice to quit the premises. When Gerrish refused, Garner commenced this summary proceeding to have him evicted. Petitioner contended that the lease created a tenancy at will because it failed to state a definite term. In his answering affidavit, the tenant alleged that he had always paid the rent specified in the lease. He also contended that the lease granted him tenancy for life, unless he elects to surrender possession during his lifetime.

The County Court granted summary judgment to petitioner on the ground that the lease is "indefinite and uncertain ... as regards the length of time accorded respondent to occupy the premises. Although the writing specifies the date of commencement of the term, it fails to set forth the determination of continuance, and the date or event of termination." The court concluded that the original landlord leased the premises to the tenant "for a month-to-month term and that petitioner was entitled to terminate the lease upon the death of the lessor effective upon the expiration of the next succeeding monthly term of occupancy." In support of its decision the court quoted the following statement from our opinion in Western Transp. Co. v. Lansing, 49 N.Y. 499, 508: "A lease . . . for so long as the lessee shall please, is said to be a lease at will of both lessor and lessee."

The Appellate Division affirmed for the same reasons in a brief memorandum (99 A.D.2d 608, 471 N.Y.S.2d 717).

On appeal to our court, the parties conceded that the agreement creates a lease. The only question is whether it should be literally construed to grant to the tenant alone the right to terminate at will, or whether the landlord is accorded a similar right by operation of law.

At early common law according to Lord Coke, "when the lease is made to have and to hold at the will of the lessee, this must be also at the will of the lessor" (1 Co. Litt., §55a). This rule was generally adopted in the United States during the 19th century and at one time was said to represent the majority view (see Ann., 137 A.L.R. 362, 367; 51C C.J.S., Landlord and Tenant, §167, p.475). However, it was not universally accepted (see, e.g., Effinger v. Lewis, 32 Pa. 367; Gunnison v. Evans, 136 Kan. 791, 18 P.2d 191; Thompson v. Baxter, 107 Minn. 122, 119 N.W. 797) and has been widely criticized, particularly in this century, as an antiquated notion which violates the terms of the agreement and frustrates the intent of the parties (1 Tiffany, Real Property [3d ed.], §159; 1 American Law of Real Property [Casner ed., 1952], §3.30; Schoshinski, American Law of Landlord and Tenant, §2:7; see, also, Restatement, Property 2d, Landlord and Tenant §1.6).

It has been noted that the rule has its origins in the doctrine of livery of seisin (Tiffany, op. cit., §159; Effinger v. Lewis, supra), which required physical transfer of a clod of earth, twig, key, or other symbol on the premises in the presence of witnesses, to effect a conveyance of land interest (2 Blackstone's Comm., pp. 315, 316; Black's Law Dictionary [Fourth ed.], p. 1084). Although this ceremony was not required for leases, which were generally limited to a specified term of years, it was necessary to create a life tenancy which was viewed as a freehold interest. Thus, if a lease granting a tenant a life estate was not accompanied by livery of seisin, the intended conveyance would fail and a mere tenancy at will would result. The corollary to Lord Coke's comment is that the grant of a life estate would be enforceable if accompanied by livery of seisin and the other requisites for a conveyance. Because such a tenancy was terminable at the will of the grantee, there was in fact no general objection at common law to a tenancy at the will of the tenant. The express terms of a lease granting a life tenancy would fail, and a tenancy at will would result, only when livery of seisin, or any other requirement for a conveyance, had not been met (see, generally, Tiffany, op. cit., §159; Effinger v. Lewis, supra; Tennant v. Tennant Mem. Home, 167 Cal. 570, 140 P. 242; Myers v. East Ohio Gas Co., 51 Ohio St. 2d 121, 5 O.O.3d 103, 364 N.E.2d 1369).

Because livery of seisin, like the ancient requirement for a seal, has been abandoned, commentators generally urge that there is no longer any reason why a lease granting the tenant alone the right to terminate at will, should be converted into a tenancy at will terminable by either party

(Tiffany, *op. cit.*, §159; 1 American Law of Property, *op. cit.*, §3.30; Schoshinski, *op. cit.*, §2:16, pp. 61, 62). The Restatement adopts this view and provides the following illustration: "L leases a farm to T 'for as long as T desires to stay on the land.' The lease creates a determinable life estate in T, terminable at T's will or on his death." (Restatement, Property 2d, Landlord and Tenant, §1.6, Comment *g*, illustration 6.) This rule has increasingly gained acceptance in courts which have closely examined the problem (Myers v. East Ohio Gas Co., *supra;* Collins v. Shanahan, 34 Colo. App. 82, 523 P.2d 999; Thompson v. Baxter, *supra;* Gunnison v. Evans, *supra;* Effinger v. Lewis, *supra*).

This court has never specifically addressed the issue. In 1872 we applied the Coke dictum by analogy, and without attribution, in Western Transp. Co. v. Lansing, 49 N.Y. 499, *supra*. The case did not deal with a tenant's right to terminate a lease, but with the right of a tenant to renew a lease beyond its initial term "for such further time, after the expiration of said term, as said party of the second part (the lessee) shall choose or elect" (Western Transp. Co., v. Lansing, *supra,* at p. 502). The initial term was for 15 years. At its expiration the original lessor had died and the lessee had assigned the lease to a corporate tenant which sought specific performance of the right to renew. Although on that occasion the assignor only requested renewal for an additional 15 years, we held that the renewal clause itself was indefinite and unenforceable. In the course of the opinion we observed (at p. 508), that the renewal clause "is similar to a provision for such time as both parties please . . . or a lease giving a right to occupy as long as lessee pleases . . . A lease for so long as both parties shall please, or for so long as the lessee shall please, is said to be a lease at the will of both lessor and lessee."

Several years later, however, in Hoff v. Royal Metal Furniture Co., 117 App. Div. 884, 103 N.Y.S. 371, where the initial term of the lease was for one year renewable "from year to year" by the tenant, "its successors or assigns," our earlier *Western Transp.* case was held by the Appellate Division to pose no obstacle to enforcing the original tenant's requesting for a one-year renewal made during the life of the lessor who had signed the lease. On appeal to this court we affirmed without opinion (189 N.Y. 555, 82 N.E. 1128). These cases illustrate that seemingly perpetual leases are not favored by the law, and will not be enforced unless the lease clearly grants to the tenant or his successors the right to extend beyond the initial term by renewing indefinitely.

In the case now before us the lease does not provide for renewal, and its duration cannot be said to be perpetual or indefinite. It simply grants a personal right to the named lessee, Lou Gerrish, to terminate at a date of his choice, which is a fairly typical means of creating a life tenancy terminable at the will of the tenant (Restatement, Property 2d, *op. cit.,*

Illustration 6; Collins v. Shanahan, *supra*). Thus the lease will terminate, at the latest, upon the death of the named lessee. The fact that it may be terminated at some earlier point, if the named tenant decides to quit the premises, does not render it indeterminate. Leases providing for termination upon the occurrence of a specified event prior to the completion of an otherwise fixed term, are routinely enforced even when the event is within the control of the lessee (Schoshinski, *op. cit.*, §2:7, pp. 41-42).

In sum, the lease expressly and unambiguously grants to the tenant the right to terminate, and does not reserve to the landlord a similar right. To hold that such a lease creates a tenancy terminable at the will of either party would violate the terms of the agreement and the express intent of the contracting parties.

Accordingly, the order of the Appellate Division should be reversed and the petition dismissed.

COOKE, C.J., and JASEN, JONES, MEYER, SIMONS and KAYE, JJ., concur.

Order reversed, with costs, and petition dismissed.

Chapter Fourteen

Concurrent Ownership

Insert the following material on page 256 at the end of Problem 14.5.

See also Harms v. Sprague, 105 Ill. 2d 315, 473 N.E.2d 930 (1984), which held that a mortgage by one joint tenant on his interest in the joint tenancy does not sever the joint tenancy. In regard to what happens to the mortgage when the joint tenant who gave the mortgage dies survived by the other joint tenant, the court said: "Further, we find that the mortgage executed by John Harms does not survive as a lien on plaintiff's property. A surviving joint tenant succeeds to the share of the deceased joint tenant by virtue of the conveyance which created the joint tenancy, not as the successor of the deceased."

Part 5

Before and After the Statute of Uses

Chapter Fifteen

Conveyancing and Future Interests Before the Statute of Uses

Insert the following material on page 290 before the problems.

Case concerned with whether deed conveyed fee simple title or determinable fee simple.

HARRISON v. MARCUS

Supreme Judicial Court of Massachusetts, 1985
396 Mass. 424, 486 N.E.2d 710

ABRAMS, Justice.

The plaintiffs brought suit to quiet title to two parcels of land in South Yarmouth. At issue is the title granted to the trustees of the two parcels. The plaintiffs argue that the trustees acquired a fee simple determinable. The defendants argue that the trustees acquired a fee simple absolute. A judge in the Land Court allowed the defendants' motion for summary judgment and held that the conveyance created a charitable trust, the purpose of which had failed, and ordered the trustees to convey the parcels to the heirs. The Appeals Court summarily reversed. Harrison v. Marcus, 19 Mass. App. 1103, 471 N.E.2d 1373 (1984).[3] We granted further appellate review. We affirm the judgment of the Land Court.

---

3. The Appeals Court issued an unpublished memorandum in which it concluded that the deeds and declarations of trust created an equitable estate in fee simple determinable. The court published the following order: "Judgment reversed. Judgment shall enter instructing the plaintiff trustees to convey to Cape Cod and Islands Council, Inc., Boy Scouts of America, free of trust the two parcels of land held by them in trust. On that occurrence, Cape Cod and Islands Council, Inc., will hold title to the land in fee simple absolute, free of trust and free of any possibility of reverter." 19 Mass. App. at 1103, 471 N.E.2d 1373.

The judge found the following undisputed facts. By deed and declaration of trust dated November 14, 1936, and recorded in the Barnstable Country registry of deeds, Irving K. Taylor conveyed in trust a parcel of land on the shore line of James Pond in South Yarmouth to Harold E. Hallett, Fred M. Angus, and Hervey L. Small, for the use of Troop 59, Bass River, Boy Scouts of America. Relevant portions of the deed and declaration of trust are set out in the margin.[4] Taylor died in New York in 1939 and devised a second parcel of land in South Yarmouth to the same trustees under the same terms and conditions. By deed and declaration of trust dated February 6, 1940, William L. Taylor, as executor of the will of Irving K. Taylor, conveyed the second parcel of land to the trustees "for the purposes declared in and by [the] deed and declaration of trust dated November 14, 1936, and subject to all the same conditions therein set forth, with like effect as though the granted premises had been conveyed to said grantees in and by said deed, all pertinent provisions of which shall be deemed to be herein incorporated and made a part hereof."

Troop 59, Bass River, Boy Scouts of America, is no longer in existence.[5] The trustees and Cape Cod and Islands Council, Inc., successor in interest to Troop 59,[6] brought suit to quiet title to the parcels. The defendants are the heirs of Irving K. Taylor, the executor of Taylor's

---

4. To have and to hold all and singular the above granted premises unto the said Harold E. Hallett, Fred M. Angus, and Hervey L. Small, and their successors forever, but in Trust Nevertheless, and to and for the purposes herein declared. First To permit and allow Troop 59-Bass River-Boy Scouts of America to enjoy the unrestricted use of the same for Boy Scout purposes so long as said Troop 59 shall continue its organization, and to function as a boy scout troop under the rules, regulations, and practices of similar Boy Scout organizations as now existing and to pay or discharge, all taxes, assessments, betterments and all other levies or liens of like nature levied upon said property, when due and payable. Second in the event of a breach of any of the foregoing conditions, this trust shall terminate and be at an end, and the trustees, or their successors for the time being shall deed and reconvey said aforedescribed real estate free and discharged of all trust, to the grantor Irving K. Taylor or to his heirs or his or their assigns. The judgment of the trustees or their successors or a majority of them as to the existence of a breach of any said conditions shall be final and conclusive on all parties in interest and a recital thereof in any instrument of reconvenance [sic] hereof shall be final and conclusive evidence thereof. Third in the event of the decease, resignation or incapacity of any of the trust[ees] to forewith nominate and appoint a successor or successors and to record in the Registry of Deeds for the County of Barnstable a statement of said appointment, duly accepted by the appointee or appointees, whereupon the same title, duties and obligations shall vest in said appointee or appointees as though he or they had been originally appointed and named as trustee in this instrument.

5. The record does not indicate when Troop 59 disbanded.

6. The Cape Cod and Islands Council alleged in its complaint that it is the successor of interest to Troop 59. For purposes of this decision, we assume without deciding that this characterization is proper.

estate and of the estate of his deceased daughter (the defendants), and the Attorney General. See G.L. c. 12, §8 (1984 ed.).[7]

The parties agree that Taylor created a charitable trust. The point of controversy is the nature of the estate granted to the trustees, see Selectmen of Provincetown v. Attorney Gen., 15 Mass. App. 639, 643-644, 447 N.E.2d 677 (1983), and the future interest in the heirs. The plaintiffs argue that the trustees took title in fee simple determinable, which left a possibility of reverter in the heirs. Under G.L. c. 184A, §3,[8] a fee simple determinable becomes a fee simple absolute if the specified contingency giving rise to the possibility of reverter does not occur within thirty years from the date the fee simple determinable interest becomes possessory. General Laws c. 260, §31A,[9] bars proceedings on any possibility of reverter created before January 2, 1955, unless a written statement was recorded in the registry of deeds on or before January 1, 1964. Apparently, no such statement was filed with respect to the land in question. The plaintiffs argue that, based on the provisions of G.L. c. 184A, §3, and G.L. c. 260, §31A, Cape Cod and Islands Council, Inc., as the successor in interest to Troop 59, is vested with title in fee simple absolute.

7. The Attorney General has not participated in this case.

8. General Laws c. 184A, §3 (1984 ed.), states:

A fee simple determinable in land or a fee simple in land subject to a right of entry for condition broken shall become fee simple absolute if the specified contingency does not occur within thirty years from the date when such fee simple determinable or fee simple subject to a right of entry becomes possessory. If such contingency occurs within said thirty years the succeeding interest, which may be an interest in a person other than the person creating the interest or his heirs, shall become possessory or the right of entry exercisable notwithstanding the rule against perpetuities.

9. General Laws c. 260, §31A (1984 ed.), states in part:

No proceeding based upon any right of entry for condition broken or possibility of reverter, to which a fee simple or fee simple determinable in land is subject, created before the second day of January, nineteen hundred and fifty-five, shall be maintained in any court after the first day of January, nineteen hundred and sixty-four, unless on or before the first day of January, nineteen hundred and sixty-four, (a) the condition has been broken or the reverter has occurred, and a person or persons having the right of entry or reverter shall have taken possession of the land, and in case of entry made after January first, nineteen hundred and fifty-seven, shall have filed a certificate of entry pursuant to section nineteen of chapter one hundred and eighty-four, or (b) a person or persons having the right of entry, or who would have it if the condition were broken, or would be entitled if the reverter occurred, or one of them if there be more than one, shall by himself, or by his attorney, agent, guardian, conservator, or parent, have filed in the registry of deeds, or in the case of registered land, in the registry of the land court, for the district in which the land is situated, a statement in writing, duly sworn to, describing the land and the nature of the right and the deed or other instrument creating it, and where it may be found if recorded or registered, and, in case of registered land, naming the holder or holders of the outstanding certificate of title and stating the number of said certificate, and, in case of land not registered, naming the person or persons appearing of record to own the fee subject to such right or possibility, or shown by the records of the tax assessors at the last prior assessment date to be the owner or owners thereof.

The defendants argue that the trustees originally were vested with title in fee simple absolute, subject to a duty to convey title to the grantor's heirs when the charitable trust terminated. The defendants argue that the trustees held the legal interest, while both Troop 59 and the heirs had equitable interests.

We begin our analysis by considering the nature and quality of the legal estate created by the instruments. Proprietors of the Church in Brattle Square v. Grant, 3 Gray 142, 146 (1855). In the 1936 deed and declaration of trust,[10] Taylor granted the first parcel to the trustees

> to have and to hold all and singular the above granted premises unto the said Harold E. Hallett, Fred M. Angus, and Hervey L. Small, and their successors, forever, but in trust nevertheless, and to and for the purposes herein declared. First to permit and allow Troop 59 Bass River Boy Scouts of America to enjoy the unrestricted use of the same for Boy Scout purposes so long as said Troop 59 shall continue its organization, and to function as a boy scout troop under the rules, regulations, and practices of similar Boy Scout organizations as now existing and to pay or discharge, all taxes, assessments, betterments and all other levies or liens of like nature levied upon said property, when due and payable.

As we read the 1936 instrument, the deed portion begins with the description of the property and ends with the sentence of conveyance, "to have and to hold all and singular the above granted premises unto the said Harold E. Hallett, Fred M. Angus, and Hervey L. Small, and their successors forever, but in Trust nevertheless, and to and for the purposes herein declared." The portion of the instrument following that sentence constitutes the declaration of trust. Under this construction, there is no question but that the deed conveyed the property in fee simple absolute to the trustees. All the terms and conditions are in the trust instrument. The words of the deed convey a fee simple absolute. Neither the parties nor the judge read the instrument as bifurcated. We therefore turn to the arguments of the parties.

The instrument in question is both a deed and a declaration of trust. The rules of construction are similar. Trust instruments must be construed to give effect to the intention of the settlor as ascertained from the language of the whole instrument considered in the light of the attendant circumstances. Groden v. Kelley, 382 Mass. 333, 335, 415 N.E.2d 850 (1981). Deeds should be so "construed as to give effect to the intent of the parties, unless inconsistent with some law or repugnant to the terms of the grant." Bass River Sav. Bank v. Nickerson, 303 Mass. 332, 334, 21 N.E.2d 717 (1939), and cases cited. When land is conveyed in trust, the trustees generally take such an estate as is necessary to enable

---

10. We consider the 1936 conveyance by deed and declaration of trust. None of the parties argue that the 1940 devise ought to be interpreted differently from the 1936 conveyance.

them to perform the trust. 1 A. Scott, Trusts §88, at 751 (3d ed. 1967). See Richardson v. Warfield, 252 Mass. 518, 520, 148 N.E. 141 (1925). Under the terms of the trust, the trustees must hold the land for the use and enjoyment of Troop 59. The trustees must also decide whether any of the conditions have been broken, and, if they so decide, then they must convey title to the heirs.[11] To carry out all these responsibilities, the trustees needed to hold title in fee simple absolute.

The plaintiffs focus on the words "so long as" and argue that those words indicate that the trustees took title in fee simple determinable. See Brown v. Independent Baptist Church, 325 Mass. 645, 646, 91 N.E.2d 922 (1950); Institution for Sav. v. Roxbury Home for Aged Women, 244 Mass. 583, 586, 139 N.E. 301 (1923); First Universalist Soc'y v. Boland, 155 Mass. 171, 174, 29 N.E. 524 (1892). The plaintiffs misconstrue the deed. Typically, the words "so long as" do create a fee simple determinable when used to define the nature of the interest granted. See, e.g., Brown v. Independent Baptist Church, *supra*, G. G. & G. T. Bogert, Trusts and Trustees §419, at 481 (rev. 2d ed. 1977); Restatement of Property §44 comment a, illustration 1 (1936). However, "particular forms of expression standing alone and without resort to the purpose of the instrument in question are not determinative." Oldfield v. Stoeco Homes, Inc., 26 N.J. 246, 256, 139 A.2d 291 (1958). See Simonds v. Simonds, 199 Mass, 552, 557, 85 N.E. 860 (1908).

Examining the instrument as a whole, we find no intent to grant a fee simple determinable. If Taylor had so intended, he could simply have deeded the parcel to the trustees "so long as Troop 59 exists." Instead, Taylor created an express trust and recorded it. He required the trustees and their successors to record their appointments. He charged the trustees with the responsibility to determine the existence of a breach of conditions and on such determination to convey title to the heirs. By these provisions, Taylor sought to eliminate any uncertainty in the chain

11. The trustees stand in a fiduciary relationship to the beneficiaries, Briggs v. Crowley, 352 Mass. 194, 200, 224 N.W.2d 417 (1967), and must carry out the directions of the settlor as expressed in the terms of the trust. G. G. & G. T. Bogert, Trusts and Trustees, §541, at 154-155 (1978). Where there are successive beneficiaries, the trustees "owe[ ] a duty to them to administer the trust with impartial consideration for the interests of all the beneficiaries." Id. at 156. See Boston Safe Deposit and Trust Co. v. Stone, 348 Mass. 345, 350, 203 N.E.2d 547 (1965). Taylor clearly intended that the parcels be reconveyed to his heirs on the breach of any of the conditions, and the trustees are obliged to protect the heirs' interest. We note that the trustees did not file any statement in the Registry of Deeds pursuant to G.L. c. 260, §31A (note 9 *supra*). If the trustees believed that they held title in fee simple determinable which would, under G.L. c. 184A, §3 (note 8 *supra*), become a fee simple absolute in Troop 59 and divest the heirs of the possibility of reverter, their fiduciary duties to the heirs obliged them to save the gift to the heirs by registering the heirs' interest pursuant to G.L. c. 260, §31A.

of title.[12] Title would always be in the trustees until, in their sole discretion, they determined that the charitable trust had failed, and then the trustees would convey the property to the heirs.[13] This elaborate mechanism is inconsistent with an estate in fee simple determinable in which a breach of conditions would cause title automatically to revert to the heirs, without any action of the trustees. Thus, we conclude that the trustees took title in fee simple absolute.[14]

12. It was precisely that uncertainty that led the Legislature in 1954 to adopt G.L. c. 184A, §3, limiting fees simple determinable to thirty years' duration. See Leach, Perpetuities Legislation, Massachusetts Style, 67 Harv.L.Rev. 1349, 1362-1363 (1954). Our construction of this conveyance as a fee simple absolute takes it outside the scope of §3. We note, however, that the purposes of §3 are served here by the settlor's requirement that the trustees' appointments be recorded at the Registry of Deeds and that they be arbiters of any breach of condition. Thus, the status of title to the property could always be quickly and easily ascertained.

13. The conveyance to the heirs is subject to the rule against perpetuities. Under the rule against perpetuities, interests must vest, if at all, within twenty-one years plus the life or lives in being at the time of creation of the interest. G.L. c. 184A, §§1, 2 (1984 ed.). See Brown v. Independent Baptist Church, 325 Mass. 645, 646-649, 91 N.E.2d 922 (1950). The judge found that the gift over in this case would not be void under the rule against perpetuities because it was saved under the "second look" doctrine. See Warner v. Whitman, 353 Mass. 468, 472, 233 N.E.2d 14 (1968). Apart from the argument that the heirs' interest is a possibility of reverter to which G.L. c. 184A, §3 applies, the plaintiffs do not argue that the judge erred in the application of the "second look" doctrine to the heirs' interest. The judge also considered whether the doctrine of cy pres should be applied to direct the trust for the general benefit of the Boy Scouts of America. The judge found no general charitable intent by the settlor and declined to apply the doctrine of cy pres. On appeal the plaintiffs do not challenge this ruling.

14. The plaintiffs also argue that the words "to the grantor Irving K. Taylor or to his heirs or his or their assigns" were words of limitation — defining the quantum of interest given to the grantee — rather than words of purchase — indicating who is the grantee. We disagree. The plaintiffs' construction would leave open the question of who was to receive the interest after the breach of conditions. Moreover, the plaintiffs' argument appears to resurrect the doctrine of worthier title. Under the doctrine of worthier title, "a limitation to an heir in a devise is void, and . . . the heir cannot be a purchaser." Ellis v. Page, 7 Cush. 161, 163 (1851). See National Shawmut Bank v. Joy, 315 Mass. 457, 463, 53 N.E.2d 113 (1944). That is, a conveyor cannot "limit a fee simple to his own heirs." C. Moynihan, Real Property 149 (1962). See generally L. Simes & A. Smith, Future Interests c. 46 (2d ed. 1956). The doctrine of worthier title has been abolished in Massachusetts by G.L. c. 184, §33A and 33B (1984 ed.). Section 33B states,

> When any interest in real or personal property is limited, in an otherwise effective inter vivos conveyance, in form or in effect, to the heirs or next of kin of the conveyor, which conveyance creates one or more prior interests in favor of a person or persons in existence, such interest that the conveyor purports to create operates in favor of such heirs or next of kin by purchase and not by descent.

The plaintiffs' argument that the grant to the heirs should be construed as words of limitation rather than words of purchase amounts to an argument that the heirs should take by descent a possibility of reverter rather than take by purchase a gift over. Section 33B precludes such a construction.

Finally, if the trustees had acquired title in fee simple determinable, that would not compel the conclusion that Cape Cod and Islands Council of the Boy Scouts now is entitled to the property. As we read G.L. c. 184A, §3, title in fee simple absolute would vest in the original grantees of the fee simple determinable—the trustees. The trustees, of course, must carry out the intent of the settlor of the trust. See note 11 *supra*. A statute cannot extinguish the terms of a trust. General Laws c. 184A, §3, does not purport to do so. Thus, when Troop 59 ceased to exist, the trustees as holders of a fee simple absolute by virtue of §3 would have been obliged to convey the property to Taylor's heirs.

Judgment affirmed.

Part 6

Landlord and Tenant

Chapter Eighteen

Means Available to Assure Lease Performance

Add the following on page 426 to the last paragraph of the note on security deposits.

The Massachusetts statute was applied in Vinton v. Demetrion, 473 N.E.2d 207 (Mass. App. 1985), in a case where the landlord terminated the lease and sold the leased premises to another without returning the tenant's security deposit. The court held that the purchaser of the leased premises was liable for the security deposit under the Massachusetts statute. The following reference to the statute is quoted from the court's opinion:

> Section 15B(5), as appearing in St. 1978, c. 553, §2, provides that when a lessor sells the premises to another, he shall transfer the deposit to the successor; in case he fails to do so, the successor "shall . . . assume liability for payment of the security deposit to the tenant in accordance with the provisions of this section," with the proviso that "if the tenant still occupies the dwelling unit for which the security deposit was given, said successor . . . may satisfy such obligation by granting the tenant free occupation and use of the dwelling unit for a period of time equivalent to that period of time for which the dwelling unit could be leased . . . if the security deposit were deemed to be rent. . . ."

The court did say that whether the successor would be liable for the security deposit if the termination of the tenancy may have long antedated the succession to ownership need not be considered in this case. See also Castenholz v. Caira, 490 N.E.2d 494 (Mass. App. 1986), which discusses the treble damages penalty available against the landlord for failure to place the security deposit in a separate escrow account, for which the landlord may be liable even though he has transferred the leased land and delivered the security deposit to his successor.

Chapter Nineteen

When Parties Are Excused From Performance

Insert the following material on page 518 before the note on promise by the tenant to keep leased property in repair.

Case adopting Implied Warranty of Habitability that discusses tenant's remedies.

HILDER v. ST. PETER

Supreme Court of Vermont, 1984
144 Vt. 150, 478 A.2d 202

BILLINGS, Chief Justice.

Defendants appeal from a judgment rendered by the Rutland Superior Court. The court ordered defendants to pay plaintiff damages in the amount of $4,945.00, which represented "reimbursement for all rent paid and additional compensatory damages" for the rental of a residential apartment over a fourteen month period in defendants' Rutland apartment building. Defendants filed a motion for reconsideration on the issue of the amount of damages awarded to the plaintiff, and plaintiff filed a cross-motion for reconsideration of the court's denial of an award for punitive damages. The court denied both motions. On appeal, defendants raise three issues for our consideration: first, whether the court correctly calculated the amount of damages awarded the plaintiff; secondly, whether the court's award to plaintiff of the entire amount of rent paid to defendants was proper since the plaintiff remained in possession of the apartment for the entire fourteen month period; and finally, whether the court's finding that defendant Stuart St. Peter acted on his own behalf and with the apparent authority of defendant Patricia St. Peter was error.

The facts are uncontested. In October, 1974, plaintiff began occupying an apartment at defendants' 10-12 Church Street apartment building in Rutland with her three children and new-born grandson.[1] Plaintiff orally agreed to pay defendant Stuart St. Peter $140 a month and a damage deposit of $50; plaintiff paid defendant the first month's rent and the damage deposit prior to moving in. Plaintiff has paid all rent due under her tenancy. Because the previous tenants had left behind garbage and items of personal belongings, defendant offered to refund plaintiff's damage deposit if she would clean the apartment herself prior to taking possession. Plaintiff did clean the apartment, but never received her deposit back because the defendant denied ever receiving it. Upon moving into the apartment, plaintiff discovered a broken kitchen window. Defendant promised to repair it, but after waiting a week and fearing that her two year old child might cut herself on the shards of glass, plaintiff repaired the window at her own expense. Although defendant promised to provide a front door key, he never did. For a period of time, whenever plaintiff left the apartment, a member of her family would remain behind for security reasons. Eventually, plaintiff purchased and installed a padlock, again at her own expense. After moving in, plaintiff discovered that the bathroom toilet was clogged with paper and feces and would flush only by dumping pails of water into it. Although plaintiff repeatedly complained about the toilet, and defendant promised to have it repaired, the toilet remained clogged and mechanically inoperable throughout the period of plaintiff's tenancy. In addition, the bathroom light and wall outlet were inoperable. Again, the defendant agreed to repair the fixtures, but never did. In order to have light in the bathroom, plaintiff attached a fixture to the wall and connected it to an extension cord that was plugged into an adjoining room. Plaintiff also discovered that water leaked from the water pipes of the upstairs apartment down the ceilings and walls of both her kitchen and back bedroom. Again, defendant promised to fix the leakage, but never did. As a result of this leakage, a large section of plaster fell from the back bedroom ceiling onto her bed and her grandson's crib. Other sections of plaster remained dangling from the ceiling. This condition was brought to the attention of the defendant, but he never corrected it. Fearing that the remaining plaster might fall when the room was occupied, plaintiff moved her and her grandson's bedroom furniture into the living room and ceased using the back bedroom. During the summer months an odor of raw sewage permeated plaintiff's apartment. The odor was so strong that the plaintiff was ashamed to have company in her apartment. Responding to plaintiff's complaints, Rutland City work-

---

1. Between October, 1974, and December, 1976, plaintiff rented apartment number 1 for $140.00 monthly for 18 months, and apartment number 50 for $125.00 monthly for 7 months.

ers unearthed a broken sewage pipe in the basement of defendant's building. Raw sewage littered the floor of the basement, but defendant failed to clean it up. Plaintiff also discovered that the electric service for her furnace was attached to her breaker box, although defendant had agreed, at the commencement of plaintiff's tenancy, to furnish heat.

In its conclusions of law, the court held that the state of disrepair of plaintiff's apartment, which was known to the defendants, substantially reduced the value of the leasehold from the agreed rental value, thus constituting a breach of the implied warranty of habitability. The court based its award of damages on the breach of this warranty and on breach of an express contract. Defendant argues that the court misapplied the law of Vermont relating to habitability because the plaintiff never abandoned the demised premises and, therefore, it was error to award her the full amount of rent paid. Plaintiff counters that, while never expressly recognized by this Court, the trial court was correct in applying an implied warranty of habitability and that under this warranty, abandonment of the premises is not required. Plaintiff urges this Court to affirmatively adopt the implied warranty of habitability.

Historically, relations between landlords and tenants have been defined by the law of property. Under these traditional common law property concepts, a lease was viewed as a conveyance of real property. See Note, Judicial Expansion of Tenants' Private Law Rights: Implied Warranties of Habitability and Safety in Residential Urban Leases, 56 Cornell L.Q. 489, 489-90 (1971) (hereinafter cited as Expansion of Tenants' Rights). The relationship between landlord and tenant was controlled by the doctrine of caveat lessee; that is, the tenant took possession of the demised premises irrespective of their state of disrepair. Love, Landlord's Liability for Defective Premises: Caveat Lessee, Negligence, or Strict Liability? 1975, Wis. L. Rev. 19, 27-28. The landlord's only covenant was to deliver possession to the tenant. The tenant's obligation to pay rent existed independently of the landlord's duty to deliver possession, so that as long as possession remained in the tenant, the tenant remained liable for payment of rent. The landlord was under no duty to render the premises habitable unless there was an express covenant to repair in the written lease. Expansion of Tenants' Rights, *supra*, at 490. The land, not the dwelling, was regarded as the essence of the conveyance.

An exception to the rule of caveat lessee was the doctrine of constructive eviction. Lemle v. Breeden, 51 Haw. 426, 430, 462 P.2d 470, 473 (1969). Here, if the landlord wrongfully interfered with the tenant's enjoyment of the demised premises, or failed to render a duty to the tenant as expressly required under the terms of the lease, the tenant could abandon the premises and cease paying rent. Legier v. Deveneau, 98 Vt. 188, 190, 126 A. 392, 393 (1924).

Beginning in the 1960's, American courts began recognizing that this approach to landlord and tenant relations, which had originated during the Middle Ages, had become an anachronism in twentieth century, urban society. Today's tenant enters into lease agreements, not to obtain arable land, but to obtain safe, sanitary and comfortable housing.

> [T]hey seek a well known package of goods and services—a package which includes not merely walls and ceilings, but also adequate heat, light and ventilation, serviceable plumbing facilities, secure windows and doors, proper sanitation, and proper maintenance. Javins v. First National Realty Corp., 428 F.2d 1071, 1074 (D.C. Cir.), *cert. denied*, 400 U.S. 925, 91 S. Ct. 186, 27 L. Ed. 2d 185 (1970).

Not only has the subject matter of today's lease changed, but the characteristics of today's tenant have similarly evolved. The tenant of the Middle Ages was a farmer, capable of making whatever repairs were necessary to his primitive dwelling. Green v. Superior Court, 10 Cal. 3d 616, 622, 517 P.2d 1168, 1172, 111 Cal. Rptr. 704, 708 (1974). Additionally, "the common law courts assumed that an equal bargaining position existed between landlord and tenant . . . ." Note, The Implied Warranty of Habitability: A Dream Deferred, 48 UMKC L. Rev. 237, 238 (1980) (hereinafter cited as A Dream Deferred).

In sharp contrast, todays' residential tenant, most commonly a city dweller, is not experienced in performing maintenance work on urban, complex living units. Green v. Superior Court, *supra*, 10 Cal. 3d at 624, 517 P.2d at 1173, 111 Cal. Rptr. at 707-08. The landlord is more familiar with the dwelling unit and mechanical equipment attached to that unit, and is more financially able to "discover and cure" any faults and breakdowns. Id. at 624, 517 P.2d at 1173, 111 Cal. Rptr. at 708. Confronted with a recognized shortage of safe, decent housing, see 24 V.S.A. §4001(1), today's tenant is in an inferior bargaining position compared to that of the landlord. Park West Management Corp. v. Mitchell, 47 N.Y.2d 316, 324-325, 391 N.E.2d 1288, 1292, 418 N.Y.S.2d 310, 314, *cert. denied*, 444 U.S. 992, 100 S. Ct. 523, 62 L. Ed. 2d 421 (1979). Tenants vying for this limited housing are "virtually powerless to compel the performance of essential services." Id. at 325, 391 N.E.2d at 1292, 418 N.Y.S.2d at 314.

In light of these changes in the relationship between tenants and landlords, it would be wrong for the law to continue to impose the doctrine of caveat lessee on residential leases.

> The modern view favors a new approach which recognizes that a lease is essentially a contract between the landlord and the tenant wherein the landlord promises to deliver and maintain the demised premises in habitable con-

dition and the tenant promises to pay rent for such habitable premises. These promises constitute interdependent and mutual considerations. Thus, the tenant's obligation to pay rent is predicated on the landlord's obligation to deliver and maintain the premises in habitable condition. Boston Housing Authority v. Hemingway, 363 Mass. 184, 198, 293 N.E.2d 831, 842 (1973).

Recognition of residential leases as contracts embodying the mutual covenants of habitability and payment of rent does not represent an abrupt change in Vermont law. Our case law has previously recognized that contract remedies are available for breaches of lease agreements. Clarendon Mobile Home Sales, Inc. v. Fitzgerald, 135 Vt. 594, 596, 381 A.2d 1063, 1065 (1977); Keene v. Willis, 128 Vt. 187, 188, 191-92, 260 A.2d 371, 371-372, 374 (1969); Breese v. McCann, 52 Vt. 498, 501 (1879). More significantly, our legislature, in establishing local housing authorities, 24 V.S.A. §4003, has officially recognized the need for assuring the existence of adequate housing.

> [S]ubstandard and decadent areas exist in certain portions of the state of Vermont and ... there is not ... an adequate supply of decent, safe and sanitary housing for persons of low income, and/or elderly persons of low income, available for rents which such persons can afford to pay ... this situation tends to cause an increase and spread of communicable and chronic disease ... [and] constitutes a menace to the health, safety, welfare and comfort of the inhabitants of the state and is detrimental to property values in the localities in which it exists.... 24 V.S.A. §4001(4).

In addition, this Court has assumed the existence of an implied warranty of habitability in residential leases. Birkenhead v. Coombs, 143 Vt. 167, 172, 465 A.2d 244, 246 (1983).

Therefore, we now hold expressly that in the rental of any residential dwelling unit an implied warranty exists in the lease, whether oral or written, that the landlord will deliver over and maintain, throughout the period of the tenancy, premises that are safe, clean and fit for human habitation. This warranty of habitability is implied in tenancies for a specific period or at will. Boston Housing Authority v. Hemingway, *supra*, 363 Mass. at 199, 293 N.E.2d at 843. Additionally, the implied warranty of habitability covers all latent and patent defects in the essential facilities of the residential unit.[2] Id. Essential facilities are "facilities vital to the use of the premises for residential purposes...." Kline v. Burns, 111 N.H. 87, 92, 276 A.2d 248, 252 (1971). This means that a

---

2. The warranty also covers those facilities located in the common areas of an apartment building or duplex that may affect the health or safety of a tenant, such as common stairways, or porches. Javins v. First National Realty Corp., *supra*, 428 F.2d at 1082 n. 62; King v. Moorehead, 495 S.W.2d 65, 76 (Mo. App. 1973).

tenant who enters into a lease agreement with knowledge of any defect in the essential facilities cannot be said to have assumed the risk, thereby losing the protection of the warranty. Nor can this implied warranty of habitability be waived by any written provision in the lease or by oral agreement.

In determining whether there has been a breach of the implied warranty of habitability, the courts may first look to any relevant local or municipal housing code; they may also make reference to the minimum housing code standards enunciated in 24 V.S.A. §5003(c)(1)-5003(c)(5). A substantial violation of an applicable housing code shall constitute prima facie evidence that there has been a breach of the warranty of habitability. "[O]ne or two minor violations standing alone which do not affect" the health or safety of the tenant, shall be considered de minimus and not a breach of the warranty. Javins v. First National Realty Corp, *supra*, 428 F.2d at 1082 n.63; Mease v. Fox, 200 N.W.2d 791, 796 (Iowa 1972); King v. Moorehead, *supra*, 495 S.W.2d at 76. In addition, the landlord will not be liable for defects caused by the tenant. Javins v. First National Realty Corp, *supra*, 428 F.2d at 1082 n.62.

However, these codes and standards merely provide a starting point in determining whether there has been a breach. Not all towns and municipalities have housing codes; where there are codes, the particular problem complained of may not be addressed. Park West Management Corp. v. Mitchell, *supra*, 47 N.Y.2d at 328, 391 N.E.2d at 1294, 418 N.Y.S.2d at 316. In determining whether there has been a breach of the implied warranty of habitability, courts should inquire whether the claimed defect has an impact on the safety or health of the tenant. Id.

In order to bring a cause of action for breach of the implied warranty of habitability, the tenant must first show that he or she notified the landlord "of the deficiency or defect not known to the landlord and [allowed] a reasonable time for its correction." King v. Moorehead, *supra*, 495 S.W.2d at 76.

Because we hold that the lease of a residential dwelling creates a contractual relationship between the landlord and tenant, the standard contract remedies of rescission, reformation and damages are available to the tenant when suing for breach of the implied warranty of habitability. Lemle v. Breeden, *supra*, 51 Haw. at 436, 462 P.2d at 475. The measure of damages shall be the difference between the value of the dwelling as warranted and the value of the dwelling as it exists in its defective condition. Birkenhead v. Coombs, *supra*, 143 Vt. at 172, 465 A.2d at 246. In determining the fair rental value of the dwelling as warranted, the court may look to the agreed upon rent as evidence on this issue. Id. "[I]n residential lease disputes involving a breach of the implied warranty of habitability, public policy militates against requiring expert testimony" concerning the value of the defect. Id. at 173, 465 A.2d at 247. The tenant will be liable only for "the reasonable rental value [if any] of the property in its imperfect condition during his period of occupancy." Berzito v. Gambino, 63 N.J. 460, 469, 308 A.2d 17, 22 (1973).

We also find persuasive the reasoning of some commentators that damages should be allowed for a tenant's discomfort and annoyance arising from the landlord's breach of the implied warranty of habitability. See Moskovitz, The Implied Warranty of Habitability: A New Doctrine Raising New Issues, 62 Calif. L. Rev. 1444, 1470-73 (1974) (hereinafter cited as A New Doctrine); A Dream Deferred, *supra,* at 250-51. Damages for annoyance and discomfort are reasonable in light of the fact that

> the residential tenant who has suffered a breach of the warranty . . . cannot bathe as frequently as he would like or at all if there is inadequate hot water; he must worry about rodents harrassing his children or spreading disease if the premises are infested; or he must avoid certain rooms or worry about catching a cold if there is inadequate weather protection or heat. Thus, discomfort and annoyance are the common injuries caused by each breach and hence the true nature of the general damages the tenant is claiming. Moskovitz, A New Doctrine, *supra,* at 1470-71.

Damages for discomfort and annoyance may be difficult to compute; however, "[t]he trier [of fact] is not to be deterred from this duty by the fact that the damages are not susceptible of reduction to an exact money standard." Vermont Electric Supply Co. v. Andrus, 132 Vt. 195, 200, 315, A.2d 456, 459 (1974).

Another remedy available to the tenant where there has been a breach of the implied warranty of habitability is to withhold the payment of future rent.[3] King v. Moorehead, *supra,* 495 S.W.2d at 77. The burden and expense of bringing suit will then be on the landlord who can better afford to bring the action. In an action for ejectment for nonpayment of rent, 12 V.S.A. §4773, "[t]he trier of fact, upon evaluating the seriousness of the breach and the ramification of the defect upon the health and safety of the tenant, will abate the rent at the landlord's expense in

---

3. Because we hold that the tenant's obligation to pay rent is contingent on the landlord's duty to provide and maintain a habitable dwelling, it is no longer necessary for the tenant to first abandon the premises. Northern Terminals, Inc. v. Smith Grocery & Variety, Inc., 138 Vt. 389, 396-97, 418 A.2d 22, 26-27 (1980); Legier v. Deveneau, *supra,* 98 Vt. at 190, 126 A. at 393; thus, the doctrine of constructive eviction is no longer a viable or needed defense in an action by the landlord for unpaid rent. Lemle v. Breeden, *supra,* 51 Haw. at 435-36, 462 P.2d at 475; Boston Housing Authority v. Hemingway, *supra,* 363 Mass. at 199-200, 293 N.E.2d at 843; see also Expansion of Tenants' Rights, *supra,* at 491 (constructive eviction "[w]ith its absolute requirement of abandonment . . . is utterly unsatisfactory for a tenant faced with today's urban housing shortage").

accordance with its findings." A Dream Deferred, *supra,* at 248. The tenant must show that: (1) the landlord had notice of the previously unknown defect and failed, within a reasonable time, to repair it; and (2) the defect, affecting habitability, existed during the time for which rent was withheld. See A Dream Deferred, *supra,* at 248-50. Whether a portion, all or none of the rent will be awarded to the landlord will depend on the findings relative to the extent and duration of the breach.[4] Javins v. First National Realty Corp., *supra,* F.2d at 1082-83. Of course, once the landlord corrects the defect, the tenant's obligation to pay rent becomes due again. Id. at 1083 n.64.

Additionally, we hold that when the landlord is notified of the defect but fails to repair it within a reasonable amount of time, and the tenant subsequently repairs the defect, the tenant may deduct the expense of the repair from future rent. 11 Williston on Contracts §1404 (3d ed. W. Jaeger 1968); Marini v. Ireland, 56 N.J. 130, 146, 265 A.2d 526, 535 (1970).

In addition to general damages, we hold that punitive damages may be available to a tenant in the appropriate case. Although punitive damages are generally not recoverable in actions for breach of contract, there are cases in which the breach is of such a willful and wanton or fraudulent nature as to make appropriate the award of exemplary damages. Clarendon Mobile Home Sales, Inc. v. Fitzgerald, *supra,* 135 Vt. at 596, 381 A.2d at 1065. A willful and wanton or fraudulent breach may be shown "by conduct manifesting personal ill will, or carried out under circumstances of insult or oppression, or even by conduct manifesting . . . a reckless or wanton disregard of [one's] rights. . . ." Sparrow v. Vermont Savings Bank, 95 Vt. 29, 33, 112 A. 205, 207 (1921). When a landlord, after receiving notice of a defect, fails to repair the facility that is essential to the health and safety of his or her tenant, an award of punitive damages is proper. 111 East 88th Partners v. Simon, 106 Misc. 2d 693, 434 N.Y.S.2d 886, 889 (N.Y. Civ. Ct. 1980).

> The purpose of punitive damages . . . is to punish conduct which is morally culpable . . . . Such an award serves to deter a wrongdoer . . . from repetitions of the same or similar actions. And it tends to encourage prosecution of a claim by a victim who might not otherwise incur the expense and inconvenience of private action . . . . The public benefit and a display of ethical indig-

---

4. Some courts suggest that, during the period rent is withheld, the tenant should pay the rent as it becomes due, into legal custody. See, e.g., Javins v. First National Realty Corp., *supra,* 42 F.2d at 1083 n. 67; see also King v. Moorehead, *supra,* 495 S.W.2d at 77 (*King* requires the deposit of the rent into legal custody pending the litigation). Such a procedure assures the availability of that portion, if any, of the rent which the court determines is due to the landlord. King v. Moorehead, *supra,* 495 S.W.2d at 77; see A Dream Deferred, *supra,* at 248-50.

nation are among the ends of the policy to grant punitive damages. Davis v. Williams, 92 Misc. 2d 1051, 402 N.Y.S.2d 92, 94 (N.Y. Civ. Ct. 1977).

In the instant case, the trial court's award of damages, based in part on a breach of the implied warranty of habitability, was not a misapplication of the law relative to habitability. Because of our holding in this case, the doctrine of constructive eviction, wherein the tenant must abandon in order to escape liability for rent, is no longer viable. When, as in the instant case, the tenant seeks, not to escape rent liability, but to receive compensatory damages in the amount of rent already paid, abandonment is similarly unnecessary. Northern Terminals, Inc. v. Smith Grocery & Variety, Inc., *supra*, 138 Vt. at 396-97, 418 A.2d at 26-27. Under our holding, when a landlord breaches the implied warranty of habitability, the tenant may withhold future rent, and may also seek damages in the amount of rent previously paid.

In its conclusions of law the trial court stated that the defendants' failure to make repairs was compensable by damages to the extent of reimbursement of all rent paid and additional compensatory damages. The court awarded plaintiff a total of $4,945.00; $3,445.00 represents the entire amount of rent plaintiff paid, plus the $50.00 deposit. This appears to leave $1500.00 as the "additional compensatory damages." However, although the court made findings which clearly demonstrate the appropriateness of an award for compensatory damages, there is no indication as to how the court reached a figure of $1500.00. It is "crucial that this Court and the parties be able to determine what was decided and how the decision was reached." Fox v. McLain, 142 Vt. 11, 16, 451 A.2d 1122, 1124 (1982).

Additionally, the court denied an award to plaintiff of punitive damages on the ground that the evidence failed to support a finding of willful and wanton or fraudulent conduct. See Clarendon Mobile Home Sales, Inc. v. Fitzgerald, *supra*, 135 Vt. at 596, 381 A.2d at 1065. The facts in this case, which defendants do not contest, evince a pattern of intentional conduct on the part of defendants for which the term "slumlord" surely was coined. Defendants' conduct was culpable and demeaning to plaintiff and clearly expressive of a wanton disregard of plaintiff's rights. The trial court found that defendants were aware of defects in the essential facilities of plaintiff's apartment, promised plaintiff that repairs would be made, but never fulfilled those promises. The court also found that plaintiff continued, throughout her tenancy, to pay her rent, often in the face of verbal threats made by defendant Stuart St. Peter. These findings point to the "bad spirit and wrong intention" of the defendants, Glidden v. Skinner, 142 Vt. 644, 648, 458 A.2d 1142, 1144 (1983), and would support a finding of willful and wanton or fraudulent conduct, contrary to the conclusions of law and judgment of the trial judge. However, the plaintiff did not appeal the court's denial of punitive damages, and issues not appealed and briefed are waived. R. Brown & Sons, Inc. v. International Harvester Corp., 142 Vt. 140, 142, 453 A.2d 83, 84 (1982).

We find that defendants' third claimed error, that the court erred in finding that both defendant Stuart St. Peter and defendant Patricia St. Peter were liable to plaintiff for the breach of the implied warranty of habitability, is meritless. Both defendants were named in the complaint as owners of the 10-12 Church Street apartment building. Plaintiff's complaint also alleged that defendant Stuart St. Peter acted as agent for defendant Patricia St. Peter. Defendants fail to deny these allegations; under V.R.C.P. 8(d) these averments stand as admitted.

Affirmed in part; reversed in part and remanded for hearing on additional compensable damages, consistent with the views herein.

ON REARGUMENT

On the motion for reargument, defendants claim that equitable relief was sought below and that pursuant to Soucy v. Soucy Motors, Inc., 143 Vt. 615, 471 A.2d 224 (1983), the trial court had no jurisdiction since the cause was heard by the presiding judge and one assistant judge. An examination of the record reveals that plaintiff's equitable claims were directed against other defendants who were dismissed prior to trial; at trial only compensatory and punitive damages were sought against the defendants here. See Vermont National Bank v. Dowrick, 144 Vt. 504, 481 A.2d 396 (1984).

Motion for reargument denied.

Note: Implied Warranty of Habitability — the Minority Viewpoint

Kentucky has refused to recognize the implied warranty of habitability. See Miles v. Shauntee, 664 S.W.2d 512 (S. Ct. Ky. 1983, *rehg. denied,* 1984). The following is quoted from the court opinion.

II.   Whether an Implied Warranty of Habitability Exists in a Landlord-Tenant Relationship

At early common law, a lease was considered a conveyance of an estate in land and was equivalent to a sale of the premises to the lessee for the term of the demise. The lessee, as a purchaser of the estate of land, was subjected to the strict common law property rule of caveat emptor. The lessee had the duty to inspect the property for defects and took the land as he found it. King. v. Moorehead, 495 S.W.2d 65 (Mo. App. 1973). There was no implied warranty by the lessor that the demised premises were habitable or fit for the purpose leased. A lessee wishing to protect himself as to the fitness of the premises had to exact an express covenant from the landlord for that purpose. *King, supra,* at 69.

Kentucky courts have followed other common law jurisdictions in applying the strict property rule of caveat emptor to leaseholds. As is often the case with strict rules, however, exceptions to concept of caveat emptor were created. In Holzhauer v. Sheeny, 127 Ky. 28, 104 S.W. 1034 (1907), the then Court of Appeals of Kentucky stated:

> The rule of caveat emptor applies to a contract of letting. The tenant must take the premises as he may find them. There is no implied covenant on the part of the landlord that they are fit for the purpose for which they are rented, or that they are in particular condition; but there is extension of the rule: If the landlord knows that the premises are defective or dangerous, and such defect is not discoverable by the tenant by ordinary care and the landlord conceals or fails to disclose the dangerous condition, he is liable to the tenant, his family and servants, or even his guests, for injuries sustained therefrom. Holzhauer v. Sheeny, 104 S.W. at 1035.

This extension was carefully limited in application to cases where actual knowledge was brought home to the landlord. Franklin v. Tracy, 117 Ky. 267, 77 S.W. 1113 (1904).

Kentucky courts have also recognized exceptions to this general rule of law where a portion of the demised premises was retained by the lessor for the common use and benefit of a number of tenants, Carver v. Howard, Ky., 280 S.W.2d 708 (1955); Richmond v. Standard Elkhorn Coal Co., 222 Ky. 150, 300 S.W. 359 (1928); Home Realty Co. v. Carius, 189 Ky. 228, 224 S.W. 751 (1920); Offutt v. O'Leary, 204 Ky. 726, 265 S.W. 296 (1924); Cohen v. White, 206 Ky. 209, 266 S.W. 1078 (1924); and where actions by the landlord constitutes a constructive eviction. Estes v. Gatliff, et al., 291 Ky. 93, 163 S.W.2d 273 (1942).

As stated in the case of Milby v. Mears, 580 S.W.2d 724 (Ky. Ct. App. 1979), at page 728:

> It has been a long standing rule in Kentucky that a tenant takes the premises as he finds them. The landlord need not exercise even ordinary care to furnish reasonably safe premises, and he is not generally liable for injuries caused by defects therein.

The general rule in effect in Kentucky, is that the tenant takes premises as he finds them. Whitehouse v. Lorch, Ky., 347 S.W.2d 512 (1961). In the absence of a special agreement to do so, made when the contract is entered into, there is no obligation upon the landlord to repair the leased premises. Hortsman v. Newman, Ky., 291 S.W.2d 567 (1956); Mahan-Jellico Coal Company v. Dulling, 282 Ky. 698, 139 S.W.2d 749 (1940).

Appellants argue that an implied warranty of habitability should arise from local housing or health codes absent an express provision in the contract of lease and absent such a provision in the ordinance or regulation in question. Absent an expression to the contrary such provisions do not create an implied warranty of habitability, or create a cause of action in the tenants. The remedies for violations are found within the codes, ordinances or regulations themselves. It is for the legislature to create rights and duties nonexistent under the common law. Absent legislation to the contrary the established doctrine in effect in Kentucky is that the tenant takes possession of the premises as he first finds them, *Whitehouse, supra,* and the landlord, absent an express covenant to the contrary, has no obligation to repair the premises, *Horstman, supra,* and *Mahan-Jellico Coal Company, supra.* No implied warranty of habitability exists under Kentucky law. The judgments of the Jefferson and Warren Circuit Courts, and the decision of the Court of Appeals on this issue are affirmed.

Case concerning tenant withholding rent for breach of implied warrant of habitability.

BERMAN v. JEFFERSON

Supreme Judicial Court of Massachusetts, 1979
379 Mass. 196, 396 N.E.2d 981

LIACOS, Justice.

Cynthia Jefferson (tenant) leased for one year, beginning March 1, 1976, at $245 a month an apartment in Peabody from Berman & Sons, Inc. (landlord). From late August until October 8, 1976, a series of breaks in underground heating pipes caused the tenant to receive intermittent heat. The landlord repaired each leak promptly. On October 8, the pipe burst completely, and the tenant was without heat until the pipe was repaired on October 20. Furthermore, from time to time, the apartment was without adequate hot water. These failures continued sporadically through June, 1977. The tenant withheld $35 from her November, 1976, rent. The landlord returned the check and in January, 1977, brought an action for summary process in the District Court of Peabody. The tenant answered and counterclaimed, alleging, inter alia, breach of the implied warranty of habitability. The judge denied the landlord's claim for possession and awarded the tenant $310 damages. In February, 1977, the landlord appealed to the Superior Court, which heard the case on written stipulations. On October 23, 1978, the judge entered findings of fact, conclusions of law, and an order awarding the tenant

$310 for breach of the warrant of habitability. The landlord appealed from the judgment. We granted the landlord's application for direct appellate review. We affirm the judgment.[1]

The Superior Court judge found there was insufficient evidence to conclude that the landlord acted intentionally, negligently, or in bad faith.[2] He found and ruled that the losses of heat and hot water were material breaches of the warranty of habitability. The judge ruled further that the tenant is allowed to abate the rent from the date the landlord had notice of the breach of the warranty of habitability. We must decide (1) whether a tenant must pay full rent without abatement when the landlord, acting without fault or bad faith, fails to maintain a dwelling in a habitable condition and (2) whether the tenant's obligation to pay full rent persists until the landlord has had a reasonable time to repair the defect. We hold that the tenant's obligation abates as soon as the landlord has notice that the premises failed to comply with the requirements of the warrant of habitability. The landlord's lack of fault and reasonable efforts to repair do not prolong the duty to pay full rent.

In Boston Hous. Auth. v. Hemingway, 363 Mass. 184, 293 N.E.2d 831 (1973), we found that social changes in landlord-tenant relations[3] and legislative changes in landlord obligations and tenant remedies[4] were inconsistent with medieval notions of the lease as a conveyance of prop-

---

1. We have been aided in our consideration of the issues raised by this appeal by amicus briefs filed by the Greater Boston Real Estate Board and a coalition of legal assistance groups led by the Housing Allowance Project, Inc., and the Massachusetts Law Reform Institute.

2. The landlord and the tenant disagree as to whether the landlord effected repairs within a reasonable time after learning of the defect, and the trial judge made no finding. For the purposes of argument, however, we assume that the landlord did accomplish the repairs within a reasonable time.

3. We noted that the factual assumptions underlying the common law exception of Ingalls v. Hobbs, 156 Mass. 348, 31 N.E. 286 (1892), had come to describe the rule: "Modern tenants rightfully expect that the premises they rent . . . will be suitable for occupation." Boston Hous. Auth. v. Hemingway, 363 Mass. 184, 197, 293 N.E.2d 831, 841 (1973). And we quoted the decision in Javins v. First Nat'l Realty Corp., 138 U.S. App. D.C. 369, 428 F.2d 1071, 1078-1079 (D.C. Cir. 1970), which describes the differences between the old agrarian and modern urban tenant's expectations concerning repairs of a dwelling.

4. For example, the State Sanitary Code, adopted pursuant to authority granted in G.L. c.111, §5 (since amended, see G.L. c.111, §127A, for the current version), imposed on the landlord a duty to maintain an apartment in habitable condition, so the landlord could fairly expect and be expected to keep his rented premises habitable. Moreover, the Legislature had created tenant's remedies for private enforcement of the Code, G.L. c.111, §§2127A-127H, and for self-help through rent withholding, G.L. c.239, §8A. The creation of private remedies negated any argument that the Legislature was content with purely public enforcement of the Code. The rent-withholding provision embodies a legislative judgment that the tenant's rental obligation is bound up with the landlord's obligation to provide habitable premises.

erty. The changes in social and legal circumstances changed the parties' expectations. It was in this context that we chose to recast our theory of the landlord-tenant relationship in a form congenial with the Legislature's tendency: "[A] lease is essentially a contract between the landlord and the tenant wherein the landlord promises to deliver and maintain the demised premises in habitable condition and the tenant promises to pay rent for such habitable premises. These promises constitute interdependent and mutual considerations. Thus, the tenant's obligation to pay rent is predicated on the landlord's obligation to deliver and maintain the premises in habitable condition." Id. at 198, 293 N.E.2d at 842. We held that a tenant is entitled to a rent abatement, in whole or in part, during the period that an apartment remains uninhabitable after the landlord has notice of the defects.[5] Id. at 203, 293 N.E.2d 831.

The landlord argues that, on the present facts, he has done no wrong. He argues that to impose strict liability would penalize the landlord who is acting reasonably and would impose a duty impossible to meet. Moreover, he claims the expectations of the parties support the landlord's position. Both landlord and tenant expect less than perfect upkeep of apartments; systems break down; maintenance takes time; the law should reflect this reality.[6] Furthermore, Berman contends, the purpose of the warranty is "to provide tenants with a mechanism to encourage the repair of serious and dangerous defects" connected with a residential dwelling unit or the common areas. This purpose can be achieved without imposing strict liability on landlords.

These contentions have no place in the framework established in *Hemingway*. Considerations of fault do not belong in an analysis of warranty. Nowhere does the landlord point us to an analogous body of warranty law that incorporates a fault standard,[7] nor has Berman persuaded us to make

5. The trial judge found that the measure of damages was "the difference between the value of the apartment as warranted and the rental value of the apartment in its defective condition." See McKenna v. Begin, 5 Mass. App. 304, —, 362, N.E.2d 548 (1977). Apart from the question whether the tenant's rent abates only after the landlord has had a reasonable time to repair, damages are not in dispute in this case.

6. The landlord seems further to suggest that the presence of an exculpatory clause in the tenant's lease should be evidence of the tenant's expectations. The clause stated that the landlord would provide hot water and reasonable heat, but that failure to do so would not give rise to a damage claim. As the landlord appears to concede, this clause is void. It is an attempt to limit the landlord's duties and liabilities under the Sanitary Code and is therefore of no effect. Boston Hous. Auth. v. Hemingway, *supra* at 199, 293 N.E.2d 831. A tenant has a right to expect that the landlord will comply with the law. It is this right that we protect.

7. Amicus Greater Boston Real Estate Board cites language in Beck v. Wickes Corp., — Mass. —, — (Mass. Adv. Sh. [1978] 1874, 1883) 378 N.E.2d 964, 969 (1978). We said that "[w]arrant liability is not absolute liability. [A] manufacturer must anticipate the environment in which its product will be used, and it must design against the reasonably foresee-

an exception here. The landlord may be correct in characterizing itself as an innocent party, and we are cognizant of the economic burdens that a landlord typically bears.[8] Nevertheless, we note that the landlord's liabilty without fault is merely an economic burden; the tenant living in an uninhabitable buidling suffers a loss of shelter, a necessity. Moreover, the warranty of habitability is not designed to penalize the landlord for misbehavior. In the rent abatement context, the doctrine imposes a duty quite apart from notions of moral sanction or deterrence.[9]

---

able risks attending the product's use in that setting." This quotation, of course, states the proximate cause limitation on the warranty of a manufacturer of goods. There is no suggestion that proof of fault or bad faith is a prerequisite for recovery under such a warranty. Furthermore, in contrast to a claim for injury to person or property, considerations of proximate cause do not affect validity of a claim for rent abatement.

8. The landlord suggests, and the amicus Greater Boston Real Estate Board argues at length, that to make the landlord the insurer of apartment maintenance will have deleterious economic effects on landlords and on the housing market generally. Increased costs derived from the warranty will result in increased rents. Older buildings, whose maintenance is hardest to ensure, tend to house low income tenants who cannot pay increased rents. Thus, imposing full warranty protection will ultimately reduce the stock of low income housing.

This argument assumes that tenants will frequently enforce the rent abatement remedy or that landlords will spend a great deal of money on preventive maintenance. Yet empirical evidence tends to show a very low rate of tenant enforcement. Abbott, Housing Policy, Housing Codes and Tenant Remedies: An Integration, 56 B.U.L. Rev. 1, 63 (1976). Hirsch, Hirsch & Margolis, Regression Analysis of the Effects of Habitability Laws Upon Rent: An Empirical Observation on the Ackerman-Komesar Debate, 63 Cal. L. Rev. 1098, 1130 (1975). A study has failed to find a statistically significant relationship between the presence of most habitability laws, including rent abatement, and increased rents. Hirsch, Hirsch & Margolis, *supra* at 1130-1132. In addition, we request the virtue of relying on a theory of economic efficiency at the expense of legal analysis. Precedent, legislative policy, and common law principles support the result we reach today. See Michelman, Norms and Normativity in the Economic Theory of Law, 62 Minn. L. Rev. 1015, 1015 (1978) ("[W]ell-conducted, systematic, convincing, behaviorally focused research can entrap as well as liberate, can help engender as well as dispel false belief about social reality, insofar as it invites the reduction of reality to observed regularities of behavior").

9. The landlord relies in part on case law relating to tort liability for injuries caused by failure to repair defective premises. We have held that, when the defect occurs in the common areas, the landlord is subject to a duty of reasonable care. King v. G & M Realty Corp., 373 Mass. 658, —-— (Mass. Adv. Sh. [1977] 2372, 2375-2376), 370 N.E.2d 413 (1977). When the defect occurs in the rented premises, the question is not one of negligence, but one of breach of warranty. In the latter instance, the landlord must comply at least with minimum standards prescribed by the State building and sanitary codes. Whether the scope of the warranty is broader is an open question. Crowell v. McCaffrey, — Mass. —, —-— (Mass. Adv. Sh. [1979] 568, 578-579), 386 N.E.2d 1256 (1979). But see Boston Hous. Auth. v. Hemingway, *supra* at 218, 293 N.E.2d 831. (Quirico, J., dissenting).

Crowell left open a second question as well. "[W]e think the jury would have been warranted in finding that the landlord, by the exercise of reasonable care, . . . could have

The landlord would have us avert our eyes from the clear teaching of *Hemingway:* "[T]he essential objective of the leasing transaction is to provide a dwelling suitable for habitation." Boston Hous. Auth. v. Hemingway, *supra* at 196-197, 293 N.E.2d at 841. A dwelling afflicted with a substantial Sanitary Code violation is not habitable. The essential objective of the warranty is to make sure that the tenant receives what she is paying for. The tenant may not excuse her obligation with mere reasonable efforts to pay rent. Nor may the landlord avoid his duty with mere reasonable efforts to provide a habitable dwelling. The contract between the parties, seen through the law's clarifying lens, requires such symmetry.

The landlord argues that the existence of a serious defect in an apartment is a potential breach of the warranty; the breach becomes actual only after the landlord has been notified of the defect and has had a reasonable time to repair.[10] In *Hemingway,* however, we set out a very different picture of the warranty: "[The warranty] means that at the inception of the rental there are no latent [or patent] defects in facilities vital to the use of the premises for residential purposes and that these essential facilities will remain during the entire term in a condition which makes the property livable." Boston Hous. Auth. v. Hemingway, *supra* at 199, 293 N.E.2d at 843, quoting from Kline v. Burns, 111 N.H. 87, 92, 276 A.2d 248 (1971). Neither at the inception nor during the term of the lease did we leave room for a reasonable time to repair.[11] Admittedly a

---

brought the premises into compliance. We do not pass on the question whether such a finding is essential to liability." Crowell v. McCaffrey, *supra* at —-— (Mass. Adv. Sh. [1979] at 579-580), 386 N.E.2d at 1262. Whatever standard of liability for personal injury under a theory of breach of warranty is appropriate, however, the tenant's right to abate rent in the present case arises from mutual obligations, not from an interest in freedom from harm. See W. Prosser, Torts §92 (4th ed. 1971).

10. In support of this proposition, the landlord points out that three States require that a landlord have a reasonable time to repair. Hinson v. Delis, 26 Cal. App. 3d 62, 70, 102 Cal. Rptr. 661 (1972). King v. Moorehead, 495 S.W.2d 65 (Mo. App. 1973). Berzito v. Gambino, 63 N.J. 460, 469, 308 A.2d 17 (1973). We note that these cases did not squarely present the issue and that the courts stated the proposition without explanation.

11. See King v. G & M Realty Corp., 373 Mass. 658, n.6 (Mass. Adv. Sh. [1977] 2372, 2376 n.6), 370 N.E.2d 413 (1977). See also Love, Landlord's Liability for Defective Premises: Caveat Lessee, Negligence, or Strict Liability?, 1975 Wis. L. Rev. 19, 105 ("[T]he notice [and reasonable time to repair] requirement reflects the continuing vitality of the notion that a lease is a conveyance of property").

Amicus Real Estate Board presses an analogy based on G.L. c.106 §2-508(2) of the Uniform Commercial Code, as appearing in St. 1957, c.765, §1: "Where the buyer rejects a non-conforming tender which the seller had reasonable grounds to believe would be acceptable with or without money allowance the seller may if he seasonably notifies the buyer have a further reasonable time to substitute a conforming tender." The argument that the landlord has a comparable right to cure fails on two grounds. First, the seller may cure only if the buyer rejects, or, arguably, revokes acceptance of the goods. Here the tenant did

tenant must notify her landlord of defects as a prerequisite to a rent abatement,[12] but the purpose of this requirement is not to assure the landlord a reasonable time to repair. The requirement is designed to minimize the time the landlord is in breach and hence mitigate the permissible period of abatement of rent. The rent abatement begins when notice is given, not at a reasonable time after notice. Time for repairs has no place in the calculus.[13]

Our position follows as a corollary of *Hemingway*. However, *Hemingway* is not the only source of guidance for rejecting the landlord's theory. When the tenant's loss of heat occurred, G.L. c.239, §8A, permitted the tenant to withhold rent for Code violations only if "the owner . . . had not taken reasonable steps to remedy such conditions." St. 1973, c.471. In 1977, the Legislature struck this provision. St. 1977, c.963. The tenant may now withhold rent without considering whether the landlord is at fault or is taking reasonable steps to repair. As was the case in *Hemingway*, this statute provides for rent withholding, not rent abatement; but, as in *Hemingway*, we choose to permit a rent abatement as a matter of common law.[14] We consider the result we reach here to be consistent not

---

neither. By not vacating her apartment, she accepted the goods, then sought damages under the warranty. In that circumstance, §2-508(2) does not afford a right to cure. See, e.g., Bonebrake v. Cox, 499 F.2d 951, 957 (8th Cir. 1974).

Second, the amicus relies on the statement of official Comment 2 that "reasonable grounds can lie in prior course of dealing, course of performance or usage of trade. . . ." Here the landlord appears to have proceeded in a responsible manner consistent with landlords' trade usage. However, the State Sanitary Code, not such usage, provides the proper yardstick for measuring the landlord's conduct. The *Hemingway* court removed the landlord's duties under the Code from the realm of private ordering. Boston Hous. Auth. v. Hemingway, *supra* at 199, 293 N.E.2d 831. Those duties cannot be waived, bargained away, or qualified by customary practice. The Code puts the landlord on notice that it must supply adequate heat and hot water. State Sanitary Code, Art. II, Regulations 5, 6 (1969) (current version at 105 Code of Mass. Regs. 410.190, 410.200, 410.201). The landlord can have no reasonable grounds to believe that noncompliance will be acceptable.

12. The landlord's knowledge of the defect is also sufficient. McKenna v. Begin, 3 Mass. app. 168, 172-173, 325 N.E.2d 587 (1975). Crowell v. McCaffrey, — Mass. —, —·— (1979) (Mass. Adv. Sh. [1979] 568, 579-80), 386 N.E.2d 1256, 1262 (1979), left open the question whether a landlord without notice or actual knowledge of a Code violation can be liable if "by the exercise of reasonable care, [he] could have discovered whatever violations of the codes . . . existed."

13. "[T]he possibility that the residence could be made habitable within a reasonable time," is a factor in determining the materiality of a breach of warranty. Boston Hous. Auth. v. Hemingway, *supra* at 201, 293 N.E.2d at 844. However, there is no mechanical relationship between this possibility and a characterization of the breach as "potential" or "actual." Here the trial judge's ruling that the landlord's breach was material was not in error.

14. Amicus Real Estate Board points to language in the State Sanitary Code to show that the Code contemplates a reasonable time to repair as a prerequisite for punishment of a

only with Hemingway, but also with the law dealing with breach of warranty and with express legislative policy.

Judgment affirmed.

Case concerning tort liability of landlord based on breach of implied warranty of habitability.

BECKER v. IRM CORPORATION

Supreme Court of California, 1985
213 Cal. Rptr. 213, 698 P.2d 116

BROUSSARD, Justice.

In this personal injury action plaintiff's complaint asserted causes of action of strict liability and negligence against defendant landlord. Defendant moved for summary judgment urging that a landlord is not liable to a tenant for a latent defect of the rented premises absent concealment of a known danger or an expressed contractual or statutory duty to repair.

---

violation. An enforcement agency's order "shall indicate the time limit for compliance" and "may suggest action which, if taken, will effect compliance with this Chapter." State Sanitary Code, Art. II, Regulation 33.4(c) and (e), adopted in 67 Mass.Reg. 40 (1977) (currently codified in 105 Code of Mass.Regs 410.832[B][3] & [5]). Failure to comply with such an order is a prerequisite for a fine. Id. at 410.910.

First, we note that the language quoted appears in a version of the State Sanitary Code not in effect at the time of events in this case. See 67 Mass. Reg. 21 (effective Aug. 1, 1977). The version in effect in 1976 required the enforcing agency to "allot a reasonable time for any action [the order] requires." State Sanitary Code, Art. II, Regulation 33.4(b) (1969). The 1977 amendment changed the "reasonable time" requirement to a specific time limit. State Sanitary Code, 105 Code of Mass. Regs. 410.830. For a failure to provide heat, the Code now requires that the board of health, within twelve hours of the inspection, shall order the landlord to make a good faith effort to correct the violation within twenty-four hours. Id. at 410.830(A)(2). We believe that this change indicates dissatisfaction with the vagueness of the term "reasonable time."

Second, even though the Code has consistently provided some grace period during which the landlord may attempt to comply, there is a distinction between the Code's criminal penalty and the rent abatement at issue here. The landlord "violates" the Code by failing to comply. State Sanitary Code, Art. II, Regulation 1 (1969) (currently codified in 105 Code of Mass. Regs. 410.044). Only the penalty is delayed during the grace period. And under the new version of the Code, every enforcement order must be accompanied by notice to the landlord that "the conditions which exist may permit the occupant . . . to exercise one or more statutory remedies." State Sanitary Code, 105 Code of Mass. Regs. 410.832(B)(6). We read the Code to imply that civil remedies for violations are available during the landlord's time to repair. This result is consistent with the 1977 amendment to G.L. c.239, §8A.

The trial court granted the motion and denied a motion for reconsideration. Plaintiff appeals.[1]

We have concluded that the trial court erred as to both causes of action.

The complaint alleges that plaintiff was injured when he slipped and fell against the frosted glass shower door in the apartment he leased from defendant. The door was made of untempered glass. It broke and severely lacerated his arm. It is undisputed that the risk of serious injury would have been substantially reduced if the shower door had been made of tempered glass rather than untempered glass.

Defendant's affidavits in support of the motion for summary judgment may be summarized as follows: Plaintiff's apartment is part of a 36-unit apartment complex built in 1962 and 1963 and acquired by defendant in 1974. Prior to the acquisition, two officers of defendant walked through most of the apartments and observed that all of the shower doors were of frosted glass and appeared to be the same. The officials, one of whom managed the property from the time of its acquisition, stated that prior to plaintiff's accident in 1978 there were no accidents involving the shower doors and that they were not advised that any of the shower doors were made of untempered glass. They first learned that some of the shower doors were untempered glass after the accident. Their inspection of shower doors after the accident provided "no visible difference between the tempered and untempered glass in terms of visible appearance."

Defendant's maintenance man stated that after the accident he examined the glass doors, and that 31 of the doors with untempered glass were replaced by him. He also stated that in looking for the untempered glass shower doors "there was no way the layperson could tell any difference by simply looking at the shower doors. The only way that I was able to differentiate . . . was by looking for a very small mark in the corner of each piece of glass."

Plaintiff did not file affidavits in opposition to defendant's.

The summary judgment procedure is drastic and should be used with caution so that it will not become a substitute for a full trial. A summary judgment is proper only if the affidavits of the moving party would be sufficient to support a judgment in his favor and doubts as to the merits of the motion should be resolved in favor of the party opposing the motion. (Rowland v. Christian (1968) 69 Cal.2d 108, 111, 70 Cal. Rptr. 97, 443 P.2d 561.)

---

1. We have been advised that while the case was pending in this court plaintiff settled with the builder and a door assembler and installer for $150,000 plus $50,000 in the event plaintiff is unsuccessful against the remaining defendants. Apparently, the case remains pending in the trial court against a component part supplier. Defendant landlord will be referred to as defendant herein.

STRICT LIABILITY

In Greenman v. Yuba Power Products, Inc. (1963) 59 Cal. 2d 57, 62, 27 Cal. Rptr. 697, 377 P.2d 897, we established the rule: "A manufacturer is strictly liable in tort when an article he places on the market, knowing that it is to be used without inspection for defects, proves to have a defect that causes injury to a human being. Recognized first in the case of unwholesome food products, such liability has now been extended to a variety of other products that create as great or greater hazards if defective. [Citations.]" The court recognized that the cases imposing strict liability had "usually been based on the theory of an express or implied warranty running from the manufacturer to the plaintiff." (59 Cal. 2d at p.63, 27 Cal. Rptr. 697, 377 P.2d 897.) The justification for departing from warranty theory and for establishing a doctrine of strict liability in tort was the recognition that the liability was imposed by law and the refusal to permit the manufacturer to define the scope of its own liability for defective products. (Ibid.)

Our concern was not that warranty law failed to adequately define the manufacturer's duty but that the " 'intricacies of the law of sales' " applicable to commercial transactions might defeat the obvious representation of safety for intended use made by the manufacturer. (Id. at pp.63-64, 27 Cal. Rptr. 697, 377 P.2d 897.) In declining to discuss the basis of the strict liability, *Greenman* pointed out that the basis of it had been fully articulated, citing to the classical concurring opinion in Escola v. Coca Cola Bottling Co. (1944) 24 Cal. 2d 453, 461, 150 P.2d 436. (Id., 59 Cal. 3d at p.63, 27 Cal. Rptr. 697, 377 P.2d 897.) In the concurring opinion in *Escola,* Justice Traynor pointed out: "The retailer, even though not equipped to test a product, is under an absolute liability to his customer, for the implied warranties of fitness for proposed use and merchantable quality include a warranty of safety of the product. [Citations.]" (24 Cal. 2d at p.464, 150 P.2d 436.) It was also pointed out that the retailer should not bear the burden of his warranty alone but that he could recoup any losses by means of the warranty of safety attending the wholesaler's or manufacturer's sale to him. (Ibid.)

Greenman also noted that the purpose of strict liability in tort is "to insure that the costs of injuries resulting from defective products are borne by the manufacturers that put such products on the market rather than by the injured persons who are powerless to protect themselves." (59 Cal. 2d at p.63, 27 Cal. Rptr. 697, 377 P.2d 897; see Daly v. General Motors (1978) 20 Cal. 3d 725, 732-733, 736, 144 Cal. Rptr. 380, 575 P.2d 1162.)

We follow a stream of commerce approach to strict liability in tort and extend liability to all those who are part of the "overall producing and marketing enterprise that should bear the cost of injuries from defective products." (Vandermark v. Ford Motor Co. (1964) 61 Cal. 2d 256, 262 et seq., 37 Cal. Rptr. 896, 391 P.2d 168.) The doctrine of strict liability in tort has been applied not only to manufacturers but to the various links in the commercial marketing chain including a retailer (id.), a wholesale-retail distributor (Barth v. B.F. Goodrich Tire Co. (1968) 265 Cal. App. 2d 228, 251 et seq., 71 Cal. Rptr. 306), personal property lessors and bailors (Price v. Shell Oil Co. (1970) 2 Cal. 3d 245, 251-253, 85 Cal. Rptr. 178, 466 P.2d 722), and a licensor of personalty (Garcia v. Halsett (1970) 3 Cal. App. 3d 319, 324-326, 82 Cal. Rptr. 420). In holding that strict liability in tort was applicable to lessors and bailors in Price v. Shell Oil Co., *supra*, 2 Cal. 3d at page 254, 85 Cal. Rptr. 178, 466 P.2d 722, it was pointed out that strict liability does not apply to isolated transactions such as the sale of a single lot.

Application of warranty doctrine has not been limited to those engaged in commerce in personalty but has been applied where appropriate to those engaged in the real estate business. Traditionally, the courts applied the doctrine of caveat emptor with the buyer assuming the risk on quallity unless there was express warranty, fraud or misrepresentation. (E.g., Gustafson v. Dunman, Inc. (1962) 204 Cal. App. 2d 10, 13, 22 Cal. Rptr. 161.)

However, the courts have recognized that a contract to build is in effect one of material and labor, and that implied warranties are not limited to sales transactions, and that building contracts give rise to a warranty of merchantability and suitability for ordinary use. (Aced v. Hobbs-Sesack Plumbing Co. (1961) 55 Cal. 2d 573, 580-583, 12 Cal. Rptr. 257, 360 P.2d 897; Pollard v. Saxe & Yolles Dev. Co. (1974) 12 Cal. 3d 374, 378, 115 Cal. Rptr. 648, 525 P.2d 88; Green v. Superior Court (1974) 10 Cal. 3d 616, 626, 111 Cal. Rptr. 704, 517 P.2d 1168.) And in Pollard v. Saxe & Yolles Dev. Co., *supra*, 12 Cal. 3d 374, 377-380, 115 Cal. Rptr. 648, 525 P.2d 88, it was held that an implied warranty of quality attaches to the sale of new construction. The court pointed out that the doctrine of implied warranty in a sales contract is based on the actual and presumed knowledge of the seller, reliance on the seller's skill and judgment, and the ordinary expectations of the parties. The court reasoned that "the builder or seller of new construction—not unlike the manufacturer or merchandiser of personalty—makes implied representations, ordinarily indispensable to the sale, that the builder has used reasonable skill and judgment in constructing the building. On the other hand, the purchaser does not usually possess the knowledge of the builder and is unable to fully examine a completed house and its components without disturbing the finished product." (12 Cal. 3d at p.379, 115 Cal. Rptr. 648, 525 P.2d 88.) The court concluded that "builders and sellers of new construction should be held to what is impliedly represented—that the completed structure was designed and constructed in a reasonably workmanlike manner." (Id. at p.380, 115 Cal. Rptr. 648, 525 P.2d 88.)

Similarly, application of strict liability in tort has not been limited to those engaged in commerce in personalty but has been applied where appropriate to those engaged in real estate businesses who impliedly represent the quality of their product. In Kriegler v. Eichler Homes, Inc. (1969) 269 Cal. App. 2d 224, 74 Cal. Rptr. 749, a builder who mass-produced homes was held strictly liable when the heating system placed in a home failed. The court relied upon Schipper v. Levitt & Sons, Inc. (1965) 44 N.J. 70, 207 A.2d 314, 325-326, where the court pointed out that when in our modern society a person purchases a tract house from an advertised model, he relies upon the skill of the developer and the implied representation that the house will be erected in a reasonably workmanlike manner and reasonably fit for habitation, that the purchaser ordinarily does not have the means to protect himself either by hiring experts to supervise and inspect or by provision in the deed, and that the public interest dictates that the cost of injury from defects should be borne by the developer who created the danger and who is in a better economic position to bear the loss rather than the injured party who relied on the developer's skill and implied representation. In Avner v. Longridge Estates (1969) 272 Cal. App. 2d 607, 615, 77 Cal. Rptr. 633, it was held that a manufacturer of a residential lot may be held strictly liable in tort for damages suffered by the owner as the result of defect in the manufacturing process causing subsidence.

A similar development appears with respect to the landlord-tenant relationship. The earlier legal concepts regarded the lease as an equivalent to a sale of the premises for the term and under traditional common law rules the landlord owed no duty to place leased premises in a habitable condition and no obligation to repair absent an agreement. (Green v. Superior Court (1974) 10 Cal. 3d 616, 622, 111 Cal. Rptr. 704, 517 P.2d 1168; McNally v. Ward (1961) 192 Cal. App. 2d 871, 878, 14 Cal. Rptr. 260.)

> The common law placed the risk on the tenant as to whether the condition of the leased property made it unsuitable for the use contemplated by the parties. In recent years, the definite judicial trend has been in the direction of increasing the responsibility of the landlord, in the absence of a valid contrary agreement, to provide the tenant with property in a condition suitable for the use contemplated by the parties. This judicial trend has been supported by the statutes that deal with this problem. This judicial and statutory trend reflects a view that no one should be allowed or forced to live in unsafe and unhealthy housing." (Rest. 2d Property, Landlord and Tenant, ch. 5, introductory note, p.150.)

The Restatement draws a distinction as to defective conditions in leased dwellings existing at the time of the lease and those arising thereafter. In the former situation the tenant may recover damages in the absence of lessor fault while in the latter damages are recoverable only if the landlord is at fault. (Compare id., §5.1, subd. (2)(a), pp. 168-169 with §§5.2, subd. (2)(a), p.184, and 5.4, subd. (2)(a), pp.194-195.)

Departures from the traditional common law rule applicable to landlords evolved in California both by statute and judicial decision. Civil Code section 1941 requires that the lessor of a building intended for use as a dwelling put it in fit condition for such use and repair all subsequent dilapidations. However, the tenant's remedies for violation of the statute are limited to the making of necessary repairs and deducting costs from one month's rent, or to abandon the premises with discharge from rental obligations. (Civ. Code, §1942, subd. (a).) And the landlord's duty does not arise if the tenant has breached certain of his obligations relating to the maintenance of the premises. (Id. §1941.2.) An agreement by the lessee waiving his rights under section 1941 is void as contrary to public policy except that the lessee may agree as part of the rental to improve, repair, or maintain stipulated portions of the dwelling. (Id., see §1942.1.)

Pointing out that the traditional common law rule that the landlord had no duty to make the dwelling habitable arose in the agrarianism of the Middle Ages and is incompatible with contemporary social conditions and modern legal values, California courts have recognized that a lease for a dwelling contains an implied warranty of habitability. (Hinson v. Delis (1972) 26 Cal. App. 3d 62, 68-71, 102 Cal. Rptr. 661; Green v. Superior Court, *supra,* 10 Cal. 3d 616, 622 et seq., 111 Cal. Rptr. 704, 517 P.2d 1168; Knight v. Hallsthammar (1981) 29 Cal. 3d 46, 51-53, 171 Cal. Rptr. 707, 623 P.2d 268.) In *Green,* the court reasoned that the typical city dweller leasing an apartment cannot realistically be viewed as merely acquiring an interest in land but rather contracts for a place to live, that modern apartment buildings are complex, difficult and expensive to repair and adequate inspection by tenants is a virtual impossibility, that repairs will often be outside the reach of abilities or finances of tenants, that the scarcity of adequate low-cost housing has left tenants with little bargaining power and rendered the common law remedies inadequate, and that the widespread enactment of comprehensive housing codes show that public policy compels landlords to bear "the primary responsibility for maintaining safe, clean and habitable housing in our state." (10 Cal. 3d at pp. 623-628, 111 Cal. Rptr. 704, 517 P.2d 1168.)

Green analogized to the parallel dramatic changes in the law of commercial transactions where modern decisions have recognized that the consumer in an industrial society should be entitled to rely on the skill of the supplier to assure that goods and services are of adequate quality and, discarding the caveat emptor approach, have implied a warranty of merchantability and fitness. Pointing out that the modern urban tenant is in the same position as any normal consumer of goods, it was concluded that a tenant may reasonably expect that the product purchased is fit as a living unit and that since the lease specifies a term the tenant may reasonably expect that the premises will be fit for habitation for the term. (10 Cal. 3d at p.627, 111 Cal. Rptr. 704, 517 P.2d 1168.)

Green held that breach of the implied warranty of habitability may be urged as a defense in an unlawful detainer proceeding and that in such cases the court could determine that the breach warranted a partial or total reduction in rent. (10 Cal. 3d at p.631 et seq., 111 Cal. Rptr. 704, 517 P.2d 1168.) Neither *Green* nor our subsequent decision in Knight v. Hallsthammar, *supra,* 29 Cal. 3d 46, 171 Cal. Rptr. 707, 623 P.2d 268, discussed whether or to what extent breach of the implied warranty of habitability might provide a basis for recovery of tort damages for injuries caused by the breach.[2]

Developments in the law of landlord liability for injuries due to defective condition of the demised premises have not lagged far behind. The traditional common law rule was that a landlord is not liable to the tenant for injuries due to a defective condition or faulty construction of the demised premises in the absence of fraud, concealment or covenant of the lease. (E.g., Del Pino v. Gualtieri (1968) 265 Cal. App. 2d 912, 919-920, 71 Cal. Rptr. 716; Forrester v. Hoover Hotel & Inv. Co. (1948) 87 Cal. App. 2d 226, 232, 196 P.2d 825.) The rule was not only based on traditional property concepts and caveat emptor but also on the landlord's lack of possession and control. (E.g., Brennan v. Cockrell Investments, Inc. (1973) 35 Cal. App. 3d 796, 799-800, 111 Cal. Rptr. 122.) A number of exceptions have developed to the rule of landlord nonliability—where the landlord voluntarily undertakes to repair, where the landlord had knowledge of defects, where a safety law was violated, where the landlord retained a part of the premises for common use, and where the lease was for a semi-public purpose. (3 Witkin, Summary of Cal. Law (8th ed. 1973) pp. 2135-2136.)

Strict liability for the conditions of the demised premises has been applied to landlords. Prior to *Greenman,* it was held that where a landlord represented that a wallbed was safe, secure and in fit condition at the time of letting, the plaintiff could maintain an action based on the express warranty. (Shattuck v. St. Francis Hotel & Apts. (1936) 7 Cal. 2d 358, 360-361, 60 P.2d 855.) Also, prior to *Greenman,* it was held that a lessee could recover for breach of an implied warranty of fitness for use when a door to which a folding bed was attached fell and injured him.

2. As will appear, subsequent Court of Appeal cases have considered this issue.

(Fisher v. Pennington (1931) 116 Cal. App. 248, 249-251, 2 P.2d 518.) *Fisher* was followed in Charleville v. Metropolitan Trust Co. (1934) 136 Cal. App. 349, 355, 29 P.2d 241 which also involved a folding bed and Hunter v. Freeman (1951) 105 Cal. App. 2d 129, 131 et seq., 233 P.2d 65, involving an explosion of a detachable heater. In all four cases, the accident occurred shortly after the tenant went into possession, and it was also held that the warranty liability was limited to "the condition of the premises at the beginning of the term and not to conditions which, unknown to the lessor, subsequently arise." (Forrester v. Hoover Hotel & Inv. Co., *supra,* 87 Cal. App. 2d 226, 232, 196 P.2d 825.)[3] Each of the above cases involved a furnished apartment and the accident was arguably attributed to the furnishings as well as the condition of the demised premises.

Subsequent to *Greenman,* strict liability in tort was applied to landlords for injuries to tenants in Fakhoury v. Magner (1972) 25 Cal. App. 3d 58, 62-63, 101 Cal. Rptr. 473 and Golden v. Conway (1976) 55 Cal. App. 3d 948, 960-963, 128 Cal. Rptr. 69. In *Fakhoury,* a couch in a furnished apartment collapsed, and the court held that the landlord is strictly liable in tort for defective furniture, pointing out that the liability was not for defective premises. (25 Cal. App. 3d at p.63, 101 Cal. Rptr. 473.) In *Golden,* the landlord employed a contractor to install a heater, and because of defective manufacture or installation there was a fire. Although acknowledging the distinction made in *Fakhoury* between defective fixtures and defective furniture, the court rejected it and held that the landlord engaged in the business of leasing property is strictly liable in tort when he equips the premises with an appliance which proves to have defects causing injury. (55 Cal. App. 3d at pp.960-963, 128 Cal. Rptr. 69.) Defendant points out that *Fakhoury* differs from the instant case because injury resulted from defective personalty rather than the condition of the premises and that *Golden* differs because the landlord installed the heater whereas the shower door was apparently installed by the builder.

We are satisfied that the rationale of the foregoing cases, establishing the duties of a landlord and the doctrine of strict liability in tort, requires us to conclude that a landlord engaged in the business of leasing dwellings is strictly liable in tort for injuries resulting from a latent defect in

---

3. Stowe v. Fritzie Hotels, Inc. (1955) 44 Cal. 2d 416, 424, 282 P.2d 890, stated that *Forrester* and *Hunter* disapproved a statement in *Fisher* that the landlord of a furnished apartment warrants the safety of the premises and the furnishings to the same extent as an innkeeper. The citation to *Forrester* and *Hunter* reflects approval of the limited implied warranty recognized in the former case and applied in the latter of a warranty of the condition of the premises at the beginning of the term. Thus, *Stowe* should not be read as rejecting implied warranties by landlords generally but only the equation of such warranties to an innkeeper's warranties.

the premises when the defect existed at the time the premises were let to the tenant.[4] It is clear that landlords are part of the "overall producing and marketing enterprise" that makes housing accommodations available to renters. (Cf. Vandermark v. Ford Motor Co., *supra*, 61 Cal. 2d at p.262, 37 Cal. Rptr. 896, 391 P.2d 168; Green v. Superior Court, *supra*, 10 Cal. 3d at pp.623, 627, 111 Cal. Rptr. 704, 517 P.2d 1168.) A landlord, like defendant owning numerous units, is not engaged in isolated acts within the enterprise but plays a substantial role. The fact that the enterprise is one involving real estate may not immunize the landlord. Our courts have long recognized that contracts relating to realty may give rise to implied warranties. (Aced v. Hobbs-Sesack Plumbing Co., *supra*, 55 Cal. 2d 573, 580-583, 12 Cal. Rptr. 257, 360 P.2d 897.)

Absent disclosure of defects, the landlord in renting the premises makes an implied representation that the premises are fit for use as a dwelling and the representation is ordinarily indispensable to the lease. (Pollard v. Saxe & Yolles Dev. Co., *supra*, 12 Cal. 3d 374, 377-380, 115 Cal. Rptr. 648, 525 P.2d 88.) The tenant purchasing housing for a limited period is in no position to inspect for latent defects in the increasingly complex modern apartment buildings or to bear the expense of repair whereas the landlord is in a much better position to inspect for and repair latent defects. (Green v. Superior Court, *supra*, 10 Cal. 3d at p. 626, 111 Cal. Rptr. 704, 517 P.2d 1168.) The tenant's ability to inspect is ordinarily substantially less than that of a purchaser of the property. (Cf. Pollard v. Saxe & Yolles Dev. Co., *supra*, 12 Cal. 3d at p.379, 115 Cal. Rptr. 648, 525 P.2d 88.)

The tenant renting the dwelling is compelled to rely upon the implied assurance of safety made by the landlord. It is also apparent that the landlord by adjustment of price at the time he acquires the property, by rentals or by insurance is in a better position to bear the costs of injuries due to defects in the premises than the tenants.

In these circumstances, strict liability in tort for latent defects existing at the time of renting must be applied to insure that the landlord who markets the product bears the costs of injuries resulting from the defects "rather than the injured persons who are powerless to protect themselves." (Greenman v. Yuba Power Products, Inc., *supra*, 59 Cal. 2d at p.653, 27 Cal. Rptr. 697, 377 P.2d 897.)

Defendant argues that a landlord who purchases an existing building which is not new should be exempt from strict liability in tort for latent defects because, like dealers in used personalty, he assertedly is not part of the manufacturing and marketing enterprise. Defendant relies on a

---

4. We do not determine whether strict liability would apply to a disclosed defect. (See Luque v. McLean (1972) 8 Cal. 3d 136, 141-146, 104 Cal. Rptr. 443, 501 P.2d 1163.)

statement in Vandermark v. Ford Motor Co., *supra,* 61 Cal. 2d 256, 262-263, 37 Cal. Rptr. 896, 391 P.2d 168: "Strict liability on the manufacturer and retailer alike afford maximum protection to the injured plaintiff and works no injustice to defendants, for they can adjust the costs of such protection between them in the course of their continuing business relationship." Defendant states that it has never been in a business relationship with the builder and that purchasers of used rental properties do not have a continuing business relationship with builders permitting adjustments of the costs of protecting tenants.

In several cases, it has been held that a seller of used machinery who does not rebuild or rehabilitate the machinery is not strictly liable in tort. (Wilkinson v. Hicks (1981) 126 Cal. App. 3d 515, 520 et seq., 179 Cal. Rptr. 5; LaRosa v. Superior Court (1981) 122 Cal. App. 3d 741, 748 et seq., 176 Cal. Rptr. 224; Tauber-Arons Auctioneers Co., Inc. v. Superior Court (1980) 101 Cal. App. 3d 268, 273 et seq., 161 Cal. Rptr. 789.) Each of these cases relied at least in part on the theory that the used machinery dealer simply by offering machinery for sale does not make any representation as to quality or durability and thus does not generate the expectation of safety involved in the sale of new goods. (*Wilkinson, supra,* 126 Cal. App. 3d at pp.520-521, 179 Cal. Rptr. 5; *LaRosa, supra,* 122 Cal. App. 3d at pp. 760-761, 176 Cal. Rptr. 224; *Tauber-Arons, supra,* 101 Cal. App. 3d at p.278 et seq., 161 Cal. Rptr. 789.) When the seller of the used goods makes extensive modifications or reconditions, he is treated as a manufacturer — there is an expectation that the safety of the product has been addressed. (Green v. City of Los Angeles (1974) 40 Cal. App. 3d 819, 838, 115 Cal. Rptr. 685.)

LaRosa v. Superior Court, *supra,* 122 Cal. App. 3d 741, 756-757, 176 Cal. Rptr. 224 and Tauber-Arons Auctioneers Co., Inc. v. Superior Court, *supra,* 101 Cal. App. 3d 268, 282, 161 Cal. Rptr. 789, also suggested that the used machinery dealer ordinarily is not part of the manufacturing and marketing enterprise.

However, a continuing business relationship is not essential to imposition of strict liability. The unavailability of the manufacturer is not a factor mitigating against liability of others engaged in the enterprise. The paramount policy of the strict products liability rule remains the spreading throughout society of the cost of compensating otherwise defenseless victims of manufacturing defects. (Ray v. Alad Corp. (1977) 19 Cal. 3d 22, 33-34, 136 Cal. Rptr. 574, 560 P.2d 3; Price v. Shell Oil Co. (1970) 2 Cal. 3d 245, 251, 85 Cal. Rptr. 178, 466 P.2d 722; Rawlings v. D. M. Oliver, Inc. (1979) 97 Cal. App. 3d 890, 899 et seq., 159 Cal. Rptr. 119.) If anything, the unavailability of the manufacturer is a factor militating in favor of persons engaged in the enterprise who can spread the cost of compensation. (See Ray v. Alad Corp., *supra,* 19 Cal. 3d 22, 33-34,

136 Cal. Rptr. 574, 560 P.2d 3.) Just as the unavailability of the manufacturer does not militate against liability, the absence of a continuing business relationship between builder and landlord is not a factor warranting denial of strict liability of the landlord.

Landlords are an integral part of the enterprise of producing and marketing rental housing. While used machinery is often scrapped or discarded so that resale for use may be the exception rather than the rule, landlords are essential to the rental business. They have more than a random or accidental role in the marketing enterprise. In addition, landlords have a continuing relationship to the property following the renting in contrast to the used machinery dealer who sells. As we have seen, in renting property the landlord, unlike the used machinery dealer, makes representations of habitability and safety.

The cost of protecting tenants is an appropriate cost of the enterprise. Within our marketplace economy, the cost of purchasing rental housing is obviously based on the anticipated risks and rewards of the purchase, and thus it may be expected that along with numerous other factors the price of used rental housing will depend in part on the quality of the building and reflect the anticipated costs of protecting tenants, including repairs, replacement of defects and insurance. Further, the landlord after purchase may be able to adjust rents to reflect such costs. The landlord will also often be able to seek equitable indemnity for losses.

We conclude that the absence of a continuing business relationship between builder and landlord does not preclude application of strict liability in tort for latent defects existing at the time of the lease because landlords are an integral part of the enterprise and they should bear the cost of injuries resulting from such defects rather than the injured persons who are powerless to protect themselves. (Greenman v. Yuba Power Products, Inc., *supra,* 59 Cal. 2d 57, 63, 27 Cal. Rptr. 697.)[5]

Negligence

Civil Code section 1714, subdivision (a) establishes the fundamental principle of negligence liability, providing: "Every one is responsible, not only for the result of his willful acts, but also for an injury occasioned to another by his want of ordinary skill in the management of his property or person, . . ."

Rejecting the prior distinctions made by the common law as to invitees, licensees, and trespassers, the landmark case of Rowland v. Christian, *supra,* 69 Cal. 2d 108, 111 et seq., 70 Cal. Rptr. 97, 443 P.2d 561 held that

---

5. In view of our conclusion it is unnecessary to determine whether the landlord is strictly liable for defects which develop after the property is leased.

the fundamental rule was applicable to the liability of owners and occupiers of land. The fundamental principle is applicable to the landlord's liability to the tenant, and the landlord owes a tenant a duty of reasonable care in providing and maintaining the rented premises in a safe condition. (Stoiber v. Honeychuck (1980) 101 Cal. App. 3d 903, 924, 162 Cal. Rptr. 194; Evans v. Thomason (1977) 72 Cal. App. 3d 978, 985, 140 Cal. Rptr. 525; Golden v. Conway, *supra*, 55 Cal. App. 3d 948, 955, 128 Cal. Rptr. 69; Brennan v. Cockrell Investments, Inc., *supra*, 35 Cal. App. 3d 796, 800-801, 111 Cal. Rptr. 122.)

Any departure from the fundamental principle involves the

balancing of a number of considerations; the major ones are the foreseeability of the harm to the plaintiff, the degree of certainty that the plaintiff suffered injury, the closeness of the connection between the defendant's conduct and the injury suffered, the moral blame attached to the defendant's conduct, the policy of preventing future harm, the extent of the burden to the defendant and consequences to the community of imposing a duty to exercise care with resulting liability for breach, and the availability, cost, and prevalence of insurance for the risk involved. [Citations.] (Rowland v. Christian, *supra*, 69 Cal. 2d at pp.112-113, 70 Cal. Rptr. 97, 443 p.2d 561.)

"In the typical situation involving a dwelling house, the foreseeability of harm to a tenant from the landlord's failure to maintain the premises in a habitable condition is obvious; the degree of certainty that the tenant suffered injury and the closeness of the connection between the landlord's conduct and the injury is readily ascertainable by proof in each case; the moral blame attached to the landlord's conduct in not complying with the habitability requirements articulated in the Civil Code and the policy of preventing future harm arè present. Nor can we say that the imposition of a duty to exercise care with resulting liability for breach would unduly extend a landlord's burden insofar as the availability, cost and prevalence of insurance for the risk involved. In short, we believe that under the policy standards articulated in *Rowland*, a due regard for human safety and health compels the imposition on a landlord of a duty of due care in the maintenance of the premises." (Stoiber v. Honeychuck, *supra*, 101 Cal. App. 3d 903, 924, 162 Cal. Rptr. 194.)

Accordingly, a landlord in caring for his property must act toward his tenant as a reasonable person under all of the circumstances, including the likelihood of injury, the probable seriousness of the injury, the burden of reducing or avoiding the risk, and his degree of control over the risk-creating defect. (Golden v. Conway, *supra*, 55 Cal. App. 3d 948, 955, 128 Cal. Rptr. 69; Brennan v. Cockrell Investments, Inc., *supra*, 35 Cal. App. 3d 796, 800-801, 111 Cal. Rptr. 122.)

Defendant urges that in the absence of knowledge of the defective condition or of prior accidents it was not under a duty to inspect for defective shower doors and that imposition of a duty to inspect would conflict with the Civil Code section 1954 limiting the landlord's right to enter a rented dwelling unit. So far as appears in the instant case, the dangerous shower doors were installed by the builder at the time of the construction and were in position at the time defendant purchased the building.

A person contemplating purchase of rental property, in the exercise of due care, will examine its condition. Maintenance of rental property in a safe and habitable condition is the primary responsibility of the landlord. (Green v. Superior Court, *supra,* 10 Cal. 3d 616, 627, 111 Cal. Rptr. 704, 517, P.2d 1168.) In the exercise of ordinary care, the purchaser of rental property may be expected to inspect the premises not only to determine whether they are aesthetically pleasing but also to determine whether they meet bare living standards, including whether they are safe. The prospective purchaser may be expected to make such inspection in the absence of knowledge of any existing defects or of any prior accidents. Similarly, a landlord at time of letting may be expected to inspect an apartment to determine whether it is safe.

The mere fact that a particular kind of accident has not happened before does not show that such accident is one which might not reasonably have been anticipated. (Weirum v. RKO General, Inc. (1975) 15 Cal. 3d 40, 47, 123 Cal. Rptr. 468, 539 P.2d 36.) Defective glass doors provide a substantial risk of injury which reasonably may be anticipated.

Civil Code section 1954 limiting the right of the landlord to enter the tenant's premises provides that he may enter to exhibit the dwelling unit "to prospective or actual purchasers" and to make necessary repairs, and the section does not provide a bar to recognition of a duty to inspect in the instant case. Defendant's officials inspected the apartments.

We conclude that a duty to inspect for dangerous conditions in the exercise of due care may properly be found in the instant case and that lack of awareness of the dangerous condition does not necessarily preclude liability.

In urging that there was no duty to inspect, defendant relies upon cases where the defect developed after purchase of the building by the defendant and while the apartment was in possession of the tenant. (E.g., Uccello v. Laudenslayer (1975) 44 Cal. App. 3d 504, 510 et seq., 118 Cal. Rptr. 741.) Those cases are distinguishable because, in the instant case, the dangerous condition existed at the time of purchase and the time the property was leased.

The duty to inspect should charge the defendant only with those matters which would have been disclosed by a reasonable inspection. In the instant case, the undisputed affidavits are to the effect that there was "no visible difference between the tempered and untempered glass in terms of visible appearance," but that there was a "very small mark" in the corner of each piece of glass which apparently showed that the glass was untempered. The glass was not before the trial court when it granted the motion for summary judgment, and the record does not disclose the nature of the "mark." If the "mark" was "untempered" a trier of fact could properly conclude that a reasonable inspection would have, at least, included a visual inspection which disclosed the danger. In resolving doubts in favor of the party opposing the motion for summary judgment (Rowland v. Christian, *supra,* 69 Cal. 2d 108, 111, 70 Cal. Rptr. 97, 443 P.2d 561), defendant's failure to fully identify the "mark" requires us to assume that it would have disclosed the danger to a reasonable inspection.

As to each cause of action the trial court erred in granting summary judgment in favor of the defendant.

The judgment is reversed.

KAUS, REYNOSO and GRODIN, JJ., concur.

BIRD, Chief Justice, concurring.

Justice Newsom wrote a fine opinion in the Court of Appeals with which I agree. It is adopted herewith as my own.*

This is an appeal from a summary judgment dismissing appellant's causes of action for negligence and strict products liability. Declarations submitted by respondent in support of its motion for summary judgment reveal the following pertinent facts, which we summarize as necessary to a resolution of the issues raised on appeal.

Appellant was seriously injured on November 21, 1978, when he slipped and fell against the *untempered* glass shower door of his rented apartment, which is in a 36-unit apartment complex owned, operated and maintained by respondent. The apartment complex was built in 1963 and acquired by IRM Corporation in 1974 [IRM]. According to undisputed evidence, had the shower door been made of *tempered* glass, the risk of serious injury to appellant would have been reduced.

The declarations submitted in support of the summary judgment motion state that between the time respondent acquired the building and appellant's injury none of the tenants either complained that the shower doors were made of unsafe untempered glass or reported injuries similar to those suffered by appellant. Appellant's shower door was in place when IRM purchased the apartment complex. Of the 36 showers in the apartment building prior to appellant's accident, 31 had untempered and 5 had tempered glass.

It is difficult to visually distinguish tempered from untempered glass. The

---

* Brackets together, in this manner [], without enclosing material, are used to indicate deletions from the opinion of the Court of Appeal; brackets enclosing material (other than the editor's added parallel citations) are, unless otherwise indicated, used to denote my insertions or additions.

apartment manager for IRM declared that he walked through most of the bathrooms prior to appellant's accident, and found the two types of shower doors to be highly similar: he said both had a "frosted glass" appearance. After the accident, at respondent's request, a maintenance man for IRM and an expert from Diablo Glass & Paint Company inspected the shower doors. According to the maintenance man, "from my own examination following the . . . accident, there was no visible difference between the tempered or the nontempered glass in terms of visible appearance.

But he also explained: "The only way that I was able to differentiate . . . was by looking for a very small mark in the corner of each piece of glass." After the inspection, the 31 shower doors without tempered glass were replaced with doors made of tempered glass.

The summary judgment procedure authorized by section 437c of the Code of Civil Procedure is a " ' "drastic procedure to be used sparingly and with circumspection." . . . ' " (Harris v. De La Chapelle (1976) 55 Cal. App. 3d 644, 647, 127 Cal. Rptr. 695, *disapproved on another point* in Sprecher v. Adamson Companies (1981) 30 Cal. 3d 358, 372, fn. 9, 178 Cal. Rptr. 783, 636 P.2d 1121.) A defendant moving for summary judgment has the burden of establishing that the action is without merit; a factual showing negating all causes of action on all theories is required. (Tresemer v. Barke (1978) 86 Cal. App. 3d 656, 666, 150 Cal. Rptr. 384, 12 A.L.R. 4th 27; *Harris, supra,* 55 Cal. App. 3d at p. 647, 127 Cal. Rptr. 695.) "If he fails in that burden, summary judgment must be denied despite the lack of opposing declarations." (*Tresemer, supra,* 86 Cal. App. 3d at p.666, 150 Cal. Rptr. 384.) But if all material issues of fact are eliminated and the declarations filed in support of the motion establish that the defendant is entitled to judgment as a matter of law, summary judgment should be granted. (Tauber-Arons Auctioneers Co. v. Superior Court (1980) 101 Cal. App. 3d 268, 273-274, 161 Cal. Rptr. 789.) " 'Applicable substantive law determines the facts necessary to support a particular theory of relief and hence the sufficiency of properly framed factual statements in declarations to support a summary judgment.' " (*Tresemer, supra,* 86 Cal. App. 3d at pp.666-667, 150 Cal. Rptr. 384.)

Appellant claims that his negligence cause of action presents issues of fact which must be litigated at trial. He insists that respondent's declarations do not sufficiently negate the elements of his action for negligence.

Respondent submits that it had no *duty* of care to appellant, absent actual notice of the dangerous condition of the shower doors, and that its declarations disprove such notice.

The essential elements of a cause of action for negligence are: (1) defendant's legal duty of care to plaintiff, (2) defendant's breach of duty—by negligent act or omission, (3) injury to plaintiff as the result of the breach, and (4) compensable damages. (Rosales v. Stewart (1980) 113

Cal. App. 3d 130, 133, 169 Cal. Rprt. 660; 3 Witkin, Cal. Procedure (2d ed. 1971) Pleading, §450, p.2103.) Liability for negligent conduct may only be imposed where it is found that defendant owed a duty of care to the plaintiff or to a class of persons of which the plaintiff is a member. (J'Aire Corp v. Gregory (1979) 24 Cal. 3d 799, 803, 157 Cal. Rptr. 407, 598 P.2d 60; Rogers v. Jones (1976) 56 Cal. App. 3d 346, 350, 128 Cal. Rptr. 404.) The duty may arise by statute, contract, the general character of the activity in which the defendant engaged, the relationship of the parties, or even the interdependent nature of human society. (J'Aire, supra, 24 Cal. 3d at p.803, 157 Cal. Rptr. 407, 598 P.2d 60.) "Whether a duty is owed is simply a shorthand way of phrasing what is ' "the essential question—whether the plaintiff's interests are entitled to legal protection against the defendant's conduct." ' " (Ibid.)

The crucial issue before us is, therefore, whether plaintiff has established that his corporate landlord owed a duty of care to protect him against the particular risk of harm which caused his injury. ([See] Evans v. Thomason (1977) 72 Cal. App. 3d 978, 984, 140 Cal. Rptr. 525.) " 'While the question whether one owes a duty to another must be decided on a case-by-case basis, every case is governed by the rule of general application that all persons are required to use ordinary care to prevent others from being injured as a result of their conduct. . . .' " (J'Aire, supra, 24 Cal. 3d at p.806, 157 Cal. Rptr. 407, 598 P.2d 60; Weirum v. RKO General, Inc. (1975) 15 Cal. 3d 40, 46, 123 Cal. Rptr. 468, 539 P.2d 36.) In Rowland v. Christian (1968) 69 Cal. 2d 108, 113, 70 Cal. Rptr. 97, 443 P.2d 561, 32 A.L.R.3d 496, our high court enumerated the following factors as relevant to a determination of whether a possessor or owner of land owes a duty of care to injured victims: the foreseeability of the harm to the plaintiff; the degree of certainty that the plaintiff suffered injury; the closeness of the connection between defendant's conduct and the injury suffered; the moral blame attached to the defendant's conduct; the policy of preventing future harm; the extent of the burden to the defendant and the consequences to the community of imposing a duty to exercise care with resulting liability for breach; and the availability, cost and prevalence of insurance for the risk involved. (See also Thompson v. County of Alameda (1980) 27 Cal. 3d 741, 750, 167 Cal. Rptr. 70, 614, P.2d 728, 12 A.L.R.4th 701; Sun N' Sand Inc. v. United California Bank (1978) 21 Cal. 3d 671, 695, 148 Cal. Rptr. 329, 582 P.2d 920; Rosales v. Stewart, supra, 113 Cal. App. 3d 130, 134, 169 Cal. Rptr. 660; DeSuza v. Andersack (1976) 63 Cal. App. 3d 694, 702, 133 Cal. Rptr. 920.)

But in all cases, the primary consideration in establishing the element of duty is the foreseeability of the risk. (Sun N' Sand, supra, 21 Cal. 3d at p.695, 148 Cal. Rptr. 329, 582 P.2d 920; Weirum, supra, 15 Cal. 3d at p.46, 123 Cal. Rptr. 468, 539 P.2d 36; *DeSuza, supra,* 63 Cal. App. 3d at p.702, 133 Cal. Rptr. 920.) " 'As a general principle, a "defendant owes a duty of care to all persons who are *foreseeably* endangered by his conduct, with respect to all risks which make the conduct unreasonably dangerous" ' " (Tresemer v. Barke, *supra,* 86 Cal. App. 3d 656, 670, 150 Cal. Rptr. 384.) The question of whether legal duty exists is one of law (Thompson v. County of Alameda [, *supra,*] 27 Cal. 3d 741, 750, 167 Cal. Rptr. 70, 614 P.2d 728, 12 A.L.R.4th 701), but if the issue depends upon the foreseeability of the risk it becomes a question of fact for resolution by the jury (*Weirum* [], *supra,* 15 Cal. 3d 40, 46, 123 Cal. Rptr. 468, 539 P.2d 36; Harris v. De La Chapelle, *supra,* 55 Cal. App. 3d 644, 647, 127 Cal. Rptr. 695).[1]

It is now settled that a landlord generally owes a tenant a duty of reasonable care in maintaining the rented premises in a safe condition. (Evans v. Thomason, *supra,* 72 Cal. App. 3d 978, 985, 140 Cal. Rptr. 525; Golden v. Conway (1976) 55 Cal. App. 3d 948, 955, 128 Cal. Rptr. 69; Brennan v. Cockrell Investments, Inc. (1973) 35 Cal. App. 3d 796, 800-801, 111 Cal. Rptr. 122.) In Stoiber v. Honeychuck (1980) 101 Cal. App. 3d 903, 924, 162 Cal. Rptr. 194, the court explained:

> In the typical rental situation involving a dwelling house, the foreseeability of harm to a tenant from the landlord's failure to maintain the premises in a habitable condition is obvious; the degree of certainty that the tenant suffered injury and the closeness of the connection between the landlord's conduct and the injury is readily ascertainable by proof in each case; the moral blame attached to the landlord's conduct in not complying with the habitability requirements articulated in the Civil Code and the policy of preventing future harm are present. Nor can we say that the imposition of a duty to exercise care with resulting liability for breach would unduly extend a landlord's burden insofar as the availability, cost and prevalence of insurance for the risk involved. In short, we believe that under the policy standards articulated in *Rowland,* a due regard for human safety and health compels the imposition on a landlord of a duty of due care in the maintenance of the premises.

And in Golden v. Conway, *supra,* 55 Cal. App. 3d at page 955, 128 Cal. Rptr. 69, this court adopted the standard expressed in Brennan v. Cockrell Investments, Inc., *supra,* 35 Cal. App. 3d 796, 111 Cal. Rptr. 122, that ". . . a landlord must act toward his tenant as a reasonable person under all of the circumstances, including the likelihood of injury, the probable seriousness of such injury, the burden of reducing or avoiding the risk, and his degree of control over the risk-creating defect. . . ."

---

1. The reasonableness of the defendant's conduct is also a question for the trier of fact. (Slater v. Alpha Beta Acme Markets, Inc. (1975) 44 Cal. App. 3d 274, 278, 118 Cal. Rptr. 561, 72 A.L.R.3d 1264.)

But like any other business proprietor or owner of property, the landlord is not an insurer of a tenant's safety. (Riley v. Marcus (1981) 125 Cal. App. 3d 103, 109, 177 Cal. Rptr. 827; Rogers v. Jones, *supra*, 56 Cal. App. 3d 346, 351, 128 Cal. Rptr. 404.) And, we repeat, as in all cases, foreseeability is the key factor to be considered. (Coulter v. Superior Court (1978) 21 Cal. 3d 144, 152, 145 Cal. Rptr. 534, 577 P.2d 669, superseded by statute as stated in Strang v. Cabrol (1984) 37 Cal. 3d 720, 724, 209 Cal. Rptr. 347, 691 P.2d 1013; *Riley, supra,* 125 Cal. App. 3d at p.109, 177 Cal. Rptr. 827.) Consequently, we must decide whether the unsafe nature of the shower doors was reasonably foreseeable by respondent.

The uncontradicted evidence offered by respondent establishes that IRM had no actual notice of the dangerous condition of the premises either from complaints or previous accidents. According to undisputed declarations, it was also difficult to distinguish the untempered glass shower doors from those made of tempered glass; only a "very small mark in the corner of each piece of glass," observed upon a careful inspection following appellant's accident, set the two types of doors apart.

But foreseeability does not require that prior identical or even similar events must have occurred. (Kwaitkowski v. Superior Trading Co. (1981) 123 Cal. App. 3d 324, 329, 176 Cal. Rptr. 494.) As noted in Weirum v. RKO General, Inc., *supra*, 15 Cal. 3d 40, 47, 123 Cal. Rptr. 468, 539 P.2d 36: " 'The mere fact that a particular kind of [an] accident has not happened before does not . . . show that such accident is one which might not reasonably been anticipated.' " Appellant's accident cannot be characterized as unforeseeable simply because it was the first of its time at the apartment complex.

And although the dangerous condition of the shower door may not have been readily apparent, the evidence indicates that it was discoverable upon reasonably careful inspection. In light of the landlord's control over the premises and ability to insure against the risk of injury, we think it reasonable to conclude that foreseeability of risk presented a triable issue of fact best left for resolution by the jury. That IRM had no actual notice of the risk should not, we repeat, absolve it from a duty of care as a matter of *law*. Maintenance of rental property, particularly fixtures and appliances, in a safe and habitable condition, has been recognized as an important obligation of the landlord. (Green v. Superior Court (1974) 10 Cal. 3d 616, 626-627, 111 Cal. Rptr. 704, 517 P.2d 1168; Stoiber v. Honeychuck, *supra,* 101 Cal. App. 3d 903, 914, 924, 162 Cal. Rptr. 194.)[2] Since it was possible if not likely that IRM would have

---

2. In *Stoiber, supra,* 101 Cal. App. 3d 903, 162 Cal. Rptr. 194, the court noted that "public policy requires landlords to bear the primary responsibility for maintaining safe, clean and habitable housing" (id., at p. 914, 162 Cal. Rptr. 194), and added: ". . . we believe

learned of the dangerous condition of the property had it devoted closer attention to the safety of its tenants, particularly given the direct and serious harm which the hazard posed to IRM's tenants, we think that the trial court erred in granting summary judgment and dismissing appellant's negligence action.

Appellant also argues that respondent's declarations do not negate his strict liability cause of action since the doctrine of strict products liability applies to respondent as a supplier of housing. Respondent submits that, on the contrary, as a matter of law a landlord does not incur liability under a theory of strict liability for the defective condition of rented premises.

In the landmark case of Greenman v. Yuba Power Products, Inc. (1963) 59 Cal. 2d 57, 62, 27 Cal. Rptr. 697, 377 P.2d 897, 13 A.L.R.3d 1049, our high court announced the rule that, "A manufacturer is strictly liable in tort when an article he places on the market, knowing that it is to be used without inspection for defects, proves to have a defect that causes injury to a human being." (See also McGee v. Cessna Aircraft Co. (1978) 82 Cal. App. 3d 1005, 1012, 147 Cal. Rptr. 694.) "That rule is equally applicable to the manufacturer and the retailer." (Barrett v. Atlas Powder Co. (1978) 86 Cal. App. 3d 560, 564, 150 Cal. Rptr. 339.)[3]

The courts have freely applied strict liability in tort law link by link in the manufacturing chain—"from manufacturer to distributor, to retailer, and so forth." (Kasel v. Remington Arms Co.[, *supra*,] 24 Cal. App. 3d 711, 724, 101 Cal. Rptr. 314 [].) California follows a "stream-of-commerce" approach to strict liability, under which

". . . no precise legal relationship to the member of the enterprise causing the defect to be manufactured or to the member most closely connected with the

---

that under the policy standards articulated in Rowland [v. Christian (1968) 69 Cal. 2d 108, 70 Cal. Rptr. 97, 443 P.2d 561], a due regard for human safety and health compels the imposition on a landlord of a duty of due care in the maintenance of the premises." (Id., at p. 924, 162 Cal. Rptr. 194.)

3. In fact, as noted in Kasel v. Remington Arms Co. [1972] 24 Cal. App. 3d 711, 724, 101 Cal. Rptr. 314: "The following entities besides the manufacturer, obviously the principal one, have been found to be integral components of the particular enterprise responsible for placing alleged defective products on the market: a lessor (McClaflin v. Bayshore Equipment Rental Co., 274 Cal. App. 2d 446 [79 Cal. Rptr. 337] . . . [stepladder] and Price v. Shell Oil Co., 2 Cal. 3d 245 [85 Cal. Rptr. 178, 466 P.2d 722] . . . [gasoline truck]; a developer (Kriegler v. Eichler Homes, Inc., 269 Cal. App. 2d 224 [74 Cal. Rptr. 749] . . . [a builder engaged in mass tract development of homes]); a licensee (Garcia v. Halsett, 3 Cal. App. 3d 319 [82 Cal. Rptr. 420] . . . [a launderette owner who was said to have licensed the use of a washing machine to plaintiff]); a retailer (Vandermark v. Ford Motor Co., *supra*, 61 Cal. 2d 256 [37 Cal. Rptr. 896, 391 P.2d 168] [retailer of a defective automobile]); and a wholesale-retail distributor (Barth v. B. F. Goodrich Tire Co., 265 Cal. App. 2d 228 [71 Cal. Rptr. 306] . . . [who merely distributed tires from his stock on order of the manufacturer])."

customer is required before the courts will impose strict liability. It is the defendant's participatory connection, for his personal profit or other benefit, with the injury-producing product and with the enterprise that created consumer demand for and reliance upon the product (and not the defendant's legal relationship (such as agency) with the manufacturer or other entities involved in the manufacturing-marketing system) which calls for imposition of strict liability." (Tauber-Arons Auctioneers Co. v. Superior Court, *supra*, 101 Cal. App. 3d 268, 275-276, 161 Cal. Rptr. 789, quoting from Kasel v. Remington Arms Co., *supra* 24 Cal. App. 3d 711, 725, 101 Cal. Rptr. 314.)

The strict products liability doctrine extends to all those who are "engaged in the business of distributing goods to the public" as an "integral part of the overall producing and marketing enterprise" for the product in question. (Vandermark v. Ford Motor Co. (1964) 61 Cal. 2d 256, 262-263, 37 Cal. Rptr. 896, 391 P.2d 168; *Tauber-Arons, supra,* 101 Cal. App. 3d. at pp.274-275, 161 Cal. Rptr. 789.) Thus, participation in the marketing enterprise by which distribution of the product to the consuming public is effected in more than a " 'random and accidental role' " justifies imposition of strict liability. (*Tauber-Arons, supra,* at p.277, 161 Cal. Rptr. 789; Garcia v. Halsett (1970) 3 Cal. App. 3d 319, 326, 82 Cal. Rptr. 420.)[4]

Landlords have been included within the scope of the strict products liability doctrine. For example, in Fakhoury v. Magner (1972) 25 Cal. App. 3d 58, 101 Cal. Rptr. 473, the lessee of a furnished apartment — injured when the couch supplied by her landlord collapsed under her — sued on a theory of strict liability. The court concluded that the landlord was strictly liable as lessor of the defective furniture rather than as lessor of furnished real property. (Id., at p. 63, 101 Cal. Rptr. 473.)

Subsequently, in Golden v. Conway, *supra,* 55 Cal. App. 3d 948, 128 Cal. Rptr. 69, this court extended the doctrine of strict products liability to a landlord who supplied and installed, through an independent contractor, a defective wall heater in an unfurnished apartment. Relying upon *Fakhoury,* we found no reason to distinguish between furniture and appliances attached to realty, and concluded that a "lessor of real property who, as the landlord in this case, is engaged in the business of leasing apartments and appurtenant commercial premises, equips the premises with an appliance without knowing whether or not it is defective because

4. In *Garcia* a launderette owner who maintained four rows of coin-operated washing machines manufactured by Philco-Bendix in continuous operation for public use, was held liable as a marketer. The court observed: "Although respondent is not engaged in the distribution of the product, in the same manner as a manufacturer, retailer, or lessor, he does provide the product to the public for use by the public, and consequently does play more than a random and accidental role in the overall marketing enterprise of the product in question." (3 Cal. App. 3d at p.326, 82 Cal. Rptr. 420.)

of the manner in which it is manufactured or installed, and it proves to
have defects which cause injury to persons or property when used in a
normal manner, is strictly liable in tort." (Id., at pp. 961-962, 128 Cal.
Rptr. 69.)

Here, respondent is in the business of leasing apartments, including
appliances and fixtures, and is therefore part of the marketing enterprise by which the shower door in question reached the user public. In
Green v. Superior Court, *supra,* 10 Cal. 3d 616, 627, 111 Cal. Rptr. 704,
517 P.2d 1168, our high court observed:

> In most significant respects, the modern urban tenant is in the same position
> as any other normal consumer of goods. [Citation.] Through a residential
> lease, a tenant seeks to purchase "housing" from his landlord for a specified
> period of time. The landlord "sells" housing, enjoying a much greater opportu-
> nity, incentive and capacity than a tenant to inspect and maintain the condition
> of his apartment building. A tenant may reasonably expect that the product he
> is purchasing is fit for the purpose for which it is obtained, that is, a living unit.
> Moreover, since a lease contract specifies a designated period of time during
> which the tenant has a right to inhabit the premises, the tenant may legiti-
> mately expect that the premises will be fit for such habitation for the duration
> of the term of the lease. It is just such reasonable expectations of consumers
> which the modern "implied warranty" decisions endow with formal, legal
> protection.

The landlord is a vital link in the commercial chain, and directly profits
from the consumer's use of products provided as part of the rental unit.
We think it a reasonable rule that a landlord should be treated as a
"retailer" of rental housing, subject to liability for defects in the premises
rented.

In reaching this conclusion, we have considered that the salutary policies underlying the strict products liability doctrine will be furthered by
inclusion of landlords within its scope. According to our high court, "the
paramount policy to be promoted by the rule is the protection of otherwise defenseless victims of manufacturing defects and the spreading
throughout society of the cost of compensating them." (Price v. Shell Oil
Co. (1970) 2 Cal. 3d 245, 251, 85 Cal. Rptr. 178, 466 P.2d 722; see also
Tauber-Arons Auctioneers Co. v. Superior Court, *supra,* 101 Cal. App. 3d
268, 283, 161 Cal. Rptr. 789.) "Placing the economic burden of injuries on
those best able to pay for those costs while permitting the transfer of that
burden to those most culpable is consistent with the equitable considerations inherent in the resolution of the difficult problems which have been
judicially posed." (Rawlings v. D. M. Oliver, Inc. (1979) 97 Cal. App. 3d
890, 901, 159 Cal. Rptr. 119.) The landlord receives the financial benefit
from the tenants' use of appliances included in rental housing, and has the
ability to spread the cost of compensation throughout the marketing sys-

tem by obtaining insurance or otherwise accounting for the risk of loss. In addition, the landlord has control over the rental premises, which provides the means by which the possible harm from defective appliances or fixtures can be eliminated.

We find the cases relied upon by respondent unpersuasive. In both Tauber-Arons Auctioneers Co. v. Superior Court, *supra*, 101 Cal. App. 3d 268, 161 Cal. Rptr. 789, and La Rosa v. Superior Court (1981) 122 Cal. App. 3d 741, 176 Cal. Rptr. 224 it was held that a dealer in used products acting merely as an agent for the seller or manufacturer, and who has no other connection with the product, cannot be held strictly liable in tort for its defective condition. In contrast, here respondent played no such random and accidental role in the marketing of the untempered glass shower doors; rather, it directly provided the product to tenants for their use, thus actively entering the marketing enterprise for that product.

It is vigorously argued as a reason for exclusion of respondent from liability as a matter of law, that it was not the owner of the building when the allegedly defective product was installed. Once IRM became the landlord, however, it acted in effect as distributor or supplier of housing, with authority and ability to monitor all products so furnished, including appliances and fixtures in the apartments. And by failing to remove shower doors made of untempered glass, respondent maintained the distribution of these appliances to its tenants.

Respondent argues with equal force that it reasonably ought not to incur liability for the defective shower doors because it had no notice of the defect. We disagree, since we regard notice as irrelevant to the strict liability analysis.

The doctrine of strict products liability is based upon a defect in the product, and can arise from an unsafe design as well as from faults attributable to the manufacturing process. (Pike v. Frank G. Hough Co. (1970) 2 Cal. 3d 465, 475, 85 Cal. Rptr. 629, 467 P.2d 229.)

While the operative term "defect" is not capable of precise definition, and is concededly an amorphous and elusive concept, it does *not* require proof that the defective design renders the product "unreasonably dangerous" to the unsuspecting customer. (Cronin v. J. B. E. Olson Corp. (1972) 8 Cal. 3d 121, 133, 104 Cal. Rptr. 433, 501 P.2d 1153; McGee v. Cessna Aircraft Co., *supra*, 82 Cal. App. 3d 1005, 1015, 147 Cal. Rptr. 694; Buccery v. General Motors Corp. (1976) 60 Cal. App. 3d 533, 544, 132 Cal. Rptr. 605.) On the other hand, of course, neither does the concept of strict liability make the manufacturer an absolute insurer of its product. (Daly v. General Motors Corp. (1978) 20 Cal. 3d 725, 733, 144 Cal. Rptr. 380, 575 P.2d 1162.)

Our high court has suggested that issue of defectiveness can best be resolved by resort to the "cluster of precedents" forming the crucible in which the products liability doctrine has been forged and shaped. (Barker v. Lull Engineering Co. (1978) 20 Cal 3d 413, 428, 143 Cal. Rptr. 225, 573 P.2d 443, 96 A.L.R.3d 1; Cronin v. J. B. E. Olson Corp., *supra*, 8 Cal. 3d at p.134, 104 Cal. Rptr. 433, 501 P.2d 1153.) In *Barker, supra,* the court enumerated the following as standards to be employed in determining whether a product is defectively designed:

> First, a product may be found defective in design if the plaintiff establishes that the product failed to perform as safely as an ordinary consumer would expect when used in an intended or reasonably foreseeable manner. Second, a product may alternatively be found defective in design if the plaintiff demonstrates that the product's design proximately caused his injury and the defendant fails to establish, in light of the relevant factors, that, on balance, the benefits of the challenged design outweigh the risk of danger inherent in such design. (Id., 20 Cal. 3d at p.432, 143 Cal. Rptr. 225, 573 P.2d 443.)

In evaluating the adequacy of a product's design pursuant to these standards, a jury may consider, among other relevant factors: the gravity of the danger posed by the challenged device; the likelihood that such danger would occur; the mechanical feasibility of a safer alternative design; the financial cost of an improved design; and the adverse consequences to the product and the consumer that would result from an alternative design. (Barker v. Lull Engineering Co., *supra,* 20 Cal. 3d 413, 431, 143 Cal. Rptr. 225, 573 P.2d 443; Horn v. General Motors Corp. (1976) 17 Cal. 3d 359, 367, 131 Cal. Rptr. 78, 551 P.2d 398; Southern Cal. Edison Co. v. Harnischfeger Corp. (1981) 120 Cal. App. 3d 842, 854, 175 Cal. Rptr. 67.) The cases have recognized the "need to 'weigh' competing considerations in an *overall* product design, in order to determine whether the design was 'defective.' " (Daly v. General Motors Corp., *supra,* 20 Cal. 3d 725, 746, 144 Cal. Rptr. 380, 575 P.2d 1162, italics added.)

The strict liability doctrine also " 'requires a manufacturer to foresee some degree of misuse and abuse of his product, either by the user or by third parties, and to take reasonable precautions to minimize the harm that may result from misuse and abuse. . . .' " (Buccery v. General Motors Corp., *supra,* 60 Cal. App. 3d 533, 546, 132 Cal. Rptr. 605; Self v. General Motors Corp. (1974) 42 Cal. App. 3d 1, 7, 116 Cal. Rptr. 575.) Strict liability should not be imposed upon a manufacturer when injury results from a use of its product that is not reasonably foreseeable. (Cronin v. J. B. E. Olson Corp., *supra,* 8 Cal. 3d 121, 126, 104 Cal Rptr. 433, 501 P.2d 1153; *Self, supra,* 42 Cal. App. 3d at p.7, 116 Cal. Rptr. 575.) But as the court acknowledged in *Cronin, supra:* "The design and manufacture of products should not be carried out in an industrial vacuum but with recognition of the realities of their everyday use." (Id., 8 Cal. 3d at p.126, 104 Cal. Rptr. 433, 501 P.2d 1153; *Buccery, supra,* 60 Cal. App. 3d at p.546, 132 Cal. Rptr. 605; *Self, supra,* 42 Cal. App. 3d at p.7, 116 Cal. Rptr. 575.) The prospect of liability for injuries resulting from foreseeable abuse and misuse "keeps the manufacturer on his toes and thereby serves a socially useful purpose." (Self v. General Motors, *supra,* 42 Cal. App. 3d at p.8, 116 Cal. Rptr. 575.) []"

LUCAS, Justice, concurring and dissenting.

I concur in that portion of the majority opinion which holds that a landlord may be held liable for dangerous conditions of which he knew or should have known. However, I cannot join in imposing upon landlords strict liability for latent defects in any component of their property no matter who built or installed the defective item.

Taking an unprecedented leap, the majority imposes "an unusual and unjust burden on property owners . . . [T]he landlord [will] be faced with liability for every injury claim resulting from any untoward condition in every cranny of the building, whether it is reasonably foreseeable or not." (Dwyer v. Skyline Apartments, Inc. (N.J. App. 1973) 123 N.J. Super. 48, 301 A.2d 463, 467, *aff'd obiter dictum,* 63 N.J. 577, 311 A.2d 1.) Any landlord, even one renting the family home for a year, will now be insurer for defects in any wire, screw, latch, cabinet door, pipe or other article on and in his premises at the time they are let despite the fact that he neither installed the item nor had any knowledge or reason to know of the defect. I believe, in conformance with the almost unanimous judgment of other jurisdictions considering this issue, that such imposition of liability is inappropriate. As one authority has remarked, "One problem in analyzing product liability law is our tendency to study rule changes in isolation and not to analyze their aggregate effect on liability costs or primary behavior." (Epstein, Commentary (1983) 58 N.Y.U.L. Rev. 930, 931.) My colleagues here have taken just such an "isolated" viewpoint.

Justice Traynor, over 40 years ago in his classic concurrence, reasoned that "it should now be recognized that a manufacturer incurs an absolute liability when a product that he has placed on the market, knowing that it is to be used without inspection, proves to have a defect that causes injury to human beings." (Escola v. Coca Cola Bottling Co. (1944) 24 Cal. 2d 453, 461, 150 P.2d 436.) Thereafter, in Greenman v. Yuba Power Products, Inc. (1963) 59 Cal. 2d 57, 63, 27 Cal. Rptr. 697, 377 P.2d 897, speaking for a unanimous court, Justice Traynor explained that "The purpose of such liability is to insure that the costs of injuries resulting from defective products are borne by the manufacturers that put such products on the markets rather than by the injured persons who are powerless to protect themselves." In other words, the one who *makes* the product should be held responsible for its defects.

The next year, strict liability was extended to retailers. (Vandermark v. Ford Motor Co. (1964) 61 Cal. 2d 256, 37 Cal. Rptr. 896, 391 P.2d 168.) The rationale articulated in support of this extension was that

> Retailers like manufacturers are engaged in the business of distributing goods to the public. They are an integral part of the overall producing and marketing enterprise that should bear the cost of injuries resulting from defective products. . . . Strict liability on the manufacturer and retailer alike affords maximum protection to the injured plaintiff and *works no injustice to the defendants, for they can adjust the costs of such protection between them in the course of their continuing business relationship.*" (Id., at pp. 262-263, 37 Cal. Rptr. 896, 391 P.2d 168, italics added.)

We later held that lessors and bailors of personal property similarly might be held strictly liable, after stressing "the necessity for a continuous course of business as a condition to application of the rule. . . ." (Price v. Shell Oil Co. (1970) 2 Cal. 3d 245, 253-254, 85 Cal. Rptr. 178, 466 P.2d 722.) As I shall discuss, this requirement of a continuing relationship which avoids "injustice" to defendants is given no meaningful consideration in the majority approach.

The potential liability of *producers* of residences was addressed in Kriegler v. Eichler Homes, Inc. (1969) 269 Cal. App. 2d 224, 74 Cal. Rptr. 749, a case cited with approval in *Price, supra* (2 Cal. 3d at p.251, fn. 6, 85 Cal. Rptr. 178, 466 P.2d 722), for the proposition that manufacturers placing products on the market, including mass producers of homes, should be held strictly liable for defects in their products. The *Kriegler* court concluded that "there are no meaningful distinctions between Eichler's mass production and sale of homes and the mass production and sale of automobiles and that the pertinent overriding policy considerations are the same." (269 Cal. App. 2d at p.227, 74 Cal. Rptr. 749; see Del Mar Beach Club Owners Assn. v. Imperial Contracting Co. (1981) 123 Cal. App. 3d 898, 911-912, 176 Cal. Rptr. 886.) *Kriegler*'s holding rested on the identification of Eichler as essentially a "manufacturer of homes," a situation undeniably very different from the one present here. IRM Corporation *purchased* an already "produced" and used property.

The distinction between a party actually selecting, installing, constructing, and buying the defective product and a party who plays no such role and *therefore has no connection with anyone up the ladder of distribution,* was fundamentally adhered to by the Court of Appeals in two cases dealing with defects allegedly present in items found on or in leased premises. In Fakhoury v. Magner (1972) 25 Cal. App. 3d 58, 101 Cal. Rptr. 473, the plaintiff was injured when a couch in a rented apartment collapsed. She sued her landlord in strict liability asserting latent defects in the furniture. The court concluded that the landlord could be held liable "not as lessor of real property, but as lessor of the furniture" (P.63, 101 Cal. Rptr. 473.) The requirement that the property be placed in the stream of commerce was met because "a casual or isolated transaction will not bring the doctrine into play. [However, in] the case at hand, the landlord furnished two apartments in San Francisco and three in Sacramento at the same time with the same kind of couch purchased from the same seller." (P.64, 101 Cal. Rptr. 473.) In the instant case, the shower door was a fixture and the defendant is being sued as a lessor of property not as a lessor of furniture. Moreover, the shower doors had not been purchased by defendant.

The role of strict liability in landlord-tenant relationships was further explored in Golden v. Conway (1976) 55 Cal. App. 3d 948, 128 Cal. Rptr. 69. The plaintiff sued the landlord in strict liability after suffering damages in a fire caused by a wall heater installed by a contractor at the landlord's behest approximately one year before. The court permitted maintenance of the cause of action on the ground "that a lessor of real property who . . . is engaged in the business of leasing apartments and appurtenant commercial premises, equips the premises with an appliance without knowing whether or not it is defective because of the manner in which it was manufactured or installed, and it proves to have defects which cause injury to persons or property when used in a normal manner, is strictly liable in tort." (Pp. 961-962, 128 Cal. Rptr. 69.) The installation of the heater assertedly created the dangerous condition, and the court was careful to distinguish the facts from those in Ruiz v. Minnesota Mining & Mfg. Co. (1971) 15 Cal. App. 3d 462, 93 Cal. Rptr. 270. In the latter case, the *Golden* court stressed, a product used on the premises was defective "and the property owner merely failed to take corrective action because he did not discover the defect" and therefore was not strictly liable. (55 Cal. App. 3d at p.963, 128 Cal. Rptr. 69.) In our case, there is no allegation that the landlord was aware of the defect in the already present product.[1]

The treatment of cases involving used goods and their sale better high-

---

1. The *Golden* court did *not* discuss whether the transaction at issue here was an isolated one and therefore not normally the subject of an action in strict liability. The relevant continuing relationship usually is the one between the party sought to be held strictly liable and those up the chain of distribution to the manufacturer. Neither the relationship of the landlord to the marketing chain, nor between landlord and tenant was considered for this purpose, and I therefore consider *Golden* to be of limited assistance in evaluating the underlying policy problems.

lights relevant concerns ignored by the majority. In Tauber-Arons Auctioneers Co. v. Superior Court (1980) 101 Cal. App. 3d 268, 161 Cal. Rptr. 789, the Court of Appeals held that an auctioneer of used machinery who did not perform any maintenance or repair on the equipment, did not inspect it, and sold it "as is," could not be held strictly liable for any defects in the items. The court stated that when considering the requirement that a potential defendant be a participant "in the manufacturing-marketing system" before he be held subject to strict liability, one significant factor is "the requirement that defendant have a participatory connection with the enterprise which 'created consumer demand for and reliance upon' the particular 'injury-producing product' [citation] not just products of the same classification." (101 Cal. App. 3d at p.276, 161 Cal. Rptr. 789; see also Brejcha v. Wilson Machinery, Inc. (1984) 160 Cal. App. 3d 630, 639, 206 Cal. Rptr. 688.) The court further emphasized participation in the "initial distribution of the particular manufacturer's products. . . ." (P.277, 206 Cal. Rptr. 688.) Because a used machinery dealer normally

> has no continuing business relationship with the manufacturer in the course of which he can adjust the cost of protection from strict liability . . . the rationale which underlies *Vandermark* simply is inapplicable to such a dealer. Moreover, the risk reduction which was sought in *Vandermark* on the assumption that "the retailer himself may play a substantial part in insuring that the product is safe or may be in a position to exert pressure on the manufacturer to that end" (61 Cal. 2d at p. 262, 37 Cal. Rptr. 896, 391 P.2d 168) . . . is simply unattainable because the "used-goods dealer is normally entirely outside the original chain of distribution of the product. . . ." (Tillman v. Vance Equipment Co. [(1979) 286 Or. 747, 596 P.2d 1299, 1304].) (101 Cal. App. 3d at p.283, 161 Cal. Rptr. 789, fn. omitted; see also Wilkinson v. Hicks (1981) 126 Cal. App. 3d 515, 521, 179 Cal. Rptr. 5; LaRosa v. Superior Court (1981) 122 Cal. App. 3d 741, 753-754, 176 Cal. Rptr. 224.)

Analogous considerations apply in the case of the "used property" lessor.

Discounting other crucial and long-recognized justifications for imposition of strict liability, my colleagues focus primarily on the "risk-spreading" function of this form of liability. Essentially they ignore the fact that landlords of used property have no special position with regard to original manufacturers and sellers and thus have no influence to wield in order to improve product safety. Moreover, contrary to the majority's implication, the landlord, while impliedly representing that the premises are habitable, is not representing to tenants that he has expertise and guarantees the perfection of every item forming the premises. Instead of considering what role landlords of used property realistically play with regard to that property, the majority concentrates narrowly on the advancement of "The paramount policy of the strict products liability rules [namely] the spreading throughout society of the cost of compensating otherwise defenseless victims of manufacturing defects." (*Ante,* p.220 of 213 Cal. Rptr., at p.123 of 696 P.2d.) Next my colleagues observe that "landlords are essential to the rental business. They have more than a random or accidental role in the marketing enterprise [and] a continuing relationship to the property following the renting. . . ." In addition, "it may be expected that along with numerous other factors the price of used rental housing will depend in part on the quality of the building and reflect the anticipated costs of protecting tenants, including repairs, replacement of defects and insurance," and that rentals may be adjusted to cover such costs. (*Ante,* at p.221 of 213 Cal. Rptr., at p.124 of 696 P.2d.)[2]

One major difficulty with this approach is the concentration on the wrong "stream of commerce." Unquestionably the landlord has more than an "accidental role" in the marketing of rental property. Except for those who on a one-time basis rent out a piece of property for a reasonably short term, every landlord of both multiple and single properties has a continuing role in the rental market. But those same landlords in all likelihood will have absolutely no direct or continuing relationships with the *manufacturers and marketers* of the particular defective products found on the premises. We are not discussing here those who *build* the property; we are discussing those who purchase already existing multiple residence properties. In fact, applying the majority's analysis, those who decide to rent out the family home on a regular basis are also now strictly liable for defects in any item located therein. Under the majority's formulation, where the relevant relationship is that of landlord to his property and tenants, any landlord is now strictly liable for defects of which he or she has no knowledge or reason to know and which appear in any part of the property no matter how esoteric the understanding necessary to compre-

---

2. One Court of Appeal recently undertook an extensive review of strict liability in the context of sellers of used machinery which "they neither inspected, repaired nor modified." (LaRosa v. Superior Court, *supra,* 122 Cal. App. 3d 741, 743, 176 Cal. Rptr. 224.) It reviewed five "policy predicates" for strict liability described in Note, Sales of Defective Used Products: Should Strict Liability Apply? (1979) 52 So. Cal. L. Rev. 805, namely, (1) enterprise liability (forcing the enterprise to bear costs of injuries caused by its defective products); (2) deterrence; (3) risk distribution; (4) practicality (problems of proof made easier by application of strict liability) and (5) implied representations of safety because product is present on the market. (122 Cal. App. 3d at pp.756-760, 176 Cal. Rptr. 224.) The Court of Appeal found that as to the risk distribution rationale, so heavily relied upon here by the majority, "the very pervasiveness of the . . . rationale suggests that it is probably insufficient, by itself, to justify *strict* liability." (122 Cal. App. 3d at p.759, 176 Cal. Rptr. 224.) As to diminishing problems of proof, the court observed "ease of recovery is not really a *rationale* for strict liability; more precisely it describes the *effect* strict liability was expected to have. Obviously if ease of recovery *were* a pervasive rationale for strict liability then strict liability would be the universal rule." (Id. at p.760, 176 Cal. Rptr. 224.) These conclusions have validity in our context as well.

hend the working of that part.[3] Nothing in the majority's approach is necessarily confined to landlords of multiple residences.

The weakness of the majority's analysis of the relevant stream of commerce is revealed by consideration of its basis for concluding that "a continuing business relationship is not essential to imposition of strict liability." It relies upon Ray v. Alad Corp. (1977) Cal. 3d 22, 136 Cal. Rptr. 574, 560 P.2d 3, for the proposition that unavailability of a manufacturer militates in favor of the imposition of liability on "persons engaged in the enterprise who can spread the cost of compensation." (See *ante*, pp. 220-221, of 213 Cal. Rptr., at pp.123-124 of 696 P.2d.) In *Alad*, we held that a corporation which had acquired all assets of the manufacturer of the defective product and which continued to run the business in a manner almost identical to its original form, could be held strictly liable for defects in a product manufactured by the predecessor corporation. "By taking over and continuing the established business of producing and distributing Alad ladders, Alad II became 'an integral part of the overall producing and marketing enterprise that should bear the cost of injuries resulting from defective products (Vandermark v. Ford Motor Co., *supra*, 61 Cal. 2d 256, 262 [37 Cal. Rptr. 896, 391 P.2d 168]).' " (Ray v. Alad Corp., *supra*, 19 Cal. 3d at p.34, 136 Cal. Rptr. 574, 560 P.2d 3.) Under those narrow circumstances, we held the successor could be held liable.

Similar complete unavailability of the manufacturer or others in the original chain of distribution simply is not at issue here. As the majority states in its recitation of facts, the plaintiff here settled with the builder and a door assembler and installer for a minimum of $150,000 and has actions pending against defendants in addition to the landlord. No legal unavailability of the kind occurring in *Alad* presented a problem for plaintiff's recovery. Moreover, there is no reasonable suggestion that the relationship between the landlord here and any party participating in the original manufacture and distribution of the shower door can be analogized to the almost complete overlap of the corporate entities in *Alad*. It is illogical to conclude that the landlord here became part of the

---

3. This sharply contrasts with the general view that "Only a seller who can be regarded as a merchant or as one engaged in the business of supplying goods of the kind involved in the case is subject to strict liability. . . ." (Prosser & Keeton on the Law of Torts (5th ed. 1984) Products Liability, §100 at p.705.) We conformed to this viewpoint in *Price* where the court concluded "that for the doctrine of strict liability in tort to apply to a lessor of personalty, the lessor should be found to be in the business of leasing, in the same general sense as the seller of personalty is found to be in the business of manufacturing or retailing." (2 Cal. 3d at p.254, 85 Cal. Rptr. 178, 466 P.2d 722.) The majority makes landlords "merchants" of anything contained in or on their property, no matter what the expertise or familiarity entailed, or the actual role of the landlord with regard to the particular product at issue.

overall *marketing* scheme for the shower doors merely by purchasing property in which they had long since been installed.

Unlike retailers, lessors, bailors, wholesalers or others in the original chain of distribution of the product, the landlord owning used property cannot adjust the costs of production up the chain. He may only do it, at best, *down* the chain of "distribution," namely by charging more to his tenants. Unlike the others mentioned above, such a "merchant" has no opportunity to enter into indemnification agreements with those more closely linked with the making of the product — he will have little idea if any when he buys the property as to the origin of items such as the wiring found in the walls, and without doubt even if he has such knowledge will have no bargaining power to enter into any agreements with such suppliers. Moreover, his responsibility extends to a myriad of products, unlike the situation faced by a retailer of a particular line of goods. Landlords henceforth are in a risky business. No matter how carefully they inspect, and no matter how impossible to discern the defect, they are now the last outpost of liability for countless unrelated products in which they have no particular expertise.[4]

Consideration of the inherent problems — and unfairness — in extending strict liability to landlords has led almost every other jurisdiction deciding this issue to decide that imposition of such liability is unwarranted. In 1973, a New Jersey appellate court so held in a decision affirmed by that state's highest court. The opinion contained a cogent discussion of some of the reasons why use of this theory of recovery is inappropriate in this context:

> The underlying reasons for the enforcement of strict liability against the manufacturer, seller or lessor of products or the mass builder-vendor of homes do not apply to the ordinary landlord of a multiple family dwelling.
>
> Such a landlord is not engaged in mass production whereby he places his product — the apartment — in the stream of commerce exposing it to a large number of consumers. He has not created the product with a defect which is preventable by greater care at the time of manufacture or assembly. He does

---

4. One court summed up the difference between extending strict liability to lessors of commercial products and to motel owners in a manner which has general application in our context as well:

> A major consideration in holding lessors of commercial products strictly liable was that such lessors possessed expert knowledge of the characteristics of the equipment or machines they leased. [Citations.] Another consideration is that such lessors, like retailers, deal continually with their suppliers, giving them an enduring relationship which permits them to seek contribution and indemnification. These considerations do not apply when a motel operator makes a one-time purchase of furnishings and fixtures about which he has no special expertise. Therefore, we hold that a motel operator is not strictly liable for defects in the fixtures and furnishings of the rooms he held out to the public. (Livingston v. Begay (1982) 98 N.M. 712, 652 P.2d 734, 738-739.)

not have the expertise to know and correct the condition so as to be saddled with responsibility for a defect regardless of negligence.

An apartment involves several rooms with many facilities constructed by many artisans with differing types of expertise, and subject to constant use and deterioration from many causes. It is a commodity wholly unlike a product which is expected to leave the manufacturer's hands in a safe condition with an implied representation upon which the consumer justifiably relies.

The tenant may expect that at the time of the letting there are no hidden dangerous defects known to the landlord and of which the tenant has not been warned. But he does not expect that all will be perfect in his apartment for all the years of his occupancy with the result that his landlord will be strictly liable for all consequences of any deficiency regardless of fault. He expects only that in the event anything goes wrong with the accommodations or the equipment therein, the landlord will repair it when he knows or should know of its existence; and that if injury results liability will attach. (Dwyer v. Skyline Apartments, Inc., *supra*, 301 A.2d at p. 467.)

Several other courts have reached similar conclusions in reviewing analogous cases. As the Kansas [*sic*] Court of Appeal observed, "No case has been cited, nor has one been found, imposing strict liability upon the nonbuilder landlord for latent defects, rendering the premises unsafe or dangerous, absent some actual or constructive notice of the defects." (Henderson v. W.C. Haas Rlty. Management, Inc. (Mo. App. 1977) 561 S.W.2d 382, 387.)[5] Cases rejecting application of liability without knowledge have utilized various approaches. (See, e.g., Meyer v. Parkin (Minn. App. 1984) 350 N.W.2d 435, 438-439 [recent legislation did not eliminate requirement of scienter on part of landlord before he has duty to warn lessee of concealed defects]; George Washington University v. Weintraub (D.C. App. 1983) 458 A.2d 43, 49 and fn. 9 [landlord exercising reasonable care may not be held liable for losses caused from defects of which he neither knew nor should have known]; Livingston v. Begay, *supra*, 652 P.2d 734 [lessor of motel room not strictly liable; theory not meant to apply to "unsafe design of a hotel room"]; Boudreau v. General Elect. Co. (1981) 2 Haw. App. 10, 625 P.2d 384, 389-390 [strict liability requires lessor to be engaged in business of supplying goods in which defect is claimed]; Segal v. Justice Court Mut. Housing Co-op (N.Y. Civ. Ct. 1980) 105 Misc. 2d 453, 432 N.Y.S.2d 463, 467, *aff'd* (1981) 108 Misc. 2d 1074, 442 N.Y.S.2d 686 [no strict liability of landlords under public policy or legislation; they are not insurers of property"; Kidd v. Price

---

5. The one apparent exception is in Louisiana where *pursuant to statute* a landlord may be held liable for defects in the absence of actual knowledge of the defective condition of his property. (See Parr v. Head (La. App. 1983) 442 So. 2d 1234, 1235; Buxton v. Allstate Ins. Co. (La. App. 1983) 434 So. 2d 605, 607-608.)

(Ky.1970) 461 S.W.2d 565, 567 [liability for latent defect depends on notice or knowledge thereof].)

I would hold that a subsequent purchaser of property who has not installed, altered or created the item or condition which is claimed to be defective, and who has no actual or constructive knowledge of any defect therein, should not be held strictly liable. If the landlord knows or should know of the defect, then he has a duty to take appropriate action to correct or warn of the problem. However, where the landlord has no continuing relationship with the chain of marketing leading back to the manufacturer of the defective product, and thus has no way of influencing the production or design of the product or of adjusting potential costs of the *manufacturer's* enterprise or others in the business of marketing the item at issue, imposition of strict liability is inappropriate. The only rationales supporting such responsibility are ease of proof for the injured party and "distributing" the risk of damages to the landlord. The costs of such an extension of liability to those *without* expertise or continuing relationships for the multiple products and parts for which they may now bear responsibility will entail a significant shift in how our tort system has heretofore operated. It amounts, in effect, to insurance for tenants,[6] because it does nothing to aid in the goals of deterrence or product safety.

I would affirm the trial court's decision to the extent that it granted summary judgment to defendant on the cause of action sounding in strict liability, while joining in the majority's reversal as to the negligence cause of action.

MOSK, J., concurs.

---

6. The majority never considers the economic effect of its holding. The only logical result is that the price of rental housing will increase because of the increased cost of insurance, assuming insurance can be obtained for this purpose. Even if landlords can sue participants in the original line of manufacture and marketing, the litigation costs involved will likely also have an effect on the price of rental housing. Arguably, instead of risk distribution, the majority's conclusion will result in a general increased cost attributable to the risks involved without a concurrent benefit. Someone will have to pay for the additional litigation today's decision is likely to create.

Insert the following material on page 522 before heading D. Retaliatory Conduct

Case concerned with the landlord's liability for criminal acts committed against tenants on leased premises.

FELD v. MERRIAM

Supreme Court of Pennsylvania, 1984
506 Pa. 383, 485 A.2d 742

Opinion[1]

McDermott, Justice.

Peggy and Samuel Feld were tenants in the large Cedarbrook Apartment complex, consisting of 150 acres and 1,000 apartments housed in three high rise buildings. For an extra rental fee the apartments are serviced by parking garages adjacent to the apartment buildings. On the evening of June 27, 1975, about 9:00 P.M., the Felds, returning from a social engagement, drove as usual to their allotted space in the parking garage. Then began the events that brings before us the question of a landlord's liability for the criminal acts of unknown third persons. We are not unaware of the social, economic and philosophic dimensions of the questions posed.

While the Felds were parking their car, they were set upon by three armed felons. At gun point, accompanied by two of the felons, they were forced to the back seat of their car. Followed by the third felon in an "old, blue broken down car," they were driven past the guard on duty at the gate, out into the night, to the ferine disposal of three criminals. To clear the car for their main criminal purpose, the felons started to force Mr. Feld into the trunk of the car. Mrs. Feld pled her husband's illness and to save him, offered herself for her husband's life. Thereupon the felons released Mr. Feld on a deserted street corner and drove Mrs. Feld to the lonely precincts of a country club. There is no need to recite the horrors that brave and loving woman suffered. Suffice it to say they extorted a terrible penalty from her defenseless innocence.

The Felds brought suit against the appellees, owners of the complex,[2] alleging a duty of protection owed by the landlord, the breach of duty,

1. This case was reassigned to this author on May 16, 1984.

2. Cedarbrook is owned by John W. Merriam, and Thomas Wynne, Inc. Merriam and Thomas Wynne, Inc., were co-venturers in a company trading as the Cedarbrook Joint Venture. Merriam owns all of Thomas Wynne, Inc.'s stock, and, at trial, was appropriately treated as Cedarbrook's sole owner.

and injuries resulting therefrom. Named as defendants were John Merriam, Thomas Wynne, Inc., the Cedarbrook Joint Venture, and Globe Security Systems, Inc. Following an eight-day trial, the jury returned a plaintiff's verdict and a judgment totaling six million dollars against Merriam, Thomas Wynne, Inc., and the Cedarbrook Joint Venture.[3] The jury absolved Globe Security of any liability. Common Pleas, per the Honorable Jacob Kalish, denied motions for a new trial, judgment N.O.V. and remittitur.

On appeal the Superior Court affirmed the lower court, with the exception that the award of punitive damages to Samuel Feld was reduced by one half. Both Cedarbrook and Mr. Feld filed petitions for allowance of appeal, which were granted. We now reverse.

I

The threshold question is whether a landlord has any duty to protect tenants from the forseeable criminal acts of third persons, and if so, under what circumstances. Well settled law holds landlords to a duty to protect tenants from injury arising out of their negligent failure to maintain their premises in a safe condition. See Smith v. M.P.W. Realty Co. Inc., 423 Pa. 536, 225 A.2d 227 (1967). Lopez v. Gukenback, 391 Pa. 359, 137 A.2d 771 (1958). That rule of law is addressed to their failure of reasonable care, a failure of care caused by their own negligence, a condition, the cause of which was either known or knowable by reasonable precaution. The criminal acts of a third person belong to a different category and can bear no analogy to the unfixed radiator, unlighted steps, falling ceiling, or the other myriad possibilities of one's personal negligence. To render one liable for the deliberate criminal acts of unknown third persons can only be a judicial rule for given limited circumstances.

The closest analogy is the duty of owners of land who hold their property open to the public for business purposes. See Leary v. Lawrence Sales Corp., 442 Pa. 389, 275 A.2d 32 (1971). They are subject to liability for the accidental, negligent or intentionally harmful acts of third persons, as are common carriers, innkeepers and other owners of places of public resort. Section 344, comment (f) of the Restatement (Second) of Torts, adopted by this court in Moran v. Valley Forge Drive-In Theater, Inc., 431 Pa. 432, 246 A.2d 875 (1968), requires that they

---

3. Samuel Feld was awarded $1 million in compensatory damages and $1.5 million in punitive damages. Peggy Feld was awarded $2 million in compensatory damages and $1.5 million in punitive damages. Delay damages, pursuant to Pa. R. Civ. P. 238, were assessed against Cedarbrook in the amount of $83,835.24.

take reasonable precaution against that which might be reasonably antici-pated. The reason is clear; places to which the general public are invited might indeed anticipate, either from common experience or known fact, that places of general public resort are also places where what men can do, they might. One who invites all may reasonably expect that all might not behave, and bears responsibility for injury that follows the absence of reasonable precaution against that common expectation. The common areas of an apartment complex are not open to the public, nor are the general public expected or invited to gather there for other purposes than to visit tenants.

Tenants in a huge apartment complex, or a tenant on the second floor of a house converted to an apartment, do not live where the world is invited to come. Absent agreement, the landlord cannot be expected to protect them against the wiles of felonry any more than the society can always protect them upon the common streets and highways leading to their residence or indeed in their home itself.

An apartment building is not a place of public resort where one who profits from the very public it invites must bear what losses that public may create. It is of its nature private and only for those specifically invited. The criminal can be expected anywhere, any time, and has been a risk of life for a long time. He can be expected in the village, monastery and the castle keep.

In the present case the Superior Court departed from the traditional rule that a person cannot be liable for the criminal acts of third parties when it held "that in all areas of the leasehold, particularly in the area under his control, the landlord is under a duty to provide adequate security to protect his tenants from the forseeable criminal actions of third persons." Feld v. Merriam, et al., 314 Pa. Super. 414, 427, 461 A.2d 225, 231 (1983).

The Superior Court viewed the imposition of this new duty as merely an extension of the landlord's existing duty to maintain the common areas to be free from the risk of harm caused by physical defects. How-ever, in so holding that court failed to recognize the crucial distinction between the risk of injury from a physical defect in the property, and the risk from the criminal act of a third person. In the former situation the landlord has effectively perpetuated the risk of injury by refusing to correct a known and verifiable defect. On the other hand, the risk of injury from the criminal acts of third persons arises not from the con-duct of the landlord but from the conduct of an unpredictable indepen-dent agent. To impose a general duty in the latter case would effectively require landlords to be insurers of their tenants' safety: a burden which could never be completely met given the unfortunate realities of modern society.

Our analysis however does not stop here, for although there is a general rule against holding a person liable for the criminal conduct of another absent a preexisting duty, there is also an exception to that rule, i.e., where a party assumes a duty, whether gratuitously or for consideration, and so negligently performs that duty that another suffers damage. Pascarella v. Kelley, 378 Pa. 18, 105 A.2d 70 (1954). See Rehder v. Miller, 35 Pa. Super. 344 (1908).

This exception has been capsulized in Section 323 of the Restatement (Second) of Torts, which provides:

§323.   Negligent Performance of Undertaking to Render Services
One who undertakes, gratuitously or for consideration, to render services to another which he should recognize as necessary for the protection of the other's person or things, is subject to liability to the other for physical harm resulting from his failure to exercise reasonable care to perform his undertaking if
(a) his failure to exercise such care increases the risk of such harm, or
(b) the harm is suffered because of the other's reliance upon the undertaking.

Previously we adopted this section as an accurate statement of the law in this Commonwealth. Gradel v. Inouye, 491 Pa. 534, 421 A.2d 674 (1980). DeJesus v. Liberty Mutual Insurance Co., 423 Pa. 198, 223 A.2d 849 (1966).[4]

Expounding on the proper application of Section 323 the drafters indicated that

[T]his Section applies to any undertaking to render services to another which the defendant should recognize as necessary for the protection of the other's person or things. It applies whether the harm to other or his things results from the defendant's negligent conduct in the manner of his performance of the undertaking, or from his failure to exercise reasonable care to complete it or to protect the other when he discontinues it. Comment (a) §323 Restatement (Second) of Torts.

These comments are particularly relevant in a situation such as the present where a landlord undertakes to secure the areas within his control and possibly fosters a reliance by his tenants on his efforts.

Absent therefore an agreement wherein the landlord offers or voluntarily proffers a program, we find no general duty of a landlord to protect tenants against criminal intrusion. However, a landlord may, as

4. Although in DeJesus v. Liberty Mutual Insurance Co., 423 Pa. 198, 201, 223 A.2d 849, 850 (1966), we held that both subsections (a) *and* (b) would have to be met to support liability, later application of Section 323 indicates that a party need only satisfy subsection (a) *or* (b) See Hamil v. Bashline, 481 Pa. 256, 392 A.2d 1280 (1978). See also, Morena v. South Hills Hospital, 501 Pa. 634, 462 A.2d 680 (1983).

indicated, incur a duty voluntarily or by specific agreement if to attract or keep tenants he provides a program of security.[5] A program of security is not the usual and normal precautions that a reasonable home-owner would employ to protect his property. It is, as in the case before us, an extra precaution, such as personnel charged to patrol and protect the premises. Personnel charged with such protection may be expected to perform their duties with the usual reasonable care required under standard tort law for ordinary negligence. When a landlord by agreement or voluntarily offers a program to protect the premises, he must perform the task in a reasonable manner and where a harm follows a reasonable expectation of that harm, he is liable. The duty is one of reasonable care under the circumstances. It is not the duty of an insurer and a landlord is not liable unless his failure is the proximate cause of the harm.

A tenant may rely upon a program of protection only within the reasonable expectations of the program. He cannot expect that a landlord will defeat all the designs of felonry. He can expect, however, that the program will be reasonably pursued and not fail due to its negligent exercise. If a landlord offers protection during certain periods of the day or night a tenant can only expect reasonable protection during the periods offered. If, however, during the periods offered, the protection fails by a lack of reasonable care, and that lack is the proximate cause of the injury, the landlord can be held liable. A tenant may not expect more than is offered. If, for instance, one guard is offered, he cannot expect the same quality and type of protection that two guards would have provided, nor may he expect the benefits that a different program might have provided. He can only expect the benefits reasonably expected of the program as offered and that that program will be conducted with reasonable care.

In the present case the trial judge, when instructing the jury, was placed in the unenviable position of predicting how we would resolve this difficult question. Although we commend him on his endeavor, we are constrained to reverse the verdict, since the jury instructions which were given imposed upon the landlord a duty greater than that which we today hold to have existed.

II

Cedarbrook also argues that the evidence of negligence failed to support the jury's punitive damages award, and that the introduction of

5. See Phillips v. Chicago Housing Authority, 89 Ill. 2d 122, 59 Ill. Dec. 281, 431 N.E.2d 1038 (1982); Pippin v. Chicago Housing Authority, 78 Ill. 2d 204, 35 Ill. Dec. 530, 399 N.E.2d 596 (1979); Scott v. Watson, 278 Md. 160, 359 A.2d 548 (1976).

evidence concerning appellant's considerable wealth was so prejudicial as to taint the jury's compensatory damages award. In light of our grant of a new trial on the issue of liability, the issues regarding damages are moot. However, in anticipation of the same issues arising at retrial, we will address them.

A. PUNITIVE DAMAGES

This Court has embraced the guideline of Section 908(2) of the Restatement (Second) of Torts regarding the imposition of punitive damages: "Punitive damages may be awarded for conduct that is outrageous, because of the defendant's evil motive or his reckless indifference to the rights of others." See Chambers v. Montgomery, 411 Pa. 339, 192 A.2d 355 (1963). Punitive damages must be based on conduct which is " 'malicious,' 'wanton,' 'reckless,' 'willful,' or 'oppressive' . . ." Id. at 344-45, 192 A.2d at 358, *citing* Hughes v. Babcock, 349 Pa. 475, 37 A.2d 551 (1944).

Further, one must look to "the act itself together with all the circumstances including the motive of the wrongdoers and the relations between the parties . . ." Chambers v. Montgomery, *supra,* 411 Pa. at 345, 192 A.2d at 358. See also, Pittsburgh Outdoor Advertising Co. v. Virginia Manor Apartments Inc., 436 Pa. 350, 260 A.2d 801 (1970).

The state of mind of the actor is vital. The act, or the failure to act, must be intentional, reckless, or malicious.

The danger here was not an easily perceptible one. While a jury might find that Cedarbrook failed to reasonably perform the duty it undertook, the evidence presented was insufficient to support a finding that they acted with the state of mind necessary to impose punitive damages. While the record indicates that the security systems might have been inadequate under the circumstances, there was no evidence of an evil motive or a reckless indifference to the safety of the tenants.

In deciding whether to impose punitive damages a court should not look to the third party's criminal conduct, which in this case was truly outrageous; a court should not look at the end result, which in this case also was outrageous; rather, the court should examine the actor's conduct. As a matter of law, on this record, a jury could not conclude that appellants' conduct was outrageous. Thus the trial court erred in submitting this issue to the jury.

B. COMPENSATORY DAMAGES

As a result of the trial judge's determination that the issue of punitive damages was a jury question, evidence was allowed concerning appellant's considerable wealth. Cedarbrook argues that this evidence had a prejudicial effect on the jury and thus the compensatory damage award of three million dollars should be vacated. We agree.

A jury may not consider a defendant's wealth in setting compensatory damages. It is "improper, irrelevant, prejudicial, and clearly beyond the legally established boundaries." Trimble v. Merloe, 413 Pa. 408, 410, 197 A.2d 457, 458 (1964). However, a defendant's wealth is relevant to set punitive damages. Arye v. Dickstein, 337 Pa. 471, 474, 12 A.2d 19, 20 (1940).

As we stated earlier, the outrageous conduct necessary to send the issue of punitive damages to the jury was not present in this case. Here, evidence showed that appellant's financial net worth was $40 million. The trial court resisted Cedarbrook's effort to try the issue of punitive damages separately, and refused to deliver Cedarbrook's suggested instruction that consideration of appellant's wealth was not relevant in fixing the amount of compensatory damages. Rather, a broader cautionary instruction was delivered which was inadequate to overcome any prejudice which might have resulted from the introduction of evidence regarding appellant's wealth.

Where the issue of punitive damages incorrectly goes to the jury, and where the trial court fails to sufficiently warn the jury that they may not look to a defendant's wealth in setting compensatory damages, evidence of the wealth of a defendant may improperly prejudice the jury and a compensatory damage award should be set aside.[6]

For the reasons stated above, this case must be remanded to the lower court for a new trial, in accordance with the standards stated.

ZAPPALA, J., joins in this Opinion, and files a separate Concurring Opinion.

Add the following material to note 64 on page 537.

See Scofield v. Berman and Sons, 393 Mass. 95, 469 N.E.2d 805 (1984), for a retaliatory eviction case that prevented the landlord from terminating a tenancy at will.

Insert the following material at the end of page 552.

Note

Should a landlord be allowed to restrict property he is offering for rent to adults only? If so, what happens to the tenants who have a child after they have rented the property? The following case considers the rental of property to "adults only."

---

6. The dramatic remedy of a new trial is not required in every case. In some cases a sufficient cautionary instruction may overcome the prejudice triggered by the introduction of evidence of a defendant's wealth.

HALET v. WEND INV. CO.

United States Court of Appeals, Ninth Circuit, 1982
672 F.2d 1305

CHOY, Circuit Judge:
Robert Halet applied for an apartment in a complex owned by the Wend Investment Company in Marina del Rey. His application was denied because Wend had an adults-only rental policy and Halet had a child in his household. Halet brought his suit against Wend and Los Angeles County, which leases the land to Wend, charging that the adults-only rental policy violated his right to live with his family and was racially discriminatory.[1] Specifically, he claimed that the County and Wend violated the fourteenth amendment, Civil Rights statutes, 42 U.S.C. §§1981, 1982, 1983, and 2000d, and the Fair Housing Act, 42 U.S.C. §3604. He sought a declaratory judgment that the rental policy was unlawful and an injunction prohibiting such a policy.

The district court dismissed Wend on the grounds that the case was moot and that Halet failed to state a claim upon which relief could be granted. The district court dismissed the County of Los Angeles on the grounds that there was no invidious discrimination and that the complaint failed to allege sufficient facts to show state action. Finally, the district court denied Halet's request for attorney's fees.

I. Mootness

After Halet filed his complaint, the City of Los Angeles adopted an ordinance prohibiting adults-only rental policies. Wend then announced a new policy under which it would rent to households with minor children. Although the complex that is the subject of this suit is not located in the city of Los Angeles, Wend has a complex in the city and stated that it wanted to maintain a uniform policy for all its complexes.

The voluntary cessation of allegedly illegal conduct does not ordinarily make a case moot. County of Los Angeles v. Davis, 440 U.S. 625, 631 99 S. Ct. 1379, 1383, 59 L. Ed. 2d 642 (1979); United States v. Concentrated Phosphate Export Assn., 393 U.S. 199, 203, 89 S. Ct. 361, 364, 21 L. Ed. 2d 344 (1968); T.R.W. Inc. v. FTC, 647 F.2d 942, 953 (9th Cir. 1981). Such circumstances may make a case moot, however, if it is absolutely clear that: (1) there is no reasonable expectation that the alleged violation will recur; and (2) interim relief or events have completely eradicated the effects of the violation. County of Los Angeles, 440 U.S. at 631,

---

1. Halet's claims of racial discrimination are based on the greater effect that an adults-only policy has on Blacks and Hispanics because more of those households include minor children.

99 S. Ct. at 1383; Lodge 1380, Brotherhood of Railway Clerks, etc. v. Dennis, 625 F.2d 819, 822 (9th Cir. 1980). The defendant bears a heavy burden to demonstrate mootness. *County of Los Angeles,* 440 U.S. at 631, 99 S. Ct. at 1383; *Concentrated Phosphate,* 393 U.S. at 203, 89 S. Ct. at 364; *TRW, Inc.,* 647 F.2d at 953. But see Halvonik v. Reagan, 457 F.2d 311, 313 (9th Cir. 1972). A promise to refrain from future violations likewise is not sufficient to establish mootness. United States v. W. T. Grant Co., 345 U.S. 629, 633, 73 S. Ct. 894, 897, 97 L. Ed. 1303 (1953). In *Grant,* the government sued three corporations and an individual who was director of all three for violations of the Clayton Act. The individual resigned and the companies told the Court that they had no intention to revive the interlocks. The Court held, however, that because the companies were free to return to their old ways and because of the public interest in having the legality of the practice settled, the case was not moot. 345 U.S. at 632, 73 S. Ct. at 897. Further, it held that the defendants' representations of intent were not sufficient to moot the case.

Similarly, in *Concentrated Phosphate* a new regulation made it uneconomical for the defendants to continue their alleged violations for which they had formed an association. They disbanded and said they would not engage in future joint operations. The Court held that such a statement standing alone "cannot suffice to satisfy the heavy burden of persuasion" resting on those claiming mootness. *Concentrated Phosphate,* 393 U.S. at 203, 89 S. Ct. at 364.

This court cannot rely on Wend's statement alone. Wend could revert to an adults-only policy in the future, and Wend has not demonstrated that there is no reasonable expectation of such an occurrence. Moreover, it is not clear that Wend's new policy has completely eradicated the effect of Wend's adults-only policy. Accordingly, Wend has not demonstrated that the case is moot.

II. Standing

The County asserts that Halet, who is white, does not have standing to challenge racial discrimination against Blacks and Hispanics. The district court did not dismiss any claims on this basis, but this court can affirm the dismissal on any ground fairly presented in the record. Shipley v. United States, 608 F.2d 770, 773-74 (9th Cir. 1979).

The standing requirements of Article III are only that the party be injured by the challenged conduct. However, the Supreme Court has further limited standing, as a prudential matter, requiring that a party assert its own rights and interests not those of third parties. Duke Power Co. v. Carolina Environmental Study Group, 438 U.S. 59, 80, 98 S. Ct. 2620, 2634, 57 L. Ed. 2d 595 (1978); Warth v. Seldin, 422 U.S. 490, 499,

95 S. Ct. 2197, 2205, 45 L. Ed. 2d 343 (1974). The Court has waived this standing requirement in some discrimination cases where it appears that a white person is the only effective adversary. Sullivan v. Little Hunting Park, 396 U.S. 299, 90 S. Ct. 400, 24 L. Ed. 2d 386 (1969); Barrows v. Jackson, 346 U.S. 249, 73 S. Ct. 1031, 97 L. Ed. 1586 (1952). Here, however, Halet is not the only effective adversary; he is in no better position to bring this action than a black person denied an apartment because of minor children.

Thus, Halet does not have standing to assert his racial discrimination claims under the fourteenth amendment, or under §§1981, 1982, 1983 and 2000d. The dismissal of Halet's claims under §§1981, 1982 and 2000d is therefore not erroneous because §§1981 and 1982 are limited to the protection against racial discrimination. See Patterson v. American Tobacco Co., 535 F.2d 257, 270 (4th Cir.), *cert. denied*, 429 U.S. 920, 97 S. Ct. 314, 50 L. Ed. 2d 286 (1976) (§1981). Also §2000d is limited by its terms to types of discrimination not present in this case.[2]

Halet does, however, have standing to raise a racial discrimination claim under the Fair Housing Act. Congress expanded standing under that Act to the full extent of Article III. The Supreme Court, in Gladstone Realtors v. Village of Bellwood, 441 U.S. 91, 99-100, 103 n.9, 99 S. Ct. 1601, 1607-08, 1609-10 n.9 (1979), held that a plaintiff who has suffered an actual injury is permitted to prove that the rights of another are infringed.[3] Here, Halet claims that he was denied an apartment because of a policy that allegedly infringes on the rights of Blacks and Hispanics. Under *Gladstone* this is sufficient to support Halet's standing under the Act.

III. Failure to State a Claim

Although Halet lacked standing to raise racial discrimination claims under §1983 and the fourteenth amendment, he clearly has standing to

2. These claims are not saved by the fact that Halet filed a class action. Prior to class certification, the named plaintiffs must have standing to raise race discrimination claims before they can assert them on behalf of a class. O'Shea v. Littleton, 414 U.S. 488, 494, 94 S. Ct. 669, 675, 38 L. Ed. 2d 674 (1974); see East Texas Motor Freight v. Rodriguez, 431 U.S. 395, 403-06, 97 S. Ct. 1891, 1896-98, 52 L. Ed. 2d 453 (1977). This is true even if they have standing on other claims. Payne v. Travenol Laboratories, Inc., 565 F.2d 895, 898 (5th Cir.), *cert. denied*, 439 U.S. 835, 99 S. Ct. 118, 58 L. Ed. 2d 131 (1978). Cf. Harris v. White, 479 F. Supp. 996, 1009 (D. Mass. 1979) (if named plaintiff has standing to raise one substantial claim, he may seek class-wide relief on claims on which he has no standing).

3. This extended to suits brought under 42 U.S.C. §3612, such as this one, the standing rule the Court had previously held applicable to suits brought under 42 U.S.C. §3610, in Trafficante v. Metropolitan Life Ins. Co., 409 U.S. 205, 93 S. Ct. 364, 34 L. Ed. 2d 415 (1972). *Gladstone*, 441 U.S. at 96-97, 99 S. Ct. at 1606-07.

challenge the adults-only policy under §1983 and the fourteenth amendment on the grounds that it violates his right to raise a family and discriminates against families with children. We must now proceed to consider whether the district court's dismissal of Wend for failure to state a claim, and its dismissal of Los Angeles County on the grounds that the complaint was insufficient to show state action and that there was no invidious discrimination, were correct.

A dismissal for failure to state a claim upon which relief can be granted is a ruling on a question of law and as such is freely reviewable by this court. Alonzo v. ACF Property Management, Inc., 643 F. 2d 578, 579 (9th Cir. 1981). Such a dismissal cannot be upheld unless it appears to a certainty that the plaintiff would be entitled to no relief under any state of facts that could be proved. Beneficial Life Insurance Co. v. Knobelauch, 653 F.2d 393, 395 (9th Cir. 1981). On a motion to dismiss, the court presumes that the facts alleged by the plaintiff are true. California Motor Transport Co. v. Trucking Unlimited, 404 U.S. 508, 515, 92 S. Ct. 609, 614, 30 L. Ed. 2d 642 (1972); Ernest W. Hahn, Inc. v. Codding, 615 F. 2d 830, 834 (9th Cir. 1980).

A. FAMILY RIGHTS

"Freedom of personal choice in matters of marriage and family life is one of the liberties protected by the Due Process Clause of the Fourteenth Amendment." Moore v. City of East Cleveland, 431 U.S. 494, 499, 97 S. Ct. 1932, 1935, 52 L. Ed. 2d 531 (1977) (quoting Cleveland Board of Education v. Lafleur, 414 U.S. 632, 639-640, 94 S. Ct. 791, 796, 39 L. Ed. 2d 52 (1974)). Halet contends that the adults-only policy infringed this due process right and discriminated against families with children in violation of the equal protection clause.

1. State Action

To maintain an action under the fourteenth amendment or §1983, Halet must show state involvement. The under-color-of-state-law requirement of §1983 is equivalent to the state action requirement of the fourteenth amendment. Arnold v. IBM Corp., 637 F. 2d 1350, 1355 n.2 (9th Cir. 1981).

Halet's complaint alleged that the County leased the land to Wend. In Halet's opposition to the motion to dismiss he offered to amend his complaint to allege additional facts regarding state action. He again offered to amend his complaint at the hearing of the motion to dismiss. Nevertheless, the complaint was dismissed without leave to amend.[4]

---

4. Wend contends that the dismissal constituted summary judgment. It is, however, apparent from the district court's orders that its dismissal for failure to state a claim was not a summary judgment.

A denial of leave to amend is within the discretion of the district court and will be reversed if the district court abused its discretion. Waits v. Weller, 653 F. 2d 1288, 1290 (9th Cir. 1981). The facts regarding state action provided by Halet in his opposition to the motion to dismiss in the district court and in his brief in this court, if true, establish state action. The district court abused its discretion in dismissing without leave to amend,[5] see Scott v. Eversole Mortuary, 522 F. 2d 1110, 1116 (9th Cir. 1975), and a dismissal for lack of state action in light of these facts is erroneous.

In his opposition and in his brief, Halet alleges that: (1) the County owns the land leased to Wend for the apartment complex; (2) the County acquired and prepared the land using federal and state funds and used federal services in dredging the harbor in the redevelopment area; (3) the purchase of land was part of a large redevelopment program; (4) the County leased the land to Wend for the benefit of the public in providing housing; (5) the lease prohibits race or religious discrimination; (6) the County oversees the development of the area and the design of the buildings and had final approval of all plans; (7) the County controls the use and purpose of the apartment and the rent charged; (8) Wend pays a percentage of the rentals to the County; and (9) Wend must abide by all the conditions of the lease.

These allegations, if proved, would place the County in a position of interdependence such that it is a joint participant with Wend. See Burton v. Wilmington Parking Authority, 365 U.S. 715, 81 S. Ct. 856, 6 L. Ed. 2d 45 (1961) (city leased space in garage to restaurant, costs of acquisition and construction defrayed by city, benefit to city of proceeds in exchange for tax benefit to restaurant, city could have required nondiscrimination); Geneva Towers Tenants Organization v. Federal Mortgage Investors, 504 F. 2d 483 (9th Cir. 1974); Male v. Crossroads Assn., 469 F. 2d 616 (2d Cir. 1972); Smith v. Holiday Inns of America, 336 F. 2d 630 (6th Cir. 1964). Thus, there are sufficient allegations of state action to require reversal of the district court's dismissal of the County as a defendant and to permit Halet's claims under the fourteenth amendment.

2. Infringement of Rights

The district court also explained its dismissal of the County saying that children are not an "insular minority," see United States v. Carolene Products Co., 304 U.S. 144, 152-53 n.4, 58 S. Ct. 778, 783-84 n.4, 82 L. Ed. 1234 (1938), and that the policy therefore withstood the lesser de-

---

5. Further, because neither Wend nor the County had filed a responsive pleading, Halet had the right to amend his complaint as a matter of course. Nolen v. Fitzharris, 450 F.2d 958, 958-59 (9th Cir. 1971).

gree of scrutiny required in equal protection claims when no suspect class is involved. Strict scrutiny is required, however, when the classification impermissibly interferes with the exercise of a fundamental right or operates to the peculiar disadvantage of a suspect class. Tsosie v. Califano, 630 F. 2d 1328, 1337 (9th Cir. 1980) (quoting Massachusetts Board of Retirement v. Murgia, 427 U.S. 307, 312 96 S. Ct. 2562, 49 L. Ed. 2d 520 (1976)), *cert. denied,* 451 U.S. 940, 101 S. Ct. 2022, 68 L. Ed. 2d 328 (1981). A fundamental right may also require strict scrutiny under the due process clause. See Moore v. City of East Cleveland, 431 U.S. 494, 498-99, 97 S. Ct. 1932, 1935, 52 L. Ed. 2d 531 (1976) (plurality opinion); Roe v. Wade, 410 U.S. 113, 155, 93 S. Ct. 705, 728, 35 L. Ed. 2d 137 (1973).

Family life, in particular the right of family members to live together, is part of the fundamental right of privacy. *Moore,* 431 U.S. at 498-99, 97 S. Ct. 1932, 1935, 52 L. Ed. 2d 531 (plurality opinion) *cited with approval in Zablocki v. Redhail,* 434 U.S. 375 at 385, 98 S. Ct. 673 at 680, 54 L. Ed. 2d 618. The plurality opinion in *Moore* stated that "when the government intrudes on choices concerning family living arrangements, this court must examine carefully the importance of the governmental interests advanced and the extent to which they are served by the challenged regulation." *Moore,* 431 U.S. at 499, 97 S. Ct. at 1935. The ordinance in *Moore* prohibited a household from including certain extended family members. The policy in this case prohibits a household from including immediate family members—that is children. A fundamental right is even more clearly involved here because the rental policy infringes the choice of parents to live with their children rather than the choice of more distant relations. *Moore,* 431 U.S. at 500, 97 S. Ct. at 1936 (plurality opinion), 431 U.S. at 536, 97 S. Ct. at 1954 (Stewart dissenting); Stanley v. Illinois, 405 U.S. 645, 92 S. Ct. 1208, 31. L. Ed. 2d 551 (1972). A fundamental right to be free from state intrusion in decisions concerning family relationships in the nuclear family has been clearly recognized. Prince v. Massachusetts, 321 U.S. 158, 166, 64 S. Ct. 438, 442, 88 L. Ed. 145 (1944), *cited in Zablocki,* 434 U.S. at 384-86, 98 S. Ct. at 679-81; *Stanley,* 405 U.S. at 651, 92 S. Ct. at 1212.

Not every state action that infringes upon a fundamental right triggers strict scrutiny. See *Tsosie,* 630 F.2d at 1337; Socialist Workers Party v. March Fong Eu, 591 F.2d 1252, 1260 (9th Cir. 1978), *cert. denied,* 441 U.S. 946, 99 S. Ct. 2167, 60 L. Ed. 2d 1049 (1979). Because the state action in this case infringes upon a fundamental right, we must reverse the district court's dismissal of Halet's due process and equal protection claims to enable it to consider whether, under the recently-decided Hawaii Boating Ass'n v. Water Transportation Facilities Division, 651 F.2d 661 (9th Cir. 1981), a "genuinely significant deprivation" of a fundamental right has occurred. Id. at 664-65. If such a deprivation has occurred, then the court must determine whether the adults-only policy can survive strict scrutiny.

B   FAIR HOUSING ACT

Significant discriminatory effects flowing from rental decisions may be sufficient to demonstrate a violation of the Fair Housing Act. See United States v. Mitchell, 580 F.2d 789, 791 (5th Cir. 1978); Resident Advisory Board v. Rizzo, 564 F.2d 126, 146-48 (3d Cir. 1977); Metropolitan Housing Development Co. v. Village of Arlington Heights, 558 F.2d 1283, 1289-90 (7th Cir. 1977) (on remand); Smith v. Anchor Building Corp., 536 F.2d 231, 233 (8th Cir. 1976). As these cases show, the circuits have applied different standards in determining how important a discriminatory effect is in proving a Fair Housing Act violation. We prefer to address the issue of which standard should apply when it is presented in the context of a fully-developed record.

The documents attached to the complaint seem to show some possibility of discriminatory effect.[6] Halet has made sufficient allegations to state a cause of action under the Act.

Conclusion

We affirm the dismissal of Halet's claim of race discrimination under the fourteenth amendment, 42 U.S.C. §§1981, 1982, 1983, and 2000d. We reverse and remand Halet's claim under the fourteenth amendment and 42 U.S.C. §1983 of a denial of his right to live together with immediate family members, and his race discrimination claim under 42 U.S.C. §3604. Because the case is remanded, the issue of attorney's fees for Halet's district court work is premature. The parties shall bear their own costs on this appeal.

KEEP, District Judge, concurs in the result.

---

6. Halet provided a table showing the percentage of Blacks, Hispanics, whites, female-headed households with children. For example, the table shows, that in Los Angeles, 38 percent of white households, 62 percent of black households, and 69 percent of Hispanic households have children.

Part 7

The Modern Land Transaction

Chapter Twenty-five

The Contract for the Sale of Land (Herein the Law of Vendor and Purchaser)

Insert the following material on page 700 at the end of the first full paragraph.

The following discussion relates to the last sentence in the first full paragraph on page 700. It is a portion of a letter received from the National Association of Realtors.

A former member of the National Association who is now a first year law student in Virginia has called to our attention a statement contained in the third Edition of your book Cases and Text on Property on page 700 that:

> Real estate boards—which are broker's organizations—fix standard rates for particular localities, and these are generally accepted as criteria of reasonable compensation.

Up until 1970, this statement may well have been accurate. But in 1971 the NATIONAL ASSOCIATION OF REALTORS categorically prohibited boards of REALTORS across the country from adopting *any* type of commission schedule, regardless of whether the rates set forth on such a schedule were mandatory or merely recommended. Of course, in 1975 the United States Supreme Court in Goldfarb v. Virginia State Bar Association held that fee schedules, whether recommended or mandatory, published by professional associations were per se illegal under Section 1 of the Sherman Act.

Indeed, during the late 1970s and early 1980s there has been a significant amount of litigation brought by the United States Department of Justice and private litigants contending that real estate brokers were continuing to establish their rates of compensation by reference to board published commission schedules.

As part of a comprehensive antitrust compliance program, the NA-

TIONAL ASSOCIATION OF REALTORS has attempted since 1971 to insure that any and all vestiges of fee schedules are eliminated from the bylaws or other governing documents of local boards of REALTORS. We firmly believe that we have been successful in this regard.

Insert the following material at the end of page 705.

Note

See Bennett v. McCabe, 808 F.2d 178 (1st Cir. 1987), in which the Federal Court undertook to interpret Massachusetts law as developed in the Tristram's Landing case in regard to when the broker's commission is earned. In the *Bennett* case a binding contract had been entered into but the deal finally fell through because of a late discovered defect in the title, which the seller could not clear up. The First Circuit in the Bennett case held that the broker's commission had to be paid.

Insert the following material on page 706 before the Sample Contract for the sale of land.

Note

The negotiations between the seller and buyer of land that will determine the detailed terms of contract for the sale of land may take some time. It may be desirable to have some kind of a binder executed before undertaking the work involved in preparing a contract for the sale of land. Set out below, on pp. 156-157, is an example of such a binder prepared by the Massachusetts Conveyancer's Association, which is reproduced here with permission.

Insert the following material as an addition to note 30 on page 727.

See Johnson v. United States, 82-2 U.S.T.C. ¶9643 (8th Cir. 1986), which took the position that the vendor under a contract of sale of real property retained legal title after the vendee forfeited his rights under the contract. Consequently, the cancellation of the contract extinguished perfected tax liens placed on the property to satisfy the vendee's tax liability. The forfeiture did not constitute a non-judicial sale and the Internal Revenue Service was not entitled to a notice of cancellation.

MCA FORM NO. 9

OFFER TO PURCHASE REAL ESTATE

TO: _____

Date: _____

_____

(Seller)

Re: The property at _____,

_____ (the "Premises")

(For title, see: _____)

We hereby offer to buy the Premises which have been offered to me by your broker, _____, as your agent, subject to the following terms and conditions:

1. We will pay for the Premises $ _____, of which

   (a) $ _____ is paid herewith as a deposit to validate this Offer;

   (b) $ _____ is to be paid as an additional deposit upon the execution of the Purchase and Sale Agreement provided for below; and

   (c) $ _____ is to be paid at the time of delivery of the Deed.

2. This Offer is good until _____ A.M./P.M. on _____, 19 _____, at or before which time a copy of this Offer must be signed by you and returned to us or this Offer shall be void and the money paid with this Offer shall be returned to us immediately.

3. The Closing shall take place at _____ A.M./P.M. on _____, 19 _____, at the appropriate Registry of Deeds.

4. If this Offer is accepted by you, then our obligation to buy the Premises is subject to and conditioned upon:

   (a) Obtaining, on or before _____ days from your acceptance of this Offer, an inspection of the Premises satisfactory to us; and

   (b) Execution by you and us, on or before _____ 7 days from your acceptance of this Offer, of a mutually satisfactory Purchase and Sale Agreement setting forth all of the terms and conditions of this transaction, which shall then become the agreement of the parties; and

   (c) Our obtaining, on or before _____ 30 days from the execution of the Purchase and Sale Agreement, a satisfactory commitment letter from an institutional lender for a first mortgage loan not in excess of $ _____ at prevailing rates and terms.

   If the above conditions are not satisfied after the acceptance of this Offer, this agreement shall terminate, you shall refund our deposit, and neither party shall have further recourse against each other.

5. If we do not fulfill our obligations under this Offer after it has been accepted by you, the deposit shall immediately become your property without further liability by us to you.

6. Time is of the essence of this Offer.

7. The riders, if any, attached hereto are incorporated by reference.
FOR RESIDENTIAL PROPERTY CONSTRUCTED PRIOR TO 1978, ATTACH LEAD PAINT RIDER.

8. When, as and if the deed is delivered and recorded and the purchase price is paid, you, the Seller, shall pay a brokerage commission of
$_____ to _____.

NOTICE: This is a legal document. Consult an attorney. Upon acceptance by the Seller, it constitutes a binding agreement on both parties. Both parties acknowledge that they have been offered the opportunity to seek and confer with legal counsel of their choice prior to signing this agreement.

_____ _____
Buyer (or spouse)   Buyer
Address of Buyer:

ACCEPTANCE

This Offer is hereby accepted upon the foregoing terms and conditions and the receipt of the deposit of $_____ is hereby acknowledged.

_____ _____
Seller (or spouse)   Seller
Address of Seller:

RECEIPT FOR DEPOSIT

_____, 19____

Received from Buyer the sum of $_____ as a deposit under the terms of the above Offer. In the event of any disagreement between the parties, the Broker may retain the deposit pending instructions mutually given by the Seller and the Buyer.

_____
Broker

11/28/88

MASSACHUSETTS CONVEYANCERS ASSOCIATION

Copyright © 1987
Massachusetts Conveyancers Association

157

Insert the following material before Note in page 737.

Case concerning effect on real estate transaction of non-disclosure by vendor of structural defect in real estate.

LAYMAN v. BINNS

Supreme Court of Ohio, 1988
35 Ohio St. 3d 176, 519 N.E.2d 642

HERBERT R. BROWN, Justice.

The determinative issue raised on appeal is whether recovery is barred by application of the doctrine of caveat emptor (let the buyer beware). We find that it is for the reasons set forth below.

The doctrine of caveat emptor, although virtually abolished in the area of personal property, remains a viable rule of law in real estate sales. 7 Williston, Contracts (Jaeger 3 Ed. 1963) 779, Section 926; Friedman, Contracts and Conveyances of Real Property (4 Ed. 1984) 37, Section 1.2(n); Kafker, Sell and Tell: The Fall and Revival of The Rule on Nondisclosure in Sales of Used Real Property (1986), 12 U. Dayton L. Rev. 57, 58-63.

In Traverse v. Long (1956) 165 Ohio St. 249, 252, 59 O. O. 325, 326-327, 135 N.E.2d 256, 259, this court articulated the rule as follows:

> The principle of caveat emptor applies to sales of real estate relative to conditions open to observation. Where those conditions are discoverable and the purchaser has the opportunity for investigation and determination without concealment or hindrance by the vendor, the purchaser has no just cause for complaint even though there are misstatements and misrepresentations by the vendor not so reprehensible in nature as to constitute fraud. . . ." (Citations omitted.)

The doctrine of caveat emptor is one of long standing. Since problems of varying degree are to be found in most dwellings and buildings, the doctrine performs a function in the real estate marketplace. Without the doctrine nearly every sale would invite litigation instituted by a disappointed buyer. Accordingly, we are not disposed to abolish the doctrine of caveat emptor. A seller of reality is not obligated to reveal all that he or she knows. A duty falls upon the purchaser to make inquiry and examination.

To make the doctrine operate fairly, courts have established certain conditions upon the rule's application. We summarize and adopt these conditions as follows: (1) the defect must be open to observation or discoverable on reasonable inspection, (2) the purchaser must have an unimpeded opportunity to examine the property and (3) the vendor may not engage in fraud. We measure the case before us against these requirements.

I

The defect here was open to observation. Mr. Layman (one of the purchasers) saw the steel bracing that supported the defective wall. The Laymans contend that Mr. Layman was not an expert and should not be held to have knowledge of the defect simply because he saw a symptom of it. If the issue were the cause of the defect or the remedial effectiveness of the beams, we might agree. However, the test is whether the defect was open to observation. Here, witnesses who viewed the basement detected the bow and steel beams with little effort. The defect was described as obvious and highly visible. The basement wall was bulging.

II

The purchasers had an unhindered opportunity to examine the basement. Mr. Layman saw the steel beams, yet failed to inspect the wall in detail or to ask about the purpose of the beams. The purchasers had a duty to inspect and inquire about the premises in a prudent, diligent manner. See Traverse v. Long, *supra*, at 252, 59 O.O. at 326-327, 135 N.E.2d at 259; Foust v. Valleybrook Realty Co. (1981), 4 Ohio App. 3d 164, 4 OBR 264, 446 N.E.2d 1122.

III

This brings us to the final, and pivotal, question. On the facts in this case, did the vendors engage in fraud?

The purchasers admit that no active misrepresentation or misstatement of material fact was made. However, they argue that failure to disclose the bow in the wall constituted fraudulent concealment.

An action for fraud may be grounded upon failure to fully disclose facts of a material nature where there exists a duty to speak. 37 American Jurisprudence 2d (1968) 196-201, Fraud and Deceit, Sections 144 and 145. This court has held that a vendor has a duty to disclose material facts which are latent, not readily observable or discoverable through a purchaser's reasonable inspection. Miles v. McSwegin (1979), 58 Ohio St. 2d 97, 12 O. O.3d 108, 388 N.E.2d 1367. See also Hadley v. Clinton Cty. Importing Co. (1862), 13 Ohio St. 502, 506; Klott v. Associates Real Estate (1974), 41 Ohio App. 2d 118, 121-122, 70 O. O.2d 129,

131-132, 322 N.E.2d 690, 692-693. Other jurisdictions adhere to a similar rule.[1]

The non-disclosure in this case does not rise to the level of fraud for the reason that the defect here was not latent. It could have been detected by inspection. Thus, the purchasers must show an affirmative misrepresentation or a misstatement of a material fact in order to demonstrate fraud and thereby preclude application of the doctrine of caveat emptor. This, they failed to do.

IV

We hold that the doctrine of caveat emptor precludes recovery in an action by the purchaser for a structural defect in real estate where (1) the condition complained of is open to observation or discoverable upon reasonable inspection, (2) the purchaser had the full and unimpeded opportunity to examine the premises, and (3) there is no evidence of fraud on the part of the vendor. The judgment of the court of appeals is reversed and final judgment is hereby entered in favor of appellants.

Judgment reversed.

MOYER, C.J., and SWEENEY HOLMES, DOUGLAS and WRIGHT, JJ., concur.

LOCHER, J., concurs in part and dissents in part.

LOCHER, Justice, concurring in part and dissenting in part.

Although I have no quarrel with the law expressed in the syllabus, I cannot concur in its application by the majority to the facts of this case.

In my view, the trial court properly found that the structural defect in the basement wall was not readily apparent upon reasonable inspection by persons inexperienced in such matters, like the Laymans. The observability or discoverability of such a defect is a factual issue best resolved by the trier of fact, who has firsthand exposure to the evidence and can observe the demeanor of the witnesses. This is especially true where

1. See *e.g.*, Lingsch v. Savage (1963), 213 Cal. App. 2d 729, 29 Cal. Rptr. 201; Cohen v. Vivian (1960), 141 Colo. 443, 349 P.2d 366; Wedig v. Brinster (1983), 1 Conn. App. 123, 469 A.2d 783, *cert. denied* (1984), 192 Conn. 803, 472 A.2d 1284; Lock v. Schreppler (Del. Super.1981), 426 A.2d 856; Johnson v. Davis (Fla. 1985), 480 So.2d 625; Wilhite v. Mays (1976), 140 Ga. App. 816, 232 S.E.2d 141, *affirmed* (1977), 239 Ga. 31, 235 S.E.2d 532; Bursey v. Clement (1978), 118 N.H. 412, 387 A.2d 346; Posner v. Davis (1979), 76 Ill. App.3d 638, 32 Ill. Dec. 186, 395 N.E.2d 133; Loghry v. Capel (1965), 257 Iowa 285, 132 N.W.2d 417; Jenkins v. McCormick (1959), 184 Kan. 842, 339 P.2d 8; Kaze v. Compton (Ky. 1955), 283 S.W.2d 204; Maguire v. Masino (La. App. 1975), 325 So. 2d 844; Williams v. Benson (1966), 3 Mich. App. 9, 141 N.W.2d 650; Weintraub v. Krobatsch (1974), 64 N.J. 445, 317 A.2d 68; Taylor v. Heisinger (1963), 39 Misc. 2d 955, 242 N.Y.S.2d 281; Brooks v. Ervin Constr. Co. (1960), 253 N.C. 214, 116 S.E.2d 454; Holcomb v. Zinke (N.D. 1985), 365 N.W.2d 507; Lawson v. Citizens & So. Natl. Bank of S.C. (1972), 259 S.C. 477, 193 S.E.2d 124; Ware v. Scott (1979), 220 Va. 317, 257 S.E.2d 855; Obde v. Schlemeyer (1960), 56 Wash. 2d 449, 353 P.2d 672; Thacker v. Tyree (W. Va. 1982), 297 S.E.2d 885.

there is conflicting testimony, because the trier of fact is best able to evaluate the credibility of the testimony.

In the case sub judice, there was conflicting testimony as to the observability of the defect. On the one hand, there was testimony that the bow in the basement wall was very slight, varying from only one to three inches in depth. So inconspicuous was the defect that the Laymans' sales agent, Ramona Olding, did not notice it even though she showed the house twice.[2] Mr. Layman testified that he saw the steel bracing on the wall, but merely assumed that it was part of the structure of the house. On the other hand, there was testimony by expert witnesses in the areas of real estate construction, appraisal and sales to the effect that they thought the bow in the wall was obvious and plainly visible.

The trial court, after reviewing all the testimony and evidence, found that the defect was not observable upon reasonable inspections by purchasers such as the Laymans. The majority, however, fails to give due deference to the trial court's findings, choosing instead to reweigh the evidence and come to its own conclusion. In doing so, the majority usurps the role of the trial court. I would uphold the trial court's judgment as being supported by some competent, credible evidence. See, e.g., C. E. Morris Co. v. Foley Constr. Co. (1978), 54 Ohio St. 2d 279, 8 O. O.3d 261, 376 N.E.2d 578, syllabus.

Furthermore, the majority's analysis applies an unreasonably high standard for the purpose of determining whether the Laymans should have observed or discovered the defective wall. In concluding that the defect was open to observation, the majority states that "witnesses who viewed the basement detected the bow and steel beams with little effort." These witnesses were persons with experience in the construction, appraisal and sales of homes. However, the standard by which purchasers of real property should be measured in order to determine whether they should have observed or discovered a structural defect is that of "ordinarily prudent persons of their station and experience confronted with the same or similar circumstances." Traverse v. Long (1956), 165 Ohio St. 249, 252, 59 O.O. 325, 326, 135 N.E.2d 256, 259. See also Crum v. McCoy (1974), 41 Ohio Misc. 34, 38, 70 O.O.2d 76, 79, 322 N.E.2d 161, 164. Because the Laymans have little or no experience in the construction or buying of homes, it is simply unreasonable to compare them to persons with specialized knowledge in the fields of construction and real estate, as opposed to ordinarily prudent persons of like experience. Accordingly, I would affirm the trial court's judgment that persons of the

2. Mr. Binns informed his realtor of the defect and instructed him to tell the Laymans about the problem. However, the realtor failed to bring this information to the attention of either the Laymans or their agent, Ramona Olding.

Laymans' experience would not have discovered the defect upon reasonable inspection.

For these reasons, I respectfully dissent.

Insert the following material on page 737 to the note on implied warranty of habitability in a contract for the sale of land.

See Freyfogle, Real Estate Sales and the New Implied Warranty of Lawful Use, 71 Conn. L. Rev. 1 (1985). See also, Kennedy, The Effect of the Warranty of Habitability on Low Income Housing: "Milking" and Class Violence, 15 Fla. St. U. L. Rev. 485 (1987).

Insert the following material after note on page 737.

Note: Return Required in the Case of Real Estate Transactions

Section 6045(e) of the Internal Revenue Code provides as follows:

(e) Return Required in the Case of Real Estate Transactions.

(1) In General. — In the case of a real estate transaction, the real estate reporting person shall file a return under subsection (a) and a statement under subsection (b) with respect to such transaction.

(2) Real Estate Reporting Person. — For purposes of this subsection, the term "real estate reporting person" means any of the following persons involved in a real estate transaction in the following order:

   (A) the person (including any attorney or title company) responsible for closing the transaction,

   (B) the mortgage leader,

   (C) the seller's broker,

   (D) the buyer's broker,

   (E) such other person designated in regulations prescribed by the Secretary.

Any person treated as a real estate reporting person under the preceding sentence shall be treated as a broker for purposes of subsection (c)(1).

(3) Prohibition of Separate Charge for Filing Return. — It shall be unlawful for any real estate reporting person to separately charge any customer for complying with any requirement of paragraph (1).

(4) Whether Seller's Financing was Federally Subsidized. — In the case of a real estate transaction involving a residence, the real estate broker shall specify on the return under subsection (a) and the statement under subsection (b) whether or not the financing (if any) of the seller was federally-subsidized indebtedness (as defined in section 143(m)(3)).

Chapter Twenty-seven
The Deed

Insert the following material on page 780 before the problems.

Case involving resolution of conflict in deeds' description of property conveyed.

BERNARD v. NANTUCKET BOYS' CLUB, INC.

Supreme Judicial Court of Massachusetts, 1984
391 Mass. 823, 465 N.E.2d 236

HENNESSEY, C.J. The plaintiff brought this action in the Land Court alleging that the defendant had fraudulently registered land owned by the plaintiff, and seeking imposition of a constructive trust and an order requiring a conveyance to him. The Land Court judge found that the plaintiff was not the owner of the land at the time it was registered by decree of the Land Court in January, 1976, and he dismissed the complaint. Thus the judge did not reach the issue of fraud in the registration process. The plaintiff appealed. The Appeals Court summarily affirmed. 15 Mass. App. Ct. 1107 (1983). We allowed the plaintiff's application for further appellate review. We affirm.

The case arises from a conflict in the description of the property conveyed by a deed from one Maude Adams to the defendant in 1957. It is agreed that the deed conveyed the lots designated B and C on an accompanying diagram (see Figure One); the subject of the dispute is the lot designated A. If the deed conveyed lot A, then the defendant owned it prior to the registration and the plaintiff's allegation of fraud in the registration process is of no consequence. If the deed did not convey lot A, then the plaintiff, as the sole beneficiary of the estate of Adams, owned it prior to the registration, and his allegation that the defendant fraudulently failed to notify him of the registration proceeding must be considered.

In 1955, Adams owned lots A, B, C, and 3. Lot 1 was owned by one

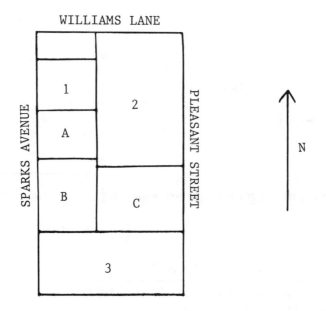

Figure One (Schematic Representation)

Potter, who had purchased it from Adams's father in the 1920's. Lot 2 was owned by one Manuel Morris. In September, 1955, Adams conveyed lot A to one John Walsh. Approximately one month later, Walsh reconveyed lot A to Adams, and Adams conveyed lot 3 to Walsh. According to his testimony, Walsh found lot A "to low" and so he decided to "trade up" to lot 3.

In 1957, Adams executed the deed in question. The deed grants to the defendant

> [t]he land in ... Nantucket bounded and described as follows: Easterly by Pleasant Street; Southerly by land of John B. Walsh et ux; Westerly by Sparks Avenue; Northerly by other land of grantor; Easterly by land of Manuel Morris; Northerly by land of said Morris. Said property being entirely enclosed by fences. For my title see Estates of Marcia A. Adams and Edgar Adams probated in Nantucket Probate Court.

In 1965, lot 2 was acquired by the defendant. Adams died in 1972, leaving her entire estate to the plaintiff. In 1974, the defendant registered a tract of land comprising lots A, B, C, and 2.

The Land Court found, and an enlarged aerial photograph taken ten days before Adams's conveyance to the defendant clearly shows, that there was a fence around lots A, B, and C, but no fence between lots A and B at the time of the conveyance. Thus there is a conflict in the

description of the property conveyed.[1] If Adams intended to convey lot
A, then she must have mistakenly thought that she owned lot 1, else the
call, "Northerly by other land of grantor," would be meaningless. If she
did not intend to convey lot A, then she was mistaken as to the existence
of a fence between lots A and B.

The plaintiff contends that the title reference resolves the conflict
because, while the estates of Marcia and Edgar Adams were the source of
Maude Adams's title to lots B and C, they were not, because of the
conveyance to and reconveyance from Walsh, the source of her title to
lot A. But, although not the immediate source of her title, the Adams
estates were the original source of her title. Thus the title reference,
being itself ambiguous, does not help to clarify the grantor's intent. Cf.
Sawyer v. Kendall, 10 Cush. 241, 246 (1852).

The parties' subsequent conduct does not indicate clearly that they
construed the deed one way or other. There was evidence that Adams
was assessed for, and thus presumably paid, real estate taxes on lot A
through 1957, and then again from 1965 until her death. (Apparently,
for some unexplained reason, no one was assessed for the property from
1958 through 1964.) Payment of taxes evidences a claim of ownership.
Blanchard v. Lowell, 177 Mass. 501, 505-506 (1901). Elwell v. Hinckley,
138 Mass. 225, 227 (1885). See Amee v. Boston & Albany R.R., 212 Mass.
421, 424 (1912). In addition, Adams's attorney and conservator, Wayne
Holmes, testified that he drew a will, on Adams's instructions, which,
because of her death, was never executed, and which left her "Sparks
Avenue property" to the defendant.[2] However, Mr. Holmes also testified
that Adams told him that "she had nothing left on Sparks Avenue, that
the property had gone to the Boys Club." There was evidence that the
defendant's board of directors considered purchasing lot A in 1973, but
there was also evidence that the defendant's executive director considered lot A to be the defendant's property in 1965. Finally, there was
evidence that lot A was used and graded by the defendant in the early
1960's, without objection by Adams, who lived nearby. See Dow v. Dow,
243 Mass. 587, 593 (1923). The Land Court judge made no findings on
the parties' subsequent construction of the deed. We think the evidence

---

1. As Figure One shows, lot B is bounded easterly by lot 2 for a very short distance.
Thus the call, "Easterly by land of Manuel Morris," is correct whether or not lot A was
intended to be conveyed.

2. This testimony was the subject of a motion to correct the transcript. At the hearing
on the motion, Mr. Holmes testified that his testimony at the trial was that by the terms of
the unexecuted will Adams left the remainder of her estate to the defendant without any
reference to "Sparks Avenue property." The Land Court judge declined to rule on the
motion because, in the view he took of the case, it makes no difference. The same is true for
us.

construction of the deed. We think the evidence is too equivocal to permit a conclusion that the parties to the deed shared a common interpretation one way or the other.

In the absence of any satisfactory evidence of the actual intent of the parties to the deed, we must look to rules of construction. The Land Court judge adopted a rule of the Massachusetts Conveyancers' Association that provides: "When a deed contains two inconsistent descriptions of a parcel of land, the more specific will govern." M. E. Park & D. D. Park, Real Estate Law, §241 at 313-314 (1981). He concluded that the reference to the property "being entirely enclosed by fences" is more specific than the call, "Northerly by other land of grantor." We disagree. Neither description is more specific than the other. Even if it is assumed that we would adopt the rule of preference for specificity, it has no applicability to this case.

The plaintiff urges that we adopt a rule of construction preferring natural monuments, including boundaries of other property, over artificial monuments, such as fences. See United States v. Gallas, 269 F. Supp. 141 (D. Md. 1967). Such a rule has the advantage of encouraging reliance on relatively permanent monuments and discouraging references to monuments likely to disappear. In the instant case, however, the rule might well contravene the parties' intent. In the absence of any evidence that she either viewed the property or reviewed her property holdings generally at the time she made the deed, we cannot say whether Adams was more likely mistaken as to the existence of the fence or as to her ownership of lot 1. It seems likely, however, that the defendant, the officers of which presumably viewed the property, would more readily rely on a physically observable fence than on the state of the title to an adjacent lot. See Wheeler v. Randall, 6 Met. 529, 535 (1843).

We prefer to resolve the case by applying a long-established rule of construction which, although not cited by the parties, is entirely dispositive of the controversy. "It is a rule in the construction of deeds, that the language, being the language of the grantor, is to be construed most strongly against him." Thayer v. Payne, 2 Cush. 327, 331 (1848). "If, therefore, there be two descriptions of the land conveyed, which do not coincide, the grantee is entitled to hold by that which will be most beneficial to him." Melvin v. Proprietors of the Locks & Canals on Merrimack River, 5 Met. 15, 27 (1842). See, e.g., E. Whitehead, Inc. v. Gallo, 357 Mass. 215, 219 (1970); Fulgenitti v. Cariddi, 292 Mass. 321, 326 (1935); Moran v. Somes, 154 Mass. 200, 202-203 (1891); Morse v. Marshall, 13 Allen 288 (1866); Salisbury v. Andrews, 19 Pick. 250, 253 (1837); Adams v. Frothingham, 3 Mass. 352, 361 (1807). We assume that the defendant paid a valuable consideration for the conveyance. The deed recites consideration, and there was no evidence that the conveyance was a gift. On the contrary, the plaintiff stated several times in his testimony that the property was "sold" to the defendant. Thus we need not decide the difficult question whether a gratuitous conveyance should be construed against the grantor. Compare Cleaveland v. Norton, 6 Cush. 380, 383-384 (1850), with Eliot v. Thatcher, 2 Met. 44, 45 (1822), quoting Bacon's Abridgment, Grant, I. See also Lynnfield v. Peabody, 219 Mass. 322, 330 (1914).

Resolving the conflict in the deed in favor of the grantee, it is clear that the reference to the fence controls, and the defendant thus became the owner of lot A in 1957. Even if we assume all facts as alleged by the plaintiff as to the registration proceeding, they are without consequence and the complaint was correctly dismissed. We add that there are allegations here that the attorney who represented the defendant in the registration, who was an active member and leader of the Nantucket Boys' Club, and who also represented Adams's estate, was well aware of the doubtful state of the title to lot A. These allegations are argued in light of the fact that the attorney neither informed the Land Court of the plaintiff's claim nor notified the plaintiff of the pendency of the proceeding. Without deciding whether these allegations concerning the attorney's conduct are true, we comment that a petitioner for registration, and indeed his attorney who has personal knowledge, have a duty to disclose all adverse claims, however dubious. See Kozdras v. Land/Vest Properties, Inc., 382 Mass. 34 (1980). It is the province of the Land Court, not the petitioner, to determine which claims are meritorious.

Judgment affirmed.

Chapter Twenty-eight

Recording (Herein Bona Fide Purchaser of Real Property)

Insert the following material on page 814 before the problems.

IN RE WALKER

United States Bankruptcy Court (C.D. Cal. 1986)
67 Bankr. L. Rep. 811

I. INTRODUCTION

SAMUEL L. BUFFORD, Bankruptcy Judge.

The debtor Georgia B. Walker ("Walker") brings this adversary proceeding to set aside a foreclosure sale of real property, conducted in violation of the automatic stay, on the grounds that the purchaser failed to record his trustee's deed until after the debtor had recorded a notice of the bankruptcy filing. The Court holds that, under the California race-notice recording statute, the transfer of the property to the third party purchaser may be avoided by the debtor, because the debtor recorded her notice of the bankruptcy before the purchaser recorded his trustee's deed.

II. FACTS

In 1976 Walker gave a promissory note to California Mortgage Service ("California Mortgage") as security for a loan on her real property in Inglewood, California. Debtor also gave California Mortgage a deed of trust on the property, which named California Mortgage as beneficiary and as trustee, and which included a provision granting a power of sale to California Mortgage upon default. On November 30, 1984, Guardian Trust Deed Service ("Guardian"), the servicing agent for California

Mortgage, recorded a notice of default and election to sell[1] in the Los Angeles County recorder's office in consequence of default in payment on the note by Walker. After the passage of the three-month statutory period under California Civil Code §2924 (West 1974 & Supp. 1986), Guardian published (and presumably recorded) a notice of trustee's sale, which set the foreclosure sale on April 5, 1985.

On April 2, 1985, three days prior to the trustee's sale, the debtor filed this Chapter 13 bankruptcy case. She notified Guardian of the bankruptcy case filing, and Guardian postponed the trustee's sale. The sale was ultimately postponed nine times before it was actually conducted.[2]

The Court confirmed the debtor's Chapter 13 plan on June 17, 1985. The plan provided that the prepetition arrearages of $4,000 owing to California Mortgage would be paid over a period of 36 months.

After confirmation of the plan, Walker fell behind in her monthly mortgage payments. In consequence, California Mortgage brought a motion for relief from the automatic stay.[3] At the hearing on December

1. The California procedure for exercising a power of sale in a deed of trust is set forth in California Civil Code §§2924-2924h (West 1974 & Supp. 1986). The holder of the deed of trust must first record a notice of default in the county recorder's office, and give notice to the owner and other lienholders. The owner and junior lienholders have a right to cure by paying the amount of default up to five days before the date of sale. If the default is uncured after three months, the holder of the deed of trust may post and publish a notice of sale at least twenty days before the sale date. The notice of sale must be recorded at least fourteen days before the sale.

2. California Civil Code §2924g(c) (West 1974 & Supp. 1986) authorizes up to three postponements of a sale under a deed of trust on instruction of the beneficiary, and one additional postponement upon written request of the trustor (to obtain cash to pay the encumbrance or to bid at the sale). The only notice of any such postponement is an announcement at the time and place previously set for the sale. Any additional postponement requires a new notice of sale as prescribed by section 2924f (West 1974 & Supp. 1986).

Section 2924g(c)(2) provides that any postponement by operation of law or by order of court is not counted in the maximum number of postponements. The automatic stay of Bankruptcy Code §362(a) thus frequently results in many postponements, which may cover a period of years: Cases have come before the Court involving more than thirty postponements over a period of several years. If no additional notice of sale is required, the public sale contemplated by California Civil Code §§ 2924-2924h is converted into a private sale, where the mortgagee is normally the only bidder. Even the property owner normally does not know the date on which a final sale is set.

The propriety and constitutionality of this procedure appears dubious. Apparently the California legislature has left it to the bankruptcy courts to impose republication requirements in appropriate circumstances.

3. As to post-confirmation mortgage payments, the automatic stay normally terminates upon confirmation of a Chapter 13 plan. In re Dickey, 64 B.R. 3, 4 (Bankr. E.D. Va. 1985); In re Mason, 51 B.R. 548, 550 (D. Ore. 1984). This results from the vesting of all property of the estatee in the debtor upon confirmation, pursuant to Bankruptcy Code §1327(b), 11 U.S.C. §1327(b) (1979). However, paragraph X of Walker's plan provides: "Property of the

4, 1985, the debtor brought the post-petition payments current, and the parties stipulated to an order for adequate protection, which was entered on December 26, 1985. Upon further default, the order required a further motion for relief from stay, which could be brought on shortened notice pursuant to this Court's "ex parte" procedures,[4] before a foreclosure sale could be conducted. California Mortgage has not sought any such further relief from stay.

Notwithstanding the continuation of the automatic stay, Guardian conducted a foreclosure sale on behalf of California Mortgage on February 28, 1986.[5] Defendant Frank Dorman ("Dorman") purchased the property for $70,350 at the sale, but he failed to record the trustee's deed until March 24, 1986 (according to the admission of his counsel at oral argument). Although the parties dispute whether Dorman was a good faith purchaser, the Court assumes for the purpose of its ruling herein that the purchase was made in good faith.

Walker recorded a notice of the filing of the Chapter 13 case in the Los Angeles County recorder's office on March 13, 1986. Dorman recorded his trustee's deed eleven days thereafter. Walker continues in possession of the property, and has transmitted her monthly payments to her attorney, who holds them in his trust account pending this Court's ruling herein.

Walker filed this adversary proceeding against California Mortgage, Guardian and Dorman, seeking restoration of title and compensatory and punitive damages for violation of the automatic stay. California Mortgage has cross-claimed against Dorman to rescind the sale. Various other cross-claims have also been filed.

Both Walker and Dorman have brought motions for summary judgment, and have submitted declarations and deposition testimony in sup-

---

estate shall revest in the Debtor at such time as a discharge is granted or the case is dismissed." Thus the automatic stay remained in effect as to post-confirmation defaults in current payments to California Mortgage, and California Mortgage was required to obtain relief from stay before it was authorized to proceed with foreclosure. Ellis v. Parr (In re Ellis), 60 B.R. 432 (Bankr. 9th Cir.1985).

4. Where a debtor defaults under a prior adequate protection order that has been granted in a Chapter 13 case, the Court authorizes a creditor to bring a motion for relief from stay on its Wednesday afternoon calendar. The motion must be scheduled no later than 3:00 p.m. the prior Thursday, after which telephonic notice must be given immediately to the debtor (if possible) and his counsel of record (if any). Moving papers must be served and filed no later than noon on the Monday preceding the hearing.

5. California Mortgage also failed to republish its notice of the sale before conducting its foreclosure sale, even though republication is required before a sale pursuant to a deed of trust may take place (unless the Court orders otherwise). Ellis v. Parr (In re Ellis), 60 B.R. 432, 436 (Bankr. 9th Cir. 1985).

port thereof. Dorman's summary judgment motions are brought against both Walker and California Mortgage.

III. DISCUSSION

Section 549(a) of the Bankruptcy Code, 11 U.S.C. §549(a) (Supp. 1986), authorizes the avoidance of certain post-petition property transfers:

> Except as provided in subsection (b) or (c) of this section, the trustee, may avoid a transfer of property of the estate —
> (1) made after the commencement of the case; and
> (2) . . . (B) that is not authorized under this title or by the court.

Dorman contends that the transfer to him is not avoidable because he qualifies under section 549(c), 11 U.S.C. §549(c) (1979 & Supp. 1986), which provides in relevant part:

> The trustee may not avoid . . . a transfer of real property to a good faith purchaser without knowledge of the commencement of the case and for present fair equilvalent value unless a copy or notice of the petition is filed, where a transfer of such real property may be recorded to perfect such transfer, before such transfer is so perfected that a bona fide purchaser of such property, against whom applicable law permits such transfer to be perfected, could not acquire an interest that is superior to the interest of such good faith purchaser.

The recording requirement of section 549(c) was amended by Congress in 1984 in the Bankruptcy Amendments and Federal Judgeship Act ("BAFJA"). Prior to 1984, recording was required only in a county different from the county in which the bankruptcy case was filed. The purpose of this amendment was to permit a bona fide purchaser to obtain good title at a foreclosure sale, even if the sale is conducted in violation of an automatic stay, unless the filing of a bankruptcy case appears in the chain of the title of the property. Thus, under section 549(c) as amended, a bona fide purchaser without knowledge of the filing of a bankruptcy case may rely upon the title records.

Under section 549(c), a debtor can cut off the rights of a third party purchaser of property sold in violation of the automatic stay if, at the time that he records his notice of the filing of the bankruptcy, he could have conveyed the property to a good faith purchaser who could have obtained superior title to the actual purchaser at the foreclosure sale.

The California recording statute governs whether Dorman sufficiently perfected his interest in the property to prevent a good faith purchaser from acquiring a superior interest as of March 13, 1986, when Walker recorded her notice of the bankruptcy petition. The California recording statute is a "race-notice" type of recording statute. It provides:

Every conveyance of real property, other than a lease for a term not exceeding one year, is void as against any subsequent purchaser or mortgagee of the same property, or any part thereof, in good faith and for a valuable consideration, whose conveyance is first duly recorded. . . . California Civil Code §1214 (West 1982).

There are three[6] principal types of recording acts in the United States.[7] See, generally, J. Cribbett, Principles of the Law of Property 285 (1975); L. Simes, A Handbook for More Efficient Conveyancing 18-31 (1961); 4 American Law of Property §§7.4-17.36 (Casner ed. 1952); R. Patton & C. Patton, Patton on Land Titles 28-45 (2d ed. 1957) ("Patton").

Under a "race" statute the grantee who first records his deed prevails over all other conveyances from the same source of title.[8] The first party to record is protected even though he has notice of a prior unrecorded conveyance. Patton, *supra*, at 33.

A second type of recording act is a "notice" statute, which protects a later purchaser only if he paid value at a time when he was without notice of a prior unrecorded conveyance.[9] Patton, *supra*, at 39. The subsequent purchaser need not record first to protect his interest. Id.

A "race-notice" statute, such as that in California, combines elements of both "race" and the "notice" recording statutes. As under a "notice"

6. A fourth type of recording statute, a "grace period" statute, was formerly in force in several states. It permitted the recordation of a real estate conveyance to relate back to the date of the conveyance, if it was recorded within a short statutory period of time after the conveyance. However, as to real property, all such statutes have disappeared. The concept is still alive in the Uniform Commercial Code, which provides a grace period for the filing of a financial statement (the equivalent of the recordation of a conveyance) for certain transactions. *See*, UCC § 9-301(2), 9-304 and 9-306 (1972).

7. No up-to-date list of the kinds of recording acts in the various states has been discovered. The classification of the various states as of 1952 is set forth in 4 American Law of Property 545 n.63 (1952).

8. Apparently the only state with a "race" statute for the equity ownership of real property is North Carolina. Its recording statute provides:

No (i) conveyance of land, or (ii) contract to convey, or (iii) option to convey, or (iv) lease of land for more than three years shall be valid to pass any property interest as against lien creditors or purchasers for a valuable consideration from the donor, bargainor or lessor but from the time of registration thereof in the country where the land lies.

N.C. Gen. Stat. §47-18(a) (1984). Several other states have "race" statutes for the recordation of mortgages.

9. A typical "notice" statute is the recording statute in Massachusetts, which provides:

A conveyance of an estate in fee simple, fee tail or for life, or a lease for a term of seven years, or an assignment of rents or profits from an estate or lease, shall not be valid as against any person, except the grantor or lessor, his heirs and devisees and persons having actual notice of it, unless it . . . is recorded in the registry of deeds for the county or district in which the land to which it relates lies. Mass. Gen. Laws Ann. c. 183, §4 (1977).

statute, a subsequent purchaser receives protection only if he is a bona fide purchaser without notice of the prior conveyance at the time of his conveyance. As under a "race" statute, he must record first to protect his interest. Patton, *supra*, at 43-44. Thus under the California statute a subsequent purchaser is entitled to priority if (1) he is without notice at the time that the conveyance is made and the consideration paid, and (2) he records first.

The recordation of a copy of or a notice of a bankruptcy petition under section 549(c) has the same effect as the recordation of a subsequent conveyance by the debtor on the same date to a bona fide purchaser without notice of the bankruptcy case. Under a "race-notice" recording statute a recorded subsequent conveyance would take priority. Thus under the California recording statute the recordation of a notice of bankruptcy cuts off the rights of a purchaser with a prior unrecorded deed.

In this case Walker recorded the notion of her bankruptcy case in time to cut off Dorman's rights. While Dorman had purchased the property at the foreclosure sale and had given value prior to the recordation of the notice of bankruptcy, he failed to record his trustee's deed promptly. In the intervening period of time, Walker recorded her notice. On the date that she recorded her notice, she could have sold the property to a bona fide purchaser, who could have recorded a deed that would have taken priority over Dorman's unrecorded deed. In consequence, Walker is entitled to set aside the conveyance to Dorman.

Dorman argues that Walker could not convey the property to a good faith purchaser on March 13, 1986, because the recordation by California Mortgage of its notice of default would put such a purchaser on notice of the pending foreclosure. Dorman further argues that reasonable inquiry by such a purchaser would have led to the discovery of the foreclosure sale.

The Court does not find this argument persuasive. The Court holds that a prospective purchaser has no duty to inquire about a California notice of default or notice of sale that is more than six months old. Under California law, a foreclosure sale normally takes place from four to six months after a notice of default is recorded, and within a month after a notice of sale is recorded. Defaults often are cured after the recordation of a notice of default or a notice of sale. Although California Civil Code §2924c(a)(2) (West 1974 & Supp. 1986) authorizes upon demand the recordation of a notice of rescission of a notice of default after cure, such notices of recission often are not recorded. If six months has elapsed since the recordation of a notice of default or a notice of sale, a prospective purchaser is entitled to assume that the default has been cured.

In this case the notice of default was recorded more than sixteen months prior to the date of the foreclosure sale. Any purchaser was entitled to assume that the default had been cured. In consequence, the notice of default that appeared in the title records would not put a prospective purchaser on inquiry notice sufficient to prevent him from being a good faith purchaser.

In setting aside the conveyance to Dorman, Walker is not entitled to be put in a better position than she would have had if the foreclosure sale had not taken place in violation of the automatic stay. In consequence, the title that this Court orders restored to Walker is subject to the deed of trust in favor of California Mortgage, and to all junior encumbrances of record at the time of the foreclosure sale. Walker is required to bring the post-petition payments current by the transmission to California Mortgage of the payments held in trust by her attorney. Because Walker remains in possession of the property, no remedy is needed in this regard.

Dorman has also brought a summary judgment motion against California Mortgage on its cross-claim against him. Because of the Court's ruling in favor of Walker on the principal complaint, summary judgment is granted against Dorman on the cross-complaint:[10] The sale to Dorman is null and void.

However, Dorman is equally entitled to the benefits of the rescission of the foreclosure sale. He is entitled to the return by California Mortgage of the $70,350 that he paid at the foreclosure, plus interest at the legal rate.

There are further issues that are not ripe for summary judgment. Walker's complaint includes a claim for compensatory damages (chiefly her attorneys fees) and punitive damages. Dorman has not yet filed his answer to the California Mortgage cross-complaint: he may be entitled to further damages if he files a counter-claim. The remaining cross-claims are also not ripe for summary judgment.

---

10. If it appears to the Court, under the evidence brought before the Court on a summary judgment motion, that partial summary judgment should be granted *against* the moving party and that there is no genuine issue as to any material fact relating thereto, the Court has the power to enter such judgment. Scoggins v. Boeing Co., 742 F.2d 1225, 1227 n.1 (9th Cir.1984); Golden State Transit v. Los Angeles, 726 F.2d 1430, 1431 n.1 (9th Cir.1984), *cert. denied*, 471 U.S. 1003, 105 S. Ct. 1865, 85 L. Ed. 2d 159 (1985); Cool Fuel, Inc. v. Connett, 685 F.2d 309, 311 (9th Cir. 1982); 10A C. Wright, A. Miller & M. Kane, Federal Practice & Procedure §2720, at 27-35 (2d ed. 1983). The party against whom such summary judgment is to be rendered must be given a full and fair opportunity to explore the issues involved in the motion. Heinz v. Commissioner of Internal Revenue, 770 F.2d 874, 876 (9th Cir. 1985); Cool Fuel, *supra.* 685 F.2d at 312. In this case California Mortgage has had a full and fair opportunity to explore the issues involved in this partial summary judgment, including Dorman's right to recover the $70,350 that he paid for the property if the Court should award the property to plaintiff.

IV. CONCLUSION

The Court concludes that the foreclosure sale of Walker's property, conducted by California Mortgage, must be set aside, and that title to the property must be restored to Walker, subject to the trust deed of California Mortgage and the other encumbrances of record as of the date of the foreclosure sale. In addition, the Court grants summary judgment against Walker on California Mortgage's cross-complaint to rescind the foreclosure sale, and holds that Dorman is entitled to the repayment from California Mortgage of the $70,350 that he paid for the purchase of the property plus interest at the legal rate. The remaining issues are subject to further proceedings before the Court.

The foregoing constitutes the Court's findings of fact and conclusions of law.

Part 8

Land Use Planning and Development

Chapter Thirty-two

Private Law Devices

Insert the following material at the end of page 947.

Revenue Ruling 85-132, I.R.B. 1985-34, 14, provides as follows:

REV. RUL. 85-132

ISSUE

Will the exchange of stock in a cooperative housing corporation for legal title to a condominium unit and an undivided interest in the common elements, under the facts described below, result in nonrecognition of gain under section 1034 of the Internal Revenue Code?

FACTS

A resides in a building that contains residential units. Prior to January 1985, the building was owned and operated on a cooperative basis by *COOP*, a cooperative housing corporation, as that term is defined in section 216(b)(1) of the Code. *A* was a tenant-stockholder in *COOP* and used the apartment that *A* was entitled to occupy as such stockholder as *A*'s principal residence.

In January 1985, *A* and the other tenant-stockholders of *COOP* converted their equity interests from cooperative ownership to condominium ownership pursuant to the following plan: *COOP* recorded a condominium declaration under which each apartment comprised a separate condominium unit. Initially *COOP* owned legal title to all condominium units and to the common elements. Following recordation of the condominium declaration, *COOP* adopted a plan of complete liquidation. Under the plan, *A* and the other tenant-shareholders surrendered for cancellation all of their shares of *COOP* stock and, in exchange therefor, received only legal title to their respective condominium units and an undivided interest in the elements. *COOP* was then dissolved.

Pursuant to the plan *A* surrendered all of *A*'s shares of stock in *COOP* and received legal title to the condominium unit that *A* occupied and an undivided interest in the common elements. At the time, the value of the condominium unit and A's undivided interest in the common elements exceeded the adjusted basis of A's stock in *COOP*. A continues to occupy the unit as A's principal residence.

A did not, within 2 years before the date of the exchange, sell at a gain other property used by A as A's principal residence.

LAW AND ANALYSIS

Section 1034(a) of the Code provides that if property (the "old residence") used by the taxpayer as the taxpayer's principal residence is sold by the taxpayer and, within the period beginning 2 years before the date of such sale and ending 2 years after such date, property (the "new residence") is purchased and used by the taxpayer as the taxpayer's principal residence, gain (if any) from such sale shall be recognized only to the extent that the taxpayer's adjusted sales price of the old residence exceeds the taxpayer's cost of purchasing the new residence.

Section 1034(c)(1) of the Code provides that an exchange by the taxpayer of the taxpayer's residence for other property shall be treated as a sale of such residence, and that the acquisition of a residence on the exchange of property shall be treated as a purchase of such residence.

Section 1034(f) of the Code provides, in part, that for purposes of section 1034, references to property used by the taxpayer as the taxpayer's principal residence, and references to the residence of a taxpayer, shall include stock held by a tenant-stockholder (as defined in section 216) in a cooperative housing corporation (as defined in section 216) if, in the case of stock sold, the house or apartment which the taxpayer was entitled to occupy as such stockholder was used by the taxpayer as the taxpayer's principal residence and, in the case of stock purchased, the taxpayer used as the taxpayer's principal residence the house or apartment which the taxpayer was entitled to occupy as such stockholder.

Rev. Rul. 64-31, 1964-1 (Part 1) C.B. 300, holds that an individual who sells a principal residence and uses the proceeds, within 1 year after the sale, to purchase an apartment in a condominium project which is used as the individual's new principal residence is entitled to the relief provided by section 1034(a) of the Code.

Under section 1034(f) of the Code, the *COOP* stock is considered to be A's principal residence for purposes of section 1034(a). Furthermore, an exchange of the taxpayer's residence for other property constituting a residence is considered to be a sale of a residence and a purchase of another residence under section 1034(c)(1). Accordingly, the exchange of *COOP* stock for the condominium unit and an undivided interest in the common elements is considered to be a sale of the taxpayer's residence, and the receipt of the condominium unit and an undivided interest in the common elements for the stock is considered to be a purchase of a residence for the purposes of section 1034.

HOLDING

Based on the facts and circumstances presented, the exchange of *A*'s shares of stock in *COOP* for legal title to the condominium unit occupied by *A* and an undivided interest in the common elements will qualify as a sale within the meaning of section 1034(a) of the Code, and no gain or loss will be recognized to *A* on such sale, subject to the limitations of section 1034(a) of the Code and section 1.1034-1 of the Income Tax Regulations.

Add the following material to note 34 on page 990.

For a recent article relating to the touch and concern test, see Stake, Toward An Economic Understanding of Touch and Concern, Duke L. J., No. 5, p. 925 (1988).

Insert the following material after the note on page 1028.

Case considering statutory requirements to record currently ancient restrictions.

MANNING v. NEW ENGLAND MUTUAL LIFE INSURANCE CO.

Supreme Judicial Court of Massachusetts, 1987
399 Mass. 730, 506 N.E.2d 870

HENNESSEY, Chief Justice.

The plaintiffs appeal from a judgment of a Land Court judge denying specific enforcement of restrictions in deeds to a parcel of land owned by the defendant. We conclude that the judge correctly ruled that the restrictions could not be enforced because of the failure to re-record them as required by G.L. c.184, §28.

New England Mutual Life Insurance Co. (defendant) owns land in the Back Bay section of Boston, bounded by Boylston Street, Berkeley Street, Clarendon Street, and St. James Avenue. The defendant purchased the parcel in two parts, the portion bordering Boylston Street from the Commissioners of Public Lands of the Commonwealth, and the portion bordering St. James Avenue from the Boston Water Power Company. The entire parcel had once been part of tidal flats which the Commonwealth filled, beginning in the 1850's. The Commonwealth then sold lots in the area for dwellings, subject to restrictions in conformity with a comprehensive land use plan. See Blakeley v. Gorin, 365 Mass. 590, 592, 313 N.E.2d 903 (1974). These restrictions, known as the Commonwealth Restrictions, or the Back Bay Restrictions, include "[t]hat the front wall [of any building] on Boylston Street, shall be set back, twenty-five feet from said Boylston Street,"[3] and "[t]hat a passageway twenty five feet wide, is to be laid out in the rear of the premises, the same to be filled in by the Commonwealth and to be kept open and maintained by the abutters in common. . . ."

The defendant plans to erect a building on its parcel which will be set back only ten feet, and will cover the alley which formerly ran down the middle of the parcel between the buildings on Boylston Street and those on St. James Avenue. The defendant has received certain zoning relief from the Boston Redevelopment Authority, the Boston Zoning Commission, and the board of appeal of Boston. Appeals from those board and agency actions are pending in separate actions.

Most of the plaintiffs are residents of the Back Bay. Several plaintiffs own property which was originally conveyed by the Commonwealth subject to the Commonwealth Restrictions. No plaintiff owns land which either lies in a block surrounded by the same streets as the defendant's parcel or is contiguous to the defendant's parcel. The plaintiffs concede that they would suffer no money damages, and seek specific enforcement of the restrictions.

The Land Court judge concluded that the restrictions were never brought forward as required by G.L. c.184, §28, and therefore could not be enforced against the defendant. The judge also concluded that, even if §28 were not applicable, §30 would bar the enforcement of the restrictions.[4]

1.

The plaintiffs argue that the judge erred in finding that G.L. c.184, §28, barred enforcement of the restrictions.[5] Section 28 provides in part:

3. The deed for the parcel bordering St. James Avenue required a setback of ten feet, later amended to fifteen feet. The plaintiffs seek to enforce the setback restriction only with regard to Boylston Street, and not St. James Avenue, and also the restriction requiring that a "passageway" be kept open.

4. General Laws c.184, §30, inserted by St. 1961, c.448, §1, provides that no restriction shall be enforced or declared to be enforceable unless it is determined that the restriction is, at the time of the proceeding, of actual and substantial benefit to a person claiming rights of enforcement. Further, even if a restriction is found to be of such benefit, it shall not be enforced except by award of money damages if any of several enumerated conditions are found to exist. See Blakeley v. Gorin, *supra* at 592-593, 313 N.E.2d 903. Because the application of §28 is dispositive of the case, we need not consider the correctness of the judge's conclusions as to §30.

5. The plaintiffs have not argued that §28 does not apply to the covenant to keep the passageway open. Compare Labounty v. Vickers, 352 Mass. 337, 347-348, 225 N.E.2d 333 (1967), with Myers v. Salin, 13 Mass. App. Ct. 127, 134-136, 431 N.E.2d 233 (1982). Therefore, we need not address that issue.

No restriction imposed before January first, nineteen hundred and sixty-two shall be enforceable after the expiration of fifty years from its imposition unless a notice of restriction is recorded before the expiration of such fifty years or before January first, nineteen hundred and sixty-four, whichever is later, and in case of such recording, twenty years have not expired after the recording of any notice of restriction without the recording of a further notice of restrictions. G.L. c.184, §28.

The Legislature entitled the statute: "An Act to protect land titles from uncertain and obsolete restrictions and to provide proceedings in equity with respect thereto." St. 1961, c.448.

The plaintiffs concede that no notice of restrictions was recorded as required by §28. Nevertheless, the plaintiffs argue that §28 should not bar enforcement of the restrictions. The plaintiffs contend that the "necessary implication" of this court's decision in Blakeley v. Gorin, *supra*, applying §30 although the requirements of §28 had not been satisfied, is that §28 does not bar enforcement of the Commonwealth Restrictions. We disagree. The issue of compliance with §28 was not argued or briefed in Blakeley v. Gorin, and this court did not address the issue. Nothing in Blakeley v. Gorin dictates that §28 is inapplicable in this case.

The plaintiffs next argue that subsequent legislative history indicates that the Legislature did not intend §28 to apply to restrictions contained in conveyances by the Commonwealth. In 1974, the Legislature amended §28, adding: "The provisions of this section shall not be construed to apply to, and do not apply to, lands owned and conveyed by the commonwealth, notwithstanding any lapse of time or the passage of any prior law." St. 1974, c.527, §3. This language, however, was deleted the following year. St. 1975, c.356.

We do not agree with the plaintiffs' contention that this subsequent legislative history establishes that §28 should not apply to the Commonwealth Restrictions. Even if we were to interpret the 1974 amendment as reviving restrictions previously extinguished by §28, the subsequent deletion of the 1974 amendment would operate to have the opposite effect. We are not convinced by the plaintiffs' suggestion that the Legislature repealed the 1974 amendments because it concluded that Blakeley v. Gorin, decided immediately after the 1974 amendments, had achieved the result of making the Commonwealth Restrictions enforceable despite §28. A more reasonable interpretation of the Legislature's action is that it intended to do precisely what it accomplished: the repeal of the 1974 amendment.

We therefore conclude that §28 is applicable to the restriction in this case. The plaintiffs are unable to point to any other provision exempting them from the requirement of §28 that notice of the restrictions must be re-recorded. Therefore, the restrictions on the defendant's parcel are unenforceable by virtue of §28.

2.

The plaintiffs argue that application of §28 would violate the contract clause of the United States Constitution, U.S. Const., art. I, cl. 10.[6] According to the plaintiffs, §28 impermissibly extinguished valuable contractual rights which the Commonwealth had a duty to enforce.[7] We have recognized that these restrictions can form a valuable right. See Blakeley v. Gorin, *supra*, 365 Mass. at 604, 313 N.E.2d 903.

The plaintiffs do not argue that §28 would be unconstitutional as applied to restrictions imposed in transactions between private parties. Instead, the plaintiffs assert that the fact that the Commonwealth was the original grantor imposing the restrictions requires closer scrutiny of the Legislature's subsequent enactment affecting those restrictions. Cf. United States Trust Co. v. New Jersey, 431 U.S. 1, 25-26, 97 S. Ct. 1505, 1519, 52 L. Ed. 2d 92 (1977). Even if we were to accept the plaintiffs' assertion that the Commonwealth is under some continuing contractual obligation to the successors of the original grantees subject to the restrictions, we would still find that application of §28 involved no constitutional infirmity under the contract clause. In El Paso v. Simmons, 379 U.S. 497, 85 S. Ct. 577, 13 L. Ed. 2d 446 (1965), the United States Supreme Court upheld a State statute which limited the right of grantees of land from the State to reinstate their land forfeited to the State for nonpayment of interest. Prior to the statute in question, the defaulting grantee's right to reinstate his claim by paying the interest in arrears was unlimited in time. The statute required payment of interest in arrears within five years. A subsequent amendment limited the right of reinstatement to the last purchaser from the State and his vendees or heirs. Id. at 498-501, 85 S. Ct. at 578-579. The Court concluded that, given the State's "objectives and the impediments posed to their fulfillment by timeless reinstatement rights, a statute of repose was quite clearly necessary." Id. at 516, 85 S. Ct. at 587.

In this case, §28 poses even less of a conflict with the contract clause. In El Paso v. Simmons, the land was defaulted to the State. In this case, the Commonwealth's self-interest is not similarly implicated. Moreover, §28

6. "No State shall . . . pass any . . . Law impairing the Obligation of Contracts." U.S. Const., art. I, cl. 10.

7. The plaintiffs do not argue the application of §28 violates any other Federal or State constitutional provision, such as Massachusetts Declaration of Rights, art. 10, or the United States Constitution, Amendments 5 and 14.

does not extinguish preexisting rights, but only requires that the beneficiary of the restrictions record to preserve them. Given the Commonwealth's interest in preserving the marketability of real estate titles, and of ensuring that titles are not clouded by obsolete and uncertain restrictions, §28 is a reasonable method of achieving those goals, while permitting the beneficiaries of restrictions in which there is continuing benefit to preserve those rights merely by recording notice of the restrictions. Such a requirement does not overly burden the beneficiary. Moreover, §28 allowed a reasonable time — approximately three years — for recording those restrictions already more than fifty years old when §28 was enacted. See Brookline v. Carey, 355 Mass. 424, 427, 245 N.E.2d 446 (1969). See also Opinion of the Justices, 369 Mass. 979, 986-987, 338 N.E.2d 806 (1975); Selectmen of Nahant v. United States, 293 F. Supp. 1076 (D. Mass. 1968). Thus, application of §28 here does not violate the contract clause.

3.

Finally, we deal briefly with two other contentions raised by the plaintiffs. First, the plaintiffs, relying on Boston Waterfront Dev. Corp. v. Commonwealth, 378 Mass. 629, 393 N.E.2d 356 (1979), and Newburyport Redevelopment Auth. v. Commonwealth, 9 Mass. App. Ct. 206, 401 N.E.2d 118 (1980), argue that the Commonwealth Restrictions constitute a public trust because the Back Bay is filled tidal land. Those cases, however, concerned submerged land, not tidal land. "[T]he public interest in [tidal] flats reclaimed pursuant to lawful authority may be extinguished, and, if deemed appropriate, the Legislature may act to declare that those rights have been extinguished so as to assure the marketability of title to such property." Opinions of the Justices, 383 Mass. 895, 902, 424 N.E.2d 1092 (1981). "Neither the public nor the Commonwealth has a continuing interest in these tidelands in the nature of a public trust of the character described in the Boston Waterfront case." Id. at 910, 424 N.E.2d 1092, citing Waterfront Dev. Corp. v. Commonwealth, supra, 378 Mass. at 641-649, 393 N.E.2d 356. We conclude that, even if the Commonwealth had a continuing interest of this nature, it was extinguished by the bar imposed by G.L. c.184, §28. Cf. Boston Waterfront Dev. Corp. v. Commonwealth, supra at 651-652, 393 N.E.2d 356 (discussing application of G.L. c.260, §31A, to submerged land).

The plaintiffs' second contention is that the judge erred in concluding that the Commonwealth was not required by G.L. c.91, §37, to enforce the Commonwealth Restrictions. In light of our conclusion that the restrictions were unenforceable under G.L. c.184, §28, the Commonwealth could not be under an obligation to enforce the restrictions.

4.

In sum, the judge properly concluded that the restrictions on the defendant's parcel were unenforceable by virtue of G.L. c.184, §28. There was no error.

Judgment affirmed.

Insert the following material on page 1030 after Problem 32.11.

Case enforcing restrictive covenant even though there was no common scheme or plan.

MALLEY v. HANNA

Court of Appeals of New York, 1985
65 N.Y.2d 289, 480 N.E.2d 1068

JASEN, Judge.

Plaintiffs brought this action to enforce a restrictive covenant in defendants' chain of title which prohibits the construction of two-family dwellings.

The trial court traced each of the parties' properties to an original owner, Brown Brothers Company, and found that the restrictive covenant in defendants' chain of title was clearly intended to limit residential construction to single-family dwellings. Nevertheless, the court dismissed the complaint on the ground that plaintiffs had failed to demonstrate the existence of a "general plan of development" as evidenced by a "uniform (or nearly uniform) scheme of restrictions contained in the deeds from the common grantor." The Appellate Division, 101 A.D.2d 1019, 476 N.Y.S.2d 700, reversed and granted relief to plaintiffs, finding not only that the restrictive covenant on defendants' property was intended to bar construction of the proposed dwellings, but also that the restrictive covenant was imposed by the original grantor as part of a common scheme or plan, as evidenced by the virtually identical restrictions contained in each party's respective chain of title. We now affirm for the following reasons.

Browncroft Extension, a residential neighborhood in both the City of Rochester and the Town of Brighton in Monroe County, was originally assembled by Brown Brothers Company. The parties in this action each acquired their properties through independent chains of title from that original grantor. We need only consider defendants' and plaintiff Malley's chains of title to decide this appeal.

Defendants' parcel derives directly from a deed conveyed by Brown Brothers in 1916 in which nine lots, including defendants' four, were transferred to Browncroft Realty Corporation. The conveyance was subject to the following restrictions: "Each lot in the [Browncroft] tract . . . shall be used for residence purposes only and no double house, Boston flat or apartment house, shall ever be built upon any lot in said tract." Subsequently, the property was conveyed in part several times, including in 1983 when four lots were purchased by defendants. Each conveyance, including the transfer to defendants, explicitly provided that title was taken subject to the covenants of record and specifically referred to the Browncroft Extension.

Plaintiff Malley's property, consisting of one lot located three lots east of defendants' parcel, was originally conveyed by Brown Brothers in 1929. This conveyance to Charles and Eleanore Carman provided the following conditions: "The lot hereby conveyed shall be used for the usual and ordinary purposes of a residence or dwelling and not otherwise. No double house, Boston flat or apartment house shall ever be erected thereon."

The property was transferred again the same year and, thereafter, in 1958, it was purchased by plaintiff Malley. Each conveyance was explicitly made subject to the convenants of record and specifically referred to the Browncroft Extension.

In order to establish the privity requisite to enforce a restrictive covenant, a party need only show that his property derives from the original grantor who imposed the covenant and whose property was benefited thereby, and concomitantly, that the party to be burdened derives his property from the original grantee who took the property subject to the restrictive covenant. (See, Orange & Rockland Utils. v. Philwold Estates, 52 N.Y.2d 253, 263, 437 N.Y.S.2d 291, 418 N.E.2d 1310; Nicholson v. 300 Broadway Realty Corp., 7 N.Y.2d 240, 245, 196 N.Y.S.2d 945, 164 N.E.2d 832; Neponsit Prop. Owners' Assn. v. Emigrant Indus. Sav. Bank, 278 N.Y. 248, 261, 15 N.E.2d 793.) This "vertical privity" arises wherever the party seeking to enforce the covenant has derived his title through a continuous lawful succession from the original grantor. (See, 5 Powell, The Law of Real Property ¶673[2][c], at 60-64; Clark, Real Covenants and Other Interests Which "Run With Land," at 111-137 [2d ed. 1947]; 4A Warrens' Weed, N.Y. Real Property, Restrictive Covenants §3.05, at 28-29 [4th ed.].)

Here, the undisputed facts establish the requisite vertical privity. Plaintiff Malley derives title to his property from Brown Brothers. The latter emburdened the property conveyed to defendants' predecessor by subjecting the conveyance to the restrictive covenant in question, and this covenant, in turn, accrued to the benefit of the property retained by

Brown Brothers, including that lot ultimately obtained by Malley. Additionally, the succession of conveyances from Brown Brothers to Malley was continuous and lawful. Nothing in the record indicates otherwise. Likewise, the succession of conveyances to defendants was continuous and lawful, and each transfer was subject to the covenant in question originally imposed by Brown Brothers upon defendants' predecessor in title. Vertical privity requires nothing more.

Finally, contrary to defendants' contention, plaintiff Malley's right to enforce the restrictive covenant does not depend upon his demonstrating a common plan or scheme. Indeed, once the requisite vertical privity has been established, the existence of a plan or scheme need not be determined. Rather, it is sufficient that the surrounding circumstances manifest the original grantor's intent that the covenant run with the land. (Vogeler v. Alwyn Improvement Corp., 247 N.Y. 131, 136-137, 159 N.E. 886; see, Orange & Rockland Utils. v. Philwold Estates, *supra*, 52 N.Y.2d at pp. 262-263, 437 N.Y.S.2d 291, 418 N.E.2d 1310; Bristol v. Woodward, 251 N.Y. 275, 284; Booth v. Knipe, 225 N.Y. 390, 396, 122 N.E. 202; Who May Enforce Restrictive Covenant or Agreement as to Use of Real Property, Ann., 51 A.L.R.3d 556, 568-569, 580-582; Powell, *supra*, at ¶673[2][b]; 4A Warrens' Weed, *supra*, Restrictive Covenants §19.08.)

Here, the nature of the covenant as one running with the land is clearly revealed by the following: the language of the covenant in defendants' chain of title speaks in terms of perpetuity—i.e., "no double house . . . shall ever be built" (see, Powell, *supra*, at ¶673[2][b]; Restatement of Property §531 comment d; cf. Booth v. Knipe, *supra*, at p.395, 122 N.E. 202); the land originally retained—i.e., including that now owned by Malley—necessarily benefited from the covenant (see, Orange & Rockland Utils. v. Philwold Estates, *supra*, at p.262; Post v. Weil, 115 N.Y. 361, 22 N.E. 145; Powell, *supra*, at ¶673[2][b]); every conveyance and other relevant instrument of Brown Brothers, the original grantor, included in the record contains an identical or similar covenant; and, indeed, every conveyance in each of the parties' chain of title contains the same either explicitly or by unmistakable reference. There is no requirement to establish that, in addition to the foregoing, there existed a common scheme or plan covering every deed from the original grantor of the originally entitled Browncroft Extension.

We have considered defendants' other arguments and find them to be without merit.

Accordingly, the order of the Appellate Division should be affirmed, with costs.

WACHTLER, C.J., and MEYER, SIMONS, KAYE and ALEXANDER, JJ., concur.

Order affirmed, with costs.

Insert following material at end of page 1068.

Case involving implied reservation of easements by grantor on land conveyed in relation to business properties retained by grantor.

GRANITE PROPERTIES LIMITED PARTNERSHIP v. MANNS

Supreme Court of Illinois, 1987
117 Ill. 2d 425, 512 N.E.2d 1230

Justice RYAN delivered the opinion of the court.

The plaintiff, Granite Properties Limited Partnership, brought this suit in the circuit court of Madison County, seeking to permanently enjoin the defendants, Larry and Ann Manns, from interfering with the plaintiff's use and enjoyment of two claimed easements over driveways which exist on the defendants' property. One driveway provides ingress to and egress from an apartment complex and the other to a shopping center. Both the apartment complex and the shopping center are situated on the plaintiff's property. Following a bench trial, the circuit court entered judgment against the plaintiff and in favor of the defendants as to both claimed easements. Following argument of the plaintiff's post-trial motion, the circuit court granted permanent injunctive relief as to the claimed apartment complex easement, but reaffirmed its decision denying the claimed shopping center easement. Both parties appealed from that portion of the judgment adverse to them. The appellate court, with one justice dissenting, held that the plaintiff was entitled to easements by implication over the driveways in question. (140 Ill. App. 3d 561, 94 Ill. Dec. 353, 487 N.E.2d 1230.) We granted the defendants' petition for leave to appeal (94 Ill. 2d R. 315).

The relative location of the subject properties and the claimed easements may be seen by reference to the following rough diagram adapted from the defendants' petition for leave to appeal.

As indicated, the parcels which are the subject of this appeal, are adjoining tracts located to the south of Bethalto Drive and to the north of Rou des Chateaux Street in Bethalto, Illinois. The plaintiff and its predecessors in title owned all of the subject properties from 1963 or 1964 until 1982, at which time the parcel labeled "B" was conveyed by warranty deed to the defendants. The plaintiff currently owns the parcels labeled "A" and "E," which are on the opposite sides of parcel B. The shopping center situated on the parcel designated "A" extends from lot line to lot line across the east-west dimension of that property. To the north of the shopping center is an asphalt parking lot with approximately 191 feet of frontage on Bethalto Drive. To the east of the shop-

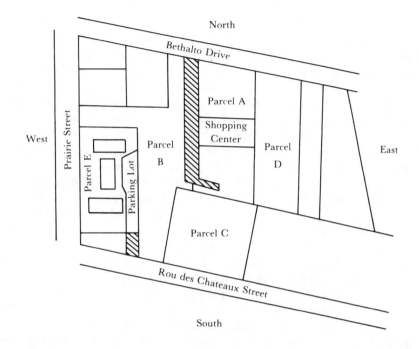

ping center on the parcel labeled "D" is a separately owned health club. To the south of parcel A on the parcel denominated "C" are five four-family apartment buildings. The distance between the back of the shopping center and the property line of parcel C is 50 feet. The shopping center's underground utility facilities are located in this area. An apartment complex, known as the Chateau des Fleurs Apartments, is located on the parcel labeled "E." Both of the plaintiff's properties were developed prior to the time parcel B was sold to the defendants. Parcel B remains undeveloped.

The first claimed easement provides access to the rear of the shopping center which is located on parcel A. The center, which was built in 1967, contains several businesses, including a grocery store, a pharmacy, and doctors' offices. The rear of the center is used for deliveries, trash storage and removal, and utilities repair. To gain access to the rear of the shopping center for these purposes, trucks use a gravel driveway which runs along the lot line between parcel A and parcel B. A second driveway, located to the east of the shopping center on parcel D, enables the trucks to circle the shopping center without having to turn around in the limited space behind the stores.

Robert Mehann, the owner of the Save-A-Lot grocery store located in the shopping center, testified on direct examination that groceries, which are delivered to the rear of the store, are loaded by forklift on a concrete pad poured for that purpose. Mehann indicated that there are large, double steel doors in the back of the store to accommodate items which will not fit through the front door. Mehann testified that semi-trailer trucks make deliveries to the rear of the grocery store four days a week, with as many as two or three such trucks arriving daily. An average of 10 to 12 trucks a day, including semitrailer trucks, make deliveries to the grocery store. Mehann further explained on direct examination that because the area behind the Save-A-Lot building extends only 50 feet to the rear property line, it would be difficult, if not impossible, for a semitrailer truck to turn around in the back and exit the same way it came in. In response to a question as to whether it would be feasible to have trucks make front-door deliveries, Mehann suggested that such deliveries would be very disruptive; pallets that would not fit through the front door would have to be broken down into parts, requiring extra work, and there would not be adequate space in the front of the store to do such work during business hours. Mehann admitted on cross-examination that he had not investigated the cost of installing a front door which would be big enough for pallets of groceries to be brought in by forklift. Further cross-examination revealed that there would not be enough space to manipulate the forklift around the front of the store, although it could be run between the shelves of food to the back of the store.

Also called as a witness for Granite Properties Limited Partnership was Darrell Layman, a limited partner. Layman noted that the shopping center had been in continuous operation since 1967 and that the pattern for deliveries had always been to the rear of the individual stores. When asked whether he had "ever seen a semi back up in the rear of the shopping center and go out the way it came in," Layman responded, "That would be impossible." On cross-examination, however, Layman admitted that, although it was very difficult, he had seen semitrailer trucks exit the same way they came in. Layman also acknowledged on cross-examination that he had not investigated the cost of expanding the size of the front doors of the building. He also claimed that it "would seem impossible" to him to put in any kind of a hallway or passageway which would allow equipment to bring supplies into the stores from the front. On redirect examination, Layman explained that the delivery trucks follow no set schedule and, therefore, their presence may overlap at times. He stated that he had seen as many as four or five delivery trucks backed up. Layman opined that there was "no way" the trucks could back up and turn around when there were multiple trucks present.

The other claimed easement concerns ingress and egress over a drive-way which leads into the parking area of the apartment complex situated on parcel E. The complex, which was erected in the 1960s prior to the conveyance of parcel B to the defendants, consists of three buildings containing 36 units. The parking lot, which is situated to the rear of the buildings, provides 72 parking spaces. The only access to the parking lot is by a driveway from Rou des Chateaux, a public street located to the south of the properties. The driveway, which cuts across a small panhandle on the southwestern corner of parcel B, has been in existence since the apartment complex was constructed. The terrain around the apartment compex is flat, including the area in front of the buildings along Prairie Street to the west.

Limited partner Darrell Layman testified at trial that if the area in front of the apartment complex, measuring 300 feet along Prairie Street and 30 feet deep, were to be converted into a parking lot, then there would be room for only 30 parking spaces. He admitted on direct examination that he had not investigated the cost of rocking or asphalting this area for that purpose. Although there was a distance of 20 feet between the apartment buildings, Layman opined that it would not be enough "usable space" to accommodate a driveway from Prairie Street to the existing parking lot because such driveway would interfere with stairways which lead to the basement apartments. Although he admitted that he did not investigate the cost of installing a driveway either between the buildings or adjacent to the end building on the north, Layman concluded that, based on his experience in the layout and design of apartment buildings, "it would be a dangerous situation" for the tenants of the apartments if a driveway were to be run between the buildings or next to their sides. Layman concluded his testimony by claiming that the plaintiff was unaware of any easement problems as to the driveways in question at the time parcel B was deeded to the defendants; otherwise, he asserted, "it would not have been deeded."

The defendant, Larry Manns, stated that he purchased parcel B from the plaintiff in the summer of 1982. Shortly afterwards, he had a survey made of the property. The survey indicated possible encroachments by the plaintiff as to the driveways in question. Finding no recorded easements following a title search, Manns stated that he notified the plaintiff to discontinue its use of the driveways. On cross-examination, Manns admitted that he saw the two driveways before he bought the subject property.

In its memorandum of judgment, the circuit court made the following findings of fact: (1) the claimed easements had been used by the plaintiff, as common grantor, prior to separation of title; (2) the driveways in question were apparent to defendant Larry Manns when he purchased the property upon which they were situated; (3) there is access from Bethalto Drive to the front of the shopping center where an all-asphalt parking lot exists; and (4) Prairie Street, which runs in front of the apartment complex, is flat in terrain, possibly allowing access to the complex. Because there was no evidence presented by the plaintiff as to the expense that would be involved in creating available alternatives affording reasonable means of ingress to and egress from these properties, the court concluded that the plaintiff created the access problems. Reasoning that it would be more convenient for the plaintiff to cross parcel B but not reasonably necessary, the circuit court refused to find easements by implications over the driveways in question and, therefore, denied the plaintiff's claims for injunctive relief.

Following a post-trial motion by the plaintiff, the circuit court vacated that portion of its judgment concerning the apartment complex easement, stating that "the court finds that the easement to the apartment complex is highly convenient and reasonably necessary for the use and enjoyment of the complex." As to the claimed easement for the shopping center, the court reasoned that because there is adequate ingress to and egress from the shopping center, as well as through the back of the shopping center, "the use of the defendants' property would be more convenient, but not reasonably necessary for the plaintiff." The court therefore affirmed its prior judgment, finding no easement as to the shopping center.

In affirming the circuit court's judgment granting injunctive relief as to the claimed apartment complex easement, the appellate court majority concluded that the circuit court's finding that such easement was highly convenient and reasonably necessary for the use and enjoyment of the complex was amply supported by the evidence at trial. 140 Ill. App. 3d 561, 573-74, 94 Ill. Dec. 353, 487 N.E.2d 1230. In reversing the circuit court's judgment denying injunctive relief as to the claimed shopping center easement, the appellate majority concluded that the circuit court, in focusing upon the degree of necessity required to sustain the implication of an easement, placed inordinate emphasis upon this requirement, thus failing to give proper consideration to the element of prior use. In light of the strong showing of prior use, the appellate majority further concluded that the evidence was sufficient to fulfill the requirement of necessity of the claimed shopping center easement. 140 Ill. App. 3d 561, 573, 94 Ill. Dec. 353, 487 N.E.2d 1230.

The plaintiff contends in this court that it acquired, by implied reservation, easements over the driveways which provide access to the rear of the shopping center located on parcel A and to the parking lot of the apartment complex situated on parcel E. Plaintiff alleges that parcels A, B and E were held in common ownership by the plaintiff and its predecessors in title until 1982, at which time the defendants received a warranty deed to parcel B, that the driveways in question were apparent and obvious, permanent, and subject to continuous, uninterrupted, and actual use by the plaintiff and its predecessors in title until the time of severance of unity of ownership, and that the driveways are highly convenient and reasonably necessary for the beneficial use and enjoyment of the shopping center and the apartment complex. Therefore, the plaintiff maintains that, upon severance of unity of title, the defendants took parcel B subject to the servitudes then existing, as the parties are presumed to convey with reference to the existing conditions of the property.

We note at the outset that the attempt here is to establish easements by implied reservation, rather than by implied grant. As the appellate court in this case correctly observed:

> While the defendant here asserts that no easement may be implied in favor of the grantor of property in derogation of his grant, Illinois courts have made no such distinction between easements implied in favor of a grantee (implied grant of easement) and those implied in favor of a grantor (implied reservation of easement). (See 16A Ill. L. & Prac. Easements sec. 16 (1971).) Rather, in stating the rule regarding the creation of easements by implication, the court in Bihss v. Sabolis (1926), 322 Ill. 350, 352, 153 N.E. 634, 685, observed:
>
> > This is not a rule for the benefit of purchasers, only, but is entirely reciprocal. Hence, if instead of a benefit a burden has been imposed upon the portion sold, the purchaser, provided the marks of this burden are open and visible, takes the property with a servitude upon it. The parties are presumed to contrast with reference to the condition of the property at the time of the sale, and neither has a right, by altering arrangements then openly existing, to change materially the relative value of the respective parts. [Citations.]
>
> Thus, Illinois may be said to follow the generally accepted view recognizing the implications of easements in favor of a grantor as well as a grantee. 28 C.J.S. Easements sec. 34 (1941); see 25 Am. Jur. 2d Easements and Licenses sec. 27, at 441 (1966); Annot., 164 A.L.R. 1001, 1003-05 (1946)." Granite Properties Limited Partnership v. Manns (1986), 140 Ill. App. 3d 561, 570, 94 Ill. Dec. 353, 487 N.E.2d 1230.

On the merits, the crucial issue is whether, in conveying that portion of its property now owned by the defendants (parcel B), the plaintiff retained easements by implication over the driveways in question. Our analysis begins with a brief, summary examination of the implied easement principles as they are stated and reflected in both the decisions of this court and the major secondary sources of American real property law.

There are two types of implied easements — the easement by necessity and the easement implied from a pre-existing use. The easement by necessity usually arises when an owner of land conveys to another an inner portion thereof, which is entirely surrounded by lands owned either by the grantor or the grantor plus strangers. Unless a contrary intent is manifested, the grantee is found to have a right-of-way across the retained land of the grantor for ingress to, and egress from, the land-locked parcel. Similarly, an easement is implied by way of necessity in the deed when the owner of lands retains the inner portion, conveying to another the balance. See, e.g., Diesenroth v. Dodge (1956), 7 Ill. 2d 340, 345, 131 N.E.2d 17; Walker v. Witt (1954), 4 Ill. 2d 16, 23, 122 N.E.2d 175; Finn v. Williams (1941), 376 Ill. 95, 99, 33 N.E.2d 226; Trapp v. Gordon (1937), 366 Ill. 102, 111, 7 N.E.2d 869; Gilfroy v. Randall (1916), 274 Ill. 128, 130-32, 113 N.E. 88; see also 2 American Law of Property sec. 8.38 (A. J. Casner ed. 1952); 3 R. Powell, The Law of Real Property sec. 410 (P. Rohan ed. 1987); 2 G. Thompson, Commentaries on the Modern Law of Real Property secs. 361-64 (rep. ed. 1980); see generally 25 Am. Jur. 2d Easements & Licenses sec. 35-37 (1966); 16A Ill. L. & Prac. Easements sec. 19 (1957).

The easement implied from a prior existing use, often characterized as a "quasi-easement," arises when an owner of an entire tract of land or of two or more adjoining parcels, after employing a part thereof so that one part of the tract or one parcel derives from another a benefit or advantage of an apparent, continuous, and permanent nature, conveys or transfers part of the property without mention being made of these incidental uses. In the absence of an expressed agreement to the contrary, the conveyance or transfer imparts a grant of property with all the benefits and burdens which existed at the time of the conveyance of the transfer, even though such grant is not reserved or specified in the deed. (See, e.g., Beloit Foundry Co. v. Ryan (1963), 28 Ill. 2d 379, 389, 192 N.E.2d 384; Bihss v. Sabolis (1926), 322 Ill. 350, 352, 153 N.E. 684; Powers v. Heffernan (1908), 233 Ill. 597, 599, 84 N.E. 661; see also 3 R. Powell, The Law of Real Property sec. 411 (P. Rohan ed. 1987); 2 G. Thompson, Commentaries on the Modern Law of Real Property secs. 351, 352 (rep. ed. 1980); Denissen, Private Ways: Title and Title Evidence, 45 Ill. B. J. 686, 689 (1957).) This court has stated on numerous occasions that an easement implied from a preexisting use is established by proof of three elements: first, common ownership of the claimed dominant and servient parcels and a subsequent conveyance or transfer separating that ownership; second, before the conveyance or transfer severing the unity of title, the common owner used part of the united parcel for the benefit of another part, and this use was apparent and obvious, continuous, and permanent; and third, the claimed easement is necessary and beneficial to the enjoyment of the parcel conveyed or retained by the grantor or transferrer. See, e.g., People ex rel. Helgeson v. Hackler (1961), 21 Ill. 2d 267, 270, 171 N.E.2d 599; Sheehan v. Sagona (1958), 13 Ill. 2d 341, 345, 148 N.E.2d 795; Partee v. Pietrobon

(1957), 10 Ill. 2d 248, 252, 139 N.E.2d 750; Gilbert v. Chicago Title & Trust Co. (1955), 7 Ill. 2d 496, 499, 131 N.E.2d 1; Kling v. Ghilarducci (1954), 3 Ill. 2d 454, 459, 121 N.E.2d 752; Carter v. Michel (1949), 403 Ill. 610, 617, 87 N.E.2d 759; Leitch v. Hine (1946), 393 Ill. 211, 226, 66 N.E.2d 90; Liberty National Bank v. Lux (1941), 378 Ill. 329, 331-32, 38 N.E.2d 6; see also R. Cunningham, W. Stoebuck & D. Whitman, The Law of Property sec. 8.4 (1984); 16A Ill. L. & Prac. Easements sec. 17 (1957); see generally Leesman, The Rationale of the Quasi-Easement in Illinois, 30 Ill. L. Rev. 963 (1936); Annot., 94 A.L.R.3d 502 (1979).

As the above discussion indicates, easements created by implication arise as an inference of the intention of the parties to a conveyance of land. This inference, which is drawn from the circumstances surrounding the conveyance alone, represents an attempt to ascribe an intention to parties who had not thought or had not bothered to put the intention into words, or to parties who actually had formed no intention conscious to themselves. To fill these common gaps resulting in incomplete thought, courts find particular facts suggestive of intent on the part of the parties to a conveyance. In the case of an easement implied from a preexisting use, proof of the prior use is evidence that the parties probably intended an easement, on the presumption that the grantor and the grantee would have intended to continue an important or necessary use of the land known to them that was apparently continuous and permanent in its nature. Where an easement by necessity is claimed, however, there is no requirement of proof of a known existing use from which to draw the inference of intention. This leaves proof of necessity alone to furnish the probable inference of intention, on the presumption that the grantor and the grantee do not intend to render the land unfit for occupancy.

This essentially is the position taken by the Restatement of Property. The Restatement describes a doctrine creating easements "by implication from the circumstances under which the conveyance was made." (Restatement of Property sec. 474 (1944).) This implication "arises as an inference of the intention of those making a conveyance." (Restatement of Property sec. 474, comment *b* (1944).) The Restatement operates on the basis of eight "important circumstances" from which the inference of intention may be drawn: whether the claimant is the conveyor or the conveyee; the terms of the conveyance; the consideration given for it; whether the claim is made against a simultaneous conveyee; the extent of necessity of the easement to the claimant; whether reciprocal benefits result to the conveyor and the conveyee; the manner in which the land was used prior to its conveyance; and the extent to which the manner of prior use was or might have been known to the parties. (Restatement of Property sec. 476 (1944).) These eight factors vary in their importance and relevance according to whether the claimed easement originates out of necessity or for another reason.

In applying the Restatement's eight important circumstances to the present case, the fact that the driveways in question had been used by the plaintiff or its predecessors in title since the 1960s, when the respective properties were developed, that the driveways were permanent in character, being either rock or gravel covered, and that the defendants were aware of the driveways' prior uses before they purchased parcel B would tend to support an inference that the parties intended easements upon severance of the parcels in question. (See Restatement of Property sec. 476, comments *i, j* (1944).) Although the prior uses which the plaintiff seeks to continue existed during the common ownership of the parcels in question, under circumstances where the defendants were fully informed by physical appearance of their existence, the defendants, nevertheless, argue that there are two factors which overwhelmingly detract from the implication of an easement: that the claimant is the conveyor and that the claimed easement can hardly be described as "necessary" to the beneficial use of the plaintiff's properties. Relying on the principle that a grantor should not be permitted to derogate from his own grant, the defendants urge this court to refuse to imply an easement in favor of a grantor unless the claimed easement is absolutely necessary to the beneficial use and enjoyment of the land retained by the grantor. The defendants further urge this court not to cast an unreasonable burden over their land through imposition of easements by implication where, as here, available alternatives affording reasonable means of ingress to and egress from the shopping center and the apartment complex allegedly exist.

While the degree of necessity required to reserve an easement by implication in favor of the conveyor is greater than that required in the case of the conveyee (Restatement of Property sec. 476, comment *c* (1944)), even in the case of the conveyor, the implication from necessity will be aided by a previous use made apparent by the physical adaptation of the premises to it. (Restatement of Property sec. 476, comment *j* (1944).) Moreover, the necessity requirement will have a different meaning and significance in the case involving proof of prior use than it will in a case in which necessity alone supports the implication; otherwise, proof of prior use would be unnecessary. (Restatement of Property sec. 476, comment *g* (1944).) Thus, when circumstances such as an apparent prior use of the land support the inference of the parties' intention, the required extent of the claimed easement's necessity will be less than when necessity is the only circumstance from which the inference of intention will be drawn. While some showing of necessity for the continuance of the use must be shown where a prior use has been made, to the extent that the prior use strengthens the implication, the degree or extent of necessity requisite for implication is reduced. (Restatement of Property sec. 476, comment *i* (1944).) As one treatise concludes:

> If a previous use is continuous and apparent, an easement may be created by implication even though the need for the use to be made is not sufficiently great to meet the test of necessity as applied in the absence of such a previous use. Hence, the test is phrased in terms of *reasonable necessity* rather than in terms of unqualified necessity. A use is necessary, it is often said, when without it no effective use could be made of the land to be benefited by it. *Where, because of a continuous and apparent previous use, the test of necessity becomes that of reasonable necessity, it is said that a use is reasonably necessary when it is reasonably convenient to the use of the land benefited.* In fact, however, reasonable necessity too is a flexible test. *The more pronounced a continuous and apparent use is, the less the degree of convenience of use necessary to the creation of an easement by implication.* (Emphasis added.) American Law of Property sec. 8.43 (A.J. Casner ed. 1952).)

As the above quote demonstrates, the "degree or extent of necessity" rubric suggests a concept with variable parameters. Professor Thompson notes the various phrases courts have used to describe the "extent of necessity" in cases in which there is proof of prior use:

> Basically, three things are essential to the creation of an easement upon the severance of an estate, upon the ground that the owner before the severance made use of an improvement in one part of the estate for the benefit of another: first, there must be a separation of the title, for, so long as there is unity of ownership, there can be no easement; second, it must appear that before the separation took place the use which gives rise to the easement shall have been so long continued and so obvious or manifest as to show that it was meant to be permanent; and, third, *the easement shall be necessary to the proper enjoyment of the land or to its reasonable, convenient or beneficial enjoyment, "reasonably necessary" to its enjoyment or use, "convenient use," or "clearly necessary" to its beneficial use.* (Emphasis added.) 2 G. Thompson, Commentaries on the Modern Law of Real Property sec. 352, at 305-07 (rep. ed. 1980).

Professor Powell, in his treatise, offers an alternative solution to the problem of stating the "extent of necessity" concept for the prior use situation that distinguishes it from the similar concept in the easement by necessity. Powell suggests that in a case with proof of prior use, the word "necessity" should be replaced by the phrase "important to the enjoyment of the conveyed quasi-dominant [or quasi-servient] parcel." As Powell explains:

> The requirement that the quasi-easement must have been "important for the enjoyment of the conveyed quasi-dominant [or quasi-servient] parcel is highly elastic. Some courts say that the use must be one which is "reasonably

necessary to the enjoyment of the [conveyed or retained] land." Others demand a use which is necessary for the beneficial, convenient, comfortable or reasonable enjoyment of such land. *When this prerequisite is phrased in terms of 'necessity,' a court is no longer properly considering the problem of implication from a quasi-easement but has crossed over (perhaps unwittingly) into the domain of easements by necessity (see* supra *par. 410).* The English courts have avoided this possible confusion by dispensing completely with this third requirement, finding easements by implication from a quasi-easement which is both "apparent" and "continuous," and without proof of its "importance." In the American courts, *"importance" strengthens the inference that the claimed easement was intended by the parties."* (Emphasis added.) 3 R. Powell, The Law of Real Property sec. 411[2] (P. Rohan ed. 1987).

Notwithstanding their difference in use of terminology, the authorities agree that the degree of extent of necessity required to create an easement by implication differs in both meaning and significance depending on the existence of proof of prior use. Hence, given the strong evidence of the plaintiff's prior use of the driveways in question and the defendants' knowledge thereof, we must agree with the appellate court majority that the evidence in this case was sufficient to fulfill the elastic necessity requirement. We approve of the appellate court majority's application of the facts of this case to the law as we have described it herein. As the appellate majority thoroughly explained:

While the trial court ruled that the driveway to the rear of the shopping center on the defendant's property was simply "more convenient . . . but not reasonably necessary" to the plaintiff's use of the property, this finding was premised on the assumption that the driveway on the other side of the shopping center provided adequate access for trucks making deliveries to the stores in the shopping center. The evidence was uncontradicted, however, that many of the deliveries were made by semitrailer trucks that would have to "jockey around quite a bit" in order to turn around behind the stores and that there may be as many as four or five trucks backed up at one time, making it impossible to turn around and go out the way they came in. For this reason, the pattern for deliveries to the stores had always been to circle around the shopping center, using the driveways on both sides. Use of the driveway on the defendant's property was thus quite beneficial to the fair enjoyment of the plaintiff's property, notwithstanding the driveway located on the other side of the shopping center. In view of these circumstances openly existing at the time of sale, it would be unreasonable to assume that the plaintiff intended to relinquish the use of this servitude on the defendant's property and assume the burden of trying to find alternate delivery routes to the stores in the shopping center. The evidence, moreover, regarding the difficulty of making deliveries to the front of the shopping center was sufficient to demonstrate the unreasonableness of such an alternative measure, despite the plaintiff's failure to establish the precise cost of reconstructing the shopping center for that purpose. We hold, therefore, that the plaintiff sustained as burden of proof as to the implied easement for the shopping center and accordingly reverse the trial court's judgment denying injunctive relief as to this easement.

Finally, with regard to the claimed easement over the defendant's property to the apartment complex parking lot, we find that the trial court's determination that such easement was "highly convenient and reasonably necessary" for the use and enjoyment of the complex was amply supported by the evidence at trial. The driveway in question had provided the only access to the parking lot behind the complex for over 15 years, and the evidence showed that the space between the buildings was inadequate to accommodate alternative driveways to the parking lot from Prairie Street, considering the plan of the buildings and the need to insure the safety of residents entering and leaving from basement apartments on the side of the buildings. The testimony indicated, moreover, that even if the plaintiff were required to construct a new parking lot in front of the buildings, there would not be adequate parking spaces for the tenants of the apartment building. We hold, therefore, that the trial court's ruling finding an implied easement for the plaintiff as to the apartment complex driveway should be affirmed. Granite Properties Limited Partnership v. Manns (1986), 140 Ill. App. 3d 561, 573-74, 94 Ill. Dec. 353, 487 N.E.2d 1230.

For the above reasons, the judgment of the appellate court is affirmed. The cause is remanded to the circuit court of Madison County.

Affirmed and remanded.

Justice GOLDENHERSH took no part in the consideration or decision of this case.

Chapter Thirty-three

Public Law Devices

Insert the following note on page 1166 before the section on eminent domain.

Note: Right-to-Farm Laws

The conversion of farmland to other uses raises concerns over the preservation of an appropriate amount of farmland for agricultural use. For a detailed discussion of this issue, see Hand, Right-to-Farm Laws: Breaking New Ground in the Preservation of Farmland, 45 U. Pitt. L. Rev. 289 (1984).

Insert the following material on page 1172 before the note on inverse condemnation.

Case concerned with when the "taking" issue is ripe for decision.

WILLIAMSON COUNTY REGIONAL PLANNING COMMISSION v. HAMILTON BANK

Supreme Court of the United States, 1985
—U.S.—, 105 S. Ct. 3108

JUSTICE BLACKMUN delivered the opinion of the Court.

Respondent, the owner of a tract of land it was developing as a residential subdivision, sued petitioners, the Williamson County [Tennessee] Regional Planning Commission and its members and staff, in United States District Court, alleging that petitioners' application of various zoning laws and regulations to respondent's property amounted to a "taking" of that property. At trial, the jury agreed and awarded respondent $350,000 as just compensation for the "taking." Although the jury's verdict was rejected by the District Court, which granted a judgment notwithstanding the verdict to petitioners, the verdict was reinstated on appeal. Petitioners and their *amici* urge this Court to overturn the jury's award on the ground that a temporary regulatory interference with an investor's profit expectation does not constitute a "taking" within the meaning of the Just Compensation Clause of the Fifth Amendment,[1] or, alternatively, on the ground that even if such interference does constitute a taking, the Just Compensation Clause does not require money damages as recompense. Before we reach those contentions, we examine the procedural posture of respondent's claim.

I

A

Under Tennessee law, responsibility for land-use planning is divided between the legislative body of each of the State's counties and regional and municipal "planning commissions." The county legislative body is responsible for zoning ordinances to regulate the uses to which particular land and buildings may be put, and to control the density of population and the location and dimensions of buildings. Tenn. Code Ann. §13-7-101 (1980). The planning commissions are responsible for more specific regulations governing the subdivision of land within their region or municipality for residential development. §§13-3-403, 13-4-303. Enforcement of both the zoning ordinances and the subdivision regulations is accomplished in part through a requirement that the planning commission approve the plat of a subdivision before the plat may be recorded. §§13-3-402, 13-4-302 (1980 & Supp. 1984).

Pursuant to §13-7-101, the Williamson County "Quarterly Court," which is the county's legislative body, in 1973 adopted a zoning ordinance that allowed "cluster" development of residential areas. Under "cluster" zoning,

> both the size and the width of individual residential lots in . . . [a] development may be reduced, provided . . . that the overall density of the entire tract remains constant — provided, that is, that an area equivalent to the total of the areas thus "saved" from each individual lot is pooled and retained as common open space. 2 N. Williams, American Land Planning Law §47.01, pp. 212-213 (1974).

Cluster zoning thus allows housing units to be grouped, or "clustered" together, rather than being evenly spaced on uniform lots.

As required by §13-3-402, respondent's predecessor-in-interest (developer) in 1973 submitted a preliminary plat for the cluster develop-

---

1. "[N]or shall private property be taken for public use, without just compensation." The Fifth Amendment's prohibition, of course, applies against the States through the Fourteenth Amendment. Chicago, B.&Q.R. Co. v. Chicago, 166 U.S. 226, 241 (1897); see also San Diego Gas & Electric Co. v. San Diego, 450 U.S. 621, 623 n.1 (1981).

ment of its tract, the Temple Hills Country Club Estates (Temple Hills), to the Williamson County Regional Planning Commission for approval. At that time, the county's zoning ordinance and the Commission's subdivision regulations required developers to seek review and approval of subdivision plats in two steps. The developer first was to submit for approval a preliminary plat, or "initial sketch plan," indicating, among other things, the boundaries and acreage of the site, the number of dwelling units and their basic design, the location of existing and proposed roads, structures, lots, utility layouts, and open space, and the contour of the land. App. in case No. 82-5388 (CA6), pp. 857, 871 (CA App.). Once approved, the preliminary plat served as a basis for the preparation of a final plat. Under the Commission's regulations, however, approval of a preliminary plat "will not constitute acceptance of the final plat." Id. at 872. Approval of a preliminary plat lapsed if a final plat was not submitted within one year of the date of the approval, unless the Commission granted an extension of time, or unless the approval of the preliminary plat was renewed. Ibid. The final plat, which is the official authenticated document that is recorded, was required to conform substantially to the preliminary plat, and, in addition, to include such details as the lines of all streets, lots, boundaries, and building setbacks. Id., at 875.

On May 3 1973, the Commission approved the developer's preliminary plat for Temple Hills. App. 246-247. The plat indicated that the development was to include 676 acres, of which 260 acres would be open space, primarily in the form of a golf course. Id., at 422. A notation on the plat indicated that the number of "allowable dwelling units for total development" was 736, but lot lines were drawn in for only 469 units. The areas in which the remaining 276 units were to be placed were left blank and bore the notation "this parcel not to be developed until approved by the planning commission." The plat also contained a disclaimer that "parcels with note 'this parcel not to be developed until approved by the planning commission' not a part of this plat and not included in gross areas." Ibid. The density of 736 allowable dwelling units was calculated by multiplying the number of acres (676) by the number of units allowed per acre (1.089). Id., at 361. Although the zoning regulations in effect in 1973 required that density be calculated "on the basis of total acreage less fifty percent (50%) of the land lying in the flood plain . . . and less fifty percent (50%) of all land lying on a slope with a grade in excess of twenty-five percent (25%)," CA App. 858, no deduction was made from the 676 acres for such land. Tr. 369.

Upon approval of the preliminary plat, the developer conveyed to the county a permanent open space easement for the golf course, and began building roads and installing utility lines for the project. App. 259-260. The developer spent approximately $3 million building the golf course, and another $500,000 installing sewer and water facilities. Defendant's Ex. 96. Before housing construction was to begin on a particular section, a final plat of that section was submitted for approval. Several sections, containing a total of 212 units, were given final approval by 1979. App. 260, 270, 278, 423. The preliminary plat, as well, was reapproved four times during that period. Id., at 270, 274, 362, 423.

In 1977, the county changed its zoning ordinance to require that calculations of allowable density exclude 10% of the total acreage to account for roads and utilities. Id., at 363; CA App. 862. In addition, the number of allowable units was changed to one per acre from the 1.089 per acre allowed in 1973. Id., at 858, 862; Tr. 1169-1170, 1183. The Commission continued to apply the zoning ordinance and subdivision regulations in effect in 1973 to Temple Hills, however, and reapproved the preliminary plat in 1978. In August 1979, the Commission reversed its position and decided that plats submitted for renewal should be evaluated under the zoning ordinance and subdivision regulations in effect when the renewal was sought. App. 279-282. The Commission then renewed the Temple Hills plat under the ordinances and regulations in effect at that time. Id., at 283-284.

In January 1980, the Commission asked the developer to submit a revised preliminary plat before it sought final approval for the remaining sections of the subdivision. The Commission reasoned that this was necessary because the original preliminary plat contained a number of surveying errors, the land available in the subdivision had been decreased inasmuch as the State had condemned part of the land for a parkway, and the areas marked "reserved for future development" had never been platted. Plaintiff's Exs. 1078 and 1079; Tr. 164-168. A special committee (Temple Hills Committee) was appointed to work with the developer on the revision of the preliminary plat. Plaintiff's Ex. 1081; Tr. 169-170.

The developer submitted a revised preliminary plat for approval in October 1980.[2] Upon review, the Commission's staff and the Temple Hills Committee noted several problems with the revised plat. App. 304-305. First, the allowable density under the zoning ordinance and subdivision regulations then in effect was 548 units, rather than the 736 units claimed under the preliminary plat approved in 1973. The difference reflected a decrease in 18.5 acres for the parkway, a decrease of 66 acres

2. The developer also submitted the preliminary plat that had been approved in 1973 and reapproved on several subsequent occasions, contending that it had the right to develop the property according to that plat. As we have noted, that plat did not indicate how all of the parcels would be developed. App. 84-85.

for the 10% deduction for roads, and an exclusion of 44 acres for 50% of the land lying on slopes exceeding a 25% grade. Second, two cul-de-sac roads that had become necessary because of the land taken for the parkway exceeded the maximum length allowed for such roads under the subdivision regulations in effect in both 1980 and 1973. Third, approximately 2000 feet of road would have grades in excess of the maximum allowed by county road regulations. Fourth, the preliminary plat placed units on land that had grades in excess of 25% and thus was considered undevelopable under the zoning ordinance and subdivision regulations. Fifth, the developer had not fulfilled its obligations regarding the construction and maintenance of the main access road. Sixth, there were inadequate fire protection services for the area, as well as inadequate open space for children's recreational activities. Finally, the lots proposed in the preliminary plat had a road frontage that was below the minimum required by the subdivision regulations in effect in 1980.

The Temple Hills Committee recommended that the Commission grant a waiver of the regulations regarding the length of the cul-de-sacs, the maximum grade of the roads, and the minimum frontage requirement. Id., at 297, 304-306. Without addressing the suggestion that those three requirements be waived, the Commission disapproved the plat on two other grounds: first, the plat did not comply with the density requirements of the zoning ordinance or subdivision regulations, because no deduction had been made for the land taken for the parkway, and because there had been no deduction for 10% of the acreage attributable to roads or for 50% of the land having a slope of more than 25%; and second, lots were placed on slopes with a grade greater than 25%. Plaintiff's Ex. 9112.

The developer then appealed to the County Board of Zoning Appeals for an "interpretation of the Residential Cluster zoning [ordinance] as it relates to Temple Hills."[3] App. 314. On November 11, 1980, the Board

---

3. The Board of Zoning Appeals was empowered:

a. To hear and decide appeals on any permit, decision, determination, or refusal made by the [County] Building Commissioner or other administrative official in the carrying out or enforcement of any provision of this Resolution; and to interpret the Zoning map and this Resolution. . . .

c. To hear and decide applications for variances from the terms of this Resolution. Such variances shall be granted only where by reason of exceptional narrowness, shallowness, or shape of a specific piece of property which at the time of adoption of this Resolution was a lot of record, or where by reason of exceptional topographic situations or conditions of a piece of property the strict application of the provisions of this Resolution would result in practical difficulties to or undue hardship upon the owner of such property. Plaintiff's Ex. 9112. See also Tenn. Code. Ann. §§13-7-106 to 13-7-109 (1980).

determined that the Commission should apply the zoning ordinance and subdivision regulations that were in effect in 1973 in evaluating the density of Temple Hills. Id., at 328. It also decided that in measuring which lots had excessive grades, the Commission should define the slope in a manner more favorable to the developer. Id., at 329.

On November 26, respondent, Hamilton Bank of Johnson City, acquired through foreclosure the property in the Temple Hills subdivision that had not yet been developed, a total of 257.65 acres. Id., at 189-190. This included many of the parcels that had been left blank in the preliminary plat approved in 1973. In June 1981, respondent submitted two preliminary plats to the Commission — the plat that had been approved in 1973 and subsequently reapproved several times, and a plat indicating respondent's plans for the undeveloped areas, which was similar to the plat submitted by the developer in 1980. Id., at 88. The new plat proposed the development of 688 units; the reduction from 736 units represented respondent's concession that 18.5 acres should be removed from the acreage because that land had been taken for the parkway. Id., at 424, 425.

On June 18, the Commission disapproved the plat for eight reasons, including the density and grade problems cited in the October 1980 denial, as well as the objections the Temple Hills Committee had raised in 1980 to the length of two cul-de-sacs, the grade of various roads, the lack of fire protection, the disrepair of the main-access road, and the minimum frontage. Id., at 370. The Commission declined to follow the decision of the Board of Zoning Appeals that the plat should be evaluated by the 1973 zoning ordinance and subdivision regulations, stating that the Board lacked jurisdiction to hear appeals from the Commission. Id., at 187-188, 360-361.

B

Respondent then filed this suit in the United States District Court for the Middle District of Tennessee, pursuant to 42 U.S.C. §1983, alleging that the Commission had taken its property without just compensation and asserting that the Commission should be estopped under state law from denying approval of the project.[4] Respondent's expert witnesses testified that the design that would meet each of the Commission's eight objections would allow respondent to build only 67 units, 409 fewer than

4. Respondent also alleged that the Commission's refusal to approve the plat violated respondent's rights to substantive and procedural due process and denied it equal protection. The District Court granted a directed verdict to petitioners on the substantive due process and equal protection claims, and the jury found that respondent had not been denied procedural due process. App. 32. Those issues are not before us.

respondent claims it is entitled to build,[5] and that the development of only 67 sites would result in a net loss of over $1 million. App. 377. Petitioners' expert witness, on the other hand, testified that the Commission's eight objections could be overcome by a design that would allow development of approximately 300 units. Tr. 1467-1468.

After a three-week trial, the jury found that respondent had been denied the "economically viable" use of its property in violation of the Just Compensation Clause, and that the Commission was estopped under state law from requiring respondent to comply with the current zoning ordinance and subdivision regulations rather than those in effect in 1973. App. 32-33. The jury awarded damages of $350,000 for the temporary taking of respondent's property. Id., at 33-34.[6] The court entered a permanent injunction requiring the Commission to apply the zoning ordinance and subdivision regulations in effect in 1973 to Temple Hills, and to approve the plat submitted in 1981. Id., at 34.

The court then granted judgment notwithstanding the verdict in favor of the Commission on the taking claim, reasoning in part that respondent was unable to derive economic benefit from its property on a temporary basis only, and that such a temporary deprivation, as a matter of law, cannot constitute a taking. Id., at 36, 41. In addition, the court modified its permanent injunction to require the Commission merely to apply the zoning ordinance and subdivisions regulations in effect in 1973 to the project, rather than requiring approval of the plat, in order to allow the parties to resolve "legitimate technical questions of whether plaintiff meets the requirements of the 1973 regulations," id., at 42, through the applicable state and local appeals procedures.[7]

A divided panel of the United States Court of Appeals for the Sixth

---

5. Id., at 377; Tr. 238-243. Respondent claimed it was entitled to build 476 units: the 736 units allegedly approved in 1973 minus the 212 units already built or given final approval and minus 48 units that were no longer available because land had been taken from the subdivision for the parkway.

6. Although the record is less than clear, it appears that the jury calculated the $350,000 award by determining a fair rate of return on the value of the property for the time between the Commission's rejection of the preliminary plat in 1980 and the jury's verdict in March 1982. See Tr. 800-805; Tr. of Oral Arg. 25, 32-33. In light of our disposition of the case, we need not reach the question whether that measure of damages would provide just compensation, or whether it would be appropriate if respondent's cause of action were viewed as stating a claim under the Due Process Clause.

7. While respondent's appeal was pending before the Court of Appeals, the parties reached an agreement whereby the Commission granted a variance from its cul-de-sac and road grade regulations and approved the development of 476 units, and respondent agreed, among other things, to rebuild existing roads, and build all new roads, according to current regulations. App. to Brief for Petitioners 35.

Circuit reversed. 729 F.2d 402 (1984). The court held that application of government regulations affecting an owner's use of property may constitute a taking if the regulation denies the owner all "economically viable" use of the land, and that the evidence supported the jury's finding that the property had no economically feasible use during the time between the Commission's refusal to approve the preliminary plat and the jury's verdict. Id., at 405-406. Rejecting petitioners' argument that respondent never had submitted a plat that complied with the 1973 regulations, and thus never had acquired rights that could be taken, the court held that the jury's estoppel verdict indicates that the jury must have found that respondent had acquired a "vested right" under state law to develop the subdivision according to the plat submitted in 1973. Id., at 407. Even if respondent had no vested right under state law to finish the development, the jury was entitled to find that respondent had a reasonable investment-backed expectation that the development could be completed, and that the actions of the Commission interfered with that expectation. Ibid.

The court rejected the District Court's holding that the taking verdict could not stand as a matter of law. A temporary denial of property could be a taking, and was to be analyzed in the same manner as a permanent taking. Finally, relying upon the dissent in San Diego Gas & Electric Co. v. San Diego, 450 U.S. 621, 636 (1981), the court determined that damages are required to compensate for a temporary taking.[8]

II

We granted certiorari to address the question whether federal, state, and local governments must pay money damages to a landowner whose property allegedly has been "taken" temporarily by the application of government regulations. — U.S. — (1984). Petitioners and their *amici* contend that we should answer the question in the negative by ruling that government regulation can never effect a "taking" within the meaning of

---

8. Judge Wellford dissented. 729 F.2d, at 409. He did not agree that the evidence supported a finding that respondent's property had been taken, in part because there was no evidence that respondent had formally requested a variance from the regulations. Even if there was a temporary denial of the "economically viable" use of the property, Judge Wellford would have held that mere fluctuations in value during the process of governmental decision-making are "incidents of ownership" and cannot be considered a "taking," id., at 410, quoting Agins v. Tiburon, 447 U.S. 255, 263, n.9 (1980). He also did not agree that damages could be awarded to remedy any taking, reasoning that the *San Diego Gas* dissent does not reflect the views of the majority of this Court, and that this Court never has awarded damages for a temporary taking where there was no invasion, physical occupation, or "seizure and direction" by the State of the landowner's property. 729 F.2d, at 411.

the Fifth Amendment. They recognize that government regulation may be so restrictive that it denies a property owner all reasonable beneficial use of its property, and thus has the same effect as an appropriation of the property for public use, which concededly would be a taking under the Fifth Amendment. According to petitioners, however, regulation that has such an effect should not be viewed as a taking. Instead, such regulation should be viewed as a violation of the Fourteenth Amendment's Due Process Clause, because it is an attempt by government to use its police power to effect a result that is so unduly oppressive to the property owner that it constitutionally can be effected only through the power of eminent domain. Violations of the Due Process Clause, petitioners' argument concludes, need not be remedied by "just compensation."

The Court twice has left this issue undecided. San Diego Gas & Electric Co. v. San Diego, *supra;* Agins v. Tiburon, 447 U.S. 255, 263 (1980). Once again, we find that the question is not properly presented, and must be left for another day. For whether we examine the Planning Commission's application of its regulations under Fifth Amendment "taking" jurisprudence, or under the precept of due process, we conclude that respondent's claim is premature.

III

We examine the posture of respondent's cause of action first by viewing it as stating a claim under the Just Compensation Clause. This Court often has referred to regulation that "goes too far," Pennsylvania Coal Co. v. Mahon, 260 U.S. 393, 415 (1922), as a "taking." See e.g., Ruckleshaus v. Monsanto Co., — U.S. —, (1984) (slip op. 16-17); Agins v. Tiburon, 447 U.S., at 260; PruneYard Shopping Center v. Robins, 447 U.S. 74, 83 (1980); Kaiser Aetna v. United States, 444 U.S. 164, 174 (1979); Andrus v. Allard, 444 U.S. 51, 65-66 (1979); Penn Central Transp. Co. v. New York City, 438 U.S. 104, 124 (1978); Goldblatt v. Hempstead, 369 U.S. 590, 594 (1962); United States v. Central Eureka Mining Co., 357 U.S. 155, 168 (1958). Even assuming that those decisions meant to refer literally to the Taking Clause of the Fifth Amendment, and therefore stand for the proposition that regulation may effect a taking for which the Fifth Amendment requires just compensation, see *San Diego,* 450 U.S., at 647-653 (dissenting opinion), and even assuming further that the Fifth Amendment requires the payment of money damages to compensate for such a taking, the jury verdict in this case cannot be upheld. Because the respondent has not yet obtained a final decision regarding the application of the zoning ordinance and subdivision regulations to its property, nor utilized the procedures Tennessee provides for obtaining just compensation, respondent's claim is not ripe.

A

As the Court has made clear in several recent decisions, a claim that the application of government regulations effects a taking of a property interest is not ripe until the government entity charged with implementing the regulations has reached a final decision regarding the application of the regulations to the property at issue. In Hodel v. Virginia Surface Mining & Reclamation Assn., Inc., 452 U.S. 264 (1981), for example, the Court rejected a claim that the Surface Mining Control and Reclamation Act of 1977, 91 Stat. 447, 30 U.S.C. §1201 et seq., effected a taking because:

> There is no indication in the record that appellees have availed themselves of the opportunities provided by the Act to obtain administrative relief by requesting either a variance from the approximate-original-contour requirement of §515(d) or a waiver from the surface mining restrictions in §522(e). If [the property owners] were to seek administrative relief under these procedures, a mutually acceptable solution might well be reached with regard to individual properties, thereby obviating any need to address the constitutional questions. The potential for such administrative solutions confirms the conclusion that the taking issue decided by the District Court simply is not ripe for judicial resolution. 452 U.S., at 297 (footnote omitted).

Similarly, in Agins v. Tiburon, *supra,* the Court held that a challenge to the application of a zoning ordinance was not ripe because the property owners had not yet submitted a plan for development of their property. 447 U.S., at 260. In Penn Central Transp. Co. v. New York City, *supra,* the Court declined to find that the application of New York City's Landmarks Preservation Law to Grand Central Terminal effected a taking because, although the Landmarks Preservation Commission had disapproved a plan for a 50-story office building above the terminal, the property owners had not sought approval for any other plan, and it therefore was not clear whether the Commission would deny approval for all uses that would enable the plaintiffs to derive economic benefit from the property. 438 U.S., at 136-137.

Respondent's claim is in a posture similar to the claims the Court held premature in *Hodel.* Respondent has submitted a plan for developing its property, and thus has passed beyond the *Agins* threshhold. But, like the *Hodel* plaintiffs, respondent did not then seek variances that would have allowed it to develop the property according to its proposed plat, notwithstanding the Commission's finding that the plat did not comply with the zoning ordinance and subdivision regulations. It appears that variances could have been granted to resolve at least five of the Commission's eight objections to the plat. The Board of Zoning Appeals had the power to grant certain variances from the zoning ordinance, including the ordinance's density requirements and its restriction on placing units on land with slopes having a grade in excess of 25%. Tr. 1204-1205, see n.3, *supra.* The Commission had the power to grant variances from the subdivision regulations, including the cul-de-sac, road grade, and frontage requirements.[9] Indeed, the Temple Hills Committee had recommended that the Commission grant variances from those regulations. App. 304-306. Nevertheless, respondent did not seek variances from either the Board or the Commission.

Respondent argues that it "did everything possible to resolve the conflict with the commission," Brief for Respondent 42, and that the Commission's denial of approval for respondent's plat was equivalent to a denial of variances. The record does not support respondent's claim, however. There is no evidence that respondent applied to the Board of Zoning Appeals for variances from the zoning ordinance. As noted, the developer sought a ruling that the ordinance in effect in 1973 should be applied, but neither respondent nor the developer sought a variance from the requirements of either the 1973 or 1980 ordinances. Further, although the subdivision regulations in effect in 1981 required that applications to the Commission for variances be in writing, and that notice of the application be given to owners of adjacent property,[10] the record contains no evidence that respondent ever filed a written request for variances from the cul-de-sac, road grade, or frontage requirements of the subdivision regulations, or that respondent ever gave the required notice.[11] App. 212-213; see also Tr. 1255-1257.

---

9. The subdivision regulations in effect in 1980 and 1981 provided:

Variances may be granted under the following conditions:
Where the subdivider can show that strict adherence to these regulations would cause unnecessary hardship, due to conditions beyond the control of the subdivider. If the subdivider creates the hardship due to his design or in an effort to increase the yield of lots in his subdivision, the variance will not be granted.
Where the Planning Commission decides that there are topographical or other conditions peculiar to the site, and a departure from their regulations will not destroy their intent. CA App. 932.

10. The Commission's regulations required that

Each applicant must file with the Planning Commission a written request for variance stating at least the following:
a. The variance requested;
b. Reason or circumstances requiring the variance;
c. Notice to the adjacent property owners that a variance is being requested.
Without the application any condition shown on the plat which would require a variance will constitute grounds for disapproval of the plat. Id., at 933.

11. Respondent's predecessor-in-interest requested, and apparently was granted, a waiver of the 10% road grade regulation for section VI of the subdivision. See Plaintiff's Exs. 1078, 9094. The predecessor-in-interest wrote a letter on January 3, 1980, that respon-

Indeed, in a letter to the Commission written shortly before its June 18, 1981, meeting to consider the preliminary sketch, respondent took the position that it would not request variances from the Commission until *after* the Commission approved the proposed plat:

> [Respondent] stands ready to work with the Planning Commission concerning the necessary variances. Until the initial sketch is renewed, however, and the developer has an opportunity to do detailed engineering work it is impossible to determine the exact nature of any variances that may be needed. Plaintiff's Ex. 9028, p.6.

The Commission's regulations clearly indicated that unless a developer applied for a variance in writing and upon notice to other property owners, "any condition shown on the plat which would require a variance will constitute grounds for disapproval of the plat." CA App. 933. Thus, in the face of respondent's refusal to follow the procedures for requesting a variance, and its refusal to provide specific information about the variances it would require, respondent hardly can maintain that the Commission's disapproval of the preliminary plat was equivalent to a final decision that no variances would be granted.

As in *Hodel, Agins,* and *Penn Central,* then, respondent has not yet obtained a final decision regarding how it will be allowed to develop its property. Our reluctance to examine taking claims until such a final decision has been made is compelled by the very nature of the inquiry required by the Just Compensation Clause. Although "[t]he question of what constitutes a 'taking' for the purposes of the Fifth Amendment has proved to be a problem of considerable difficulty," Penn Central Transp.

---

dent contends must be construed as a request for a waiver of the road-grade regulation for the entire subdivision:

> I contend that the road grade and slope question . . . is adequately provided for by both the [subdivision] Regulations and the Zoning Ordinance. In both, the Planning Commission is given the authority to approve roads that have grades in excess of 10%.
> In our particular case, it was common knowledge from the beginning that due to the character of the land involved that there would be roads that exceeded the 10% slope. In fact in our first Section there is a stretch of road that exceeds the 10%; therefore I respectfully request that this letter be made an official part of the Planning Commission Minutes of January 3, 1980 and further the Zoning Approval which has been granted be allowed to stand without any changes. Defendants' Ex. 96.

Even assuming *arguendo* that the letter constituted a request for a variance, respondent's taking claim nevertheless is not ripe. There is no evidence that respondent requested variances from the regulations that formed the basis of the other objections raised by the Commission, such as those regulating the length of cul-de-sacs. Absent a final decision regarding the application of *all* eight of the Commission's objections, it is impossible to tell whether the land retained any reasonable beneficial use or whether respondent's expectation interests had been destroyed.

Co. v. New York City, 438 U.S., at 123, this Court consistently has indicated that among the factors of particular significance in the inquiry are the economic impact of the challenged action and the extent to which it interferes with reasonable investment-backed expectations. Id., at 124. See also Ruckleshaus v. Monsanto Co., — U.S., at — (slip op. 17); PruneYard Shopping Center v. Robins, 447 U.S., at 83; Kaiser Aetna v. United States, 444 U.S., at 175. Those factors simply cannot be evaluated until the administrative agency has arrived at a final, definitive position regarding how it will apply the regulations at issue to the particular land in question.

Here, for example, the jury's verdict indicates only that it found that respondent would be denied the economically feasible use of its property if it were forced to develop the subdivision in a manner that would meet each of the Commission's eight objections. It is not clear whether the jury would have found that the respondent had been denied all reasonable beneficial use of the property had any of the eight objections been met through the grant of a variance. Indeed, the expert witness who testified regarding the economic impact of the Commission's actions did not itemize the effect of each of the eight objections, so the jury would have been unable to discern how a grant of a variance from any one of the regulations at issue would have affected the profitability of the development. App. 377; see also id., at 102-104. Accordingly, until the Commission determines that no variances will be granted, it is impossible for the jury to find, on this record, whether respondents "will be unable to derive economic benefit" from the land.[12]

---

12. The District Court's instructions allowed the jury to find a taking if it ascertained "that the regulations in question as applied to [respondent's] property denied [respondent] economically viable use of its property" Tr. 2016. That instruction seems to assume that respondent's taking theory was simply that its property was rendered valueless by the application of new zoning laws and subdivision regulations in 1980. The record indicates, however, that respondent's claim was based upon a state law theory of "vested rights," and that the alleged "taking" was the Commission's interference with respondent's "expectation interest" in completing the development according to its original plans. The evidence that it was not economically feasible to develop just the 67 units respondent claims the Commission's actions would limit it to developing was based upon the cost of building the development according to the original plan. The expected income from the sale of the 67 units apparently was measured against the cost of the 27-hole golf course and the cost of installing water and sewer connections for a large development that would not have had to have been installed for a development of only 67 units. App. 191-197; Tr. 690; see also id., at 2154-2155. Thus, the evidence appears to indicate that it would not be profitable to develop 67 units because respondent had made various expenditures in the expectation that the development would contain far more units; the evidence does not appear to support the proposition that, aside from those "reliance" expenditures, development of 67 units on the property would not be economically feasible.

We express no view of the propriety of applying the "economic viability" test when the

Respondent asserts that it should not be required to seek variances from the regulations because its suit is predicated upon 42 U.S.C. §1983, and there is no requirement that a plaintiff exhaust administrative remedies before bringing a §1983 action. Patsy v. Florida Board of Regents, 457 U.S. 496 (1982). The question whether administrative remedies must be exhausted is conceptually distinct, however, from the question whether an administrative action must be final before it is judicially reviewable. See FTC v. Standard Oil Co., 449 U.S. 232, 243 (1980); Bethlehem Steel Corp. v. EPA, 669 F.2d 903, 908 (CA3 1982). See generally, C. Wright, A. Miller & E. Cooper, Federal Practice and Procedure §3532.6 (1984). While the policies underlying the two concepts often overlap, the finality requirement is concerned with whether the initial decision-maker has arrived at a definitive position on the issue that inflicts an actual, concrete injury; the exhaustion requirement generally refers to administrative and judicial procedures by which an injured party may seek review of an adverse decision and obtain a remedy if the decision is found to be unlawful or otherwise inappropriate. Patsy concerned the latter, not the former.

The difference is best illustrated by comparing the procedure for seeking a variance with the procedures that, under Patsy, respondent would not be required to exhaust. While it appears that the State provides procedures by which an aggrieved property owner may seek a declaratory judgment regarding the validity of zoning and planning actions taken by county authorities, see Fallin v. Knox County Bd. of Commrs., 656 S.W.2d 338 (Tenn. 1983); Tenn. Code Ann. §§27-8-101, 27-9-101 to 27-9-113, and 29-14-101 to 29-14-113 (1980 and Supp. 1984), respondent would not be required to resort to those procedures before bringing its §1983 action, because those procedures clearly are remedial. Similarly, respondent would not be required to appeal the Commission's rejection of the preliminary plat to the Board of Zoning Appeals, because the Board was empowered, at most, to review that rejection, not to participate in the Commission's decision-making.

Resort to those procedures would result in a judgment whether the Commission's actions violated any of respondent's rights. In contrast, resort to the procedure for obtaining variances would result in a conclu-

---

taking claim is based upon such a theory of "vested rights" or "expectation interest." Cf. Andrus v. Allard, 444 U.S. 51, 66 (1979) (analyzing a claim that government regulations effected a taking by reducing expected profits). It is sufficient for our purposes to note that whether the "property" taken is viewed as the land itself or respondent's expectation interest in developing the land as it wished, it is impossible to determine the extent of the loss or interference until the Commission has decided whether it will grant a variance from the application of the regulations.

sive determination by the Commission whether it would allow respondent to develop the subdivision in the manner respondent proposed. The Commission's refusal to approve the preliminary plat does not determine that issue; it prevents respondent from developing its subdivision without obtaining the necessary variances, but leaves open the possibility that respondent may develop the subdivision according to its plat after otaining the variances. In short, the Commission's denial of approval does not conclusively determine whether respondent will be denied all reasonable beneficial use of its property, and therefore is not a final, reviewable decision.

B

A second reason the taking claim is not yet ripe is that respondent did not seek compensation through the procedures the State has provided for doing so.[13] The Fifth Amendment does not proscribe the taking of property; it proscribes taking without just compensation. Hodel v. Virginia Surface Mining & Recl. Assn., Inc., 452 U.S., at 297, n.40. Nor does the Fifth Amendment require that just compensation be paid in advance of, or contemporaneously with, the taking; all that is required is that a " 'reasonable, certain and adequate provision for obtaining compensation' " exist at the time of the taking. Regional Rail Reorganization Act Cases, 419 U.S. 102, 124-125 (1974) (quoting Cherokee Nation v. Southern Kansas R. Co., 135 U.S. 641, 659 (1890)). See also Ruckelshaus v. Monsanto Co., — U.S., at — (slip op. 28); Yearsley v. Ross Construction Co., 309 U.S. 18, 21 (1940); Hurley v. Kincaid, 285 U.S. 95, 104 (1932). If the government has provided an adequate process for obtaining compensation, and if resort to that process "yield[s] just compensation," then the property owner "has no claim against the Government for a taking." *Monsanto,* — U. S., at —, — n.21 (slip op. 24, and 30, n.21). Thus, we have held that taking claims against the Federal Government are premature until the property owner has availed itself of the process provided by the Tucker Act, 28 U.S.C. §1491. *Monsanto,* at —-— (slip op. 27-31). Similarly, if a State provides an adequate procedure for seeking just compensation, the property owner cannot claim a violation of the Just

13. Again, it is necessary to contrast the procedures provided for review of the Commission's actions, such as those for obtaining a declaratory judgment, see Tenn. Code Ann. §§29-14-101 to 29-14-113 (1980), with procedures that allow a property owner to obtain compensation for a taking. Exhaustion of review procedures is not required. See Patsy v. Florida Board of Regents, 457 U.S. 496 (1982). As we have explained, however, because the Fifth Amendment proscribes takings *without just compensation,* no constitutional violation occurs until just compensation has been denied. The nature of the constitutional right therefore requires that a property owner utilize procedures for obtaining compensation before bringing a §1983 action.

Compensation Clause until it has used the procedure and been denied just compensation.

The recognition that a property owner has not suffered a violation of the Just Compensation Clause until the owner has unsuccessfully attempted to obtain just compensation through the procedures provided by the State for obtaining such compensation is analogous to the Court's holding in Parratt v. Taylor, 451 U.S. 527 (1981). There, the Court ruled that a person deprived of property through a random and unauthorized act by a state employee does not state a claim under the Due Process Clause merely by alleging the deprivation of property. In such a situation, the Constitution does not require predeprivation process because it would be impossible or impracticable to provide a meaningful hearing before the deprivation. Instead, the Constitution is satisfied by the provision of meaningful postdeprivation process. Thus, the State's action is not "complete" in the sense of causing a constitutional injury "unless or until the State fails to provide an adequate postdeprivation remedy for the property loss." Hudson v. Palmer, — U.S. —, — n.12 (1984). Likewise, because the Constitution does not require pretaking compensation, and is instead satisfied by a reasonable and adequate provision for obtaining compensation after the taking, the State's action here is not "complete" until the State fails to provide adequate compensation for the taking.[14]

Under Tennessee law, a property owner may bring an inverse condemnation action to obtain just compensation for an alleged taking of property under certain circumstances. Tenn. Code Ann. §29-16-123 (1980). The statutory scheme for eminent domain proceedings outlines the procedures by which government entities must exercise the right of eminent domain. §§29-16-101 to 29-16-121. The State is prohibited from "enter-

---

14. The analogy to *Parratt* is imperfect because *Parratt* does not extend to situations such as those involved in Logan v. Zimmerman Brush Co., 455 U.S. 422 (1982), in which the deprivation of property is effected pursuant to an established state policy or procedure, and the State could provide predeprivation process. Unlike the Due Process Clause, however, the Just Compensation Clause has never been held to require pretaking process or compensation. Ruckleshaus v. Monsanto Co., — U.S. —, — (1984) (slip op. 28). Nor has the Court ever recognized any interest served by pretaking compensation that could not be equally well served by posttaking compensation. Under the Due Process Clause, on the other hand, the Court has recognized that predeprivation process is of "obvious value in reaching an accurate decision," that the "only meaningful opportunity to invoke the discretion of a decisionmaker is likely to be before the [deprivation] takes place," Cleveland Board of Education v. Loudermill, [470] U.S. [532] (1985) (slip op. 9-10), and that predeprivation process may serve the purpose of making an individual feel that the Government has dealt with him fairly. See Carey v. Piphus, 435 U.S. 247, 262 (1978). Thus, despite the Court's holding in *Logan*, *Parratt's* reasoning applies here by analogy because of the special nature of the Just Compensation Clause.

[ing] upon [condemned] land" until these procedures have been utilized and compensation has been paid the owner, §29-16-122, but if a government entity does take possession of the land without following the required procedures,

> the owner of such land may petition for a jury of inquest, in which case the same proceedings may be had, as near as may be, as hereinbefore provided; or he may sue for damages in the ordinary way. . . . §29-16-123.

The Tennessee state courts have interpreted §29-15-123 to allow recovery through inverse condemnation where the "taking" is effected by restrictive zoning laws or development regulations. See Davis v. Metropolitan Govt. of Nashville, 620 S.W.2d 532, 533-534 (Tenn. App. 1981); Speight v. Lockhart, 524 S.W.2d 249 (Tenn. App. 1975). Respondent has not shown that the inverse condemnation procedure is unavailable or inadequate, and until it has utilized that procedure, its taking claim is premature.

IV

We turn to an analysis of respondent's claim under the due process theory that petitioners espouse. As noted, under that theory government regulation does not effect a taking for which the Fifth Amendment requires just compensation; instead, regulation that goes so far that it has the same effect as a taking by eminent domain is an invalid exercise of the police power, violative of the Due Process Clause of the Fourteenth Amendment. Should the Government wish to accomplish the goals of such regulation, it must proceed through the exercise of its eminent domain power, and, of course, pay just compensation for any property taken. The remedy for a regulation that goes too far, under the due process theory, is not "just compensation," but invalidation of the regulation, and if authorized and appropriate, actual damages.[15]

---

15. See generally F. Bosselman, D. Callies, J. Banta, The Taking Issue 238-255 (1973); Sterk, Government Liability for Unconstitutional Land Use Regulation, [60] Ind. L.J. [113] (1985); Oakes, "Property Rights" in Constitutional Analysis Today, 56 Wash. L. Rev. 583 (1981); Stoebuck, Police Power, Takings, and Due Process, 37 Wash. & Lee L. Rev. 1057 (1980); Comment, Testing the Constitutional Validity of Land Use Regulations: Substantive Due Process as a Superior Alternative to Takings Analysis, 57 Wash. L. Rev. 715 (1982); Comment, Just Compensation or Just Invalidation: The Availability of a Damages Remedy in Challenging Land Use Regulations, 29 U.C.L.A.L. Rev. 711 (1982); cf. Costonis, "Fair" Compensation and the Accommodation Power: Antidotes for the Taking Impasse in Land Use Controversies, 75 Colum. L. Rev. 102 (1975) (proposing that regulation be viewed as neither an exercise of the police power, nor as a taking, but as an exercise of an "accommodation" power, which would require government to offer "fair compensation" for regulation that "goes too far").

The notion that excessive regulation can constitute a "taking" under the Just Compensation Clause stems from language in Pennsylvania Coal Co. v. Mahon, 260 U. S. 393 (1922). See *San Diego*, 450 U. S., at 649 (dissenting opinion). Writing for the *Pennsylvania Coal* Court, Justice Holmes stated: "The general rule at least is, that while property may be regulated to a certain extent, if regulation goes too far it will be recognized as a taking." 260 U.S., at 415. Those who argue that excessive regulation should be considered a violation of the Due Process Clause rather than a "taking" assert that *Pennsylvania Coal* used the word "taking" not in the literal Fifth Amendment sense, but as a metaphor for actions having the same effect as a taking by eminent domain. See, e.g., Agins v. City of Tiburon, 24 Cal. 3d 266, 274, 598 P.2d 25, 29 (1979), *aff'd*, 447 U. S. 255 (1980); Fred F. French Investing Co. v. City of New York, 39 N.Y.2d 587, 594, 350 N.E.2d 381, 385 (1976). Because no issue was presented in *Pennsylvania Coal* regarding compensation, it is argued, the Court was free to use the term loosely.[16]

The due process argument finds support, we are told, in the fact that the *Pennsylvania Coal* Court framed the question presented as "whether the police power can be stretched so far" as to destroy property rights, 260 U.S., at 413, and by the Court's emphasis upon the need to proceed by eminent domain rather than by regulation when the effect of the regulation would be to destroy property interests:

> Government hardly could go on if to some extent values incident to property could not be diminished without paying for every such change in the general law. As long recognized, some values are enjoyed under an implied limitation and must yield to the police power. But obviously the implied limitation must have its limits, or the contract and due process clauses are gone. One fact for consideration in determining such limits is the extent of the diminution. When it reaches a certain magnitude, in most if not in all cases *there must be an exercise of eminent domain and compensation to sustain the act.* Ibid. (Emphasis added.)

Further, in earlier cases involving the constitutional limitations on the exercise of police power, Justice Holmes' opinions for the Court made clear that the Court did not view overly restrictive regulation as triggering an award of compensation, but as an invalid means of accomplishing what constitutionally can be accomplished only through the exercise of

16. In *Pennsylvania Coal*, homeowners sought to enjoin a coal company from mining coal under their house in violation of Pennsylvania's Kohler Act, which prohibited the mining of coal that would cause the subsidence of any home or industrial or mercantile establishment. In defense, the coal company argued not that the regulation itself was a "taking" for which just compensation was required, but that "[i]f surface support in the anthracite district is necessary for public use, it can constitutionally be acquired only by condemnation with just compensation to the parties affected." 260 U.S., at 400.

eminent domain. See, e.g., Block v. Hirsch, 256 U.S. 135, 156 (1921); Hudson County Water Co. v. McCarter, 209 U.S. 349, 355 (1908); Martin v. District of Columbia, 205 U.S. 135, 139 (1907).

We need not pass upon the merits of petitioners' arguments, for even if viewed as a question of due process, respondent's claim is premature. Viewing a regulation that "goes too far" as an invalid exercise of the police power, rather than as a "taking" for which just compensation must be paid, does not resolve the difficult problem of how to define "too far," that is, how to distinguish the point at which regulation becomes so onerous that it has the same effect as an appropriation of the property through eminent domain or physical possession.[17] As we have noted, resolution of that question depends, in significant part, upon an analysis of the effect the Commission's application of the zoning ordinance and subdivision regulations had on the value of respondent's property and investment-backed profit expectations. That effect cannot be measured until a final decision is made as to how the regulations will be applied to respondent's property. No such decision had been made at the time respondent filed its §1983 action, because respondent failed to apply for variances from the regulations.

V

In sum, respondent's claim is premature, whether it is analyzed as a deprivation of property without due process under the Fourteenth Amendment, or as a taking under the Just Compensation Clause of the Fifth Amendment.[18] We therefore reverse the judgment of the Court of

17. The attempt to determine when regulation goes so far that it becomes, literally or figuratively, a "taking" has been called the "lawyer's equivalent of the physicist's hunt for the quark." C. Haar, Land-Use Planning 766 (3d ed. 1976). See generally, Bauman, The Supreme Court, Inverse Condemnation and the Fifth Amendment: Justice Brennan Confronts the Inevitable in Land Use Controls, 15 Rutgers L.J. 15, 20-32 (1983); Stoebuck, *supra*, at 1059-1079; Berger, A Policy Analysis of the Taking Problem, 49 N.Y.U.L. Rev. 165 (1974); Sax, Taking, Private Property and Public Rights, 81 Yale L.J. 149 (1971); Van Alstyne, Taking or Damaging by Police Power: The Search for Inverse Condemnation Criteria, 44 S. Cal. L. Rev. 1 (1971); Michelman, Property, Utility, and Fairness; Comments on the Ethical Foundations of "Just Compensation" Law, 80 Harv. L. Rev. 1165 (1967); Sax, Takings and the Police Power, 74 Yale L.J. 36 (1964).

18. In light of this disposition, we need not reach the question whether the jury's verdict that respondent's expectation interest had been "taken," see n.12, *supra*, can stand in light of the absence of any discussion in the jury instructions about the reasonableness of the alleged expectation interest. See Ruckleshaus v. Monsanto Co., — U.S. —, — (1984) (slip op. 17); Andrus v. Allard, 444 U.S., at 66. Nor do we need to reach the question whether the jury was properly allowed to determine the economic feasibility of the property, or the extent of interference with respondent's expectation interests, by reference to only that portion of the development purchased by respondent, rather than by reference to the development as a whole. Cf. Penn Central Trans. Co. v. New York City, 438 U.S. 104, 130 (1978).

Appeals and remand the case for further proceedings consistent with this opinion.

It is so ordered.

Justice WHITE dissents from the holding that the issues in this case are not ripe for decision at this time.

Justice POWELL took no part in the decision of this case.

Justice BRENNAN, with whom Justice MARSHALL joins, concurring.

Justice STEVENS, concurring in the judgment.

Insert the following material on page 1172 before the note on Inverse Condemnation.

Case on whether rent control ordinance is unconstitutional as involving a "taking" if hearing officer required to consider "hardship to a tenant" when determining whether to approve rent increase proposed by landlord.

PENNELL v. CITY OF SAN JOSE
Supreme Court of the United States, 1988
— U.S.—, 108 S. Ct. 849

Chief Justice REHNQUIST delivered the opinion of the Court.

This case involves a challenge to a rent control ordinance enacted by the City of San Jose, California, that allows a hearing officer to consider, among other factors, the "hardship to a tenant" when determining whether to approve a rent increase proposed by a landlord. Appellants Richard Pennell and the Tri-County Apartment House Owners Association sued in the Superior Court of Santa Clara County seeking a declaration that the ordinance, in particular the "tenant hardship" provisions, are "facially unconstitutional and therefore . . . illegal and void." The Superior Court entered judgment on the pleadings in favor of appellants, sustaining their claim that the tenant hardship provisions violated the Takings Clause of the 5th and 14th Amendments. The California Court of Appeal affirmed this judgment, 154 Cal. App. 3d 1019, 201 Cal. Rptr. 728 (1984), but the Supreme Court of California reversed, 42 Cal. 3d 365, 228 Cal. Rptr. 726, 721 P.2d 1111 (1986), each by a divided vote. The majority of the Supreme Court rejected appellants' arguments under the Takings Clause of the 5th and 14th Amendments and the Equal Protection and Due Process Clauses of the 14th Amendment; the dissenters in the court thought that the tenant hardship provisions were a "forced subsidy imposed on the landlord" in violation of the Takings Clause. Id., at 377, 228 Cal. Rptr., at 734, 721 P.2d, at 1119. On appellants' appeal to this Court we postponed consideration of the question of jurisdiction, 480 U.S. —, 107 S. Ct. 1346, 94 L. Ed. 2d 517 (1987), and now having heard oral argument we affirm the judgment of the Supreme Court of California.

The City of San Jose enacted its rent control ordinance (Ordinance) in 1979 with the stated purpose of

> alleviat[ing] some of the more immediate needs created by San Jose's housing situation. These needs include but are not limited to the prevention of excessive and unreasonable rent increases, the alleviation of undue hardships upon individual tenants, and the assurance to landlords of a fair and reasonable return on the value of their property. San Jose Municipal Ordinance 19696, §5701.2.[1]

At the heart of the Ordinance is a mechanism for determining the amount by which landlords subject to its provisions may increase the annual rent which they charge their tenants. A landlord is automatically entitled to raise the rent of a tenant in possession[2] by as much as eight percent; if a tenant objects to an increase greater than eight percent, a hearing is required before a "Mediation Hearing Officer" to determine whether the landlord's proposed increase is "reasonable under the circumstances." The Ordinance sets forth a number of factors to be considered by the hearing officer in making the determination, including "the hardship to a tenant." §5703.28(c)(7). Because appellants concentrate their attack on the consideration of this factor, we set forth the relevant provision of the Ordinance in full:

> 5703.29 Hardship to Tenants.   In the case of a rent increase or any portion thereof which exceeds the standard set in Section 5703.28(a) or (b), then with respect to such excess and whether or not to allow same to be part of the increase allowed under this Chapter, the Hearing Officer shall consider the economic and financial hardship imposed on the present tenant or tenants of the unit or units to which such increases apply. If, on balance, the Hearing Officer determines that the proposed increase constitutes an unreasonably severe financial or economic hardship on a particular tenant, he may order that the excess of the increase which is subject to consideration under subparagraph (c) of Section 5703-28, or any portion thereof, be disallowed. Any tenant whose household income and monthly housing expense meets

---

1. In order to be consistent with the decisions below, we refer throughout this opinion to the sections of the Ordinance as originally designated. We note, however, that the San Jose Municipal Code has recently been recodified and the Ordinance now appears at Chapter 17.23 of the new Code.

2. Under §5703.3, the Ordinance does not apply to rent or rent increases for new rental units first rented after the Ordinance takes effect, §5703.3(a), to the rental of a unit that has been voluntarily vacated, §5703.3(b)(1), or to the rental of a unit that is vacant as a result of eviction for certain specified acts, §5703.3(b)(2).

[certain income requirements] shall be deemed to be suffering under financial and economic hardship which must be weighed in the Hearing Officer's determination. The burden of proof in establishing any other economic hardship shall be on the tenant.

If either a tenant or a landlord is dissatisfied with the decision of the hearing officer, the Ordinance provides for binding arbitration. A landlord who attempts to charge or who receives rent in excess of the maximum rent established as provided in the Ordinance is subject to criminal and civil penalties.

Before we turn to the merits of appellants' contentions we consider the claim of appellees that appellants lack standing to challenge the constitutionality of the Ordinance. The original complaint in this action states that appellant Richard Pennell "is an owner and lessor of 109 rental units in the City of San Jose." Appellant Tri-County Apartment House Owners Association (Association) is said to be "an unincorporated association organized for the purpose of representing the interests of the owners and lessors of real property located in the City of San Jose." App. 2-3. The complaint also states that the real property owned by appellants is "subject to the terms of" the Ordinance. But, appellees point out, at no time did appellants allege that either Pennell or any member of the Association has "hardship tenants" who might trigger the Ordinance's hearing process, nor did they specifically allege that they have been or will be aggrieved by the determination of a Hearing Officer that a certain proposed rent increase is unreasonable on the ground of tenant hardship. As appellees put it, "[a]t this point in time, it is speculative" whether any of the Association's members will be injured in fact by the Ordinance's tenant hardship provisions. Thus, appellees contend, appellants lack standing under either the test for individual standing, see, e.g., Valley Forge Christian College v. Americans United for Separation of Church and State, Inc., 454 U.S. 464, 472, 102 S. Ct. 752, 758, 70 L. Ed. 2d 700 (1982) (individual standing requires an " 'actual injury redressable by the court' "), or the test for associational standing, see Hunt v. Washington Apple Advertising Commn., 432 U.S. 333, 343, 97 S. Ct. 2434, 2441, 53 L. Ed. 2d 383 (1977) (an association has standing on behalf of its members only when "its members would otherwise have standing to sue in their own right").[3]

3. Our cases also impose two additional requirements for associational or representational standing: the interests the organization seeks to protect must be "germane to the organization's purpose," *Hunt*, 432 U.S., at 343, 97 S. Ct., at 2441, and "neither the claim asserted nor the relief requested requires the participation of individual members in the lawsuit," ibid. See also Automobile Workers v. Brock, 477 U.S. 274, 281-282, 106 S. Ct. 2523, 2529, 91 L. Ed. 2d 228 (1986). Both of these requirements are satisfied here. The Association was "organized for the purpose of representing the interests of the owners and lessors of real

We must keep in mind, however, that "application of the constitutional standing requirement [is not] a mechanical exercise," Allen v. Wright, 468 U.S. 737, 751, 104 S. Ct. 3315, 3324, 82 L. Ed. 2d 556 (1984), and that when standing is challenged on the basis of the pleadings, we "accept as true all material allegations of the complaint, and . . . construe the complaint in favor of the complaining party," Warth v. Seldin, 422 U.S. 490, 501, 95 S. Ct. 2197, 2206, 45 L. Ed. 2d 343 (1975); see also Gladstone, Realtors v. Village of Bellwood, 441 U.S. 91, 109, 99 S. Ct. 1601, 1612, 60 L. Ed. 2d 66 (1979). Here, appellants specifically alleged in their complaint that appellants' properties are "subject to the terms of" the Ordinance, and they stated at oral argument that the Association represents "most of the residential unit owners in the city and [has] many hardship tenants," Tr. of Oral Arg. 42; see also id., at 7; Reply Brief for Appellants 2. Accepting the truth of these statements, which appellees do not contest, it is not "unadorned speculation," Simon v. Eastern Kentucky Welfare Rights Organization, 426 U.S. 26, 44, 96 S. Ct. 1917, 1927, 48 L. Ed. 2d 450 (1976), to conclude that the Ordinance will be enforced against members of the Association. The likelihood of enforcement, with the concomitant probability that a landlord's rent will be reduced below what he or she would otherwise be able to obtain in the absence of the Ordinance, is a sufficient threat of actual injury to satisfy Art. III's requirement that "[a] plaintiff who challenges a statute must demonstrate a realistic danger of sustaining a direct injury as a result of the statute's operation or enforcement." Babbitt v. Farm Workers, 442 U.S. 289, 298, 99 S. Ct. 2301, 2308, 60 L. Ed. 2d 895 (1979).[4]

This said, we recognize that the record in this case leaves much to be desired in terms of specificity for purposes of determining the standing of appellants to challenge this ordinance. Undoubtedly this is at least in part a reflection of the fact that the case originated in a state court where Art. III's proscription against advisory opinions may not apply. We strongly suggest that in future cases parties litigating in this Court under circumstances similar to those here take pains to supplement the record

---

property" in San Jose in this lawsuit, App. 3, and the facial challenge that the Association makes to the Ordinance does not require the participation of individual landlords.

4. Appellees also argue that Pennell lacks standing individually because in early 1987 he sold the properties he owned at the time the complaint in this action was filed. See Brief for Appellees 8. In a declaration submitted to the Court, Pennell admits that he sold these properties, but states that he recently repurchased and now owns one of the apartment buildings in San Jose that he formerly owned. Declaration of Richard Pennell ¶7. That property was and still is "subject to the Ordinance." Id., ¶8. Because we conclude that the Association has standing and that therefore we have jurisdiction over this appeal, we find it unnecessary to decide whether Pennell's sale and repurchase of the property affects his standing here.

in any manner necessary to enable us to address with as much precision as possible any question of standing that may be raised.

Turning now to the merits, we first address appellants' contention that application of the Ordinance's tenant hardship provisions violates the Fifth and Fourteenth Amendments' prohibition against taking of private property for public use without just compensation. In essence, appellants' claim is as follows: §5703.28 of the Ordinance establishes the seven factors that a Hearing Officer is to take into account in determining the reasonable rent increase. The first six of these factors are all objective, and are related either to the landlord's costs of providing an adequate rental unit, or to the condition of the rental market. Application of these six standards results in a rent that is "reasonable" by reference to what appellants' contend is the only legitimate purpose of rent control: the elimination of "excessive" rents caused by San Jose's housing shortage. When the Hearing Officer then takes into account "hardship to a tenant" pursuant to §5703.28(c)(7) and reduces the rent below the objectively "reasonable" amount established by the first six factors, this additional reduction in the rent increase constitutes a "taking." This taking is impermissible because it does not serve the purpose of eliminating excessive rents—that objective has already been accomplished by considering the first six factors—instead, it serves only the purpose of providing assistance to "hardship tenants." In short, appellants contend, the additional reduction of rent on grounds of hardship accomplishes a transfer of the landlord's property to individual hardship tenants; the Ordinance forces private individuals to shoulder the "public" burden of subsidizing their poor tenants' housing. As appellants point out, "[i]t is axiomatic that the Fifth Amendment's just compensation provision is 'designed to bar Government from forcing some people alone to bear public burdens which, in all fairness and justice, should be borne by the public as a whole.'" First English Evangelical Lutheran Church of Glendale v. County of Los Angeles, 482 U.S.—,—, 107 S. Ct. 2378, 2388, 96 L. Ed. 2d 250 (1987) (quoting Armstrong v. United States, 364 U.S. 40, 49, 80 S. Ct. 1563, 1569, 4 L. Ed. 2d 1554 (1960)).

We think it would be premature to consider this contention on the present record. As things stand, there simply is no evidence that the "tenant hardship clause" has in fact ever been relied upon by a Hearing Officer to reduce a rent below the figure it would have been set at on the basis of the other factors set forth in the Ordinance. In addition, there is nothing in the Ordinance requiring that a Hearing Officer in fact reduce a proposed rent increase on grounds of tenant hardship. Section 5703.29 does make it mandatory that hardship be considered—it states that "the Hearing Officer *shall* consider the economic hardship imposed on the present tenant"—but it then goes on to state that if "the proposed increase constitutes an unreasonably severe financial or economic hardship . . . he *may* order that the excess of the increase" be disallowed. §5703.29 (emphasis added). Given the "essentially ad hoc, factual inquir[y]" involved in the takings analysis, Kaiser Aetna v. United States, 444 U.S. 164, 175 100 S. Ct. 383, 390, 62 L. Ed. 2d 332 (1979), we have found it particularly important in takings cases to adhere to our admonition that "the constitutionality of statutes ought not be decided except in an actual factual setting that makes such a decision necessary." Hodel v. Virginia Surface Mining & Reclamation Assn., Inc., 452 U.S. 264, 294-295, 101 S. Ct. 2352, 2369-2370, 69 L. Ed. 2d 1 (1981). In *Virginia Surface Mining,* for example, we found that a challenge to the Surface Mining Control and Reclamation Act of 1977, 91 Stat. 447, 30 U.S.C. §1201 et seq., was "premature," 452 U.S., at 296, n.37, 101 S. Ct., at 2370, n.37, and "not ripe for judicial resolution," id., at 297, 101 S. Ct., at 2371, because the property owners in that case had not identified any property that had allegedly been taken by the Act, nor had they sought administrative relief from the Act's restrictions on surface mining. Similarly, in this case we find that the mere fact that a Hearing Officer is enjoined to consider hardship to the tenant in fixing a landlord's rent, without any showing in a particular case as to the consequences of that injunction in the ultimate determination of the rent, does not present a sufficiently concrete factual setting for the adjudication of the takings claim appellants raise here. Cf. Congress of Industrial Organizations v. McAdory, 325 U.S. 472, 475-476, 65 S. Ct. 1395, 1397, 89 L. Ed. 1741 (1945) (declining to consider the validity of a state statute when the record did not show that the statute would ever be applied to any of the petitioner's members).[5]

Appellants also urge that the mere provision in the Ordinance that a Hearing Officer may *consider* the hardship of the tenant in finally fixing a reasonable rent renders the Ordinance "facially invalid" under the Due Process and Equal Protection Clauses, even though no landlord ever has

---

5. For this reason we also decline to address appellants' contention that application of §5703.28(c)(7) to reduce an otherwise reasonable rent increase on the basis of tenant hardship violates the Fourteenth Amendment's due process and equal protection requirements. See Hodel v. Indiana, 452 U.S. 314, 335-336, 101 S. Ct. 2376, 2388-2389, 69 L. Ed. 2d 40 (1981) (dismissing as "premature" a due process challenge to the civil penalty provision of the Surface Mining Act because "appellees have made no showing that they were ever assessed civil penalties under the Act, much less that the statutory prepayment requirement was ever applied to them or caused them any injury").

Appellants and several amici also argue that the Ordinance's combination of lower rents for hardship tenants and restrictions on a landlord's power to evict a tenant amounts to a physical taking of the landlord's property. We decline to address this contention not only because it was raised for the first time in this Court, but also because it, too, is premised on a Hearing Officer's actually granting a lower rent to a hardship tenant.

its rent diminished by as much as one dollar because of the application of this provision. The standard for determining whether a state price-control regulation is constitutional under the Due Process Clause is well established: "Price control is 'unconstitutional . . . if arbitrary, discriminatory, or demonstrably irrelevant to the policy the legislature is free to adopt. . . .' " *Permian Basin Area Rate Cases*, 390 U.S. 747, 769-770, 88 S. Ct. 1344, 1361, 20 L. Ed. 2d 312 (1968) (quoting Nebbia v. New York, 291 U.S. 502, 539, 54 S. Ct. 505, 517, 78 L. Ed. 940 (1934)). In other contexts we have recognized that the Government may intervene in the marketplace to regulate rates or prices that are artificially inflated as a result of the existence of a monopoly or near monopoly, see, e.g., FCC v. Florida Power Corp., 480 U.S. —, —-—, 107 S. Ct. 1107, —-—, 94 L. Ed. 2d 282 (1987) (approving limits on rates charged to cable companies for access to telephone poles); FPC v. Texaco Inc., 417 U.S. 380, 397-398, 94 S. Ct. 2315, 2326-2327, 41 L. Ed. 2d 141 (1974) (recognizing that federal regulation of the natural gas market was in response to the threat of monopoly pricing), or a discrepancy beween supply and demand in the market for a certain product, see, e.g., Nebbia v. New York, *supra,* 291 U.S., at 530, 538, 54 S. Ct., at 513, 516 (allowing a minimum price for milk to offset a "flood of surplus milk"). Accordingly, appellants do not dispute that the Ordinance's asserted purpose of "prevent[ing] excessive and unreasonable rent increases" caused by the "growing shortage of and increasing demand for housing in the City of San Jose," §5701.2, is a legitimate exercise of appellees' police powers.[6] Cf. Block v. Hirsh, 256 U.S. 135, 156, 41 S. Ct. 458, 459, 65 L. Ed. 865 (1921) (approving rent control in Washington, D.C., on the basis of Congress' finding that housing in the city was "monopolized"). They do argue, however, that it is "arbitrary, discriminatory, or demonstrably irrelevant," Permian Basin Area Rate Cases, *supra,* 390 U.S., at 769-770, 88 S. Ct. at 1361, for appellees to attempt to accomplish the additional goal of reducing the burden of housing costs on low-income tenants by requiring that "hardship to a tenant" be considered in determining the amount of excess rent increase that is "reasonable under

---

6. Appellants do not claim, as do some amici, that rent control is per se a talking. We stated in Loretto v. Teleprompter Manhattan CATV Corp., 458 U.S. 419, 102 S. Ct. 3164, 73 L. Ed. 2d 868 (1982), that we have "consistently affirmed that States have broad power to regulate housing conditions in general and the landlord-tenant relationship in particular without paying compensation for all economic injuries that such regulation entails." Id., at 440, 102 S. Ct., at 3178 (citing, inter alia, Bowles v. Willingham, 321 U.S. 503, 517-518, 64 S. Ct. 641, 648-649, 88 L. Ed. 892 (1944)). And in FCC v. Florida Power Corp., 480 U.S. —, 107 S. Ct. 1107, 94 L. Ed. 2d 282 (1987), we stated that "statutes regulating the economic relations of landlords and tenants are not per se takings." Id., at—, 107 S. Ct., at 1112. Despite amici's urgings, we see no need to reconsider the constitutionality of rent control per se.

the circumstances" pursuant to §5703.28.[7] As appellants put it, "The objective of alleviating individual tenant hardship is . . . not a 'policy the legislature is free to adopt' in a rent control ordinance." Reply Brief for Appellants 16.

We reject this contention, however, because we have long recognized that a legitimate and rational goal of price or rate regulation is the protection of consumer welfare. See e.g., In re Permian Basin Area Rate Cases, *supra*, 390 U.S., at 770, 88 S. Ct., at 1361; *FPC v. Hope Natural Gas Co.*, 320 U.S. 591, 610-612, 64 S. Ct. 281, 291-292, 88 L. Ed. 333 (1944) ("The primary aim of [the Natural Gas Act] was to protect consumers against exploitation at the hands of natural gas companies"). Indeed, a primary purpose of rent control is the protection of tenants. See, e.g., Bowles v. Willingham, 321 U.S. 503, 513, n.9, 64 S. Ct. 641, 646, n.9, 88 L. Ed. 892 (1944) (one purpose of rent control is "to protect persons with relatively fixed and limited incomes, consumers, wage earners . . . from undue impairment of their standard of living"). Here, the Ordinance establishes a scheme in which a Hearing Officer considers a number of factors in determining the reasonableness of a proposed rent increase which exceeds eight percent *and* which exceeds the amount deemed reasonable under either §§5703.28(a) or 5703.28(b). The first six factors of §5703.28(c) focus on the individual landlord — the Hearing Officer examines the history of the premises, the landlord's costs, and the market for comparable housing. Section 5703.28(c)(5) also allows the landlord to bring forth any other financial evidence — including presumably evidence regarding his own financial status — to be taken into account by the Hearing Officer. It is in only this context that the Ordinance allows tenant hardship to be considered and, under §5703.29, "balance[d]" with the other factors set out in §5703.28(c). Within this scheme, §5703.28(c) represents a rational attempt to accommodate the conflicting interests of protecting tenants from burdensome rent increases while at the same time ensuring that landlords are guaranteed a fair return on their investment. Cf. Bowles v. Willingham, *supra*, at 517, 64 S. Ct., at 648 (considering, but rejecting the contention that rent control must be established "landlord by landlord, as in the fashion of utility rates"). We accordingly find that the Ordinance, which so carefully considers both the individual circumstances of the landlord and the tenant before determining whether to allow an *additional* increase in rent over and above certain amounts that

---

7. As we noted above, see n. 5, *supra*, to the extent that appellants' due process argument is based on the claim that the Ordinance forces landlords to subsidize individual tenants, that claim is premature and not presented by the facts before us.

are deemed reasonable, does not on its face violate the Fourteenth Amendment's Due Process Clause.[8]

We also find that the Ordinance does not violate the Amendment's Equal Protection Clause. Here again, the standard is deferential; appellees need only show that the classification scheme embodied in the Ordinance is "rationally related to a legitimate state interest." New Orleans v. Dukes, 427 U.S. 297, 303, 96 S. Ct. 2513, 2517, 49 L. Ed. 2d 511 (1976). As we stated in Vance v. Bradley, 440 U.S. 93, 99 S. Ct. 939, 59 L. Ed. 2d 171 (1979), "we will not overturn [a statute that does not burden a suspect class or a fundamental interest] unless the varying treatment of different groups or persons is so unrelated to the achievement of any combination of legitimate purposes that we can only conclude that the legislature's actions were irrational." Id., at 97, 99 S. Ct., at 943. In light of our conclusion above that the Ordinance's tenant hardship provisions are designed to serve the legitimate purpose of protecting tenants, we can hardly conclude that it is irrational for the Ordinance to treat certain landlords differently on the basis of whether or not they have hardship tenants. The Ordinance distinguishes between landlords because doing so furthers the purpose of ensuring that individual tenants do not suffer "unreasonable" hardships; it would be inconsistent to state that hardship is a legitimate factor to be considered but then hold that appellees could not tailor the Ordinance so that only legitimate hardship cases are redressed. Cf. Woods v. Cloyd W. Miller Co., 333 U.S. 138, 145, 68 S. Ct. 421, 425, 92 L. Ed. 596 (1948) (Congress "need not control all rents or none. It can select those areas or those classes of property where the needs seems the greatest"). We recognize, as appellants point out, that in general it is difficult to say that the landlord "causes" the tenant's hardship. But this is beside the point—if a landlord does have a hardship tenant, regardless of the reason why, it is rational for appellees to take that fact into consideration under §5703.28 of the Ordinance when establishing a rent that is "reasonable under the circumstances."

For the foregoing reasons, we hold that it is premature to consider appellants' claim under the Takings Clause and we reject their facial challenge to the Ordinance under the Due Process and Equal Protection Clauses of the 14th Amendment. The judgment of the Supreme Court of California is accordingly
Affirmed.

8. The consideration of tenant hardship also serves the additional purpose, not stated on the face of the Ordinance, of reducing the costs of dislocation that might otherwise result if landlords were to charge rents to tenants that they could not afford. Particularly during a housing shortage, the social costs of the dislocation of low-income tenants can be severe. By allowing tenant hardship to be considered under §5703.28(c), the Ordinance enables appellees to "fine tune" their rent control to take into account the risk that a particular tenant will be forced to relocate as a result of a proposed rent increase.

Justice KENNEDY took no part in the consideration or decision of this case.

Justice SCALIA, with whom Justice O'CONNOR joins, concurring in part and dissenting in part.

I agree that the tenant hardship provision of the Ordinance does not, on its face, violate either the Due Process Clause or the Equal Protection Clause of the Fourteenth Amendment. I disagree, however, with the Court's conclusion that appellants' takings claim is premature. I would decide that claim on the merits, and would hold that the tenant hardship provision of the Ordinance effects a taking of private property without just compensation in violation of the Fifth and Fourteenth Amendments.

I

Appellants contend that any application of the tenant hardship provision of the San Jose Ordinance would effect an uncompensated taking of private property because that provision does not substantially advance legitimate state interests and because it improperly imposes a public burden on individual landlords. I can understand how such a claim — that a law applicable to the plaintiffs is, root and branch, invalid — can be readily rejected on the merits, by merely noting that at least some of its applications may be lawful. But I do not understand how such a claim can possibly be avoided by considering it "premature." Suppose, for example, that the feature of the rental ordinance under attack was a provision allowing a Hearing Officer to consider the race of the apartment owner in deciding whether to allow a rent increase. It is inconceivable that we would say judicial challenge must await demonstration that this provision has actually been applied to the detriment of one of the plaintiffs. There is no difference, it seems to me, when the facial, root-and-branch challenge rests upon the Takings Clause rather than the Equal Protection Clause.

The Court confuses the issue by relying on cases, and portions of cases, in which the Takings Clause challenge was not (as here) that the law in all its applications took property without just compensation, but was rather that the law's application in regulating the use of particular property so severely reduced the value of that property as to constitute a taking. It is in *that* context, and not (as the Court suggests) generally, that takings analysis involves an "essentially ad hoc, factual inquir[y]," Kaiser Aetna v. United States, 444 U.S. 164, 175, 100 S. Ct. 383, 390, 62 L. Ed. 2d 332 (1979). We said as much less than a year ago, and it is surprising that we have so soon forgotten:

> In addressing petitioners' claim we must not disregard the posture in which this case comes before us. The District Court granted summary judgment to

respondents only on the facial challenge to the Subsidence Act. The court explained that ". . . *the only question before this court is whether the mere enactment of the statutes and regulations constitutes a taking.* . . .

The posture of the case is critical because we have recognized an important distinction between a claim that the mere enactment of a statute constitutes a taking and a claim that the particular impact of government action on a specific piece of property requires the payment of just compensation. This point is illustrated by our decision in Hodel v. Virginia Surface Mining & Reclamation Assn., Inc., 452 U.S. 264 [101 S. Ct. 2352, 69 L. Ed. 2d 1] (1981), in which we rejected a pre-enforcement challenge to the constitutionality of the Surface Mining Control and Reclamation Act of 1977. . . . the Court [there] explained:

> Because appellees' taking claim arose in the context of a facial challenge, it presented no concrete controversy concerning either application of the Act to particular surface mining operations or its effect on specific parcels of land. Thus, the only issue properly before the District Court and, in turn, this Court, is whether the "mere enactment" of the Surface Mining Act constitutes a taking. . . . The test to be applied in considering this facial challenge is straightforward. A statute regulating the uses that can be made of property effects a taking if it "denies an owner economically viable use of his land[.]" . . .

Petitioners thus face an uphill battle in making a facial attack on the Act as a taking. Keystone Bituminous Coal Assn. v. DeBenedictis, 480 U.S.—,—-—, 107 S. Ct. 1232, 1246-1247, 94 L. Ed. 2d 472 (1987).

While the battle was "uphill" in *Keystone,* we allowed it to be fought, and did not declare it "premature."

The same was true of the facial takings challenge in Hodel v. Virginia Surface Mining & Reclamation Assn., Inc., 452 U.S. 264, 101 S. Ct. 2352, 69 L. Ed. 2d 1 (1981). It is remarkable that the Court should point to that case in support of its position, describing the holding as follows:

> In *Virginia Surface Mining,* for example, we found that a challenge to the Surface Mining Control and Reclamation Act . . . was "premature," . . . and "not ripe for judicial resolution, . . . because the property owners in that case had not identified any property that had allegedly been taken by the Act, nor had they sought administrative relief from the Act's restrictions on surface mining. *Ante,* at 856-857.

But this holding in *Virginia Surface Mining* applied only to "the taking issue decided by the District Court," 452 U.S., at 297, 101 S. Ct., at 2371, which was the issue of the statute's validity *as applied.* Having rejected that challenge as premature, the Court then continued (in the language we quoted in *Keystone*):

> Thus, the only issue properly before the District Court and, in turn, this Court, is whether the "mere enactment" of the Surface Mining Act constitutes a taking. 452 U.S., at 295, 101 S. Ct., at 2370.

That issue was *not* rejected as premature, but was decided on its merits, id., at 295-297, 101 S. Ct., at 2370-2371, just as it was in *Keystone*, and as it was before that in Agins v. Tiburon, 447 U.S. 255, 260-263, 100 S. Ct. 2138, 2141-2142, 65 L. Ed. 2d 106 (1980).

In sum, it is entirely clear from our cases that a facial takings challenge is not premature even if it rests upon the ground that the ordinance deprives property owners of all economically viable use of their land—a ground that is, as we have said, easier to establish in an "as-applied" attack. It is, if possible, even more clear that the present facial challenge is not premature, because it does not rest upon a ground that would even profit from consideration in the context of particular application. As we said in *Agins*, a zoning law "effects a taking if the ordinance does not substantially advance legitimate state interests, . . . or denies an owner economically viable use of his land." Id. at 260, 100 S. Ct., at 2141. The present challenge is of the former sort. Appellants contend that providing financial assistance to impecunious renters is not a state interest that can legitimately be furthered by regulating the use of property. Knowing the nature and character of the particular property in question, or the degree of its economic impairment, will in no way assist this inquiry. Such factors are as irrelevant to the present claim as we have said they are to the claim that a law effects a taking by authorizing a permanent physical invasion of property. See Loretto v. Teleprompter Manhattan CATV Corp., 458 U.S. 419, 102 S. Ct. 3164, 73 L. Ed. 2d 868 (1982). So even if we were explicitly to overrule cases such as *Agins, Virginia Surface Mining,* and *Keystone,* and to hold that a facial challenge will not lie where the issue can be more forcefully presented in an "as applied" attack, there would still be no reason why the present challenge should not proceed.

Today's holding has no more basis in equity than it does in precedent. Since the San Jose Ordinance does not require any specification of how much reduction in rent is attributable to each of the various factors that the Hearing Officer is allowed to take into account, it is quite possible that none of the many landlords affected by the ordinance will ever be able to meet the Court's requirement of a "showing in a particular case as to the consequences of [the hardship factor] in the ultimate determination of the rent[.]" *Ante,* at 857. There is no reason thus to shield alleged constitutional injustice from judicial scrutiny. I would therefore consider appellants' takings claim on the merits.

II

The Fifth Amendment of the United States Constitution, made applicable to the States through the Fourteenth Amendment, Chicago, B. &

Q.R. Co. v. Chicago, 166 U.S. 226, 239, 17 S. Ct. 581, 585, 41 L.Ed. 979 (1897), provides that "private property [shall not] be taken for public use, without just compensation." We have repeatedly observed that the purpose of this provision is "to bar Government from forcing some people alone to bear public burdens which, in all fairness and justice, should be borne by the public as a whole." Armstrong v. United States, 364 U.S. 40, 49, 80 S. Ct. 1563, 1569, 4 L. Ed. 2d 1554 (1960); see also First English Evangelical Lutheran Church of Glendale v. Los Angeles County, 482 U.S.—,—, 107 S. Ct. 2378, 2388, 96 L. Ed. 2d 250 (1987); Webb's Fabulous Pharmacies, Inc. v. Beckwith, 449 U.S. 155, 163, 101 S. Ct. 446, 452, 66 L. Ed. 2d 358 (1980); Agins v. Tiburon, *supra*, 447 U.S., at 260, 100 S. Ct. at 2141; Penn Central Transportation Co. v. New York City, 438 U.S. 104, 123, 98 S. Ct. 2646, 2658, 57 L. Ed. 2d 631 (1978); Monongahela Navigation Co. v. United States, 148 U.S. 312, 325, 13 S. Ct. 622, 625, 37 L. Ed. 463 (1893).

Traditional land-use regulation (short of that which totally destroys the economic value of property) does not violate this principle because there is a cause-and-effect relationship between the property use restricted by the regulation and the social evil that the regulation seeks to remedy. Since the owner's use of the property is (or, but for the regulation, would be) the source of the social problem, it cannot be said that he has been singled out unfairly. Thus, the common zoning regulations requiring subdividers to observe lot-size and set-back restrictions, and to dedicate certain areas to public streets, are in accord with our constitutional traditions because the proposed property use would otherwise be the cause of excessive congestion. The same cause-and-effect relationship is popularly thought to justify emergency price regulation: When commodities have been priced at a level that produces exorbitant returns, the owners of those commodities can be viewed as responsible for the economic hardship that occurs. Whether or not that is an accurate perception of the way a free-market economy operates, it is at least true that the owners reap unique benefits from the situation that produces the economic hardship, and in that respect singling them out to relieve it may not be regarded as "unfair." That justification might apply to the rent regulation in the present case, apart from the single feature under attack here.

Appellants do not contest the validity of rent regulation in general. They acknowledge that the City may constitutionally set a "reasonable rent" according to the statutory minimum and the six other factors that must be considered by the Hearing Officer (cost of debt servicing, rental history of the unit, physical condition of the unit, changes in housing services, other financial information provided by the landlord, and market value rents for similar units). San Jose Municipal Ordinance 19696,

§5703.28(c) (1979). Appellants' only claim is that a reduction of a rent increase below what would otherwise be a "reasonable rent" under this scheme may not, consistently with the Constitution, be based on consideration of the seventh factor—the hardship to the tenant as defined in §5703.29. I think they are right.

Once the other six factors of the ordinance have been applied to a landlord's property, so that he is receiving only a reasonable return, he can no longer be regarded as a "cause" of exorbitantly priced housing; nor is he any longer reaping distinctively high profits from the housing shortage. The seventh factor, the "hardship" provision, is invoked to meet a quite different social problem: the existence of some renters who are too poor to afford even reasonably priced housing. But *that* problem is no more caused or exploited by landlords than it is by the grocers who sell needy renters their food or the department stores that sell them their clothes, or the employers who pay them their wages, or the citizens of San Jose holding the higher-paying jobs from which they are excluded. And even if the neediness of renters could be regarded as a problem distinctively attributable to landlords in general, it is not remotely attributable to the *particular* landlords that the ordinance singles out — namely, those who happen to have a "hardship" tenant at the present time, or who may happen to rent to a "hardship" tenant in the future, or whose current or future affluent tenants may happen to decline into the "hardship" category.

The traditional manner in which American government has met the problem of those who cannot pay reasonable prices for privately sold necessities—a problem caused by the society at large—has been the distribution to such persons of funds raised from the public at large through taxes, either in cash (welfare payments) or in goods (public housing, publicly subsidized housing, and food stamps). Unless we are to abandon the guiding principle of the Takings Clause that "public burdens . . . should be borne by the public as a whole," *Armstrong supra*, 364 U.S., at 49, 80 S. Ct., at 1569, this is the only manner that our Constitution permits. The fact that government acts through the landlord-tenant relationship does not magically transform general public welfare, which must be supported by all the public, into mere "economic regulation," which can disproportionately burden particular individuals. Here the City is not "regulating" rents in the relevant sense of preventing rents that are excessive; rather, it is using the occasion of rent regulation (accomplished by the rest of the Ordinance) to establish a welfare program privately funded by those landlords who happen to have "hardship" tenants."

Of course all economic regulation effects wealth transfer. When excessive rents are forbidden, for example, landlords as a class become poorer and tenants as a class (or at least incumbent tenants as a class) become richer. Singling out landlords to be the transferors may be within our traditional constitutional notions of fairness, because they can plausibly be regarded as the source or the beneficiary of the high-rent problem. Once such a connection is no longer required, however, there is no end to the social transformations that can be accomplished by so-called "regulation," at great expense to the democratic process.

The politically attractive feature of regulation is not that it permits wealth transfers to be achieved that could not be achieved otherwise; but rather that it permits them to be achieved "off budget," with relative invisibility and thus relative immunity from normal democratic processes. San Jose might, for example, have accomplished something like the result here by simply raising the real estate tax upon rental properties and using the additional revenues thus acquired to pay part of the rents of "hardship" tenants. It seems to me doubtful, however, whether the citizens of San Jose would allow funds in the municipal treasury, from wherever derived, to be distributed to a family of four with income as high as $32,400 a year—the generous maximum necessary to qualify automatically as a "hardship" tenant under the rental ordinance.* The voters might well see other, more pressing, social priorities. And of course what $32,400-a-year renters can acquire through spurious "regulation," other groups can acquire as well. Once the door is opened it is not unreasonable to expect price regulations requiring private businesses to give special discounts to senior citizens (no matter how affluent), or to students, the handicapped, or war veterans. Subsidies for these groups may well be a good idea, but because of the operation of the Takings Clause our governmental system has required them to be applied, in general, through the process of taxing and spending, where both economic effects and competing priorities are more evident.

That fostering of an intelligent democratic process is one of the happy effects of the constitutional prescription—perhaps accidental, perhaps not. Its essence, however, is simply the unfairness of making one citizen pay, in some fashion other than taxes, to remedy a social problem that is none of his creation. As the Supreme Court of New Jersey said in finding

---

* Under the San Jose Ordinance, "hardship" tenants include (though are not limited to) those whose "household income and monthly housing expense meets [sic] the criteria" for assistance under the existing housing provisions of §8 of the Housing and Community Development Act of 1974, 42 U.S.C. §1437f (1982 ed. and Supp. III). The United States Department of Housing and Urban Development currently limits assistance under these provisions for families of four in the San Jose area to those who earn $32,400 or less per year. Memorandum from U.S. Dept. of Housing and Urban Development, Assist. Secretary for Housing-Federal Housing Comm'r, Income Limits for Lower Income and Very Low-Income Families Under the Housing Act of 1937 (Jan. 15, 1988).

unconstitutional a scheme displaying, among other defects, the same vice I find dispositive here:

> A legislative category of economically needy senior citizens is sound, proper and sustainable as a rational classification. But compelled subsidization by landlords or by tenants who happen to live in an apartment building with senior citizens is an improper and unconstitutional method of solving the problem. Property Owners Assn. v. North Bergen, 74 N.J. 327, 339, 378 A.2d 25, 31 (1977).

I would hold that the seventh factor in §5703.28(c) of the San Jose Ordinance effects a taking of property without just compensation.

On page 1173, add the following reference to the note on Inverse Condemnation.

See First English Evangelical Lutheran Church of Glendale v. County of Los Angeles, California, — U.S. —, 107 S. Ct. 2378 (1987).

Insert the following material on page 1192 after the note on Hawaii's land reform act.

Decision of the Supreme Court of the United States reversing the Ninth Circuit Court's decision relating to the Hawaii Land Reform Act.

HAWAII HOUSING AUTHORITY v. MIDKIFF

Supreme Court of the United States, 1984
467 U.S. 229, 104 S. Ct. 2321

Justice O'CONNOR delivered the opinion of the Court.

The Fifth Amendment of the United States Constitution provides, in pertinent part, that "private property [shall not] be taken for public use, without just compensation." These cases present the question whether the Public Use Clause of that Amendment, made applicable to the States through the Fourteenth Amendment, prohibits the State of Hawaii from taking, with just compensation, title in real property from lessors and transferring it to lessees in order to reduce the concentration of ownership of fees simple in the State. We conclude that it does not.

I

A

The Hawaiian Islands were originally settled by Polynesian immigrants from the eastern Pacific. These settlers developed an economy

235

around a feudal land tenure system in which one island high chief, the ali'i nui, controlled the land and assigned it for development to certain subchiefs. The subchiefs would then reassign the land to other lower ranking chiefs, who would administer the land and govern the farmers and other tenants working it. All land was held at the will of the ali'i nui and eventually had to be returned to his trust. There was no private ownership of land. See generally Brief for Office of Hawaiian Affairs as *Amicus Curiae* 3-5.

Beginning in the early 1800's, Hawaiian leaders and American settlers repeatedly attempted to divide the lands of the kingdom among the crown, the chiefs, and the common people. These efforts proved largely unsuccessful, however, and the land remained in the hands of a few. In the mid-1960's, after extensive hearings, the Hawaii Legislature discovered that, while the State and Federal Governments owned almost 49% of the State's land, another 47% was in the hands of only 72 private landowners. See Brief for the Hou Hawaiians and Maui Loa, Chief of the Hou Hawaiians, as *Amici Curiae* 32. The legislature further found that 18 landholders, with tracts of 21,000 acres or more, owned more than 40% of this land and that, on Oahu, the most urbanized of the islands, 22 landowners owned 72.5% of the fee simple titles. Id., at 32-33. The legislature concluded that concentrated land ownership was responsible for skewing the State's residential fee simple market, inflating land prices, and injuring the public tranquility and welfare.

To redress these problems, the legislature decided to compel the large landowners to break up their estates. The legislature considered requiring large landowners to sell lands which they were leasing to homeowners. However, the landowners strongly resisted this scheme, pointing out the significant federal tax liabilities they would incur. Indeed, the landowners claimed that the federal tax laws were the primary reason they previously had chosen to lease, and not sell, their lands. Therefore, to accommodate the needs of both lessors and lessees, the Hawaii Legislature enacted the Land Reform Act of 1967 (Act), Haw. Rev. Stat., ch. 516, which created a mechanism for condemning residential tracts and for transferring ownership of the condemned fees simple to existing lessees. By condemning the land in question, the Hawaii Legislature intended to make the land sales involuntary, thereby making the federal tax consequences less severe while still facilitating the redistribution of fees simple. See Brief for Appellants in Nos. 83-141, 83-283, pp. 3-4, and nn. 6-8.

Under the Act's condemnation scheme, tenants living on single-family residential lots within developmental tracts at least five acres in size are entitled to ask the Hawaii Housing Authority (HHA) to condemn the property on which they live. Haw. Rev. Stat. §§516-1(2), (11), 516-22

(1977). When 25 eligible tenants,[1] or tenants on half the lots in the tract, whichever is less, file appropriate applications, the Act authorizes HHA to hold a public hearing to determine whether acquisition by the State of all or part of the tract will "effectuate the public purposes" of the Act. §516-22. If HHA finds that these public purposes will be served, it is authorized to designate some or all of the lots in the tract for acquisition. It then acquires, at prices set either by condemnation trial or by negotiation between lessors and lessees,[2] the former fee owners' full "right, title, and interest" in the land. §516-25.

After compensation has been set, HHA may sell the land titles to tenants who have applied for fee simple ownership. HHA is authorized to lend these tenants up to 90% of the purchase price, and it may condition final transfer on a right of first refusal for the first 10 years following sale. §§516-30, 516-34, 516-35. If HHA does not sell the lot to the tenant residing there, it may lease the lot or sell it to someone else, provided that public notice has been given. §516-28. However, HHA may not sell to any one purchaser, or lease to any one tenant, more than one lot, and it may not operate for profit. §§516-28, 516-32. In practice, funds to satisfy the condemnation awards have been supplied entirely by lessees. See App. 164. While the Act authorizes HHA to issue bonds and appropriate funds for acquisition, no bonds have issued and HHA has not supplied any funds for condemned lots. See ibid.

B

In April 1977, HHA held a public hearing concerning the proposed acquisition of some of appellees' lands. HHA made the statutorily required finding that acquisition of appellees' lands would effectuate the public purposes of the Act. Then, in October 1978, it directed appellees to negotiate with certain lessees concerning the sale of the designated properties. Those negotiations failed, and HHA subsequently ordered appellees to submit to compulsory arbitration.

Rather than comply with the compulsory arbitration order, appellees filed suit, in February 1979, in United States District Court, asking that the Act be declared unconstitutional and that its enforcement be enjoined. The District Court temporarily restrained the State from proceeding against appellees' estates. Three months later, while declaring the

1. An eligible tenant is one who, among other things, owns a house on the lot, has a bona fide intent to live on the lot or be a resident of the State, shows proof of ability to pay for a fee interest in it, and does not own residential land elsewhere nearby. Haw. Rev. Stat. §516-33(3), (4), (7) (1979).

2. See §516-56 (Supp. 1983). In either case, compensation must equal the fair market value of the owner's leased fee interest. §516-1(14). The adequacy of compensation is not before us.

compulsory arbitration and compensation formulae provisions of the Act unconstitutional,[3] the District Court refused preliminarily to enjoin appellants from conducting the statutory designation and condemnation proceedings. Finally, in December 1979, it granted partial summary judgment to appellants, holding the remaining portion of the Act constitutional under the Public Use Clause. See 483 F. Supp. 62 (Haw. 1979). The District Court found that the Act's goals were within the bounds of the State's police powers and that the means the legislature had chosen to serve those goals were not arbitrary, capricious, or selected in bad faith.

The Court of Appeals for the Ninth Circuit reversed. 702 F.2d 788 (CA 9 1983). First, the Court of Appeals decided that the District Court had permissibly chosen not to abstain from the exercise of its jurisdiction. Then, the Court of Appeals determined that the Hawaii Land Reform Act could not pass the requisite judicial scrutiny of the Public Use Clause. It found that the transfers comtemplated by the Act were unlike those of takings previously held to constitute "public uses" by this Court. The court further determined that the public purposes offered by the Hawaii Legislature were not deserving of judicial deference. The court concluded that the Act was simply "a naked attempt on the part of the state of Hawaii to take the private property of A and transfer it to B solely for B's private use and benefit." Id., at 798. One judge dissented.

On applications of HHA and certain private appellants who had intervened below, this Court noted probable jurisdiction. 464 U.S. [932], 104 S. Ct. 334, 78 L. Ed. 2d 304 (1983). We now reverse.

II

We begin with the question whether the District Court abused its discretion in not abstaining from the exercise of its jurisdiction. The appellants have suggested as one alternative that perhaps abstention was required under the standards announced in Railroad Commn. v. Pullman Co., 312 U.S. 496, 61 S. Ct. 643, 85 L. Ed. 971 (1941), and Younger v. Harris, 401 U.S. 37, 91 S. Ct. 746, 27 L. Ed. 2d 669 (1971). We do not believe that abstention was required.

---

3. As originally enacted, lessor and lessee had to commence compulsory arbitration if they could not agree on a price for the fee simple title. Statutory formulae were provided for the determination of compensation. The District Court declared both the compulsory arbitration provision and the compensation formulae unconstitutional. No appeal was taken from these rulings, and the Hawaii legislature subsequently amended the statute to provide only for mandatory negotiation and for advisory compensation formulae. These issues are not before us.

A

In Railroad Commn. v. Pullman Co., *supra*, this Court held that federal courts should abstain from decision when difficult and unsettled questions of state law must be resolved before a substantial federal constitutional question can be decided. By abstaining in such cases, federal courts will avoid both unnecessary adjudication of federal questions and "needless friction with state policies. . . ." Id., 312 U.S., at 500, 61 S. Ct., at 645. However, federal courts need not abstain on *Pullman* grounds when a state statute is not "fairly subject to an interpretation which will render unnecessary" the federal constitutional question. See Harman v. Forssenius, 380 U.S. 528, 535, 85 S. Ct. 1177, 1182, 14 L. Ed. 2d 50 (1965). *Pullman*-abstention is limited to uncertain questions of state law because "[a]bstention from the exercise of federal jurisdiction is the exception, not the rule." Colorado River Water Conservation Dist. v. United States, 424 U.S. 800, 813, 96 S. Ct. 1236, 1244, 47 L. Ed. 2d 483 (1976).

In this case, there is no uncertain question of state law. The Hawaii Land Reform Act unambiguously provides that "[t]he use of the power . . . to condemn . . . is for a public use and purpose." Haw. Rev. Stat. §516-83(a)(12) (1977); see also §§516-83(a)(10), (11), (13). There is no other provision of the Act—or, for that matter, of Hawaii law— which would suggest that §516-83(a)(12) does not mean exactly what it says. Since "the naked question, uncomplicated by [ambiguous language], is whether the Act on its face is unconstitutional," Wisconsin v. Constantineau, 400 U.S. 433, 439, 91 S. Ct. 507, 511, 27 L. Ed. 2d 515 (1971), abstention from federal jurisdiction is not required.

The dissenting judge in the Court of Appeals suggested that, perhaps, the state courts could make resolution of the federal constitutional questions unnecessary by their construction of the Act. See 702 F.2d, at 811-812. In the abstract, of course, such possibilities always exist. But the relevant inquiry is not whether there is a bare, though unlikely, possibility that state courts *might* render adjudication of the federal question unnecessary. Rather, "[w]e have frequently emphasized that abstention is not to be ordered unless the statute is of an uncertain nature, and is obviously susceptible of a limiting construction." Zwickler v. Koota, 389 U.S. 241, 251, and n.14, 88 S. Ct. 391, 397, and n.14, 19 L. Ed. 2d 444 (1967). These statutes are not of an uncertain nature and have no reasonable limiting construction. Therefore, *Pullman*-abstention is unnecessary.[4]

4. The dissenting judge's suggestion that *Pullman*-abstention was required because interpretation of the State constitution may have obviated resolution of the federal constitutional question is equally faulty. Hawaii's constitution has only a parallel requirement that a taking be for a public use. See Hawaii Const., Art. I, §20. The Court has previously determined that abstention is not required for interpretation of parallel state constitutional

B

The dissenting judge also suggested that abstention was required under the standards articulated in Younger v. Harris, *supra*. Under *Younger*-abstention doctrine, interests of comity and federalism counsel federal courts to abstain from jurisdiction whenever federal claims have been or could be presented in ongoing state judicial proceedings that concern important state interests. See Middlesex Ethics Comm. v. Garden State Bar Assn., 457 U.S. 423, 432-437, 102 S. Ct. 2515, 2521-2524, 73 L. Ed. 2d 116 (1982). *Younger*-abstention is required, however, only when state court proceedings are initiated "before any proceedings of substance on the merits have taken place in the federal court." Hicks v. Miranda, 422 U.S. 332, 349, 95 S. Ct. 2281, 2291, 45 L. Ed. 2d 223 (1975). In other cases, federal courts must normally fulfill their duty to adjudicate federal questions properly brought before them.

In this case, state judicial proceedings had not been initiated at the time proceedings of substance took place in federal court. Appellants filed their federal court complaint in February 1979, asking for temporary and permanent relief. The District Court temporarily restrained HHA from proceeding against appellants' estates. At that time, no state judicial proceedings were in process. Indeed, in June 1979, when the District Court granted, in part, appellees' motion for a preliminary injunction, state court proceedings still had not been initiated. Rather, HHA filed its first eminent domain lawsuit *after* the parties had begun filing motions for summary judgment in the District Court—in September 1979. Whether issuance of the February temporary restraining order was a substantial federal court action or not, issuance of the June preliminary injunction certainly was. See Doran v. Salem Inn, Inc., 422 U.S. 922, 929-931, 95 S. Ct. 2561, 2566-2567, 45 L. Ed. 2d 648 (1975). A federal court action in which a preliminary injunction is granted has proceeded well beyond the "embryonic stage," id., at 929, 95 S. Ct., at 2566, and considerations of economy, equity, and federalism counsel against *Younger*-abstention at that point.

The only extant proceedings at the state level prior to the September 1979 eminent domain lawsuit in state court were HHA's administrative hearings. But the Act clearly states that these administrative proceedings are not part of, and are not themselves, a judicial proceeding, for "mandatory arbitration shall be in advance of and shall not constitute any part of any action in condemnation or eminent domain." Haw. Rev. Stat.

---

provisions. See Examining Board v. Flores de Otero, 426 U.S. 572, 598, 96 S. Ct. 2264, 2279, 49 L. Ed. 2d 65 (1976); see also Wisconsin v. Constantineau, 400 U.S. 433, 91 S. Ct. 507, 27 L. Ed. 2d 515 (1971).

§516-51(b). Since *Younger* is not a bar to federal court action when state judicial proceedings have not themselves commenced, see Middlesex County Ethics Comm. v. Garden State Bar Assn., *supra,* 457 U.S., at 433, 102 S. Ct., at 2522; Fair Assessment in Real Estate Assn. v. McNary, 454 U.S. 100, 112-113, 102 S. Ct. 177, 184-185, 70 L. Ed. 2d 271 (1981), abstention for HHA's administrative proceedings was not required.

III

The majority of the Court of Appeals next determined that the Act violates the "public use" requirement of the Fifth and Fourteenth Amendments. On this argument, however, we find ourselves in agreement with the dissenting judge in the Court of Appeals.

A

The starting point for our analysis of the Act's constitutionality is the Court's decision in Berman v. Parker, 348 U.S. 26, 75 S. Ct. 98, 99 L. Ed. 27 (1954). In *Berman,* the Court held constitutional the District of Columbia Redevelopment Act of 1945. That Act provided both for the comprehensive use of the eminent domain power to redevelop slum areas and for the possible sale or lease of the condemned lands to private interests. In discussing whether the takings authorized by that Act were for a "public use," id., at 31, 75 S. Ct., at 101, the Court stated

> We deal, in other words, with what traditionally has been known as the police power. An attempt to define its reach or trace its outer limits is fruitless, for each case must turn on its own facts. The definition is essentially the product of legislative determinations addressed to the purposes of government, purposes neither abstractly nor historically capable of complete definition. Subject to specific constitutional limitations, when the legislature has spoken, the public interest has been declared in terms well-nigh conclusive. In such cases the legislature, not the judiciary, is the main guardian of the public needs to be served by social legislation, whether it be Congress legislating concerning the District of Columbia . . . or the States legislating concerning local affairs. . . . This principle admits of no exception merely because the power of eminent domain is involved. . . . Id., at 32, 75 S. Ct., at 102 (citations omitted).

The Court explicitly recognized the breadth of the principle it was announcing, noting:

> Once the object is within the authority of Congress, the right to realize it through the exercise of eminent domain is clear. For the power of eminent domain is merely the means to the end. . . . Once the object is within the authority of Congress, the means by which it will be attained is also for Congress to determine. Here one of the means chosen is the use of private enterprise for redevelopment of the area. Appellants argue that this makes the

project a taking from one businessman for the benefit of another businessman. But the means of executing the project are for Congress and Congress
alone to determine, once the public purpose has been established. Id., at 33,
75 S. Ct., at 102.

The "public use" requirement is thus coterminous with the scope of a
sovereign's police powers.

There is, of course, a role for courts to play in reviewing a legislature's
judgment of what constitutes a public use, even when the eminent domain power is equated with the police power. But the Court in *Berman*
made clear that it is "an extremely narrow" one. Id., at 32, 75 S. Ct., at
102. The Court in *Berman* cited with approval the Court's decision in Old
Dominion Co. v. United States, 269 U.S. 55, 66, 46 S. Ct. 39, 40, 70 L.
Ed. 162 (1925), which held that deference to the legislature's "public
use" determination is required "until it is shown to involve an impossibility." The *Berman* Court also cited to United States ex rel. TVA v. Welch,
327 U.S. 546, 552, 66 S. Ct. 715, 718, 90 L. Ed. 843 (1946), which
emphasized that "[a]ny departure from this judicial restraint would result in courts deciding on what is and is not a governmental function and
in their invalidating legislation on the basis of their view on that question
at the moment of decision, a practice which has proved impracticable in
other fields." In short, the Court has made clear that it will not substitute
its judgment for a legislature's judgment as to what constitutes a public
use "unless the use be palpably without reasonable foundation." United
States v. Gettysburg Electric R. Co., 160 U.S. 668, 680, 16 S. Ct. 427, 429,
40 L. Ed. 576 (1896).

To be sure, the Court's cases have repeatedly stated that "one person's
property may not be taken for the benefit of another private person
without a justifying public purpose, even though compensation be paid."
Thompson v. Consolidated Gas Corp., 300 U.S. 55, 80, 57 S. Ct. 364,
376, 81 L. Ed. 510 (1937). See, eg., Cincinnati v. Vester, 281 U.S. 439,
447, 50 S. Ct. 360, 362, 74 L. Ed. 950 (1930); Madisonville Traction Co.
v. St. Bernard Mining Co., 196 U.S. 239, 251-252, 25 S. Ct. 251, 255-256,
49 L. Ed. 462 (1905); Fallbrook Irrigation District v. Bradley, 164 U.S.
112, 159, 17 S. Ct. 56, 63 41 L. Ed. 369 (1896). Thus, in Missouri Pacific
R. Co. v. Nebraska, where the "order in question was not, *and was not
claimed to be*, . . . a taking of private property for a public use under the
right of eminent domain," the Court invalidated a compensated taking
of property for lack of a justifying public purpose. 164 U.S. 403, 416, 17
S. Ct. 130, 135, 41 L. Ed. 2d 489 (1896) (emphasis added). But where the
exercise of the eminent domain power is rationally related to a conceiv-
able public purpose, the Court has never held a compensated taking to
be proscribed by the Public Use Clause. See Berman v. Parker, *supra;*

Rindge v. Los Angeles, 262 U.S. 700, 43 S. Ct. 689, 67 L. Ed. 1186 (1923); Block v. Hirsh, 256 U.S. 135, 41 S. Ct. 458, 65 L. Ed. 865 (1921); cf. Thompson v. Consolidated Gas Corp., *supra* (invalidating an *uncompensated* taking).

On this basis, we have no trouble concluding that the Hawaii Act is constitutional. The people of Hawaii have attempted, much as the settlers of the original 13 Colonies did,[5] to reduce the perceived social and economic evils of a land oligopoly traceable to their monarchs. The land oligopoly has, according to the Hawaii Legislature, created artificial deterrents to the normal functioning of the State's residential land market and forced thousands of individual homeowners to lease, rather than buy, the land underneath their homes. Regulating oligopoly and the evils associated with it is a classic exercise of a State's police powers. See Exxon Corp. v. Governor of Maryland, 437 U.S. 117, 98 S. Ct. 2207, 57 L. Ed. 2d 91 (1978); Block v. Hirsch, *supra;* see also People of Puerto Rico v. Eastern Sugar Associates, 156 F.2d 316 (CA1), *cert. denied,* 329 U.S. 772, 67 S. Ct. 190, 91 L. Ed. 664 (1946). We cannot disapprove of Hawaii's exercise of this power.

Nor can we condemn as irrational the Act's approach to correcting the land oligopoly problem. The Act presumes that when a sufficiently large number of persons declare that they are willing but unable to buy lots at fair prices the land market is malfunctioning. When such a malfunction is signalled, the Act authorizes HHA to condemn lots in the relevant tract. The Act limits the number of lots any one tenant can purchase and authorizes HHA to use public funds to ensure that the market dilution goals will be achieved. This is a comprehensive and rational approach to identifying and correcting market failure.

Of course, this Act, like any other, may not be successful in achieving its intended goals. But "whether *in fact* the provision will accomplish its objectives is not the question: the [constitutional requirement] is satisfied if . . . the . . . [state] Legislature *rationally could have believed* that the [Act] would promote its objective." Western & Southern Life Ins. Co. v. State Bd. of Equalization, 451 U.S. 648, 671-672, 101 S. Ct. 2070, 2084-2085, 68 L. Ed. 2d 514 (1981); see also Minnesota v. Clover Leaf Creamery Co., 449 U.S. 456, 466, 101 S. Ct. 715, 725, 66 L. Ed. 2d 659 (1981); Vance v. Bradley, 440 U.S. 93, 112, 99 S. Ct. 939, 950, 59 L. Ed. 2d 171

---

5. After the American Revolution, the colonists in several states took steps to eradicate the feudal incidents with which large proprietors had encumbered land in the colonies. See, e.g., Act of May 1779, 10 Henning's Statutes At Large 64, ch. 13, §6 (1822) (Virginia statute); Divesting Act of 1779, 1775-1781 Pa. Acts 258, ch. 139 (1782) (Pennsylvania statute). Courts have never doubted that such statutes served a public purpose. See, e.g., Wilson v. Iseminger, 185 U.S. 55, 60-61, 22 S. Ct. 573, 574-575, 46 L. Ed. 804 (1902); Stewart v. Gorter, 70 Md. 242, 243, 16 A. 644, 645 (Md. 1889).

(1979). When the legislature's purpose is legitimate and its means are not irrational, our cases make clear that empirical debates over the wisdom of takings—no less than debates over the wisdom of other kinds of socioeconomic legislation—are not to be carried out in the federal courts. Redistribution of fees simple to correct deficiencies in the market determined by the state legislature to be attributable to land oligopoly is a rational exercise of the eminent domain power. Therefore, the Hawaii statute must pass the scrutiny of the Public Use Clause.[6]

B

The Court of Appeals read our cases to stand for a much narrower proposition. First, it read our "public use" cases, especially *Berman,* as requiring that government possess and use property at some point during a taking. Since Hawaiian lessees retain possession of the property for private use throughout the condemnation process, the court found that the Act exacted takings for private use. 702 F.2d, at 796-797. Second, it determined that these cases involved only "the review of . . . *congressional* determination[s] that there was a public use, *not* the review of . . . state legislative determination[s]." Id., at 798 (emphasis in original). Because state legislative determinations are involved in the instant cases, the Court of Appeals decided that more rigorous judicial scrutiny of the public use determinations was appropriate. The court concluded that the Hawaii Legislature's professed purposes were mere "statutory rationalizations." Ibid. We disagree with the Court of Appeals' analysis.

The mere fact that property taken outright by eminent domain is transferred in the first instance to private beneficiaries does not condemn that taking as having only a private purpose. The Court long ago rejected any literal requirement that condemned property be put into use for the general public. "It is not essential that the entire community, nor even any considerable portion, . . . directly enjoy or participate in any improvement in order [for it] to constitute a public use." Rindge Co. v. Los Angeles, 262 U.S., at 707, 43 S. Ct., at 692. "[W]hat in its immediate aspect [is] only a private transaction may . . . be raised by its class or character to a public affair." Block v. Hirsh, 256 U.S., at 155, 41 S. Ct., at 459. As the unique way titles were held in Hawaii skewed the land market, exercise of the power of eminent domain was justified. The Act

6. We similarly find no merit in appellees' Due Process and Contract Clause arguments. The argument that due process prohibits allowing lessees to initiate the taking process was essentially rejected by this Court in New Motor Vehicle Board v. Fox Co., 439 U.S. 96, 108-109, 99 S. Ct. 403, 411-412, 58 L. Ed. 2d 361 (1978). Similarly, the Contract Clause has never been thought to protect against the exercise of the power of eminent domain. See United States Trust Co. v. New Jersey, 431 U.S. 1, 19, and n.16, 97 S. Ct. 1505, 1516, and n.16, 52 L. Ed. 2d 92 (1977).

advances its purposes without the State taking actual possession of the land. In such cases, government does not itself have to use property to legitimate the taking; it is only the taking's purpose, and not its mechanics, that must pass scrutiny under the Public Use Clause.

Similarly, the fact that a state legislature, and not the Congress, made the public use determination does not mean that judicial deference is less appropriate.[7] Judicial deference is required because, in our system of government, legislatures are better able to assess what public purposes should be advanced by an exercise of the taking power. State legislatures are as capable as Congress of making such determinations within their respective spheres of authority. See Berman v. Parker, 348 U.S., at 32, 75 S. Ct., at 102. Thus, if a legislature, state or federal, determines there are substantial reasons for an exercise of the taking power, courts must defer to its determination that the taking will serve a public use.

IV

The State of Hawaii has never denied that the Constitution forbids even a compensated taking of property when executed for no reason other than to confer a private benefit on a particular private party. A purely private taking could not withstand the scrutiny of the public use requirement; it would serve no legitimate purpose of government and would thus be void. But no purely private taking is involved in this case. The Hawaii Legislature enacted its Land Reform Act not to benefit a particular class of identifiable individuals but to attack certain perceived evils of concentrated property ownership in Hawaii — a legitimate public purpose. Use of the condemnation power to achieve this purpose is not irrational. Since we assume for purposes of this appeal that the weighty demand of just compensation has been met, the requirements of the Fifth and Fourteenth Amendments have been satisfied. Accordingly, we reverse the judgment of the Court of Appeals, and remand these cases for further proceedings in conformity with this opinion.

It is so ordered.

Justice MARSHALL took no part in the consideration or decision of these cases.

---

7. It is worth noting that the Fourteenth Amendment does not itself contain an independent "public use" requirement. Rather, that requirement is made binding on the states only by incorporation of the Fifth Amendment's Eminent Domain Clause through the Fourteenth Amendment's Due Process Clause. See Chicago, Burlington & Quincy R. Co. v. Chicago, 166 U.S. 226, 17 S. Ct. 581, 41 L. Ed. 979 (1897). It would be ironic to find that state legislation is subject to greater scrutiny under the incorporated "public use" requirement than in congressional legislation under the express mandate of the Fifth Amendment.

Part 9
Rights Incident to Ownership of Land

Chapter Thirty-five

Water Rights

Add the following material to the listing of cases on page 1214 relating to navigable waters.

Utah Division of State Lands v. United States, — U.S. —, 107 S. Ct. 2318 (1987).

Insert the following material on page 1214 before the note on the Chicago River.

Case involving dispute between states of Mississippi and Alabama on the one hand and the United States on the other as to the ownership of seabed, minerals, and other natural resources beneath the waters of Mississippi Sound.

UNITED STATES v. LOUISIANA

Supreme Court of the United States, 1985
470 U.S. 93, 105 S. Ct. 1074

Justice BLACKMUN delivered the opinion of the Court.

This is the latest chapter in the long-lasting litigation between the Federal Government and the States of the Gulf Coast concerning ownership of the seabed, minerals, and other natural resources underlying the Gulf of Mexico. The particular and narrow issue presented here is whether the waters of Mississippi Sound are inland waters. If the Sound contains inland waters, as the States of Alabama and Mississippi contend, then these States own the lands submerged under the Sound. If the Sound in substantial part does not constitute inland waters, as the Government contends, then the United States owns the lands submerged under several "enclaves" of high seas within the Sound. We conclude that Mississippi Sound qualifies as a historic bay, and that the waters of the Sound, therefore, are inland waters.

I

The Submerged Lands Act of 1953, 67 Stat. 29, 43 U.S.C. §1301 et seq., confirms to each State title to and ownership of the lands beneath navigable waters within the State's boundaries. §1311(a). The Act also confirms in each coastal State a seaward boundary three geographical miles distant from its coastline. §1312. A State bordering on the Gulf of Mexico, however, may be entitled to a historic seaward boundary beyond three geographical miles and up to three marine leagues (approximately nine geographical miles) distant from its coastline. §§1301(b), 1312. The Act defines the term "coast line" as "the line of ordinary low water along that portion of the coast which is in direct contact with the open sea and the line marking the seaward limit of inland waters." §1301(c). The first part of this definition is relatively easy to apply. The second part — requiring determination of "the line marking the seaward limit of inland waters" — is more difficult to apply because the term "inland waters" is not defined in the Act.

In United States v. Louisiana, 363 U.S. 1, 80 S. Ct. 961, 4 L. Ed. 2d 1025 (1960), this Court determined, among other things, that the States of Alabama and Mississippi are not entitled under the Submerged Lands Act to a historic seaward boundary three marine leagues distant from their coastlines. Rather, the Court held, these two States are entitled, as against the United States, to all the lands, minerals, and other natural resources underlying the Gulf of Mexico, extending seaward from their coastlines for a distance of no more than three geographical miles. Id., at 79-82, 83, 80 S. Ct. at 1004-1006, 1007, (opinion); United States v. Louisiana, 364 U.S. 502, 503, 81 S. Ct. 258 5 L. Ed. 2d 247 (1960) (decree). The Court, however, did not express any opinion as to the precise location of the coastline from which the three-mile belt is to be measured. 363 U.S., at 82, nn. 135 and 139, 80 S. Ct., at 1006, nn. 135 and 139. The Court merely noted, in accordance with the above-mentioned definition in §2(c) of the Submerged Lands Act, 43 U.S.C. §1301(c), that "the term 'coast line' means the line of ordinary low water along that portion of the coast which is in direct contact with the open sea and the line marking the seaward limit of inland waters." 364 U.S., at 503, 81 S. Ct., at 259. See also 363 U.S., at 83, 80 S. Ct., at 1007. The Court retained jurisdiction to entertain further proceedings, including proceedings to resolve any dispute in locating the relevant coastline. Ibid.; 364 U.S., at 504, 81 S. Ct., at 259.430/

As has been noted, locating the coastline requires the determination of the seaward limit of "inland waters." Following the Court's decision in United States v. Louisiana, a disagreement arose between the United

States and the States of Alabama and Mississippi concerning the status of Mississippi Sound as inland waters. The Sound is a body of water immediately south of the mainland of the two States. It extends from Lake Borgne at the west to Mobile Bay at the east, and is bounded on the south by a line of barrier islands. These islands, from west to east, are Isle au Pitre, Cat Island, Ship Island, Horn Island, Petit Bois Island, and Dauphin Island. The Sound is approximately 80 miles long and 10 miles wide.

The two States contend that the whole of Mississippi Sound constitutes "inland waters." Under this view, the coastline of the States consists of the lines of ordinary low water along the southern coasts of the barrier islands together with appropriate lines connecting the barrier islands. These latter lines mark the seaward limit of Mississippi Sound. The United States, on the other hand, denies the inland water status of Mississippi Sound. Under its view, the coastline of the States generally consists of the lines of ordinary low water along the southern mainland and around each of the barrier islands.[1]

Under the States' view, then, the states own all the lands underlying Mississippi Sound, as well as the lands underlying the Gulf of Mexico extending seaward for a distance of three geographical miles from the southern coasts of the barrier islands and the lines connecting those islands. Under the United States' view, on the other hand, the States own only those lands underlying Mississippi Sound and the Gulf of Mexico that are within three geographical miles of the mainland coast or of the coasts of the barrier islands. There are several areas within Mississippi Sound that are more than three miles from any point on these coasts. Under the United States' view, those areas constitute "enclaves" or pockets of high seas, and the lands underlying them belong to the United States.

To resolve this dispute over the inland-water status of Mississippi

1. The United States' position actually is somewhat more complicated. First, the United States concedes that Isle au Pitre may be treated as part of the mainland, and that a bay closing line may be drawn from the eastern tip of Isle au Pitre to the eastern promontory of St. Louis Bay on the mainland. Thus, the waters of Mississippi Sound west of this bay-closing line are inland waters, and the bay-closing line forms part of the legal coastline of Mississippi. Second, the United States takes the position that if Dauphin Island at Mobile Bay is properly treated as part of the mainland — which the United States disputes — then a bay closing line may be drawn from the western tip of Dauphin Island northwesterly to Point Aux Chenes on the mainland, just west of the Alabama-Mississippi boundary. Under this secondary or fall-back position of the United States, the waters of Mississippi Sound east of this bay-closing line are inland waters, and the bay-closing line forms part of the legal coastline of Alabama and Mississippi. Finally, there are several undisputed inland rivers and bays along the shores of Alabama and Mississippi, and, as a consequence, undisputed closing lines across the mouths of these rivers and bays that, in the Government's view, form part of the legal coastline of the States.

Sound, the two States and the United States filed motions and cross-motions for the entry of a supplemental decree. The Court referred these pleadings to its Special Master, the Honorable Walter P. Armstrong, Jr., who already had been appointed in United States v. Louisiana (*Louisiana Boundary ST LINE L 445 U.S. 923, 100 S. Ct. 1306, 63 L. Ed. 2d 755 (1980). See also 457 U.S. 1115, 102 S. Ct. 2922, 73 L. Ed. 2d 1327 (1982). Following extended proceedings, the Special Master has submitted his Report to this Court.*

II

As noted above, the Submerged Lands Act employs but does not define the term "inland waters." In United States v. California, 381 U.S. 139, 161-167, 85 S. Ct. 1401, 1414-1417, 14 L. Ed. 2d 296 (1965), this Court observed that Congress had left to the Court the task of defining "inland waters" for purposes of the Submerged Lands Act. The Court for those purposes has adopted the definitions provided in the Convention on the Territorial Sea and the Contiguous Zone, [1964] 15 U.S.T. (pt. 2) 1607, T.I.A.S. No. 5639 (the Convention). 381 U.S., at 165, 85 S. Ct., at 1415. See also *Louisiana Boundary Case,* 394 U.S., at 35, 89 S. Ct., at 787; United States v. Maine (*Rhode Island and New York Boundary Case*), — U.S. —, —, 105 S. Ct. 992, 998, 83 L. Ed. 2d —.

The Convention, however, uses terminology differing somewhat from the terminology of the Submerged Lands Act. In particular, the Convention uses the term "baseline" to refer to the "coast line," and it uses the term "territorial sea" to refer to the three-geographical-mile belt extending seaward from the coastline. The territorial sea is one of the three zones into which, in international law, the sea is divided. The Court so explained in the *Louisiana Boundary Case:*

> Under generally accepted principles of international law, the navigable sea is divided into three zones, distinguished by the nature of the control which the contiguous nation can exercise over it. Nearest to the nation's shores are its inland, or internal waters. These are subject to the complete sovereignty of the nation, as much as if they were a part of its land territory, and the coastal nation has the privilege even to exclude foreign vessels altogether. Beyond the inland waters, and measured from their seaward edge, is a belt known as the marginal, or territorial, sea. Within it the coastal nation may exercise extensive control but cannot deny the right of innocent passage to foreign nations. Outside the territorial sea are the high seas, which are international waters not subject to the dominion of any single nation. 394 U.S., at 22-23, 89 S. Ct., at 780-781 (footnotes omitted).

Article 3 of the Convention provides the general rule for determining the "baseline":

> Except where otherwise provided in these articles, the normal baseline for measuring the breadth of the territorial sea is the low-water line along the coast as marked on large-scale charts officially recognized by the coastal State.

The Convention, however, provides several exceptions to the general rule pursuant to which Mississippi Sound might qualify as inland waters.

First, Article 4 of the Convention permits a nation to employ the method of straight baselines in delimiting its coastline. Article 4(1) provides in pertinent part:

> In localities where the coast line is deeply indented and cut into, or if there is a fringe of islands along the coast in its immediate vicinity, the method of straight baselines joining appropriate points may be employed in drawing the baseline from which the breadth of the territorial sea is measured.

If the method of straight baselines were applied to the coast of Alabama and Mississippi, the coastline would be drawn by connecting the barrier islands, thus enclosing Mississippi Sound as inland waters. The Court has held, however, that the method of straight baselines is applicable only if the Federal Government has chosen to adopt it. See *Louisiana Boundary Case*, 394 U.S., at 72-73, 89 S. Ct., at 806-807; United States v. California, 381 U.S., at 167-169, 85 S. Ct., at 1416-1417. In the present case, the Special Master concluded that the United States has not adopted the straight baseline method.

Second, Article 7 of the Convention provides a set of rules for determining whether a body of water qualifies as inland waters because it is a "juridical bay." Under Article 7(2), such a bay is defined to be "a well-marked indentation whose penetration is in such proportion to the width of its mouth as to contain landlocked waters and constitute more than a mere curvature of the coast." In addition, the area of the indentation must be "as large as, or larger than, that of the semi-circle whose diameter is a line drawn across the mouth of that indentation." And the closing line of the bay must not exceed 24 miles. The Special Master concluded that Mississippi Sound satisfies these criteria and thus qualifies as a juridical bay. In reaching this conclusion, the Master determined that Dauphin Island was to be treated as part of the mainland. The closing line drawn from the easternmost point of Isle au Pitre to the westernmost point of Dauphin Island, connecting each of the intervening barrier islands, crosses water gaps totaling less than 24 miles in length.

Finally, Article 7(6) of the Convention indicates that a body of water can qualify as inland waters if it is a "historic bay." The Convention does not define the term "historic bay." The Special Master concluded that Mississippi Sound qualifies as a historic bay under the tests noted in United States v. California, 381 U.S., at 172, 85 S. Ct., at 1419, and

United States v. Alaska, 422 U.S. 184, 189, 95 S. Ct. 2240, 2246, 45 L.Ed. 2d 109 (1975).

The Special Master, accordingly, recommended to this Court that a decree be entered in favor of Alabama and Mississippi.

The United States and the States of Alabama and Mississippi respectively filed exceptions to the Master's Report. The United States argued that the Master erred in concluding that Mississippi Sound is both a juridical bay and a historic bay; it claims that it is neither. Alabama and Mississippi agreed with those conclusions of the Special Master, but argued that there also were alternative grounds for concluding that Mississippi Sound constitutes inland waters. In particular, the States argued that their Acts of Admission established their boundaries along the southern coast of the barrier islands; that Mississippi Sound qualifies as inland waters under the straight baseline method of Article 4 of the Convention and prior United States practice; that Mississippi Sound qualifies as a juridical bay regardless of the characterization of Dauphin Island as a "mainland headland"; and that even if the whole of Mississippi Sound is not a juridical bay, a smaller juridical bay exists at the eastern end of the Sound.

We have independently reviewed the record, as we must. See Mississippi v. Arkansas, 415 U.S. 289, 291-292, 294, 94 S. Ct. 1046, 1047-1948, 1049, 39 L. Ed. 2d 333 (1974); Colorado v. New Mexico, — U.S. —, —, 104 S. Ct. 2433, —, 81 L. Ed. 2d 247 (1984); *Rhode Island and New York Boundary Case*, — U.S., at —, 105 S. Ct. at 994. Upon that review, we conclude that the Special Master correctly determined that Mississippi Sound is a historic bay. We therefore need not, and do not, address the exceptions presented by the States of Alabama and Mississippi or those exceptions of the United States that relate to the question whether Mississippi Sound qualifies as a juridical bay under Article 7 of the Convention.

III

The term "historic bay"[2] is not defined in the Convention and there is no complete accord as to its meaning. The Court has stated that a

---

2. In this opinion, the term "historic bay" is used interchangeably with the term "historic inland waters." It is clear that a historic bay need not conform to the geographic tests for a juridical bay set forth in Article 7 of the Convention. See *Louisiana Boundary Case*, 394 U.S. 11, 75, n.100, 89 S. Ct. 773, 808, n.100, 22 L. Ed. 2d 44 (1969). In this case, as in that one, we need not decide how unlike a juridical bay a body of water can be and still qualify as a historic bay, for it is clear from the Special Master's Report that, at minimum, Mississippi Sound closely resembles a juridical bay.

historic bay is a bay "over which a coastal nation has traditionally asserted and maintained dominion with the acquiescence of foreign nations." United States v. California, 381 U.S., at 172, 85 S.Ct., at 1419. See also United States v. Alaska, 422 U.S., at 189, 85 S. Ct., at 2246; *Louisiana Boundary Case*, 394 U.S., at 23, 89 S. Ct., at 781. The Court also has noted that there appears to be general agreement that at least three factors are to be taken into consideration in determining whether a body of water is a historic bay: (1) the exercise of authority over the area by the claiming nation; (2) the continuity of this exercise of authority; and (3) the acquiescence of foreign nations. See United States v. Alaska, 422 U.S., at 189, 95 S. Ct., at 2246; *Louisiana Boundary Case*, 394 U.S., at 23-24, n. 27, 89 S. Ct., at 781-782, n.27. An authoritative United Nations study concludes that these three factors require that "the coastal State must have effectively exercised sovereignty over the area continuously during a time sufficient to create a usage and have done so under the general toleration of the community of States." Juridical Regime of Historic Waters, Including Historic Bays 56, U.N. Doc. A/CN.4/143 (1962) (hereinafter Juridical Regime).[3] In addition, there is substantial agreement that a fourth factor to be taken into consideration is the vital interests of the coastal nation, including elements such as geographical configuration, economic interests, and the requirements of self-defense. See Juridical Regime, at 38, 56-58; 1 A. Shalowitz, Shore and Sea Boundaries 48-49 (1962). See also *Fisheries Case* (U.K. v. Nor.), 1951 I.C.J. 116, 142. In the present case, the facts establish that the United States effectively has exercised sovereignty over Mississippi Sound as inland waters from the time of the Louisiana Purchase in 1803 until 1971, and has done so without protest by foreign nations.

A

Mississippi Sound historically has been an intracoastal waterway of commercial and strategic importance to the United States. Conversely, it has been of little significance to foreign nations. The Sound is shallow, ranging in depth generally from 1 to 18 feet except for artificially maintained channels between Cat Island and Ship Island leading to Gulfport, Miss., and between Horn Island and Petit Bois Island leading to Pascagoula, Miss. Outside those channels, it is not readily navigable for ocean-going vessels. Furthermore, it is a cul de sac, and there is no reason for

---

3. The study explains that "no precise length of time can be indicated as necessary to build the usage on which the historic title must be based. It must remain a matter of judgment when sufficient time has elapsed for the usage to emerge." Juridical Regime, at 45. See also 1 A. Shalowitz, Shore and Sea Boundaries 49 (1962) (hereinafter Shalowitz).

an ocean-going vessel to enter the Sound except to reach the Gulf ports. The historic importance of Mississippi Sound to vital interests of the United States, and the corresponding insignificance of the Sound to the interests of foreign nations, lend support to the view that Mississippi Sound constitutes inland waters.[4]

Throughout most of the 19th century, the United States openly recognized Mississippi Sound as an inland waterway of importance for commerce, communications, and defense. Early in this period the Nation took steps to enhance and protect its interests in the Sound. On February 8, 1817, the House of Representatives listed among objects of national importance several "improvements requisite to afford the advantages of internal navigation and intercourse throughout the United States and its Territories," including "as a more distant object, a canal communication, if practicable, from the Altamaha and its waters to Mobile, and from thence to the Mississippi." H.R. Doc. No. 427, 14th Cong., 2d Sess. (1817), reprinted in 2 American State Papers 420, 422 (1834). This project ultimately became the Intracoastal Waterway through Mississippi Sound. On February 28, 1822, the House Committee on Military Affairs issued a report that recognized the importance of the intracoastal communication between New Orleans and Mobile Bay through what an 1820 letter reprinted in the report described as "the little interior sea, comprised between the main and the chain of islands, bounded by Cat Island to the west, and Dauphin Island to the east." H.R. Rep. No. 51, 17th Cong., 1st Sess., 7 (1823).

Defense of this important waterway has been a longstanding concern of the United States. On April 20, 1836, the Senate passed a resolution calling upon the Secretary of War to survey the most eligible sites for a fortification suitable for the defense of Mississippi Sound and the commerce along it. See S. Rep. No. 490, 26th Cong., 1st Sess., 1 (1840). A subsequent resolution instructed the Senate Committee on Military Affairs to study the expediency of erecting a fort on the western extremity of Ship Island. See S. Rep. No. 618, 26th Cong., 1st Sess., 1 (1840). In response to an inquiry pursuant to this resolution, the War Department noted: "The defenses indicated would cover one of the channels leading

---

4. United States Attorney General Edmund Randolph long ago employed similar reasoning in his opinion that Delaware Bay constitutes inland waters:

> These remarks may be enforced by asking, What nation can be injured in its rights by the Delaware being appropriated to the United States? And to what degree may not the United States be injured, on the contrary ground? It communicates with no foreign dominion; no foreign nation has ever before had a community of right in it, as if it were a main sea; under the former and present governments, the exclusive jurisdiction has been asserted. 1 Op. Atty. Gen. 32, 37 (1793).

from the gulf into the broad interior or water communication extending from Lake Borgne to the bay of Mobile." Id., at 2.[5]

Ship Island was reserved for military purposes by an executive order of August 30, 1847. In 1858, the War Department, responsive to an appropriation made by Congress, see the Act of Mar. 3, 1857, 11 Stat. 191, 192, authorized the building of a fort on the island. It was to be constructed at the island's west end, and to command the pass into Mississippi Sound between Ship and Cat Islands. Forty-eight cannons were ordered to arm the fort. During the War Between the States, the fort was occupied alternatively by Union and Confederate troops. It was finally abandoned in 1875. In 1879, the United States erected a lighthouse on the central section of the island.[6]

The United States argues that this official recognition of Mississippi Sound as an internal waterway of commercial and strategic importance has no relevance to the Sound's status as a historic bay. It would support this argument with a citation to the 1962 United Nations study of historic waters. Juridical Regime, at 56-58. The cited pages of the study discuss the view taken by some authors and governments that such circumstances as geographic configuration, requirements of self-defense, or other vital interests of the coastal state may justify a claim to historic bay status without the necessity of establishing long usage. The study notes, id., at 58, that "[t]here is undoubtedly some justification for this view,"

---

5. Ten years later, the Senate Committee on Military Affairs noted:

   The broad sheet of water which lies between the coast of Mississippi and the chain of islands parallel to it, is the channel of a commerce important in peace and indispensable in war. Through this passes the inland navigation which connects New Orleans and Mobile. This is the route of the mails and of a large part of the travel between the eastern and southwestern sections of the Union. Through this channel supplies for the naval station at Pensacola are most readily drawn from the great storehouse, the valley of the Mississippi, and its importance in this respect would be increased in a two-fold degree by the contingency of a maritime war: first, because a war would increase the requisite amount of supplies at that station; and, secondly, because it would greatly augment the difficulties of the more extended and exposed lines of communication by exterior navigation. S. Rep. No. 23, 31st Cong., 1st Sess., 2 (1850).

6. See, generally, Report of the Special Master 38; Caraway, The Story of Ship Island, 1699-1941, 4 J.Miss. Hist. 76 (1942); Weinert, The Neglected Key to the Gulf Coast, 31 J.Miss. Hist. 269 (1969).

The United States argues that the fortification of Ship Island is relevant only to the United States' suppression of its civil insurrection. But the fort was planned and construction was begun years before the outbreak of the Civil War, and it was not abandoned until some years after the conclusion of that War. The United States further argues that the abandonment of the fort suggests a retreat from any claim of inland water status for Mississippi Sound. But it seems just as likely, and perhaps more likely, that the fort eventually was abandoned because foreign nations completely acquiesced in the United States' assertion of sovereignty over the Sound, rendering the fort unnecessary.

but ultimately suggests that it does not make sense for "historic title" to be claimed in circumstances where the historic element is wholly absent. Ibid. The study, however, does not suggest that such circumstances as geographic configuration and vital interests are irrelevant to the question whether a body of water is a historic bay and, indeed, it affirmatively indicates that such circumstances can fortify a claim to "historic bay" status that is based on usage.[7]

In any event, the evidence discussed above does not merely demonstrate that Mississippi Sound is presently important to vital interests of the United States. Rather, the evidence demonstrates that the United States historically and expressly has recognized Mississippi Sound as an important internal waterway and has exercised sovereignty over the Sound on that basis throughout much of the 19th century.

B

The United States continued openly to assert the inland water status of Mississippi Sound throughout the 20th century until 1971. Prior to its ratification of the Convention on March 24, 1961,[8] the United States had adopted a policy of enclosing as inland waters those areas between the mainland and offlying islands that were so closely grouped that no entrance exceeded 10 geographical miles.[9] This 10-mile rule represented the publicly stated policy of the United States at least since the time of the Alaska Boundary Arbitration in 1903. There is no doubt that foreign nations were aware that the United States had adopted this policy. Indeed, the United States' policy was cited and discussed at length by both

---

7. The study cites Bourquin as a proponent of the view that "[t]he character of a bay depends on a combination of geographical, political, economic, historical and other circumstances." Juridical Regime, at 25 (translating and quoting Bourquin, Les Baies Historiques, in Mélanges Georges Sauser-Hall 42 (1952)). Bourquin explains:

> Where long usage is invoked by a State, it is a ground additional to the other grounds on which its claim is based. In justification of its claim, it will be able to point not only to the configuration of the bay, to the bay's economic importance to it, to its need to control the bay in order to protect its territory, etc., but also to the fact that its acts with respect to the bay have always been those of the sovereign and that its rights are thus confirmed by historical tradition. Juridical Regime, at 25-26.

8. The convention did not go into effect, however, until September 10, 1964, when the requisite number of nations had ratified it.

9. The United States confirmed this policy in a number of official communications during the period from 1951 to 1961. See Report of the Special Master 48-54. Also, the United States followed this policy in drawing the Chapman line along the Louisiana coast following the decision in United States v. Louisiana, 339 U.S. 699, 70 S. Ct. 914, 94 L. Ed. 1216 (1950). See Shalowitz, at 161. In a letter to Governor Wright of Mississippi, written on October 17, 1951, Oscar L. Chapman, then Secretary of the Interior, indicated that if the Chapman line were extended eastward beyond the Louisiana border, it would enclose Mississippi Sound as inland waters.

the United Kingdom and Norway in the celebrated *Fisheries Case* (U.K. v. Nor.), *supra*.[10] Nor is there any doubt, under the stipulations of the parties in this case, that Mississippi Sound constituted inland waters under that view.

The United States contends that its earlier adoption of and adherence to a general formulation of coastline delimitation under which Mississippi Sound would have qualified as inland waters is not a sufficiently specific claim to the Sound as inland waters to establish it as a historic bay. In the present case, however, the general principles in fact were coupled with specific assertions of the status of the Sound as inland waters. The earliest such assertion in the 20th century occurred in Louisiana v. Mississippi, 202 U.S. 1, 26 S. Ct. 408, 50 L. Ed. 913 (1906). In that case, the Court determined the location of the boundary between Louisiana and Mississippi in the waters of Lake Borgne and Mississippi Sound. The Court described the Sound as "an enclosed arm of the sea, wholly within the United States, and formed by a chain of large islands, extending westward from Mobile, Alabama, to Cat Island. The openings from this body of water into the Gulf are neither of them six miles wide." Id., at 48, 26 S. Ct., at 421. The Court ruled that the doctrine of "thalweg" was applicable to determine the exact location of the boundary separating Louisiana from Mississippi in Lake Borgne and Mississippi Sound. Under that doctrine, the water boundary between States is defined as the middle of the deepest or most navigable channel, as distinguished from the geographic center or a line midway between the banks. See Texas v. Louisiana, 410 U.S. 702, 709-710, 93 S. Ct. 1215, 1219-1220, 35 L. Ed. 2d 646 (1973); Louisiana v. Mississippi, — U.S. —, —, 104 S. Ct. 1645, 1647, 1648, 80 L. Ed. 2d 74 (1984). The Court concluded that the "principle of thalweg is applicable," not only to navigable rivers, but also to "sounds, bays, straits, gulfs, estuaries and other arms of the sea." 202 U.S., at 50, 26 S. Ct., at 421. The Court rejected the contention that the doctrine did not apply in Lake Borgne and Mississippi Sound because those bodies were "open sea." Id., at 51-52, 26 S. Ct., at 422-423. The Court noted that the record showed that Lake Borgne and the relevant part of Mississippi Sound is not open sea but "a very shallow arm of the sea, having outside of the deep water channel an inconsiderable depth." Id., at 52, 26 S. Ct., at 422. The Court clearly treated the Mississippi Sound as inland waters, under the category of "bays wholly within [the Nation's] territory not exceeding two marine leagues in width at the mouth." Ibid.

10. It is noteworthy that in the *Fisheries Case*, the International Court of Justice ruled that the consistent and prolonged application of the Norwegian system of delimiting inland waters, combined with the general toleration of foreign states, gave rise to a historic right to apply the system. See 1951 I.C.J., at 138-139.

The United States argues that the language in Louisiana v. Mississippi does not constitute a holding that Mississippi Sound is inland waters. It appears to us, however, that the Court's conclusion that the Sound was inland waters was essential to its ruling that the doctrine of thalweg was applicable. The United States also argues that it cannot be bound by the holding because it was not a party in that case. The significance of the holding for the present case, however, is not its effect as precedent in domestic law, but rather its effect on foreign nations that would be put on notice by the decision that the United States considered Mississippi Sound to be inland waters.

If foreign nations retained any doubt after Lousiana v. Mississippi that the official policy of the United States was to recognize Mississippi Sound as inland waters, that doubt must have been eliminated by the unequivocal declaration of the inland water status of Mississippi Sound by the United States in an earlier phase of this very litigation.[11] In a brief filed with this Court on May 15, 1958, the United States noted:

> [W]e need not consider whether the language, "including the islands" etc., would of itself include the water area intervening between the islands and the mainland (though we believe it would not), because it happens that all the water so situated in Mississippi is in Mississippi Sound, which this Court has described as inland water. Louisiana v. Mississippi, 202 U.S. 1, 48 [26 S. Ct. 408, 421, 50 L. Ed. 913]. The bed of these inland waters passed to the State on its entry into the Union. Pollard's Lessee v. Hagan, 3 How. 212 [11 L.Ed. 565]. Brief for United States in Support of Motion for Judgment on Amended Complaint in United States v. Louisiana, O.T.1958, No. 10 Original, p. 254.[12]

Similarly, in discussing Alabama's entitlement to submerged lands, the United States conceded that "the water between the islands and the Alabama mainland is inland water, consequently, we do not question that the land under it belongs to the State." Id., at 261.

The United States argues that the States cannot now invoke estoppel based on the Federal Government's earlier construction of Louisiana v. Mississippi as describing Mississippi Sound as inland water. The United States points out that the Court in the *Louisiana Boundary Case*, 394 U.S., at 73-74, n.97, 89 S. Ct., at 807-808, n.97, concluded that a similar concession with respect to Louisiana was not binding on the United

---

11. The United States also acknowledged that Mississippi Sound constitutes inland waters in a letter written by the Secretary of the Interior to the Governor of Mississippi on October 17, 1951, confirming that the oil and gas leasing rights inside the barrier islands belonged to the State of Mississippi. Report of the Special Master 42-44.

12. In United States v. Louisiana, 363 U.S. 1, 80 S.Ct. 961, 4 L. Ed. 2d 1025 (1960), Alabama and Mississippi argued that language in their Acts of Admission and in other historic documents entitled them to ownership of all submerged lands located within three marine leagues of their coastlines. See id., at 79-82, 80 S. Ct. at 1004-1006.

States. As with the Court's holding in 1906 in Louisiana v. Mississippi, however, the significance of the United States' concession in 1958 is not that it has binding effect in domestic law, but that it represents a public acknowledgment of the official view that Mississippi Sound constitutes inland waters of the nation.

C

In addition to showing continuous exercise of authority over Mississippi Sound as inland waters, the States must show that foreign nations acquiesced in, or tolerated, this exercise. It is uncontested that no foreign government has ever protested the United States' claim to Mississippi Sound as inland waters. This is not surprising in light of the geography of the coast, the shallowness of the waters, and the absence of international shipping lanes in the vicinity. Scholarly comment is divided over whether the mere absence of opposition suffices to establish title. See United States v. Alaska, 422 U.S., at 189, n.8, 199-200, 95 S. Ct., at 2246, n.8, 2251-2252; *Louisiana Boundary Case,* 394 U.S., at 23-24, n.27, 89 S. Ct., at 781-782, n.27. In United States v. Alaska, this Court held that, under the circumstances of that case, mere failure to object was insufficient because it had not been shown that foreign governments knew or reasonably should have known of the authority being asserted. There is substantial agreement that when foreign governments do know or have reason to know of the effective and continual exercise of sovereignty over a maritime area, inaction or toleration on the part of the foreign governments is sufficient to permit a historic title to arise. See Juridical Regime, at 48-49. See also *Fisheries Case* (U.K. v. Nor.), 1951 I.C.J, at 138-139. Moreover, it is necessary to prove only open and public exercise of sovereignty, not actual knowledge by the foreign governments. See Juridical Regime, at 54-55. In the present case, the United States publicly and unequivocally stated that it considered Mississippi Sound to be inland waters. We conclude that under these circumstances the failure of foreign governments to protest is sufficient proof of the acquiescence or toleration necessary to historic title.

IV

The United States contends that, notwithstanding the substantial evidence discussed above of the Government's assertion of sovereignty over Mississippi Sound as inland water, the States have failed to satisfy their burden of proof that Mississippi Sound is a historic bay. The United States relies on its recent disclaimer of the inland-water status of the Sound and on the absence of any evidence of actual exclusion from the Sound of foreign navigation in innocent passage. We find neither of these points persuasive.

A

In April 1971, the United States for the first time publicly disclaimed the inland waters status of Mississippi Sound by publishing a set of maps delineating the three-mile territorial sea and certain inland waters of the United States. These maps, which include the entire Gulf Coast, have been distributed to foreign governments in response to requests made upon the Department of State for documents delimiting the boundaries of the United States.

This Court repeatedly has made clear that the United States' disclaimer of historic inland waters status will not invariably be given decisive weight. In United States v. California, 381 U.S., at 175, 85 S. Ct., at 1421, the Court gave decisive effect to a disclaimer of historic inland water status by the United States only because the case involved "questionable evidence of continuous and exclusive assertions of dominion over the disputed waters." The Court suggested, however, that such a disclaimer would not be decisive in a case in which the historic evidence was "clear beyond doubt." Ibid. The Court also suggested that "a contraction of a State's recognized territory imposed by the Federal Government in the name of foreign policy would be highly questionable." Id., at 168, 85 S. Ct., at 1417. See Geofroy v. Riggs, 133 U.S. 258, 267, 10 S. Ct. 295, 297, 33 L. Ed. 642 (1890). The Court reiterated this latter theme in the *Louisiana Boundary Case,* where it stated:

> It is one thing to say that the United States should not be required to take the novel, affirmative step of adding to its territory by drawing straight baselines. It would be quite another to allow the United States to prevent recognition of a historic title which may already have ripened because of *past* events but which is called into question for the first time in a domestic lawsuit. The latter, we believe, would approach an impermissible contraction of territory against which we cautioned in United States v. California. 394 U.S., at 77, n.104, 89 S. Ct., at 809, n.104 (emphasis in original).

The maps constituting the disclaimer in the present case were published more than two years after the decree in the *Louisiana Boundary Case,* and 11 years after the decision in United States v. Louisiana, 363 U.S. 1, 80 S. Ct. 961, 4 L. Ed. 2d 1025 (1960). The Special Master concluded that "under the circumstances it is difficult to accept the disclaimer as entirely extrajudicial in its motivation." Report of the Special Master 47. Rather, according to the Master, this disclaimer "would appear to be more in the nature of an attempt by the United States to prevent recognition of any pre-existing historic title which might have already ripened because of past events but which was called into question for the first time in a domestic lawsuit." Ibid.

We conclude that historic title to Mississippi Sound as inland waters had ripened prior to the United States' ratification of the Convention in 1961 and prior to its disclaimer of the inland-water status of the Sound in 1971. That disclaimer, issued while the Court retained jurisdiction to resolve disputes concerning the location of the coastline of the Gulf Coast States, is insufficient to divest the States of their entitlement to the submerged lands under Mississippi Sound.

B

Finally, the United States argues that proof of historic inland-water status requires a showing that sovereignty was exerted to exclude from the area all foreign navigation in innocent passage. This argument is based on the principle that a coastal nation has the privilege to exclude innocent-passage foreign navigation from its inland waters, but not from its territorial sea. See *Louisiana Boundary Case,* 394 U.S., at 22, 89 S. Ct., at 780. According to the United States, such exclusion is therefore the only conduct that conclusively demonstrates that the nation exercises authority over the waters in question as inland waters and not merely as territorial sea.

This rigid view of the requirements for establishing historic inland-water status is unrealistic and is supported neither by the Court's precedents[13] nor by writers on international law.[14] To the contrary, in advocating a flexible approach to appraisal of the factors necessary to a valid claim of historic inland-waters status, two leading commentators have stated:

> It is hard to specify categorically what kind of acts of appropriation constitute sufficient evidence: the exclusion from these areas of foreign vessels or their subjection to rules imposed by the coastal State which exceed the normal scope of regulation made in the interests of navigation would obviously be acts affording convincing evidence of the State's intent. It would, however, be too strict to insist that only such acts constitute evidence. In the Grisbadarna dispute between Sweden and Norway, the judgment of 23 October 1909 mentions that "Sweden has performed various acts . . . owing to her conviction that these regions were Swedish, as, for instance, the placing of beacons, the measurement of the sea, and the installation of a light-boat, being acts which involved considerable expense and in doing which she not only thought that she was exercising her right but even more that she was performing her duty." 3 Gidel, Droit International Public de la Mer 633 (1934), translated and quoted in Juridical Regime, at 41.

A relatively relaxed interpretation of the evidence of historic assertion and of the general acquiescence of other states seems more consonant with the fre-

13. In United States v. Alaska, 422 U.S. 184, 197, 95 S. Ct. 2240, 45 L. Ed. 2d 109 (1975), the Court noted that to establish historic title to a body of water as inland waters, "the exercise of authority must have been, historically, an assertion of power to exclude all foreign vessels and navigation." It is clear, however, that a nation can assert power to exclude foreign navigation in ways other than by actual resort to the use of that power in specific instances.

14. One prominent writer has explained the "actes d'appropriation" necessary to establish effective exercise of sovereignty as follows:

quently amorphous character of the facts available to support these claims than a rigidly imposed requirement of certainty of proof, which must inevitably demand more than the realities of international life could ever yield. M. McDougal & W. Burke, The Public Order of the Oceans 372 (1962).

Similarly the 1962 United Nations study of historic waters notes that the requirement of effective exercise of sovereignty over the area by the appropriate action on the part of the claiming state

does not, however, imply that the State necessarily must have undertaken concrete action to enforce its relevant laws and regulations within or with respect to the area claimed. It is not impossible that these laws and regulations were respected without the State having to resort to particular acts of enforcement. It is, however, essential that, to the extent that action on the part of the State and its organs was necessary to maintain authority over the area, such action was undertaken. Juridical Regime, at 43.

Thus, although a coastal nation has the privilege to exclude from its inland waters foreign vessels in innocent passage, the need to exercise that privilege may never arise. Indeed, in the present case, as the United States seems to concede, the record does not indicate that there ever was any occasion to exclude from Mississippi Sound foreign vessels of innocent passage. Tr. of Oral Arg. 16. This is not surprising since, as noted above, foreign nations have little interest in Mississippi Sound and have acquiesced willingly in the United States' express assertions of sovereignty over the Sound as inland waters. We conclude that the absence in the record of evidence of any occasion for the United States to have exercised its privilege to exclude foreign navigation in innocent passage from Mississippi Sound supports rather than disproves the claim of historic title to the Sound as inland waters.

V

In sum, we conclude that the evidence discussed in the Report of the Special Master and in Part III above, considered in its entirety, is sufficient to establish that Mississippi Sound constitutes a historic bay. The exception of the United States to the Special Master's recommended ruling that the whole of Mississippi Sound constitutes historic inland waters is overruled. We repeat that we do not address the exceptions of Alabama, or those of Mississippi, or the exceptions of the United States that relate to the question whether Mississippi Sound qualifies as a juridical bay. The recommendations of the Special Master and his Report, to the extent they are consistent with this opinion, are respectively adopted and confirmed. The parties are directed promptly to submit to the Special Master a proposed appropriate decree for this Court's consideration;

if the parties are unable to agree upon the form of the decree, each shall submit its proposal to the Master for his consideration and recommendation. Each party shall bear its own costs; the actual expenses of the Special Master shall be borne half by the United States and half by Alabama and Mississippi.

The Court retains jurisdiction to entertain such further proceedings, enter such orders, and issue such writs as from time to time may be determined necessary or advisable to effectuate and supplement the forthcoming decree and the rights of the respective parties.

It is so ordered.

Justice MARSHALL took no part in the consideration or decision of this case.

Insert the following material on page 1214 before the note on the Chicago River.

Case involving further consideration of ownership rights in the bed under Mississippi Sound.

UNITED STATES v. LOUISIANA

Supreme Court of the United States, 1988
— U.S. —, 108 S. Ct. 901

Justice BLACKMUN delivered the opinion of the Court.

In the Court's most recent opinion in this extended litigation, see 470 U.S. 93, 105 S. Ct. 1074, 84 L. Ed. 2d 73 (1985), Mississippi Sound was determined to be a historic bay under the Convention on the Territorial Sea and the Contiguous Zone, [1964] 15 U.S.T. (pt. 2) 1607, T.I.A.S. No. 5639. The waters of that Sound, therefore, are inland waters, and Alabama and Mississippi own their respective portions of the bed of Mississippi Sound. The Court, as is customary in cases of this kind, stated:

> The parties are directed promptly to submit to the Special Master a proposed appropriate decree for this Court's consideration; if the parties are unable to agree upon the form of the decree, each shall submit its proposal to the Master for his consideration and recommendation. 470 U.S., at 115 [105 S. Ct., at 1086-87].

Jurisdiction was retained to entertain such further proceedings as might be determined to be necessary or advisable to effectuate and supplement the decree and to determine the rights of the parties. Ibid.

The Supplemental Report dated March 16, 1987, of the Special Master, the Honorable Walter P. Armstrong, Jr., now has been filed and is before us. The Master notes therein, p. 2, that no disagreement remains among the parties with respect to the coastline and seaward boundary of Alabama. That much has been decided and is clear. The Master further notes, however, id., at 3, that Mississippi and the United States are in disagreement as to the "seaward boundary" of Mississippi "at two points." Attached to the Report, as exhibits, are forms of a supplemental decree proposed respectively by the United States and by Mississippi. Id., at 31 and 38. The Special Master ends his Report with conclusions and recommendations. Id., at 26. Mississippi has noted exceptions. The United States is in opposition to those exceptions. Alabama at this point, of course, stands mute. Briefs had been filed and oral argument has been presented.

The Special Master concluded (a) that the decree proposed by Mississippi should *not* be entered, ibid., and (b) that, while "the line proposed by the United States," would be "a preferable solution," it "would amount to a modification of the Court's opinion of February 26, 1985," because it "would be beyond the scope of the reference" to the Master. Id., at 27. He has recommended that the Court "enter an order directing the parties to prepare and submit to the Special Master a decree" defining the seaward boundaries of Alabama and Mississippi "to the extent agreed upon"; defining Mississippi's seaward boundary between Petit Bois Island and Horn Island "as proposed in the decree submitted by the United States"; and, despite his expressed reservation noted above, defining the portion of Mississippi's seaward boundary from West Ship Island westward as a described line intersecting at its westernmost point with the already-determined Louisiana border.** Ibid.

I

The specific proceeding that culminated in this Court's opinion of February 26, 1985, reported at 470 U.S. 93, 105 S. Ct. 1074, 84 L. Ed. 2d 73 concerned, we thought, only Mississippi Sound and its boundary. See id., at 94, 105 S. Ct. at 1076; Tr. of Oral Arg. 3. The Special Master's Report and his stated reservation as to the scope of the reference to him also appear to reflect that understanding. But in its argument to the Master and in its present exceptions, Mississippi seeks to extend the scope of this litigation to include its interest in seabed south of Mississippi Sound. The State's current arguments bear little relation to earlier proceedings unless one engrafts upon our 1985 opinion, and upon our direction therein for a proposed decree fixing the southern boundary of

---

** We necessarily assume that, by his repeated use of the term "seaward boundary," the Master is referring to Mississippi's coastline and not to its ultimate offshore boundary.

Mississippi *Sound,* an implication that Mississippi's rights, if any, *south* of that Sound's boundary are to be definitively determined in this phase of the litigation.

To the south of the western part of Mississippi Sound lies Chandeleur Sound, a body of water east of Louisiana's mainland and west of the offshore Chandeleur Islands that run north and south. Chandeleur Sound and Mississippi Sound generally lie perpendicular to each other. They are separated by Cat Island, West Ship Island, and East Ship Island. The latter two at one time formed a single island but became divided by hurricane action some years ago.

An earlier phase of this litigation led to the entry of a supplemental decree issued June 16, 1975, see United States v. Louisiana (*Louisiana Boundary Case*), 422 U.S. 13, 95 S. Ct. 2022, 44 L. Ed. 2d 652, fixing the coastline (baseline) of Louisiana pursuant to the Court's decision of March 17, 1975, see 420 U.S. 529, 95 S. Ct. 1180, 43 L. Ed. 2d 373. Embodied in that decree is a line then stipulated to by the United States and the State of Louisiana delimiting Louisiana's interest in Chandeleur Sound north of the Chandeleur Islands. The Solicitor General advises us that the United States, in this litigation with Mississippi, offered to recognize Mississippi's rights "in the vicinity of Chandeleur Sound on the basis of an extension of the line stipulated" in the litigation between the United States and Louisiana (a line running from the location at that time of the northernmost of the Chandeleur Islands to a point near the middle of West Ship Island), but that Mississippi rejected that offer. Brief for United States 2-3. Mississippi acknowledges the rejection. Tr. of Oral Arg. 6. Thus, that easy solution to the controversy between the United States and Mississippi as to waters south of Mississippi Sound and in the vicinity of Chandeleur Sound proved to be unattainable. What remains in dispute is an area of about 150 square miles. Id., at 16.

II

As has been stated above, the current phase of the litigation up to this point, so far as Mississippi is concerned, has dealt only with Mississippi Sound. It has not focused on Mississippi's interest south of Mississippi Sound. This being so, we sympathize with the Special Master's unease about the scope of the reference to him. With the case in its present somewhat confused posture, we are unwilling on the present record to determine the extent of Mississippi's rights south of Mississippi Sound without the parties' complete agreement and the Special Master's ready acquiescence.

Because Mississippi's exceptions to the Special Master's Supplemental Report do not relate at all to Mississippi Sound, and do not contest the validity of that Sound's closing lines recommended by the Master, we are left with a situation where all parties are in agreement as to that Sound and its boundary. The exceptions of Mississippi, as presented to us at this time, therefore are overruled but without prejudice to the advancement of such claims as any party might have with respect to the area south of Mississippi Sound and in the vicinity of Chandeleur Sound in an appropriate separate chapter of these proceedings. The Supplemental Report dated March 16, 1987, of the Special Master and his recommendations, to the extent—and only to the extent—they are consistent with this opinion, are adopted and confirmed.

The parties once again are directed promptly to submit to the Special Master a proposed appropriate decree for this Court's consideration defining the claims of Alabama and Mississippi with respect to Mississippi Sound. If the parties are unable to agree upon the form of the decree, each shall submit its proposal to the Special Master for his consideration and recommendation. Each party shall bear its own costs; the actual expenses of the Special Master incurred with respect to this litigation since February 26, 1985, shall be borne half by the United States and half by Mississippi.

The Court retains jurisdiction to entertain such further proceedings, enter such orders, and issue such writs as from time to time may be determined to be necessary or advisable to effectuate and supplement the forthcoming decree and to determine the rights of the respective parties.

In order to facilitate the resolution of any question that might remain as to Chandeleur Sound, leave is granted the State of Mississippi and the United States, respectively, without further motion, to file a complaint with this Court setting forth its claim to any undecided portion of Chandeleur Sound. The complaint may be filed within 60 days of the date this opinion is filed. An opposing party shall have 45 days to respond. It is expected that all concerned will cooperate in expediting this remaining aspect of this phase of the litigation.

It is so ordered.

Case involving ownership of land under tidal waters that are non-navigable.

PHILLIPS PETROLEUM COMPANY v. MISSISSIPPI

Supreme Court of the United States, 1988
— U.S. —, 108 S. Ct. 791

Justice WHITE delivered the opinion of the Court.

The issue here is whether the State of Mississippi, when it entered the Union in 1817, took title to lands lying under waters that were influenced by the tide running in the Gulf of Mexico, but were not navigable-in-fact.

I

As the Mississippi Supreme Court eloquently put it: "Though great public interests and neither insignificant nor illegitimate private interests are present and in conflict, this in the end is a title suit." Cinque Bambini Partnership v. State, 491 So. 2d 508, 510 (1986). More specifically, in question here is ownership of 42 acres of land underlying the north branch of Bayou LaCroix and 11 small drainage streams in southwestern Mississippi; the disputed tracts range from under one-half acre to almost ten acres in size. Although the waters over these lands lie several miles north of the Mississippi Gulf Coast and are not navigable, they are nonetheless influenced by the tide, because they are adjacent and tributary to the Jourdan River, a navigable stream flowing into the Gulf. The Jourdan, in the area involved here, is affected by the ebb and flow of the tide. Record title to these tracts of land is held by petitioners, who trace their claims back to prestatehood Spanish land grants.

The State of Mississippi, however, claiming that by virtue of the "equal footing doctrine" it acquired at the time of statehood and held in public trust all land lying under any waters influenced by the tide, whether navigable or not, issued oil and gas leases that included the property at issue. This quiet title suit, brought by petitioners, ensued.

The Mississippi Supreme Court, affirming the Chancery Court with respect to the lands at issue here,[1] held that by virtue of becoming a

---

1. The Chancery Court had held that 140 acres of the lands claimed by petitioners were public trust lands. The Mississippi Supreme Court reversed with respect to 98 of these 140 acres, finding that these tracts were artificially created tidelands (caused by road construction), and therefore were not part of the public trust created in 1817. Since these lands were neither tidelands in 1817, nor were they added to the tidelands by virtue of natural forces of accretion, they belonged to their record title holders. 491 So. 2d, at 520.

Because the State did not cross-petition, this portion of the Mississippi Supreme Court's

State, Mississippi acquired "fee simple title to all lands naturally subject to tidal influence, inland to today's mean high water mark. . . ." Id., at 510. Petitioners' submission that the State acquired title to only lands under navigable waters was rejected.

We granted certiorari to review the Mississippi Supreme Court's decision, 479 U.S.—, 107 S. Ct. 1284, 94 L. Ed. 2d 142 (1987), and now affirm the judgment below.

II

As petitioners recognize, the "seminal case in American public trust jurisprudence is Shively v. Bowlby, 152 U.S. 1 [14 S. Ct. 548, 38 L. Ed. 331] (1894)." Reply Brief for Petitioners 11. The issue in Shively v. Bowlby, 152 U.S. 1, 14 S. Ct. 548, 38 L. Ed. 331 (1894), was whether the state of Oregon or a prestatehood grantee from the United States of riparian lands near the mouth of the Columbia River at Astoria, Oregon, owned the soil below the high-water mark. Following an extensive survey of this Court's prior cases, the English common law, and various cases from the state courts, the Court concluded:

> At common law, the title and dominion in lands flowed by the tide water were in the King for the benefit of the nation. . . . Upon the American Revolution, these rights, charged with a like trust, were vested in the original States within their respective borders, subject to the rights surrendered by the Constitution of the United States. . . .
>
> The new States admitted into the Union since the adoption of the Constitution have the same rights as the original States in the tide waters, and in the lands under them, within their respective jurisdictions. Id., at 57, 14 S. Ct., at 569.

Shively rested on prior decisions of this Court, which had included similar, sweeping statements of States' dominion over lands beneath tidal waters. Knight v. United States Land Association, 142 U.S. 161, 183, 12 S. Ct. 258, 264, 35 L. Ed. 974 (1891), for example, had stated that, "It is the settled rule of law in this court that absolute property in, and dominion and sovereignty over, the soils under the tide waters in the original States were reserved to the several States, and that the new States since admitted have the same rights, sovereignty and jurisdiction in that behalf as the original States possess within their respective borders." On many

---

decision is not before us. The only issue presented here is title to the 42 acres which the Mississippi Supreme Court found to be public trust lands.

occasions, before and since, this Court has restated and reaffirmed these words from *Knight* and *Shively*.[2]

Against this array of cases, it is not surprising that Mississippi claims ownership of all of the tidelands in the State. Other States have done as much.[3] The 13 original States, joined by the Coastal States Organization (representing all coastal States), have filed a brief in support of Mississippi, insisting that ownership of thousands of acres of tidelands under nonnavigable waters would not be disturbed if the judgment below were affirmed, as it would be if petitioners' navigability-in-fact test were adopted. See Brief for State of New York et al. as amici curiae 3-5, 26-27.

Petitioners rely on early state cases to indicate that the original States did not claim title to non-navigable tidal waters. See Brief for Petitioners 23-29. But it has been long-established that the individual States have the authority to define the limits of the lands held in public trust and to recognize private rights in such lands as they see fit. Shively v. Bowlby, 152 U.S., at 26, 14 S. Ct., at 557. Some of the original States, for example, did recognize more private interests in tidelands than did others of the 13 — more private interests than were recognized at common law, or in the dictates of our public trusts cases. See n.11, *infra*. Because some of the cases which petitioners cite come from such States (i.e., from States which abandoned the common law with respect to tidelands)[4] they are of

2. E.g., Borax Consolidated, Ltd. v. Los Angeles, 296 U.S. 10, 15, 56 S. Ct. 23, 25, 80 L. Ed. 9 (1935); Appleby v. City of New York, 271 U.S. 364, 381, 46 S. Ct. 569, 573, 70 L. Ed. 992 (1926); Illinois Central R. Co. v. Illinois, 146 U.S. 387, 435, 13 S. Ct. 110 111, 36 L. Ed. 1018 (1892); Hardin v. Jordan, 140 U.S. 371, 381, 11 S. Ct. 808, 811, 35 L. Ed. 428 (1891); McCready v. Virginia, 94 U.S. (4 Otto) 391, 394, 24 L. Ed. 248 (1877); Weber v. Harbor Comm'rs, 18 Wall 57, 65, 21 L. Ed. 798 (1873); Goodtitle v. Kibbe, 9 How. 471, 477-478, 13 L. Ed. 220 (1850).

3. See, e.g., Wright v. Seymour, 69 Cal. 122, 123-127, 10 P. 323, 324-326 (1886), which held that the State of California owned the bottom of the Russian River as far as the tide affected it, even where the River was not navigable in fact.

Earlier, Connecticut had held that the tidal flats adjoining an arm of the sea were in public ownership. Simons v. French, 25 Conn. 346, 352-353 (1856). South Carolina reached a similar conclusion concerning "salt marshes." State v. Pinckney, 22 S.C. 484, 507-509 (1885). Both of these cases, and many others like them, recognize state dominion over lands beneath non-navigable tidal waters.

4. See, e.g., Rowe v. Granite Bridge Corp., 38 Mass. 344, 347 (1838); Commonwealth v. Charlestown, 18 Mass. 179, 185-186 (1822). Massachusetts abrogated the common law for tidelands in 1641. See Shively v. Bowlby, 152 U.S. 1, 18-19, 14 S. Ct. 548, 554-555, 38 L. Ed. 331 (1894); Storer v. Freeman, 6 Mass. 435, 437-439 (1810).

Petitioners also rely quite heavily on two Connecticut cases, Groton v. Hurlburt, 22 Conn. 178, 185 (1852), and Wethersfield v. Humphrey, 20 Conn. 218, 227 (1850). See Brief for Petitioners 27. However, we think these cases are inapposite. *Groton* merely held that the erection of a highway over a tidally influenced, but not commercially navigable, creek did not offend federal control over navigable waterways (and did not require a

only limited value in understanding the public trust doctrine and its scope in those States which have not relinquished their claims to all lands beneath tidal waters.

Finally, we note that several of our prior decisions have recognized that the States have interests in lands beneath tidal waters which have nothing to do with navigation. For example, this Court has previously observed that public trust lands may be used for fishing—for both "shell-fish [and] floating fish." See. e.g., Smith v. Maryland, 18 How. 71, 75, 15 L. Ed. 269 (1855). On several occasions the Court has recognized that lands beneath tidal waters may be reclaimed to create land for urban expansion. E.g., Hardin v. Jordan, 140 U.S. 371, 381-382, 11 S. Ct. 808, 811-812, 35 L. Ed. 428 (1891); Den v. Jersey Co., 15 How. 426, 432, 14 L. Ed. 757 (1854). Because of the State's ownership of tidelands, restrictions on the planting and harvesting of oysters there have been upheld. McCready v. Virginia, 94 U.S. (4 Otto) 391, 395-397, 24 L. Ed. 248 (1877).[5] It would be odd to acknowledge such diverse uses of public trust tidelands, and then suggest that the sole measure of the expanse of such lands is the navigability of the waters over them.

Consequently, we reaffirm our longstanding precedents which hold that the States, upon entry into the Union, received ownership of all lands under waters subject to the ebb and flow of the tide. Under the well-established principles of our cases, the decision of the Mississippi Supreme Court is clearly correct: the lands at issue here are "under tide waters," and therefore passed to the State of Mississippi upon its entrance into the Union.

III

Petitioners do not deny that broad statements of public trust dominion over tidelands have been included in this Court's opinions since the early 19th century.[6] Rather, they advance two reasons why these previous

---

special grant of power under State law). *Groton,* 22 Conn., at 185-189. The decision's interest in the navigability of the creek, therefore, is unremarkable. Moreover, the *Groton* decision noted that construction of the highway put the lands to a publicly beneficial use, and that any navigation of the creek (by small boats or skiffs) was not impaired by the construction. Id., at 187-189. The decision in *Wethersfield* involved similar considerations. *Wethersfield, supra,* at 227.

5. These cases lead us to reject the dissent's assertion that "the fundamental purpose of the public trust is to protect commerce," *post,* at 801.

6. We reject petitioners' contention that our cases concerning "tidelands" are not applicable here because the term "tidelands" includes only shorelands or those lands beneath tidal waters which are immediately adjacent to the sea. Reply Brief for Petitioners 14-17. We find no basis for petitioners restriction of this term from its more common meaning;

statements of the public trust doctrine should not be given their apparent application in this case.

A

First, petitioners contend that these sweeping statements of State dominion over tidelands arise from an oddity of the common law, or more specifically, of English geography. Petitioners submit that in England practically all navigable rivers are influenced by the tide. Brief for Petitioners 19. See The Propeller Genesee Chief v. Fitzhugh, 12 How. 443, 454, 13 L. Ed. 1058 (1852). Thus, "tidewater" and "navigability" were synonyms at common law. See Illinois Central R. Co. v. Illinois, 146 U.S. 387, 436, 13 S. Ct. 110, 111, 36 L. Ed. 1018 (1892). Consequently, in petitioners' view, the Crown's ownership of lands beneath tidewaters actually rested on the navigability of those waters rather than the ebb and flow of the tide. Cf. Ibid. English authority and commentators are cited to show that the Crown did not own the soil under any non-navigable waters.[7] Petitioners also cite for support statements from this Court's opinions, such as *The Genesee Chief, supra,* and Martin v. Waddell, 16 Pet. 367, 413-414, 10 L. Ed. 997 (1842), which observed that it was "the *navigable* waters of England, and the soils under them, [which were] held by the Crown" at common law (emphasis added).

The cases relied on by petitioner, however, did not deal with tidal, non-navigable waters. And we will not now enter the debate on what the English law *was* with respect to the land under such waters, for it is perfectly clear how this Court understood the common law of royal ownership, and what the Court considered the rights of the original and the later-entering States to be. As we discuss above, this Court has consistently interpreted the common law as providing that the lands beneath waters under tidal influence were given States upon their admission into the Union. See Shively v. Bowlby, 152 U.S., at 57, 14 S. Ct., at 569. See also cases cited n. 2, *supra.* It is true that none of these cases actually dealt

---

i.e., that "tidelands" are lands "over which the tide ebbs and flows . . . land as is affected by the tide." Black's Law Dictionary 1329 (5th ed. 1979).

Furthermore, we note that this Court previously rejected a similar contention almost a century ago. See Mann v. Tacoma Land Co., 153 U.S. 273, 278, 283, 14 S. Ct. 820, 821, 38 L. Ed. 714 (1894).

7. See Brief for Petitioners 19-22 (citing, e.g., Mayor of Lynn v. Turner, 1 Cowp. 86, 98 Eng. Rep. 980, 981 (K. B. 1774); M. Hale, De Jure Maris et Brachiorum ejusdem, cap. iii (1667), reprinted in R. Hall, Essay on the Rights of the Crown and the Privileges of the Subject in the Sea Shores of the Realm, App. v (2d ed. 1875).

As we note in the text, *infra,* at 794, we do not intend to get involved in the historical debate over what the English common law was with respect to non-navigable tidal streams, if any such law existed — our concern is with how that law was understood and applied by this Court in its cases.

with lands such as those involved in this case, but it has never been suggested in any of this Court's prior decisions that the many statements included therein — to the effect that the States owned all the soil beneath waters affected by the tide — were anything less than an accurate description of the governing law.

B

Petitioners, in a related argument, contend that even if the common law does not support their position, subsequent cases from this Court developing the *American* public trust doctrine make it clear that navigability — and not tidal influence — has become the *sine qua non* of the public trust interest in tidelands in this country.

It is true that *The Genesee Chief, supra,* 12 How., at 456-457, overruled prior cases of this Court which had limited admiralty jurisdiction to waters subject to tidal influence. Cf. *The Thomas Jefferson,* 10 Wheat. 428, 429, 6 L. Ed. 358 (1825). The Court did sharply criticize the "ebb and flow" measure of admiralty inherited from England in *The Genesee Chief,* and instead insisted quite emphatically that the different topography of America — in particular, our "thousands of miles of public navigable water[s] . . . in which there is no tide" — required that "jurisdiction [be] made to depend upon the navigable character of the water, and not upon the ebb and flow of the tide." 12 How., at 457. Later, it came to be recognized as the "settled law of this country" that the lands under navigable freshwater lakes and rivers were within the public trust given the new States upon their entry into the Union, subject to the federal navigation easement and the power of Congress to control navigation on those streams under the Commerce Clause. Barney v. Keokuk, 94 U.S. (4 Otto) 324, 338, 24 L. Ed. 224 (1877). See also Illinois Central R. Co. v. Illinois, *supra,* 146 U.S., at 435-436, 13 S. Ct., at 111-112.

That States own fresh-water river bottoms as far as the rivers are navigable, however, does not indicate that navigability is or was the prevailing test for state dominion over tidelands. Rather, this rule represents the American decision to depart from what it understood to be the English rule limiting Crown ownership to the soil under tidal waters. In Oregon ex rel. State Land Board v. Corvallis Sand & Gravel Co., 429 U.S. 363, 374, 97 S. Ct. 582, 588, 50 L. Ed. 2d 550 (1977), after recognizing the accepted doctrine that States coming into the Union had title to all lands under the tidewaters, the Court stated that Barney v. Keokuk, *supra,* had "extended the doctrine to waters which were nontidal but nevertheless navigable, consistent with [the Court's] earlier extension of admiralty jurisdiction."

This Court's decisions in *The Genesee Chief* and Barney v. Keokuk extended admiralty jurisdiction and public trust doctrine to navigable fresh-waters and the lands beneath them. But we do not read those cases as simultaneously withdrawing from public trust coverage those lands which had been consistently recognized in this Court's cases as being within that doctrine's scope: *all* lands beneath waters influenced by the ebb and flow of the tide. See Mann v. Tacoma Land Co., 153 U.S. 273, 14 S. Ct. 820, 38 L. Ed. 714 (1894).[8]

C

Finally, we observe that not the least of the difficulties with petitioners' position is their concession that the States own the tidelands bordering the oceans, bays, and estuaries—even where these areas by no means could be considered navigable, as is always the case near the shore. Tr. of Oral Arg. 6. It is obvious that these waters are part of the sea, and the lands beneath them are State property; ultimately, though, the only proof of this fact can be that the waters are influenced by the ebb and flow of the tide. This is undoubtedly why the ebb-and-flow test has been the measure of public ownership of tidelands for so long.

Admittedly, there is a difference in degree between the waters in this case, and non-navigable waters on the seashore that are affected by the tide. But there is no difference in kind. For in the end, all tide waters are connected to the sea: the waters in this case, for example, by a navigable, tidal river. Perhaps the lands at issue here differ in some ways from tidelands directly adjacent to the sea; nonetheless, they still share those "geographical, chemical and environmental" qualities that make lands beneath tidal waters unique. Cf. Kaiser Aetna v. United States, 444 U.S.

---

8. *Mann* appears to be the only previous case from this Court concerning lands beneath non-navigable, tidal waters. In *Mann*, the lands at issue were "tide-flats" or "mud flats" located about one mile from the shore of Commencement Bay "covered to a uniform depth of from two to four feet (according to the run of the tides) at high water, and . . . entirely bare at low water." See Appellant's Motion to Advance in Mann v. Tacoma Land Co., O.T. 1893, No. 375, pp. 1-2.

Appellant contended in *Mann*, much as petitioners argue here, that while the ebb and flow test may have been the measure of sovereign ownership at English common law, "the [American] courts have, by the adoption of the rule of 'navigability in fact' as the test of 'navigability in law,' discarded the common law . . . [and held that w]here there is no navigation in fact, there is no State ownership by virtue of sovereignty." Supplementary Brief for Appellant 41. See also *Mann*, 153 U.S., at 277-279, 14 S. Ct. at 820. Appellee, like respondents here, argued that cases such as Barney v. Keokuk extended the public trust doctrine to cover navigable-in-fact fresh-waters, without reducing the scope of the public trust in tidelands. Brief for Appellee 2-4.

The Court, without commenting on the fact that the lands in question were beneath non-navigable tidal waters, held the lands to be within the public trust, and within the scope of its earlier decision in *Shively, Mann, supra*, at 283, 14 S. Ct., at 821. Thus, the Court implicitly rejected the argument being advanced by petitioners here that navigability-in-fact determined the scope of public trust tidelands.

164, 183, 100 S. Ct. 383, 394, 62 L. Ed. 2d 332 (1979) (BLACKMUN, J., dissenting).

Indeed, we find the various alternatives for delineating the boundaries of public trust tidelands offered by petitioners and their supporting amici to be unpersuasive and unsatisfactory.[9] As the State suggested at argument, see Tr. of Oral Arg. 22-23, and as recognized on several previous occasions, the ebb and flow rule has the benefit of "uniformity and certainty, and . . . eas[e] of application." See, e.g., Cobb v. Davenport, 32 N.J.L. 369, 379 (1867). We are unwilling, after its lengthy history at common law, in this Court, and in many state courts, to abandon the ebb and flow rule now, and seek to fashion a new test to govern the limits of public trust tidelands. Consequently, we hold that the lands at issue in this case were within those given to Mississippi when the State was admitted to the Union.

IV

Petitioners in passing, and *amici* in somewhat greater detail, complain that the Mississippi Supreme Court's decision is "inequitable" and would upset "various . . . kinds of property expectations and interests [which] have matured since Mississippi joined the Union in 1817."[10] They claim that they have developed reasonable expectations based on their record title for these lands, and that they (and their predecessors-in-interest) have paid taxes on these lands for more than a century.

We have recognized the importance of honoring reasonable expectations in property interests. Cf. Kaiser Aetna v. United States, *supra,* 444 U.S. at 175, 100 S. Ct. at 390. But such expectations can only be of consequence where they are "reasonable" ones. Here, Mississippi law appears to have consistently held that the public trust in lands under water includes "title to all the land under tidewater." Rouse v. Saucier's Heirs, 166 Miss. 704, 713, 146 So. 291, 291-292 (1933).[11] Although the Mississippi Supreme Court acknowledged that this case may be the first where it faced the question of the public trust interest in non-navigable tidelands, 490 So. 2d at 516, the clear and unequivocal statements in its earlier opinions should have been ample indication to the State's claim to tidelands. Moreover, cases which have discussed the State's public trust

9. See, e.g., Tr. of Oral Arg. 6-7; Brief for American Land Little Association as Amicus Curiae 6-7, and n. 4.

10. Brief for Petitioners 37. See also Tr. of Oral Argument 31-32; Brief for City of Elizabeth, New Jersey, et al. as amici curiae 17-20; Brief of Amicus Curiae American Land title Association as Amicus Curiae 1-3.

11. See also State ex rel. Rice v. Stewart, 184 Miss. 202, 230, 184 So. 44, 49 (1938); Martin v. O'Brien, 34 Miss. 21, 36 (1857).

interest in these lands have described uses of them not related to navigability, such as bathing, swimming, recreation, fishing, and mineral development. See, e.g., Treuting v. Bridge and Park Comm'n of City of Biloxi, 199 So. 2d 627, 632-633 (Miss.1967). These statements, too, should have made clear that the State's claims were not limited to lands under navigable waterways. Any contrary expectations cannot be considered reasonable.

We are skeptical of the suggestions by the dissent, *post*, at 800, 804, that a decision affirming the judgment below will have sweeping implications, either within Mississippi or outside the State. The State points out that only one other case is pending in its courts which raises this same issue. Tr. of Oral Arg. 19. And as for the effect of our decision today in other States, we are doubtful that this ruling will do more than confirm the prevailing understanding—which in some States is the same as Mississippi's, and in others, is quite different. As this Court wrote in Shively v. Bowlby, 152 U.S., at 26, 14 S. Ct. at 557, "there is no universal and uniform law upon the subject; but . . . each State has dealt with the lands under the tide waters within its borders according to its own views of justice and policy."

Consequently, our ruling today will not upset titles in all coastal states, as petitioners intimated at argument. Tr. of Oral Arg. 32. As we have discussed *supra*, at —, many coastal States, as a matter of state law, granted all or a portion of their tidelands to adjacent upland property owners long ago.[12] Our decision today does nothing to change ownership rights in States which previously relinquished a public trust claim to tidelands such as those at issue here.

Indeed, we believe that it would be far more upsetting to settled expectations to reverse the Mississippi Supreme Court decision. As amici note, see, e.g., Brief for State of California et al. as Amici Curiae 19, many land titles have been adjudicated based on the ebb-and-flow rule for tidelands—we cannot know how many titles would have to be adjusted if the scope of the public trust was now found to be limited to lands beneath navigable tidal waters only. If States do not own lands under non-navigable tidal waters, many State land grants based on our

12. See, e.g., Bradford v. The Nature Conservancy, 224 Va. 181, 195-198, 294 S.E.2d 866 (1982); Tinicum Fishing Co. v. Carter, 61 Pa. St. 21, 30-31 (1869); Bickel v. Polk, 5 Del. 325, 326 (1851); Storer v. Freeman, 6 Mass., at 437-439.

It is worth noting, however, that even in some of these States—i.e., even where tidelands are privately held—public rights to use the tidelands for the purposes of fishing, hunting, bathing, etc., have long been recognized. See, e.g., Bradford, *supra*, 224 Va. at 191, 197, 294 S.E.2d 866; Bickel, *supra*, at 326. Limiting the public trust doctrine to only tidelands under navigable waters might well result in a loss to the public of some of these traditional privileges.

earlier decisions might now be invalid. Cf. Hardin v. Jordan, 140 U.S., at 381-382, 11 S. Ct. at 811-812. Finally, even where States have given dominion over tidelands to private property owners, some States have retained for the general public the right to fish, hunt, or bathe on these lands. See n.11, *supra*. These long-established rights may be lost with respect to non-navigable tidal waters if we adopt the rule urged by petitioners.

The fact that petitioners have long been the record title holders, or long paid taxes on these lands does not change the outcome here. How such facts would transfer ownership of these lands from the State to petitioners is a question of state law. Here, the Mississippi Supreme Court held that under Mississippi law, the State's ownership of these lands could not be lost via adverse possession, laches, or any other equitable doctrine. 491 So. 2d, at 521. See Miss. Const., Art. 4, §104 (1890); Gibson v. State Land Comm'r, 374 So. 2d 212, 216-217 (Miss. 1979); City of Bay St. Louis v. Board of Supervisors of Hancock County, 80 Miss. 364, 371-372, 32 So. 54 (1902). We see no reason to disturb the "general proposition [that] the law of real property is, under our Constitution, left to the individual States to develop and administer." Hughes v. Washington, 389 U.S. 290, 295, 88 S. Ct. 438, 441, 19 L. Ed. 2d 530 (1967) (Stewart, J., concurring). See Davies Warehouse Co. v. Bowles, 321 U.S. 144, 155, 64 S. Ct. 474, 480, 88 L. Ed. 635 (1944); Borax Consolidated, Ltd. v. Los Angeles, 296 U.S. 10, 22, 56 S. Ct. 23, 29, 80 L. Ed. 9 (1935). Consequently, we do not believe that the equitable considerations petitioners advance divest the State of its ownership in the disputed tidelands.

V

Because we believe that our cases firmly establish that the States, upon entering the Union, were given ownership over all lands beneath waters subject to the tide's influence, we affirm the Mississippi Supreme Court's determination that the lands at issue here became property of the State upon its admission to the Union in 1817. Furthermore, because we find no reason to set aside that court's state-law determination that subsequent developments did not divest the State of its ownership of these public trust lands, the judgment below is

Affirmed.

Justice KENNEDY took no part in the consideration or determination of this case.

Justice O'CONNOR, with whom Justice STEVENS and Justice SCALIA join, dissenting.

Breaking a chain of title that reaches back more than 150 years, the Court today announces a rule that will disrupt the settled expectations of landowners not only in Mississippi but in every coastal State. Neither our precedents nor equitable principles require this result, and I respectfully dissent from this undoing of settled history.

I

As the Court acknowledges, *ante,* at 796, this case presents an issue that we never have decided: whether a State holds in public trust all land underlying tidally influenced waters that are neither navigable themselves nor part of any navigable body of water. In holding that it does, the majority relies on general language in opinions that that recognized state claims to land underlying tidewaters. But those cases concerned land lying beneath waters that were in fact navigable, e.g. Shively v. Bowlby, 152 U.S. 1, 14 S. Ct. 548, 38 L. Ed. 331 (1894) (Columbia River in Oregon), or beneath waters that were part of or immediately bordering a navigable body of water, e.g., Mann v. Tacoma Land Co., 153 U.S. 273, 14 S. Ct. 820, 38 L. Ed. 714 (1894) (shallow tidelands in Commencement Bay in Washington). Until today, none of our decisions recognized a State's public trust title to land underlying a discrete and wholly non-navigable body of water that is properly viewed as separate from any navigable body of water.

In my view, the public trust properly extends only to land underlying navigable bodies of water and their borders, bays, and inlets. This Court has defined the public trust repeatedly in terms of navigability. E.g., Utah Div. of State Lands v. United States, 482 U.S. —, 107 S. Ct. 2318, 96 L. Ed. 2d 162 (1987); Montana v. United States, 450 U.S. 544, 551, 101 S. Ct. 1245, 1251, 67 L. Ed. 2d 493 (1981); Utah v. United States, 403 U.S. 9, 10, 91 S. Ct. 1775, 1776, 29 L. Ed. 2d 279 (1971); United States v. Oregon, 295 U.S. 1, 14, 55 S. Ct. 610, 615, 79 L. Ed. 1267 (1935); United States v. Utah, 283 U.S. 64, 75, 51 S. Ct. 438, 440, 75 L. Ed. 844 (1931); United States v. Holt State Bank, 270 U.S. 49, 54-55, 46 S. Ct. 197, 198-199, 70 L. Ed. 465 (1926); Brewer-Elliott Oil & Gas Co. v. United States, 260 U.S. 77, 84-85, 43 S. Ct. 60, 63, 67 L. Ed. 140 (1922); Oklahoma v. Texas, 258 U.S. 574, 583 42 S. Ct. 406, 410, 66 L. Ed. 771 (1922); Pollard's Lessee v. Hagan, 3 How. 212, 230, 11 L. Ed. 565 (1845). It is true that these cases did not involve waters subject to the ebb and flow of the tide. But there is no reason to think that different tests of the scope of the public trust apply to salt and to fresh water. Navigability, not tidal influence, ought to be acknowledged as the universal hallmark of the public trust.

The public trust doctrine has its roots in English common law. Traditionally, all navigable waterways in England were by law common highways for the public. M. Hale, De Jure Maris et Brachiorum ejusdem, cap.

iii (1667), reprinted in R. Hall, Essay on the Rights of the Crown and the Privileges of the Subject in the Sea Shores of the Realm, App. v (2d ed. 1875). Furthermore, the King held title to the soil beneath the sea and the arms of the sea, "where the sea flows and reflows." Hale, cap. iv, reprinted in Hall, *supra,* at App. vii, ix. When the first American States became sovereign after our Revolution, their governments succeeded to the King's rights with respect to waters within their borders. Martin v. Waddell, 16 Pet. 367, 410, 10 L. Ed. 997 (1842). New States like Mississippi, upon entering the Union, acquired equivalent rights under the equal footing doctrine. Pollard's Lessee v. Hagan, *supra,* 3 How., at 228-229. Hence both petitioners and respondents have made an effort to ascertain the extent of the King's rights under English common law.

Unfortunately, English cases of the late 18th and early 19th centuries did not directly address whether the King held title to lands underlying tidally influenced, non-navigable waters. Certainly the public's right of navigation was limited to waterways that were navigable in fact, and did not extend to every waterway subject to the ebb and flow of the tide. As Lord Mansfied explained:

> How does it appear that this is a navigable river? The flowing and reflowing of the tide does not make it so, for there are many places into which the tide flows that are not navigable rivers; and the place in question may be a creek in their own private estate. Mayor of Lynn v. Turner, 1 Cowp. 86, 98 Eng. Rep. 980, 981 (K.B. 1774).

This principle of British law has proved enduring. See Rex v. Montague, 4 B. & C. 598, 602, 107 Eng. Rep. 1183, 1184 (K.B. 1825); S. Hobday, Coulson & Forbes on the Law of Waters 100-101 (6th ed. 1952). It appears, however, that the King's title to submerged land was not coextensive with the public's right of navigation. Thus in Murphy v. Ryan, 2 Ir. R.-C. L. 143, 152 (1868), the court explained that the King did not hold title to the land underlying navigable waters, unless they were influenced by the tide. Accord, Earl of Ilchester v. Raishleigh, 61 L.T.R. (n.s.) 477, 479 (Ch.D. 1889); Hobday, *supra,* at 102. It may be that the King also did not hold title to land underlying tidally influenced waters, unless they were navigable. Certainly, there are cases that describe the King's proprietary rights as pertaining to land underneath navigable water. Rex v. Smith, 2 Dougl. 441, 446, 99 Eng. Rep. 283, 285 (K.B. 1780); Lord Advocate for Scotland v. Hamilton, 1 Macqueen 46, 49 (H.L.1852); Le Roy v. Trinity House, 1 Sid. 86, 82 Eng. Rep. 986 (K.B. 1662). This strongly suggests that English common law did not authorize the claims that Mississippi makes in this case.

American cases have developed the public trust doctrine in a way that is consistent with its common law heritage. Our precedents explain that the public trust extends to navigable waterways because its fundamental purpose is to preserve them for common use for transportation.

> It is, indeed, the susceptibility to use as highways of commerce which gives sanction to the public right of control over navigation upon [navigable waterways], and consequently to the exclusion of private ownership, either of the waters or the soils under them. Packer v. Bird, 137 U.S. 661, 667 11 S.Ct. 210, 211, 34 L.Ed. 819 (1891).

Similarly, the Court has emphasized that the public trust doctrine "is founded upon the necessity of preserving to the public the use of navigable waters from private interruption and encroachment." Illinois Central R. Co. v. Illinois, 146 U.S. 387, 436, 13 S. Ct. 110, 112, 36 L. Ed. 1018 (1892).

Although the States may commit public trust waterways to uses other than transportation, such as fishing or land reclamation, this exercise of sovereign discretion does not enlarge the scope of the public trust. Even the majority does not claim that the public trust extends to every waterway that can be used for fishing or for land reclamation. Nor does the majority explain why its tidal test is superior to a navigability test for the purpose of identifying waterways that are suited to these other uses.

Because the fundamental purpose of the public trust is to protect commerce, the scope of the public trust should parallel the scope of federal admiralty jurisdiction. This Court long ago abandoned the tidal test in favor of the navigability test for defining federal admiralty jurisdiction, describing the ebb and flow test as "purely" artificial and arbitrary as well as unjust." The Propeller Genesee Chief v. Fitzhugh, 12 How. 443, 457, 13 L. Ed. 1058 (1852). The Court recognized that whether waters are influenced by the tide is irrelevant to the purposes of admiralty jurisdiction, which are to facilitate commerce in times of peace and to administer the special rules of war. Id., 12 How., at 454. Subsequent admiralty cases confirm that "the ebb and flow of the tide do not constitute the usual test, as in England, or any test at all of the navigability of waters." *The Daniel Ball*, 10 Wall. 557, 563, 19 L. Ed. 999 (1871).

Having defined admiralty jurisdiction in terms of navigability, the Court applied the same reasoning to the problem of defining the public trust. The Court explained that, "the public authorities ought to have entire control of the great passageways of commerce and navigation, to be exercised for the public advantage and convenience." Barney v. Keokuk, 94 U.S. (4 Otto) 324, 338, 24 L. Ed. 224 (1877). And it sweepingly concluded that the tidal test "had no place in American jurisprudence since the decision in the case of The Propeller Genesee Chief v. Fitzhugh, 12 How. 443." McGilvra v. Ross, 215 U.S. 70, 78, 30 S. Ct. 27, 31, 54 L. Ed. 95 (1909). These cases defined the public trust in the

context of inland waterways. But the same reasoning applies to waterways influenced by the tide. Navigability, not tidal influence, character-
izes the waterways that are suited to the purposes of the public trust.

Congress also has evidenced its belief that the States' public trusts are
limited to lands underlying navigable waters. In 1953, Congress passed
the Submerged Lands Act, 43 U.S.C. §§1301-1315. Congress intended to
confirm the States' existing rights to lands beneath navigable waters. S.
Rep. No. 133, 83d Cong., 1st Sess., pt. 1, p. 8 (1953); H.R. Rep. No.
1778, 80th Cong., 2d Sess., p. 3 (1948); Bonelli Cattle Co. v. Arizona, 414
U.S. 313, 324, 94 S. Ct. 517, 525, 38 L. Ed. 2d 526 (1973). The Act
defines "lands beneath navigable waters" as including lands "covered by
tidal waters." 43 U.S.C. §1301(a)(2). If tidal waters included discrete
bodies of *non-navigable* water, this definition would be self-contradictory.
Thus it appears that Congress understood "tidal waters" as referring to
the boundaries of the navigable ocean. As Senator Cordon explained,
"lands beneath navigable waters" identifies lands "as being under nontidal waters in the upper areas or being in tidal waters and — and I want
this emphasized — outside inland waters." 99 Cong. Rec. 2632 (1953).
Although the Submerged Lands Act is not at issue in this case, it is
evidence of Congress' interpretation of the public trust doctrine, and
that interpretation is entitled to consideration.

In sum, the purpose of the public trust, the analogy to federal admiralty jurisdiction, and the legislative history of the Submerged Lands Act
all indicate that the States hold title only to lands underlying navigable
waters. The term "navigable waters," is not self-defining, however. It
must be construed with reference to cases in which this Court has described the boundaries of the public trust.

For public trust purposes, navigable bodies of water include the non-
navigable areas at their boundaries. The question of whether a body of
water is navigable is answered waterway by waterway, not inch by inch.
The borders of the ocean, which certainly is navigable, extend to the
mean high tide line as a matter of federal common law. United States v.
Pacheco, 2 Wall. 587, 590, 17 L. Ed. 865 (1865); see Oregon ex rel. State
Land Board v. Corvallis Sand & Gravel Co., 429 U.S. 363, 376, 97 S. Ct.
582, 589, 50 L. Ed. 2d 550 (1977). Hence the States' public trusts include
the ocean shore over which the tide ebbs and flows. This explains why
there is language in our cases describing the public trust in terms of
tidewaters: each of those cases concerned the shores of a navigable body
of water. See, e.g., Borax Consolidated Ltd. v. Los Angeles, 296 U.S. 10,
16, 56 S. Ct. 23, 26, 80 L. Ed. 9 (1935); United States v. Mission Rock Co.,
189 U.S. 391, 404-405, 23 S. Ct. 606, 608-609, 47 L. Ed. 865 (1903);
Knight v. United States Land Assn., 142 U.S. 161, 183, 12 S. Ct. 258,
264, 35 L. Ed. 974 (1891). This does not imply, however, that all tidally

influenced waters are part of the sea any more than it implies that the Missouri River is part of the Gulf of Mexico.

The Court holds today that the public trust includes not only tidewaters along the ocean shore, but also discrete bodies of water that are influenced by the tide but far removed from the ocean or any navigable tidal water, such as the separate little streams and bayous at issue here. The majority doubts whether a satisfactory test could be devised for distinguishing between the two types of tidally influenced waters. *Ante,* at 797. It therefore adopts a test that will include in the public trust every body of water that is interconnected to the ocean, even indirectly, no matter how remote it is from navigable water. This is wholly inconsistent with the federal law that identifies what inland fresh waters belong to the public trust. For example, if part of a freshwater river is navigable in fact, it does not follow that all contiguous parts of the river belong to the public trust, no matter how distant they are from the navigable part. Conversely, federal law does not exclude from the public trust all non-navigable portions of a navigable river, such as shallow areas near the banks.

> The question here is not with respect to a short interruption of navigability in a stream otherwise navigable, or of a negligible part, which boats may use, of a stream otherwise non-navigable. We are concerned with long reaches with particular characteristics of navigability or non-navigability. . . . United States v. Utah, 283 U.S. 64, 77 [51 S. Ct. 438, 441, 75 L. Ed. 844] (1931)(footnote omitted). See Oklahoma v. Texas, 258 U.S. 574 [42 S. Ct. 406, 66 L. Ed. 771] (1922)(applying the navigability test to identify what parts of the Red and Arkansas Rivers belong to the public trust).

To decide whether the tidewaters at issue in this case belong to the public trust, the Court should apply the same fact-specific navigability test that it applies to inland waters. It should distinguish between navigable bodies of water and connected, but discrete, bodies of tidally influenced water. To this end, Justice Field once applied the headland to headland test, a "universal rule governing the measurement of waters," and drew a boundary dividing the navigable waters of San Francisco Bay from the tidally influenced waters of Mission Creek. Knight v. United States Land Assn., 142 U.S. 161, 207, 12 S. Ct. 258, 273, 35 L. Ed. 974 (1891)(concurring opinion). Only waterways that are part of a navigable body of water belong to the public trust.

II

The controversy in this case concerns more than cold legal doctrine. The particular facts of this case, to which the Court's opinion gives short shrift, illustrate how unfortunate it is for the Court to recognize a claim that appears belated and opportunistic.

Mississippi showed no interest in the disputed land from the time it became a State until the 1970s. Petitioners, or prior titleholders, recorded deeds on the land and paid property taxes throughout this period. App. to Pet. for Cert. 41a. In 1973, Mississippi passed the Coastal Wetlands Protection Law. Miss. Code Ann. §§49-27-1 to 49-27-69 (Supp.1987). This statute directed the Mississippi Marine Resources Council to prepare maps identifying state-owned wetlands. The maps, drawn from aerial photographs, were intended to show the probable scope of state-owned wetlands in order to aid state agencies in planning to protect them. §49-27-65. But the Mineral Lease Commission decided to use the maps as a basis for issuing oil and gas leases on what appeared to be state-owned lands. The Commission leased 600 acres to respondent Saga Petroleum U.S., Inc.

Petitioners, holders of record title, filed a complaint in Chancery Court to quiet title to the 600 contested acres and an additional 1800 acres in the area. The Chancery Court decided that the public trust included lands underlying all tidally influenced waters. Even under this test, only 140.863 acres of the land belonged to the State of Mississippi. On appeal, the Supreme Court of Mississippi reduced Mississippi's claim by another 98 acres to account for land underlying two artificial lakes. The land now claimed by Mississippi consists of slightly more than 42 acres underlying the north branch of Bayou LaCroix and 11 small drainage streams.

These waterways are not used for commercial navigation. None of the drainage streams is more than a mile long; all are nameless. Mississippi is not pressing its claim for the sake of facilitating commerce, or even to protect the public's interest in fishing or other traditional uses of the public trust. Instead, it is leasing the land to a private party for exploitation of underlying minerals. Mississippi's novel undertaking has caused it to press for a radical expansion of the historical limits of the public trust.

The Court's decision today could dispossess thousands of blameless record owners and leaseholders of land that they and their predecessors in interest reasonably believed was lawfully theirs. The Court concludes that a decision favoring petitioners would be even more disruptive, because titles may have to be adjudicated on the assumption that a tidal test defines the public trust. *Ante,* at 798-799. There is no way to ascertain, as a general matter, what assumptions about the public trust underlie existing property titles. What evidence there is suggests that the majority's rule is the one that will upset settled expectations. For example, the State of New Jersey has decided to apply the Court's test. It now claims for its public trust all land underlying non-navigable tidal waters, and all land that has been under tidal waters at any time since the American Revolution.

Due to this attempted expansion of the [public trust] doctrine, hundreds of properties in New Jersey have been taken and used for state purposes without compensating the record owners or lien holders; prior homeowners of many years are being threatened with loss of title; prior grants and state deeds are being ignored; properties are being arbitrarily claimed and conveyed by the State to persons other than the record owners; and hundreds of cases remain pending and untried before the state courts awaiting processing with the National Resource Council. Porro & Teleky, Marshland Title Dilemma: A Tidal Phenomenon, 3 Seton Hall L. Rev. 323, 325-326 (1972)(footnotes omitted). See also Brief for the City of Elizabeth, New Jersey, et al. as Amici Curiae 17-20 (confirming that these problems have not abated).

The Court's decision today endorses and encourages such action in other States.

Although there is no way to predict exactly how much land will be affected by the Court's decision, the magnitude of the problem is suggested by the fact that more than nine million acres have been classified as fresh or saline coastal wetlands. S. Shaw & C. Fredine, Wetlands of the United States, United States Department of the Interior, Fish & Wildlife Service, circular 39 p.15 (1956). The Federal Government conveyed these lands to the States, which have conveyed many of them to individuals. To the extent that the conveyances to private parties purported to include public trust lands, the States may strike them down, if state law permits. Illinois Central R. Co. v. Illinois, 146 U.S., at 452-454, 13 S. Ct. at 117-119; see Coastal Petroleum Co. v. American Cyanamid Co., 492 So. 2d 339, 342-343 (Fla. 1986), *cert. denied, sub nom.* Mobil Oil Corp v. Board of Trustees of Internal Improvement Trust Fund of Fla., 479 U.S. —, 107 S. Ct. 950, 93 L. Ed. 2d 999 (1987); Brief for the American Land Title Association as Amicus Curiae 2-3. The Court's broad definition of public trust lands will increase the amount of land that is vulnerable to such challenges.

The Court's suggestion, *ante,* at 799, that state law might honor the equitable considerations that support individual claims to public trust lands, is not persuasive. Certainly the Mississippi Supreme Court's decision in this case attached little weight to petitioners' equitable claims. Although Mississippi collected taxes on the land and made no mention of its claim for over 150 years, the Mississippi Supreme Court held that Mississippi was not estopped from dispossessing petitioners. Cinque Bambini Partnership v. State, 491 So. 2d 508, 521 (1986). The stakes are high when the land lies over valuable oil, gas, or mineral deposits.

The Court's decision departs from our precedents, and I fear that it may permit grave injustice to be done to innocent property holders in coastal States. I dissent.

Insert the following material on page 1220 before the problems.

First case applying the new rule as to surface water that was announced in Tucker v. Badoian.

VON HENNEBERG v. GENERAZIO

Supreme Judicial Court of Massachusetts, 1988
403 Mass. 519, 531 N.E.2d 563

LIACOS, Justice.

The plaintiff brought this action to recover damages for harm resulting from his defendant neighbor's interference with the flow of water from his property.[2] The defendant appeals from a denial of his motions for a directed verdict and of his motion for a judgment notwithstanding the verdict.[3] He also claims that a judge in the Superior Court erred in allowing the plaintiff to give opinion testimony as to damage; that error was committed in adding pre-judgment interest to the verdict; and that it was error to hold him individually liable for his acts as trustee of the PMG Realty Trust. We affirm.

1. Motions for a directed verdict and for judgment notwithstanding the verdict.

The same standard applies to both a motion for judgment notwithstanding the verdict and a motion for a directed verdict. Service Publications, Inc. v. Goverman, 396 Mass. 567, 571, 487 N.E.2d 520 (1986). Curtiss-Wright Corp. v. Edel-Brown Tool & Die Co., 381 Mass. 1, 3-4, 407 N.E.2d 319 (1980). "If, upon any reasonable view of the evidence, there is found a combination of facts from which a rational inference may be drawn in favor of the plaintiffs, there was an issue for decision by the

2. The plaintiff sued Generazio individually and as trustee of PMG Realty Trust. The plaintiff's complaint also contained a count for negligence and a count alleging violation of G.L. c.93A (1986 ed.). The negligence count was disposed of at trial by the allowance of the defendant's motion for a directed verdict; the c.93A count resulted in a summary judgment for the defendant. We consider only the count which went to the jury and which resulted in a verdict and a judgment for the plaintiff.

3. The jury returned a verdict in the amount of $33,500, to which the clerk of the court added interest in the amount of $22,143.50. The judge allowed Generazio's motion for a new trial, unless von Henneberg accepted a remittitur. Von Henneberg accepted the remittitur which reduced the final award to $16,750, plus $11,071.95 in interest. Final judgment was entered on May 11, 1987, in favor of von Henneberg and against Generazio individually and as trustee of the PMG Realty Trust.

jury and the motions were properly denied." Chase v. Roy, 363 Mass. 402, 404, 294 N.E.2d 336 (1973). Curtiss-Wright Corp. v. Edel-Brown Tool & Die Co., *supra*, 381 Mass. at 4, 407 N.E.2d 319. "It is axiomatic that, in reviewing the denial of the defendant's motions for directed verdict and judgment notwithstanding the verdict, we will construe the evidence most favorably to the plaintiff and disregard that favorable to the defendant." Cimino v. Milford Keg, Inc., 385 Mass. 323, 326, 431 N.E.2d 920 (1982).

We summarize the evidence in a light most favorable to the plaintiff.

Witold K. von Henneberg (Henneberg) purchased a one-acre lot on Edmands Road in Framingham from Philip Weir in 1957. Weir owned the adjacent undeveloped back lot, access to which was gained by a forty-foot strip of land which ran along the side of the plaintiff's property. Henneberg's land sloped downward toward the back lot so that water from Henneberg's property drained onto the access strip and flowed to Weir's back lot. In 1972, Weir built an earthen driveway on the access strip, which blocked the flow of the water and caused it to remain on Henneberg's land. After Henneberg complained about this flooding problem, Weir dug a drainage trench along the border of the two lots so that the water flowed from Henneberg's property onto the driveway and into the drainage trench.

In 1979, Weir sold the back lot to the defendant Generazio. Three days later Generazio conveyed the property to the PMG Realty Trust for $100. Generazio was the trustee and sole shareholder of the PMG Realty Trust. In 1980, Generazio began constructing a single-family dwelling on the back lot. He raised and paved the driveway, filled in the drainage trench, and built a berm which prevented water from flowing off Henneberg's land. Whenever there is a heavy rainfall, water floods one-third of Henneberg's property, endangering Henneberg's septic system. Photographs showing the flooded areas of the plaintiff's property were before the jury. There was evidence that, although Generazio was aware of these conditions, he made no effort to rectify them, as had Weir.

The evidence created a question of fact for the jury as to whether Generazio acted unreasonably in the circumstances. In Tucker v. Badoian, 376 Mass. 907, 384 N.E.2d 1195 (1978), a majority of the Justices announced prospectively, in a concurring opinion written by Justice Kaplan, that the "reasonable use" standard would govern water diversion cases. "[E]ach possessor is legally privileged to make a reasonable use of his land, even though the flow of surface waters is altered thereby and causes some harm to others, but incurs liability when his harmful interference with the flow of surface waters is unreasonable." Tucker v. Badoian, *supra* at 917-918 n.2, 384 N.E.2d 1195 (Kaplan, J., concurring), quoting Armstrong v. Francis Corp., 20 N.J. 320, 327, 120 A.2d 4

(1956). Jacobs v. Pine Manor College, 399 Mass. 411, 416 n.9, 504 N.E.2d 639 (1987).

The issue of reasonableness is "a question of fact to be determined in each case upon a consideration of all the relevant circumstances, including such factors as the amount of harm caused, the foreseeability of the harm which results, the purpose or motive with which the possessor acted, and all other relevant matter." Tucker v. Badoian, *supra,* 376 Mass. at 918 n.2, 384 N.E.2d 1195 (Kaplan, J., concurring), quoting Armstrong v. Francis Corp., *supra,* 20 N.J. at 330, 120 A.2d 4. Butler v. Bruno, 115 R.I. 264, 272, 341 A.2d 735 (1975).

The defendant contends that as a matter of law, his actions do not fall under conduct governed by the reasonable use standard.[4] He argues that the reasonable use standard applies only to damage caused by water flowing from one landowner's property onto another landowner's property. Because he prevented water from flowing off Henneberg's property and did not discharge water onto Henneberg's property, Generazio reasons, he cannot be liable for the harm caused under the reasonable use doctrine.

The defendant misunderstands the reasonable use doctrine. Under the reasonable use doctrine, a landowner can be held liable for the discharge of water onto another's land or for the blockage of water from another's land. The landowner "incurs liability when his *harmful interference with the flow of surface waters* is unreasonable" (emphasis added). Tucker v. Badoian, *supra,* 376 Mass. at 918 n.2, 384 N.E.2d 1195 (Kaplan, J., concurring), quoting Armstrong v. Francis Corp., *supra,* 20 N.J. at 327, 120 A.2d 4.

It is noteworthy that the concurring opinion in *Tucker* relied on two cases with facts very similar to those of the present case. In Pendergrast v. Aiken, 293 N.C. 201, 236 S.E.2d 787 (1977), the defendants blocked a stream which ran downhill from the plaintiffs' property through the defendants' property, causing flooding on the plaintiffs' property. In Butler v. Bruno, *supra,* the defendant, whose land was adjacent to and below that of the plaintiffs, built a retaining wall along the property line,

---

4. Because the defendant failed to object to the judge's charge to the jury, the standard enunciated by the judge became the law in the case. See Brady v. Nestor, 398 Mass. 184, 191, 496 N.E.2d 148 (1986) (Hennessey, C.J., dissenting): The validity of the judge's charge thus is not an issue before us. We recognize that this does not preclude the defendant from arguing that his motions for a directed verdict (made at the conclusion of the plaintiff's case and at the conclusion of the trial) should have been allowed. Tucker v. Badoian, *supra,* 376 Mass. at 915-916, 384 N.E.2d 1195. We note, however, that the judge in this case correctly charged the jury in accordance with the *Tucker* standard. We read Justice O'Connor's dissent to express no disagreement with the validity of the charge as given, but only to express disagreement with our view that the evidence was sufficient to warrant the jury's verdict.

which blocked the drainage and flooded the plaintiffs' land. In both cases, the court adopted the reasonable use doctrine, holding that the evidence presented a question to be determined by the trier of fact. Other jurisdictions have applied the reasonable use doctrine to similar fact patterns. See, e.g., Rodriguez v. State, 52 Hawaii 156, 472 P.2d 509 (1970); Mulder v. Tague, 85 S.D. 544, 186 N.W.2d 884 (1971).

The defendant contends that construction of a single-family dwelling constitutes reasonable use per se, and thus cannot result in liability. Under the *Tucker* standard, the fact finder must view the landowner's activity on his land with an eye toward the effect of that activity on the flow of surface waters. If the fact finder, after taking into account all of the relevant factors, finds that the possessor acted unreasonably, the nature of the original activity alone, whether it be constructing a shopping mall or building a single-family dwelling, will not bar liability.

Here, there was ample evidence to support a finding that the defendant acted unreasonably. Accordingly, the judge properly denied the defendant's motions for a directed verdict and for judgment notwithstanding the verdict.

2. Damages.

The defendant argues that the trial judge improperly admitted Henneberg's testimony as to damages. "An owner of property familiar with it and its uses and characteristics may testify as to its value. Rubin v. Arlington, 327 Mass. 382, 384, 99 N.E.2d 30 (1951). Evaluation of the witness's familiarity, knowledge, and experience is for the trial judge and his decision is 'conclusive unless upon the evidence it [is] erroneous as matter of law.' Id." Larabee v. Potvin Lumber Co., 390 Mass, 636, 643, 459 N.E.2d 93 (1983). Blais-Porter, Inc. v. Simboli, 402 Mass. 269, 272-273, 521 N.E.2d 1013 (1988). See P.J. Liacos, Massachusetts Evidence 118-119 (5th ed. 1981 & Supp. 1985).

The judge was well within his discretion to conclude that the plaintiff was sufficiently familiar with his land to testify as to its value. The judge did not presume familiarity from the fact of ownership alone. See Blais-Porter, Inc. v. Simboli, *supra,* at 272, 521 N.E.2d 1013. Henneberg, a professional architect, was not a mere holder of title or absentee landlord. He had cleared the land after purchasing it in 1957, had transformed a half-destroyed farmhouse into a family house, and had lived there for twenty-eight years. Henneberg demonstrated a detailed knowledge of his land in his trial testimony.

After the judge found that Henneberg was qualified to testify on the question of damages, the plaintiff was free to give his opinion of the value of the damaged property. Once a foundation for opinion testimony is properly laid, it is left to the fact finder to assess the weight and credibility in reaching a final determination of damages. Patch v. Boston, 146 Mass. 52, 57, 14 N.E. 770 (1888). The defendant's attempt, on cross-examination, to discredit Henneberg's method of reaching his dollar figure did not affect Henneberg's established competence to give his opinion. The fact that the plaintiff placed a value on the affected one-third of his land, rather than giving an opinion as to the lesser value of the whole land, is not fatal. The jury had other evidence of damages before them.[5] The value of a house lot such as the plaintiff's ($150,000) was before the jury. The jury could well have interpreted the plaintiff's testimony as evidence of a diminution of value of the entire lot as a result of the defendant's acts. See Larabee v. Potvin Lumber Co., *supra*. See also Willey v. Cafrella, 336 Mass. 623, 624, 146 N.E.2d 895 (1958).[6]

3. Individual liability.

Under G.L. c.203, §14A (1986 ed.), "[a] trustee shall be personally liable . . . for torts committed in the course of administration of the trust estate only if he was personally at fault." Generazio's unreasonable interference with surface waters constituted a private nuisance. Triangle Center, Inc. v. Department of Pub. Works, 386 Mass. 858, 863, 438 N.E.2d 798 (1982). Restatement (Second) of Torts §833 (1979). A private nuisance is a "tort" under G.L. c.203, §14A. See Triangle Center, Inc. v. Department of Pub. Works, *supra;* Tucker v. Badoian, 376 Mass. 907, 917, 384 N.E.2d 1195 (1978)(Kaplan, J., concurring); Pendergrast v. Aiken, *supra,* 293 N.C. at 216, 236 S.E.2d 787; Butler v. Bruno, 115 R.I. 264, 272, 341 A.2d 735 (1975). See also W. Prosser & R. Keeton, Torts §§87-88 (5th ed. 1984). There is no question that Generazio personally conducted the construction activities which led to the flooding of the plaintiff's property. It follows that Generazio may be held personally liable as a trustee for the damage resulting from his unreasonable interference with his neighbor's surface water.

4. Prejudgment interest.

We reject Generazio's argument that Henneberg's damages should not have included prejudgment interest under G.L. c.231 §6B (1986 ed.) As

5. There was other evidence as to damage, e.g., photographs showing the flooding of a portion of the plaintiff's land, testimony as to the danger caused by the flooding to the plaintiff's septic tank and leaching field; evidence as to the creation of a swampy area on part of the plaintiff's land; and evidence of the unsightliness of the affected area.

6. The defendant offered no evidence of value. The plaintiff testified that the value of the affected area was $50,000. The jury verdict was in the amount of $33,500. We note also that the issue of mitigation was put to the jury by the judge's charge.

we have indicated, the essence of this action is that it sounds in tort. General Laws c.231, §6B, clearly applies by its language:

> In any action in which a verdict is rendered or a finding made or an order for judgment made for pecuniary damages ... for damage to property, there shall be added by the clerk of the court to the amount of damages interest thereon at the rate of twelve percent per annum from the date of commencement of the action even though such interest brings the amount of the verdict or finding beyond the maximum liability imposed by law.

Additionally, the remittitur cured any potential error. While the original judgment was for $33,500 plus $22,143.50 in prejudgment interest, now the judgment is just under $28,000.

Judgment Affirmed.

O'Connor, Justice (dissenting).

In Tucker v. Badoian, 376 Mass. 907, 916-918, 384 N.E.2d 1195 (1978), six Justices of this court announced that, in the future, water diversion cases would be governed by a "reasonable use" standard, the "details" of which "[would] evolve and be determined in the usual way through the decisional process." This is the first case in which the court has been called upon to give shape to the new rule and to demonstrate its application. This case, then, is not only important to the parties. It also provides the court an opportunity to move forward in an area of law that has heretofore been troublesome and unsettled.

I write this separate opinion because I read the court's opinion as unwisely permitting a jury to impose liability on a defendant on the basis of evidence that, as a matter of law, demonstrates no more than that the defendant diminished the value of the plaintiff's land by obstructing the flow of water from it. Such evidence, without more, should not be legally sufficient to warrant a finding of unreasonable use.

I believe that the court should articulate standards by which reasonableness and unreasonableness must be measured, and I also believe that the reasonable use or unreasonable use issue should not be submitted to a jury unless, unlike here, the evidence is sufficient as a matter of law to warrant a finding of unreasonableness in the light of those standards.

I suggest that the standards identified by the Supreme Court of North Carolina in Pendergrast v. Aiken, 293 N.C. 201, 217, 236 S.E.2d 787 (1977), would be appropriate. In that case, the court reasoned that a determination of reasonableness requires "weighing the gravity of the harm to the plaintiff against the utility of the conduct of the defendant." Armstrong v. Francis Corp. [20 N.J. 320, 330, 120 A.2d 4 (1956)]; State v. Deetz [66 Wis. 2d 1, 224, N.W.2d 407 (1974)]; Restatement (Second) of Torts §826 (Tent. Draft No. 18, 1972). Determination of the gravity of the harm involves consideration of the extent and character of the harm to the plaintiff, the social value which the law attaches to the type of use which is invaded, the suitability of the locality for that use, the burden on plaintiff to minimize the harm, and other relevant considerations arising upon the evidence. Determination of the utility of the conduct of the defendant involves consideration of the purpose of the defendant's conduct, the social value which the law attaches to that purpose, the suitability of the locality for the use defendant makes of the property, and other relevant considerations arising upon the evidence." It is my view that the jury in the present case, guided by a consideration of those factors, could not have concluded rationally that the defendant's blockage of water flow was unreasonable.

The evidence in its light most favorable to the plaintiff, supplemented by other relevant evidence, was as follows. In 1957 Henneberg purchased a farmhose and one-acre lot at 618 Edmands Road in Framingham from Philip Weir. Weir retained ownership of an undeveloped back lot and also owned a forty-foot wide access strip connecting the back lot to Edmands Road. This right of way ran along the east side of Henneberg's property (the left side facing the property from Edmands Road). At first, there was good drainage from Henneberg's property across the right of way. The right of way was flat. In 1972, Weir piled earth on the right of way to construct a driveway on the back lot. As a result, there was a six foot high earthen bank "partially through" the right of way. When water started to collect "at the bottom of this bank," Henneberg wrote a letter to Weir complaining that the bank blocked the natural flow of water from his land. In response, Weir dug a drainage trench on Weir's land parallel to Henneberg's rear boundary line and perpendicular to and across the base of the driveway. The ditch was one foot or less deep at its easterly (left) end and became deeper as it ran westerly. The trench collected water from Henneberg's property and the earthen bank and left Henneberg's ground free of water and his lawn undamaged. After this, Henneberg had no problem with water collecting on his property until 1980.

On November 13, 1979, the defendant Generazio, a builder, purchased the back lot and right-of-way strip from Weir. In April, 1980, Henneberg noticed that water had collected at the "bottom" of his property. Generazio had dumped gravel at the "low part" of the driveway near Henneberg's land to enable vehicles to be driven "through the soft ground." This created a "barrier," so the water backed up onto Henneberg's land.

Water came from Edmands Road along the unpaved driveway and carried silt and sand onto Henneberg's property. (Nothing in the record shows that this was caused by anything Generazio had done.) Henneberg complained to Generazio about the water problem, and Generazio told him that he would eliminate the problem by running a drain on his own property.

Subsequently, Generazio built a single-family dwelling on the back lot. He filled the drainage trench that had been dug by Weir but, according to Generazio's uncontradicted testimony, he replaced Weir's trench with another trench of the same length approximately two feet away, and filled it with a perforated pipe and a filter made of one-inch stones.[1]

Generazio also paved the driveway with asphalt. Water still flowed from the driveway onto Henneberg's land and Henneberg complained to the town's building inspector. Generazio built a curb along the driveway and a catch basin at the bottom of the driveway. The catch basin did not solve the problem of water collecting at the low spot on Henneberg's property because, according to Henneberg's testimony, the catch basin "was constructed on the wrong side of the driveway"; water could not go from Henneberg's land over the "little bank" of the driveway built by Generazio, which constituted a "barrier," and thus could not drain into the catch basin.[2] After Generazio installed the drain and the curb, he did nothing further to get rid of water on Henneberg's property.

Generazio also constructed a berm across the top of his driveway where it meets Edmands Road, in order to prevent water from spilling off Edmands Road onto the driveway. As a result, water ponded on the road and leaked into Henneberg's property through a breach in the curb in front of Henneberg's property. Henneberg has never complained to the town about that breach.

Henneberg testified that he has not installed any trench or drain on his own property, has taken no action to drain water off his property, and has not contacted any contractor to see if such action on his part would be possible.

Generazio's conduct was incidental to the construction of a single-family home in a residential area. The jury would not have been warranted in finding otherwise. Thus, nothing about the "purpose of the defendant's conduct, the social value which the law attaches to that purpose, [or] the suitability of the locale for the use the defendant makes of the property," all relevant factors identified in Pendergrast v. Aiken, *supra,* weighs against Generazio or in favor of Henneberg. Furthermore, the evidence leaves entirely to speculation whether Generazio could have

1. The court's opinion notes merely that Generazio "filled in the drainage trench." *Ante* at 565. Henneberg testified that Generazio has "run a pipe along the trench." Clearly, there was no evidence that Generazio filled in the drainage trench without providing a substitute for it.

2. The evidence did not disclose whether Generazio owned land on Henneberg's side of the driveway on which an effective catch basin could have been placed.

avoided the conduct of which Henneberg complains while still making his property usable for residential purposes.

Moreover, the jury would not have been warranted in concluding that the Pendergrast v. Aiken factors bearing on the "gravity of the harm to the plaintiff" weigh in Henneberg's favor. A key factor is "the burden on plaintiff to minimize the harm." Nothing in the evidence shows that the back-up of water could not have been avoided by Henneberg. The evidence does not warrant a finding that most or all of the collected water does not come from Edmands Road through the breach in the berm at the front of Henneberg's property, a condition about which Henneberg did nothing. For all that appears in the evidence, the water collection problem could have been corrected by Henneberg's employment of simple and inexpensive methods of dealing with the source of the water or its evacuation. The evidence was insufficient to warrant the jury in concluding that the plaintiff had sustained his burden of showing that the gravity of the harm to Henneberg's property outweighed the utility of Generazio's conduct. Therefore, the evidence did not warrant a finding that the defendant's conduct was "unreasonable."

There are jurisdictions which, at least in the past, have embraced the so-called "civil law" or "natural flow" rule, subjecting a landowner to liability whenever he interferes with the natural flow of surface water to the detriment of another's property. The concurring Justices in Tucker v. Badoian, *supra,* 376 Mass. at 917, 384 N.E.2d 1195, rightly characterized that rule, which has never been the law of this Commonwealth, as "unsatisfactory." If the court is to develop a cogent body of law dealing with surface water disputes, it should not purport to reject the natural flow doctrine and then hold, as it implicitly does today, that evidence, which as a matter of law proves nothing more than the defendant's interference with the natural flow of water to the detriment of his neighbor's land, is sufficient for liability. I respectfully dissent.

Part 10
Taxation

Chapter Thirty-seven

A-B-C of Taxes for Property Lawyers (as of January 1989)

Additions to Chapter Thirty-seven that update the tax material to January 1989.

Insert the following material after carryover paragraph on page 1246.

Other recent tax law changes are the Tax Reform Act of 1984, the Tax Reform Act of 1986, the Revenue Act of 1987, and the Technical and Miscellaneous Revenue Act of 1988.

Insert the following material after the first paragraph on page 1248.

The Tax Reform Act of 1986 significantly changed the rate schedule of the individual income tax. The change reduced the number of rate brackets to two and lowered the top rate bracket to 28 percent.

Add the following material to note 1 on page 1248.

The reference to the lawyer's edition of Casner, Estate Planning, should be changed to 5th Lawyers ed. with 1989 Supp.

Add the following material to textual item 2 on page 1248.

Section 74 of the Internal Revenue Code as amended by the Tax Reform Act of 1986 requires the inclusion in the gross income of the amount of an award a person may receive after 1986. An exception described in §74 (b) is if the award is transferred by the recipient to governmental units or qualified charitable organizations.

Add the following material to textual item 3 on page 1248.

The Tax Reform Act of 1986 made some changes in regard to property transfers incident to a divorce (see §1041(c)).

Add the following material to carryover paragraph on page 1249.

An individual who gambles full time solely for his own account is engaged in a trade or business (see Commissioner v. Groetzinger, 107 S. Ct. 980 (1987)).

Add the following material to the first full paragraph on page 1249.

With a top income tax bracket of 28 percent brought in by the Tax Reform Act of 1986, the attractiveness of tax-exempt bonds is somewhat diminished.

Add the following material to the carryover paragraph on page 1250.

The so-called short-term trust has been eliminated as a practical matter as an income-shifting device by the Tax Reform Act of 1986. This is accomplished by causing the grantor of a trust to be treated as the owner of any portion of a trust in which the grantor or the grantor's spouse has a reversionary interest in either corpus or income, if, as of the inception of that portion of the trust, the value of such interest exceeds 5 percent of the value of such portion. However, if the beneficiary is a lineal descendant of the grantor and such descendant holds all the present interests in any portion of the trust, the grantor will not be treated as the owner solely by reason of a reversionary interest in such portion that takes effect on the death of such beneficiary before such beneficiary attains age 21.

Not only did the Tax Reform Act of 1986 knock out the use of a short-term trust to shift income for tax purposes to a lower bracket taxpayer, it also imposed a parent's top marginal tax rate on unearned income of a child under age 14.

Add the following material to the carryover paragraph on page 1251.

The Tax Reform Act of 1986 did not make changes in the general structure of the taxation of trust income to the trust or to a trust beneficiary, but it did require trusts to make estimated tax payments and to adopt a calendar tax year. The rate structure of income taxes for a trust was changed to follow the rate structure applicable to income taxed to individuals, that is, two brackets were adopted with the top rate bracket being 28 percent.

Add the following material to the last paragraph on page 1252.

Section 1034, referred to, provides for nonrecognition of gain if property used as the principal residence of the taxpayer is sold and within a specified period other property is purchased and used by the taxpayer as his principal residence.

Revenue Ruling 85-132, 1985-2 C.B. 182, considered a case where the tenant-stockholders in a cooperative converted their equity interest from cooperative ownership to condominium ownership. The tenant-stockholders took title to their apartments as condominium units and also received an undivided interest in the common areas. The Ruling held that this exchange qualified as a sale within the meaning of §1034(a) and that no gain or loss would be recognized. The value of the condominium unit and undivided interest in the common areas exceeded the adjusted basis of the tenant-stockholder's stock in the cooperative.

The Tax Reform Act of 1986 imposes a tax on capital gain that is the same as the tax imposed on ordinary income. This eliminates the distinction between short- and long-term capital gains (some distinction is retained until 1988).

Section 121(a) allows a one-time exclusion from gross income of gain from the sale of property if the taxpayer has attained age 55 before the date of the sale and if, during the five-year period ending on the date of the sale, such property has been owned and used by the taxpayer as his principal residence for periods aggregating three years or more. However, the amount of gain that can be excluded shall not exceed $125,000. If the residence is transferred to a trust and sold out of the trust, is the $125,000 exclusion available? I.R.S. Letter Ruling 8717010, as reported in P-H Private Letter Rulings ¶1321(87), allowed the exclusion where the trust to which the transfer was made was one under which the transferor was treated as the owner under §676(a).

In regard to the operation of §121, see Rev. Rul. 87-104, I.R.B. 1987-43, 12, which points out that a taxpayer's marital status on the date the residence is sold controls for purposes of the one-time exclusion. If two people are contemplating marriage and each owns a residence, if the sales are made before the marriage, each one may be entitled to the §121 exclusion. If they wait until after the marriage and then sell the two residences, only one §121 exclusion will be available. In the case considered by the Ruling, an individual sold his residence in January 1984. In June, he married, and the couple filed a joint return for 1984. The seller of the residence made the §121 election, and his spouse did not join in the election because they were not married when the residence was sold. The husband died in 1986, and thereafter the wife sold a residence that she had owned since before the marriage. The wife made the §121 election, and the Ruling held she was not prevented from doing so even though her deceased husband had made a §121 election. She was allowed to make the §121 election because she was not married at the time she made the sale of her residence.

Section 121(d)(4) was added by the Technical and Miscellaneous Revenue Act (TAMRA) of 1988 and gives some relief to the requirement of ownership and use as a principal residence of 3 years or more during the 5 year period ending on the date of sale under §121(a)(2). To qualify the taxpayer must be in a facility licensed by a State or local subdivision to care for an individual in the taxpayer's condition.

Add the following material to second full paragraph on page 1253.

The Technical and Miscellaneous Revenue Act (TAMRA) of 1988 amends §151(c)(1)(B)(ii) to eliminate as a dependent a full time student who reaches the age of 24 before the end of the tax year, unless his or her gross income does not exceed the exemption amount (and the other tests are met).

Add the following material to the third full paragraph on page 1253.

Wiht a top income tax bracket of 28 percent, the net cost to a taxpayer of making a deductible donative gift of $1,000 is $720.

Add the following material to the third full paragraph on page 1254.

The special tax referred to is called the alternative minimum tax (see Code §55 and following). See the amendments of this tax made by the Technical and Miscellaneous Revenue Act (TAMRA) of 1988.

Add the following material after the third full paragraph on page 1254.

The revision of the personal exemption amount resulted in the amount being $1,900 for taxable years beginning during 1987, $1,950 for taxable years beginning during 1988, and $2,000 for taxable years beginning after December 31, 1988. Starting in 1988, the benefit of the personal deduction is phased out for taxpayers with taxable income exceeding specified levels.

There is a so-called standard deduction that is a flat allowance taken in place of the itemized deduction. As of 1988, this standard deduction is as follows: single person, $3,000; head of household, $4,000; married persons filing jointly, $5,000; surviving spouse, $5,000; married persons filing separately, $2,500.

Add the following material after the carryover paragraph on page 1255.

The change made by the Tax Reform Act of 1986 to two brackets of income tax rates, with a top bracket of 28 percent, reduced the significance of the availability to husband and wife of the split-income provisions.

Married persons may have pre-marriage tax liabilities, and if so, how much of an overpayment of tax on a joint return can be allocated by the Government to payment of the pre-marriage tax liability? See Rev. Rul. 85-70, 1985-1 C.B. 361, which amplifies Rev. Rul. 74-611, 1974-2 C.B. 399, and Rev. Rul. 80-71, 1980-1 C.B. 296. A spouse's interest in an overpayment on the joint return must first be determined. This is accomplished by subtracting the spouse's share of the joint tax liability from the spouse's contribution toward the liability. Where the joint return relates to community property and by state law all community property is subject to the premarital or other separate debts of either spouse, the IRS may offset the entire amount otherwise refundable to the nonliable spouse against the separate tax liability of the other spouse.

Add the following material to item D on page 1255.

There are special rules in regard to estimated tax relating to income from farming. Revenue Ruling 80-366, 1980-2 C.B. 343 held that an income beneficiary of a trust that was engaged solely in the business of farming received income from farming for estimated tax purposes when such income represented more than two-thirds of the beneficiary's gross income.

Add the following material after the first full paragraph on page 1256.

For tax years beginning on or after January 1, 1984, an additional 5 percent (maximum of $20,250) is imposed on large corporations with taxable income of over $1 million (Tax Reform Act of 1984, §66). The Tax Reform Act of 1986 lowered the corporate tax rate to 15 percent on the first $50,000, to 25 percent between $50,000 and $75,000, and to a top of 34 percent on income over $75,000. For corporate taxable income in excess of $100,000, there is an additional 5 percent tax, but that tax cannot exceed $11,750. The benefit of graduated rates for corporations with taxable income between $100,000 and $355,000 is phased out, so that with income in excess of $335,000, a corporation pays a flat tax at a rate of 34 percent. This makes the top corporate rate higher than the top individual rate and should induce the use of the S corporation, where possible, to take advantage of the top individual rate. The dividend exclusion (§116) was repealed by the Tax Reform Act of 1986.

Add the following material to the second full paragraph on page 1258.

If, however, the state death tax is limited to the state death tax credit, §2011(f) points out that the credit shall not exceed the amount of tax imposed reduced by the amount of the unified credit.

Add the following as note 4a at the end of line 3 on page 1260.

4a. See Schoenblum, The Changing Meaning of "Gift": An Analysis of the Tax Court's Decision in Carson v. Commissioner, 32 Vand. L. Rev. 641 (1979).

Revenue Ruling 80-196, 1980-2 C.B. 32, considered whether a gift for gift tax purposes resulted in a case where A and B, individual founders of a corporation, each transferred stock they owned in the corporation to certain key employees who were considered valuable to the continued success of the corporation. The employees were not related to the transferors. After describing the income tax results of these transfers (fair market value of stock received was includible in income of the transferees; basis of stock in transferees' hands was equal to amount includible in their income; A and B were treated as having made a capital contribution to the corporation; and the corporation was entitled to a deduction for compensation paid to extent allowed by §162 and §83(h)), the Ruling turned to the gift tax result. It was concluded that no gift for gift tax purposes was made, as transfers were considered as made for an adequate and full consideration.

Kirschling v. United States, 746 F.2d 512 (9th Cir. 1984), held that allotted lands and allotment proceeds are exempt from gift tax, whether or not the transferee is an Indian. Reliance was placed on Squire v. Capolman, 351 U.S. 1 (1956), a case that exempted noncompetent Indians from capital gains tax on the timber proceeds from allotted land and observed that the allotment shall be free from all taxes.

Add the following material to the carryover paragraph on page 1261.

Section 2503(c) of the Code describes a type of gift to a minor that is really a gift of a future interest but which will be regarded as a gift of a present interest to the minor so that the annual exclusion is available with respect to the gift. A gift for the benefit of a minor is deemed a present interest under §2503(c), if (1) the gift property and the income therefrom may be expended for the benefit of the donee before the donee attains 21 and (2) any unexpended gift property or resulting income will pass to the donee at age 21 and (3) if the donee dies before attaining 21, will be payable to the donee's estate or as the donee appoints under a general power of appointment.

Add the following material to the first paragraph under item 4 on page 1261.

The unlimited gift tax marital deduction allowed spouses to achieve half and half ownership without any gift tax cost and equalized to a considerable extent the situation with respect to community and non-community property.

Add the following material to the first full paragraph on page 1262.

The so-called qualified terminable interest is generally referred to as the Q-Tip.

Add the following material to the parenthetical statement in the first sentence under item 6 on page 1263.

and the amounts described in §2503(e) referred to above.

Add the following material to the first full paragraph under item 6 on page 1263.

The Tax Reform Act of 1984 froze the top rate at 55 percent until 1988 and the Revenue Act of 1987 continued the freeze for five more years. Thus the maximum rate declines to 50 percent for decedents dying, and gifts made, after December 31, 1992.

Add the following material to the carryover paragraph on page 1285.

Add to the transfers that will not be taxable gifts the amounts described in §2503(e). Also, it is to be noted that the Revenue Act of 1987 phases out the benefit of the unified credit *and* graduated rates for transfers exceeding $10,000,000. The gift and estate tax liability for taxable transfers in excess of $10,000,000 is increased by 5 percent of such excess until the benefit of the unified credit and graduated brackets is recaptured.

Add following material as a footnote 4b appended to the first paragraph under item 1 on page 1267.

4b. Price v. United States, 470 F. Supp. 136 (N.D. Tex 1979), *aff'd,* 610 F.2d 683 (5th Cir. 1980), involved a husband and wife case where the will of each one gave the survivor all of his or her property. The husband survived the wife and died shortly thereafter and before the wife's will had been probated. The family decided not to offer it for probate. Under these circumstances, it was contended that the wife's property should not be included in the husband's gross estate. The court examined the law of Texas, the controlling state, as to the state of the title of property disposed of by a will prior to the probate of the will. The court concluded that an unprobated but apparently valid will left by a Texas citizen is effective to convey a sufficient interest in property devised by the will as to render the property includible in the devisee's gross estate for estate tax purposes.

Section 2033 of the Code refers to the inclusion in a decedent's gross estate of "the value of all property to the extent of the interest therein of the decedent at the time of his death." What is the meaning of the word "property" in this context? See First Victoria National Bank v. United States, 620 F.2d 1096 (5th Cir. 1980), which held that "rice history acreage" is "property" for purposes of the estate tax law. "The word 'property' in the statute is not limited in its scope by concepts of property that existed when the estate tax was conceived. When property rights have come into existence since the statute's enactment, the generalized term must be expanded, and the terrain cartographed, by laborers in the fields of law and government. The economy and many of the elements of life today are different than they were even a generation or less ago. The Congress in its wisdom decided to use a general word like property rather than trying to envision what the ingenuity of man would evolve as something substantial. The tax gatherer is directed to seek out the esoterics of ownership and reap his share of an individual's harvest of bundles of rice upon his demise."

Estate of Ora Summers v. United States, 85-2 U.S.T.C. §3646 (D. Or. 1985), illustrates the exclusion from the estate taxation of Indian Tribal property in certain circumstances.

Add the following material after the carryover paragraph on page 1272.

The Tax Reform Act of 1986 repealed the generation-skipping transfer tax enacted in the Tax Reform Act of 1976 and enacted an entirely new generation-skipping transfer tax. This new GST tax has been significantly amended by the Technical and Miscellaneous Revenue Act (TAMRA) of 1988.

(9) *Valuation freeze.* In view of the fact that the estate tax is based on the valuation of the property included in the gross as of the date of the decedent's death (or the valuation at the so-called alternate valuation date six months after death under some circumstances (§2032)), if the valuation of property that will go into the gross estate can be frozen at its present value, with future appreciation going to others and the future appreciation not be includible in the gross estate, considerable savings in estate taxes could be accomplished. The Technical and Miscellaneous Revenue Act (TAMRA) of 1988 attacks this problem in a new §2036(c) of the Code. This new section has its complications and may extend beyond the freeze problem in determining what is includible in the gross estate of a decedent for estate tax purposes.

Add the following material to note 7 on page 1272.

The reference to Casner, Estate Planning, Ch. 13 (4th ed.) should be changed to Casner, Estate Planning, Ch. 13 (5th ed.).

Add the following material to the first full paragraph on page 1276.

Keep in mind that the Revenue Act of 1987 defers the scheduled rate decline for estate and gift tax rates to 50 percent to decedents dying and gifts made after December 31, 1992, and also phases out the benefit of the unified credit and graduated rates for transfers exceeding $10,000,000. The gift and estate tax liability for taxable transfers in excess of $10,000,000 is increased by 5 percent of such excess until the benefit of the unified credit and graduated brackets is recaptured.

Add following material to item 2 on page 1276.

The amount of the adjusted taxable gifts for purposes of computing the estate tax is not controlled by the valuation of the gifts for gift tax purposes, but such gifts may be revalued even if the statute of limitations has run on the gift tax return in which the gifts were reported. See I.R.S. Letter Ruling 8447005, dated July 26, 1984, and reported in CCH Fed. Est. and Gift Tax Rep. ¶12153.

Add the following material as note 8 to carryover paragraph on page 1277.

8. Section 2201 provides some estate tax relief to members of the Armed Forces killed in action while serving in a combat zone or who die as a result of action in a combat zone. See Rev. Rul. 78-381, 1978-2 C.B. 347.

Add the following material to the carryover paragraph on page 1278.

The Tax Reform Act of 1986 amended §2032(c), relating to the alternate date election, to provide that the election is not available unless it will decrease the value of the gross estate and decrease the sum of the estate tax and the generation-skipping transfer tax with respect to property includible in the decedent's gross estate (reduced by credits allowable against such taxes).

Add following material as note 9 to item 4 under first centered heading of page 1278.

9. The amount includible in the gross estate with respect to the joint bank account may be only one-half or $5,000.

Add following material as note 10 to first paragraph under second centered heading of page 1278.

10. When the unlimited marital deduction came into the picture, the definition in the Code of the adjusted gross estate was eliminated. Thus if the term is to be used, the dispositive instrument should define what it means.